GOOD BEER GUIDE

TO
BELGIUM
AND
HOLLAND

TIM WEBB

D1446067

BOOKS

Author: Tim Webb
Cover design: Rob Howells
     Maps by Perrott Cartographics
     Photography: Tom Dobbie
     Beer glasses supplied by:
     The Beer Shop, 8 Pitfield Street, London N1
Typeset by T&O Graphics, Broome, Bungay, Suffolk
Printed by WSOY, Finland
Published by CAMRA, the Campaign for Real Ale, 34 Alma Road,
St Albans, Herts AL1 3BW
copyright CAMRA Ltd 1994
Reprinted 1995
ISBN 1 85249 115 9

To my daughter Jessica, whose first word was "bar".

Contents

Introduction

THE MAN FROM THE SUPERMARKET chain put it best. He said that most people's interest in special beers was at the same level as their parents' quest for fine wines twenty-five years ago. Then he pointed to the shelves of vintage clarets, Australian chardonnays and special offer Medoc, and smiled.

If he is right then the news is good for Belgium, which leads the world in the production of premium beers, without equal even in the real cask ales of Britain or the sparkling lagers of Germany and Czechoslovakia.

The Good Beer Guide to Belgium and Holland aims to introduce its readers to over a thousand different beers brewed in upwards of sixty distinct styles by more than a hundred and thirty artisanal breweries. In addition it can direct you to some of the finest cafés in Europe and take you inside two surprisingly underrated and welcoming countries right on Britain's doorstep.

Since our sell-out first edition appeared in July 1992, developments in the European beer world have been rapid. On New Year's Day 1993 the single market arrived.

In response, the giants of European brewing continue to make their takeovers and amalgamations, producing five superbrewers – BSN (based in France), Allied-Carlsberg (Britain & Denmark), Interbrew (Belgium), Guinness (Ireland) and Heineken (Netherlands). Meanwhile, in our pubs, clubs and supermarkets, strangely named brews arrive, some with with even stranger tastes, to confuse, please and mystify curious customers.

The theory goes that eighty per cent of us will drink any beer provided it does not have much flavour, while the rest want to try it all and will stick with the quality products. At least, that is what the man from the supermarket chain said.

It would not have been possible to compile this book without the invaluable guidance of Peter Crombecq, whose *Bierjaarboek* still manages somehow to keep track of every beer brewed by his country's occasionally eccentric brewers.

My thanks also go to Stephen D'Arcy and everyone in CAMRA Brussels especially for their work in Brussels and Pajottenland, to Jos Brouwer of *PINT Nieuws* for keeping tabs on the Netherlands and to Joris Pattyn for knowing me well enough to be rude about my more elementary misunderstandings.

The second edition has also been shaped by the contributions and influence of many dozens of supporters, amateur and professional, in Belgium, the Netherlands, Britain and the USA. Most will have to accept my gratitude in the unsatisfactory form of spotting their contributions in the text but I should single out Gary and Deb Yates, Andrew Dawes and Luut Claeys for special mention.

Finally, to Jan de Bruyne, Daisy Claeys, Henk Eggens, Piet de Jongh, Tejo Kromhout, Alain Mossiat, Jean-Pierre Van Roy, the De Belder brothers, Toon Denooze, Dirk van Dijk, Barend Midavaine and the hundreds of other café and brewery owners who continue to make drinking beer in their countries an unending pleasure, a heart-felt thank you and may your endeavours prosper.

Tim Webb
January 1994

General Information

BELGIUM

BELGIUM IS A COUNTRY of ten million people. It stretches from the North Sea into the heart of northern Europe and has been an independent kingdom since 1830. It is home to the EC, NATO and the European Court. It leads the world in brewing, cookery and administration.

In 1980 it was officially divided into two regions. The northern half, historically part of the Netherlands, is called Flanders. Its inhabitants are the Flemish. The southern half, historically part of France, is called Wallonia. Its inhabitants are the Walloons.

Belgium has ten "provinces", roughly equivalent to British counties. Most Belgians think there are nine so, like them, the Guide treats the northern and southern parts of Brabant as if they were one. The north of the country is largely agricultural, the central belt is industrial and the south is dominated by the forests, moors and rolling hills of the Ardennes.

The capital, Brussels, is known as the crossroads of Europe and is an international centre of government. Antwerp is a great port with an historic merchant city to support. The old industrial heartlands are based around Charleroi in the west and Liège in the east. Towns like Bruges, Ghent, Kortrijk, Tournai, Mons, Mechelen and Namur have preserved their centres so well that they could be tailor-made for tourism.

The country is awash with breweries, especially around the hop fields of West Flanders, Pajottenland on the outskirts of Brussels and the small towns of western Hainaut. Where German or British drinkers hold fast to the brands of their local brewery, many Belgians boast loyalty to a style of beer made nowhere except within a ten mile radius of where they live.

NETHERLANDS

THE NETHERLANDS IS A COUNTRY of fourteen million people. Its inhabitants are known as the Dutch and has been a nation in some form since 1579. The modern state dates from 1813 and is divided into twelve provinces.

The country is often called Holland, even by its own tourist authorities. Correctly this is only the name of the two provinces of the western Netherlands around Amsterdam, Rotterdam and Den Haag (The Hague). It is like mistaking

England for Britain but the error is so widespread that the Guide retains Holland in its title, while using Netherlands throughout its text.

The Protestant north, flat as a pancake and largely agricultural, traditionally eschews strong drink and believes in faith and hard work. The Catholic south, defined roughly as below the Ijssel river, pursues a more relaxed and tolerant path through life. The Dutch speak of having two states and then, after a pause generally add "plus Amsterdam".

The industrialised and densely populated west is known as the Randstad Holland and spreads south from Amsterdam to Rotterdam without much break. Here the business is done which has made the Netherlands a trading nation out of all proportion to its size.

Its beer culture has traditionally been fed from the breweries of Dutch Limburg and North Brabant, though its best known brewers, Heineken and Grolsch, come from the west and the northern midlands. Most welcome is the emergence in the past few years of breweries and beer cafés in the north, around Groningen, hopefully signposting better things to come.

THE LANGUAGES

ENGLISH IS SPOKEN WIDELY in both countries, especially the Netherlands. In northern Belgium they generally prefer tourists to speak English, not French.

The language of northern Belgium is Vlaams (Flemish) and of the Netherlands is Nederlands (Dutch). The differences between Vlaams and Nederlands are on the same scale as those between Scottish and English. British attempts to speak either version are generally greeted with sympathy rather than ridicule. The Walloons call the language of northern Belgium Nederlands.

Accents vary enormously. In the northern Netherlands they do not finish the word. In Amsterdam they will not use three words when two will do and only then provided a nod would not convey the complete message. The guttural splatters of the western Netherlands cannot be good for the tonsils. Antwerpers are plain speakers with a roughish tone, while for "BBC Flemish" you need to go to West Flanders.

The most obvious difference of pronunciation is between the soft Belgian "g" (a cross between "h" and "j") and the hard Dutch "g" (more like a "k").

Brussels is bilingual, though French dominates. There is also a strong, mangled dialect called Bruxellois or Brusselaer, which nobody born outside the city can understand. In Wallonia the official language is French. This is spoken with a strong accent and with a lot of local vocabulary which can vary from town to town.

The Treaty of Versailles, which divided the pickings after the First World War, left the Belgian province of Liège with a German-speaking district on its eastern border, around the town of Eupen. Inevitably, local variations have crept into common usage here.

Two other languages, both derived from Old Frankish, are spoken in southern parts of the Ardennes. Neither is officially recognised. "Walloni" reads and sounds like a cross between French and Welsh and is often incorporated in the names of shops or cafés. "Letzeburgish" is the daily language of the rural areas of the Grand Duchy of Luxembourg and is also spoken around Arlon in Belgium.

In the northern Netherlands the province of Friesland has its own language, Frysk. This bears little relation to most modern tongues but is said to have similiarities with Old English, as spoken in the Middle Ages. You can pick it up on the local radio and frequently hear it spoken, especially in villages. If you do not understand it, never mind, neither does anybody else.

GETTING THERE

DESPITE THE PROGRESS towards a single Europe, even EC citizens still need to travel with a passport or identity card.

If you take a car, the most expensive part of sea travel is the vehicle (cheaper for a party of four or five). Public transport is far better in Belgium and the Netherlands than in Britain, so consider whether you really need to take your own wheels. Our regular contributors usually only bother if they are bringing back beer.

BY SEA

WITH THE EXCEPTION of business travellers, most people arrive in Belgium and the Netherlands by sea. The ferry companies are all intent on keeping this trade even after Eurotunnel is well established. The modern North Sea ferry is no longer a warehouse with a propellor but rather a "leisure experience", seen by operators and many users as an essential part of the holiday or weekend break.

Currently, the pricing of the North Sea routes makes them better value for all cars and some foot passengers than their notoriously expensive cross-Channel competitors. When calculating the real cost of your route take account of the price of a cabin or reclining seat (compulsory on some routes), on-board purchases like meals, drinks and cinema tickets, plus the cost of getting to and from the port.

The quality of accommodation, seating areas and peripheral activities is good on most routes. Food quality tends to be better on the Dutch and French boats. Without exception, the ranges of beer are dull and unimaginative. The best advice is to stay sober and save yourself for the proper beers at your country of destination.

Note that both P&O's Dover-Zeebrugge route and Olau Lines' Sheerness-Vlissingen route have been discontinued.

The following companies all offer regular services:

Stena Sealink Ltd
Charter House
PO Box 121
Park Street
Ashford
Kent TN24 8EX
Tel: (0233) 647047

Dover-Calais
Harwich-Hook of Holland

P&O European Ferries
Channel House
Channel View Road
Dover
Kent CT17 9TJ
Tel: (0304) 203388

Dover-Calais
Felixstowe-Zeebrugge

Sally Lines
81 Piccadilly
London W1V 0JH
Tel: (071) 409 2240

Ramsgate-Dunkirk
Ramsgate-Ostend (ferry and jetfoil)

North Sea Ferries
King George Dock
Hedon Road
Hull
Humberside HU9 5QA
Tel: (0482) 77177

Hull-Zeebrugge
Hull-Rotterdam Europoort

Hoverspeed Ltd
International Hoverport
Marine Parade

Dover
Kent CT17 9TG
Tel: (0304) 240241

Dover-Calais (hovercraft)
Folkestone-Boulogne (seacat)

AIR TRAVEL

AIR TRAVEL throughout Europe is notoriously expensive and the routes between Britain and the Low Countries are no exception.

However, the profit on business flights is so high that it is usually possible to find seats for well under £100 return, especially if your stay includes a Saturday night. You are not the only person to think of flying out Friday afternoon/evening and returning Sunday evening/night and these tickets can get booked up months in advance, especially on London - Amsterdam routes.

If you collect Air Miles you will also find difficulties on the London - Amsterdam route, though London - Brussels, London - Luxembourg and eligible regional routes have fewer problems.

The convenience of using one of the smaller British regional airports can outweigh the extra expense of flying. You also avoid crippling car park charges.

Timetables and even airlines change frequently. Between our first edition going to press and the book being published three companies ceased operations, so take our listings as a rough guide only.

Amsterdam Schipol airport is 20 minutes from Amsterdam Centraal Station by fast, regular train. It has all the facilities you would expect of a top-mark international airport, except decent beer. It can get crowded at peak times. There are free direct phone lines from the arrivals area to over sixty city centre hotels, some of which are good value. Its duty-free shop is one of the cheapest and best stocked in the world.

Brussels Zaventem airport is 20 minutes from Brussels North and Central stations by regular but folksy train from the shabby airport station. Arrivals and departures use the same area, which is served by dozens of shops, bars and restaurants, few of which are duty-free. Despite Brussels being the capital of Europe, EC passport holders may take up to half an hour to clear immigration. The most expensive beers in Belgium can be found at the Interbrew-dominated beer café in the arrivals and departure area.

London Heathrow now has real ale bars in Terminal 1 and Terminal 4. Most other British airports do not.

Duty Free Goods

THERE ARE EVIL AND INCORRECT rumours that you can

now import limitless goods to Britain from other countries in the EC. This is an exaggeration.

Goods free of duty - i.e. bought on board ship or at airports - are still limited to one litre of spirits, or two litres of liqueurs/fortified wines, or two litres of sparkling wine, plus five litres of table wine. However you can now double this by re-importing any duty free goods you took with you to the continent, provided you have not opened the packaging.

There is no limit in theory to the amount of alcoholic beverages bought in shops or warehouses abroad which can be imported, provided they are for your own consumption. In practice this is taken as ten litres of spirits, 50 litres of wine and 200 litres of beer, unless you can persuade the customs officials that you are having a major party at which booze will be given away.

Note that British Airways flights from London to Brussels and Amsterdam do not have a duty-free facility but Brussels Zaventem has one on the way into the country.

BUS AND RAIL TRAVEL

BELGIUM

BELGIAN PUBLIC TRANSPORT is efficient; generally buses and trains run on time. Their routes tend to be co-ordinated with each other and reach even the most isolated parts of the country. With a few exceptions, such as the Meuse Valley, timetables are usually easy to follow, though as in Britain there are separate arrangements for weekdays and weekends.

Most Belgian main lines operate from about 06.00 to 22.00 with a few until 00.30. To give an idea of times, trains from Ostend go via Bruges (15 mins) to Ghent (40 mins) to Brussels (1 hr 20 mins) to Leuven (1 hr 40 mins) to Liège (2 hrs 20 mins). The route via Ghent to Antwerp takes 1 hr 30 mins. The Brussels to Amsterdam trains run hourly and take three hours. There is a direct train from Schipol Airport to Brussels via Antwerp.

A Benelux railcard is expensive (BFr 4.000) but worth considering if you are making long journeys. It gives you limitless travel on any five days in a calendar month anywhere within Belgium, the Netherlands and Luxembourg.

Crossing national borders can be a pain. The only links across the French border are Lille - Tournai and Lille - Kortrijk, which makes ferry connections awkward. Between Belgium and the Netherlands the only crossings are Antwerp - Roosendaal and Liège - Maastricht.

The trains are roomier than their British counterparts and do not have the sort of overcrowding problems familiar to London commuters. Belgian railway stations are a constant delight with their early 20th century architecture and decor. Antwerp Centraal is the supreme example but even the relatively simple buildings in Ostend and Bruges have their charm.

Even if you are travelling around by car, consider using public transport to get into, out of and around the larger towns and cities - driving in towns can be unpleasant and parking can be difficult, expensive and risky.

Brussels, Antwerp and other Belgian cities still run an extensive network of trams. These transports of delight add greatly to the visual appeal of their cities. In Brussels they dart in and out of tunnels, doubling as metro trains.

NETHERLANDS

DUTCH TRAINS AND BUSES run on time, almost invariably. Furthermore, most of them run at the same time every day, making route planning delightfully simple. The price of tickets is worked out on the number of kilometres travelled. A variety of special "rover ticket" deals are available at most railway stations. Some main lines run all night; most others operate from 06.00 to 24.00.

The public transport policies of the Netherlands are logical, consistent, pro-environment and incredibly sensible. Bus stations are usually next to train stations and timetables are designed to be compatible wherever possible. Train-bus tickets are often available. Bicycles are accommodated both on trains and at stations.

For areas where local access to trains is difficult, there is often a cut-price "treintaxi" which will take you from the station to your destination. You pay a little extra for your rail ticket and get the taxi at a heavily discounted rate.

Spend any length of time travelling in the Netherlands and your patience with the policies of British transport organisers - from national and local government through to public and private operators - may be sorely strained.

CAR TRAVEL

MINIMUM DRIVING AGE is 18. If you are taking your own vehicle, a GB sticker is still compulsory though nobody bothers very much. No green card is necessary for EC citizens, but take your driving licence, vehicle registration document and insurance certificate with you.

Both countries require a warning red triangle in the boot for display at an accident. Rear seat belts must be worn and no children under 12 are allowed in the front seat. Although you will be covered for Third Party insurance by your British policy, it may not cover anything else, so check. Either way, breakdowns will not be covered, so consider buying an AA, RAC or Europ Assistance policy.

There are practically no toll roads. Lead-free petrol is widely available, and cheaper than regular. Most Dutch petrol stations accept Visa/Mastercard but many Belgian ones do not, except on the motorways. The national speed limit is 120 kph (74 mph) but this is much lower in built-up areas and on minor roads. They have on-the-spot fines and humourless speed cops.

A car pulling into your path from the right may have priority, unless indicated otherwise by a solid white line. This crazy rule may lead to the odd run-in with geriatric kamikaze drivers but keeps life interesting. Speed restrictions are taken more seriously by drivers than in Britain and cruising in the overtaking lane of a major road is bad manners. They drive on the right-hand side of the road.

Neither country tolerates drink driving and with the strength of local beers being as deceptive as it is, the best rule is "DON'T DO IT!".

The motorway (or Autostrade) system throughout Belgium and the Netherlands is extensive. The ride is usually as smooth as in Britain but you will not find as much Red Cone Disease because neither country cordons off miles of roadway to resurface 50 yards at a time.

Town driving varies considerably between the two countries. In the Netherlands, war damage, land reclamation, relocation of the population and numerous other factors have allowed councils to plan their cities from first principles, so motor vehicles are directed away from areas of historic interest. There is usually plentiful parking, though this may be expensive.

In Belgian cities, inadequate parking, dozy driving, holes in the road, poor signposting and failure to name roads clearly are the norm. The worst problems are in Antwerp, Liège, Brussels and Ghent. More reasons to park at an out-of-town station and take the train into town.

Minor roads are "N" roads and major roads are "A" roads. Some "A" roads are also part of the European motorway network and may have a second designation as an "E" road. If that were not confusing enough, some ring roads around Belgian cities have a third designation as an "R" road.

Petrol is more expensive in Belgium than in Britain and more expensive again in the Netherlands. The ferries do not like you travelling with a full tank but a gallon under will save you a bit of cash.

ALTERNATIVE TRAVEL

CYCLING

IN THE NETHERLANDS, cycling is endemic and attracts many tourists. Much of the countryside is flat and cyclists are well catered for on the famous cycleways (fietspad). Many of these veer off the main road and take more picturesque but equally direct routes. The towns are not as cycle-friendly as many people think but do considerably better than in most other countries, including Belgium.

The Belgian countryside has some cycleways, especially in East and West Flanders, plus some of the rustic parts of Belgian Limburg and Antwerp province.

While the Dutch tend to bicycle like village postmen, many Belgians transform into Eddy Merckx in psychedelic frogman gear before hitting the saddle. This is an alarming and unexpected thing in a nation of normally mild-mannered people.

RAMBLING

LONG-DISTANCE WALKING is gaining in popularity in many parts of Belgium and the Netherlands. The footpaths are increasingly recognised and clearly staked out, especially in the national parks, nature reserves and other areas of natural beauty. Route maps are difficult to find and sometimes non-existent.

The most interesting hill walks are in the northern Ardennes, where hikers across the Hautes Fagnes in eastern Liège can find mile upon mile of wooden walkway suspended above the peat bogs and marsh land. Some of the long-distance paths in this area criss-cross the German border, so take your passport.

Other areas worth exploring are the Flemish Ardennes in the south of East Flanders and the old flatlands between Antwerp, Maastricht and the Lower Rhine.

HORSE RIDING

This is increasingly popular, especially in the flatlands of the southern and central Netherlands and across the border in Antwerp province. Some travel companies specialise in this type of holiday.

CANAL AND RIVER CRUISING

"Fun Boats", as the Dutch call them, are surprisingly uncommon, despite the extensive network of rivers and canals. The main reason is the continuing commercial use of the waterways for trade. Tankers of many thousand tonnes traverse the Netherlands on their way to the Ruhr and industrial barges carrying huge loads are still a common sight even in the picturesque river valleys of the Ardennes.

Hire companies are few and far between but some British operators have links. One British publication worth tracking down is "Through the Dutch and Belgian Canals" produced in one form or another since 1972 by Philip Bristow. [Editor's note: my old 1988 edition (ISBN 0-7136-5760-X; £10.95) was published by A & C Black under the Nautilus imprint.]

Given the increase of pleasure cruising in other parts of Europe it can only be a matter of time before interest grows. At present, the most commercialised boating areas are unfortunately in the beer desert of Friesland in the northern Netherlands.

ACCOMMODATION

IN BOTH COUNTRIES the European plan applies, whereby hotels and pensions (B&B places) charge per room, not per person. Breakfast is included unless stated otherwise. In effect this means that single rooms cost about twenty per cent more than in Britain while doubles cost thirty per cent less.

Budget hotels are significantly cheaper than British ones. There appear to be far more small, family-run hotels and these seem to pride themselves in attention to detail. £20.00 per head will usually buy something special. The up-market, glitz-driven, five-star hotels are as exorbitant as everywhere else but then their guests are rarely picking up the bill.

BELGIUM

IF YOU WANT TO BOOK up before you go or just want the best information about Belgian hotels, contact the Belgian Tourist Office, 29 Princes Street, London W1R 7RG, Tel: (071) 629 0230. They produce separate brochures on hotels in Flanders and Wallonia. These list details of over thirteen hundred places across the country, from the simple to the opulent, with their facilities, up-to-date tariffs, addresses, telephone and fax numbers.

Every entry in these brochures must reach certain standards laid down by Royal decree. This involves registering with the national tourist organisation and acquiring an official emblem plate displaying the standard of comfort and being inspected once a year. A few decent places evade registration but the system is definitely a great help to consumers.

Ordinary hotels are categorised "H". Extra facilities can earn between one and four stars. A hotel which fails to reach the "H" standard is described by the tourist board thus: "Possibility of spending the night, without the slightest guarantee of comfort". The Formule chain specialises in such places at budget prices.

In every large town the tourist office has details of all official accommodation and staff usually know of one or two private houses offering bed and breakfast. We recommend that you book ahead in summer for the coastal strip, city centres and especially Bruges, which can simply be "full" for weeks on end.

Campsites tend to be on the outskirts of town and to offer

reasonable facilities. Freelance camping nearer the centre of towns is about as welcome as it is in Hyde Park, except that the Belgian police are less amenable to the "I am just an ignorant foreigner" line of defence.

NETHERLANDS

EVERY DUTCH TOWN of any importance has a centrally placed, well signposted VVV tourist information office. Without exception we have found their staff to be well informed, courteous and helpful. They are sometimes so helpful that long queues build up in the busier offices. They tend to know everything there is to know about their locality and will hold information about other parts of their province. However, information about further afield, including accommodation, can be scant.

Dutch towns cannot always accommodate the volume of tourists which comes their way. Summer weekends, public holidays and Amsterdam itself are particular problems. Our advice for Amsterdam is always to book a room in advance for weekends between Easter and October and for weekdays between late June and mid September. Elsewhere you are usually okay to book on the day but be warned; if the VVV office says that the town has no vacancies, they mean it.

On one famous Easter weekend a couple of Guide stalwarts arrived at Schipol Airport early on Friday evening without a hotel booking and found 200 people camping out in the lounges waiting, they assumed, for a delayed flight. By midnight, having found floor space in the bedroom of a hotel under-manager's apartment for 75 Guilders each, they had realised that there was no hotel room available within 150 miles of the capital. One hotel owner advised them to try Belgium!

CAFÉ CULTURE

THERE ARE MANY SIMILARITIES between Belgian and Dutch cafés and their British equivalent, the pub. As always, it is the differences which cause the confusion for shy tourists and the fascination for experienced ones.

Throughout the Guide you will notice we have used the term "café" in preference to "bar". This was on advice that a café is somewhere that you pick up a beer, a coffee and sometimes a light refreshment, whereas in a bar you might pick up anything.

LICENSING

Belgian and Dutch cafés have to hold a licence, similar to the system in Britain. In some areas the number of licences available is severely restricted and a licence will tend to go with existing premises. However, it is common for a property owner to buy, say, a whole block of buildings, decide that the ground floor would do best as a café and so convert it to the purpose. Belgium has 50,000 licensed cafés. In 1900 there were four times as many for a population half the size.

In Belgium the premises and the owner are licensed separately and the person responsible for running the place has to have either a formal qualification or else substantial experience before they are accredited as a "moral person" suitable for such employment.

CHILDREN IN CAFÉS

Children are allowed into cafés in either country at any age provided they are accompanied by a responsible adult. The owner has the right to refuse admission to all or any. The age limit to enter unaccompanied and to buy or consume alcoholic drinks is 16.

The pressure not to take children into cafés is largely social. In popular tourist venues during the day, it should be no problem. In a brown café in the evenings you may be asked to remove them.

OPENING TIMES

These are generally determined by the owner and depend on commercial factors and personal preference. Licensing authorities can and do place some restrictions, but usually only when there are sound reasons.

Even in smaller towns you should have little difficulty finding a beer between 10.00 and 01.00. In most cities you should be able to find a beer at any time of day or night. There are several cafés in Liège which claim never to close, though we have not checked them out at 05.00 on a rainy Tuesday morning in late January!

CAFE STYLES

Like British pubs, Belgian and Dutch cafés come in all shapes and sizes. However, there is less tradition of having to be all things to all people. Cafés are much more likely to be unashamed specialists in trying to attract a particular type of customer to the exclusion of others. They can also change form many times during the course of a day.

An owner will often put careful thought into giving his or her café a logical combination of beers, other drinks, food, music, lighting, furnishings and opening times to reflect a particular speciality.

You can find heavily-timbered, plainly-lit cafés with candles on the table, where the music is baroque or light classical, the beers are high quality specialist ales and the food is delicious small snacks. In the next street might be a dimly-lit, boozy, cobwebbed dive with live jazz or background blues, dart boards and pool tables, with a beer list of more commercial heavyweights and food limited to plates of pasta. In the market square, perhaps there is a small restaurant renowned for its mussels or regional dishes, where there happens to be a good beer list because the owner is a beer lover and has started to serve cuisine à la bière.

Cafés can be called by a variety of names, including: auberge, bar, biercafé, bierhuis, bistro, bistrot, brasserie, café, café-biljart, café-restaurant, caves, eethuis, estaminet, gasthof, horeca, hotel, in, inn, kelder, proeflokaal, pub, restaurant, slijterij, snookertaverne, staminée, tapperij, taverne, taverne-restaurant and tea-room!

These various designations are interchangeable and do not mean much. "Hotel", "gasthof" and "auberge" do not necessarily guarantee accommodation. "Restaurant", "bistro(t)" and "eethuis" usually imply food but "café", "brasserie" and "taverne" are very unreliable in this regard.

A "proeflokaal" is theoretically a sampling room and often describes the brewery tap. However it can be used to describe cafés where you sup rather than quaff and in some cases is meaningless.

The most distinctive style of simple café is the "brown café". Typically this will be a small, single-room café where the walls and ceiling have been darkened by a century of tobacco smoke. There remain some superb examples, especially in Amsterdam and Antwerp.

The term "brown café" has become part of the politically desirable terminology of beer drinking and thus has been corrupted to include the many ill-lit dens of iniquity that decorate the average townscape. The rougher end of that spectrum is sometimes referred to as "dark brown". You will sometimes hear the owners of more up-market beer cafés describe their places as "light brown".

DECOR

The drab repetitiveness of British pub decor came about because most pubs are owned by or mortgaged to a brewery or pub chain. A small number of designers feed these chains with a small number of ideas and thus between 1960 and 1985 the great British pub drifted towards a single, dull evocation of indifferent taste.

In Belgium and the Netherlands, the average café is owned or leased by the person who runs it. Ordinary architects and designers provide the design ideas or else the landlord does the work himself. The result is often the sort of ramshackle affair which disgusts pub chain managers and delights customers. So while neither country boasts any more classic drinking establishments than Britain, they have far fewer production line models.

BEER RANGE

A typical Belgian café will carry between 12 and 20 beers. This is also true of the majority of Dutch cafés in the southern and central provinces. An exceptional range of beers would be defined as over 25 in the Netherlands and 40 in Belgium.

Cafés are often subject to "soft money" loans as in Britain. The standard Belgian deal is that the Pils from the sponsoring brewery will be stocked along with a range of other products, leaving the café owner the right to stock up to half a dozen bottled beers from other suppliers. In the Netherlands the brewer may tie one owner for five years to a wide range of products or for up to ten years to Pils only.

The Belgians import relatively little ale, though a few British brews do appear. One or two of these are brewed just for the Belgian market and are unobtainable in Britain except by re-importation. They also appear resistant to the bland, international lagers, the so-called "Wet Air" brands so beloved of North Americans. Even German and Czech lagers are fairly thin on the ground.

The Dutch beer market on the other hand is strongly influenced by imports from Belgium, Germany, Britain and literally dozens of other brewing nations. For example, you will not find Tsing Tao Porter in Hong Kong or China with any ease but we have found it in a country pub near Roermond in Dutch Limburg. The German influence is particularly noticeable around Maastricht in the south and Groningen in the north.

GETTING A DRINK

If you sit at the bar, just order. If you sit at a table they will usually come to you but not invariably. It is alright to take drinks from the bar to a table, or vice versa.

POURING A BEER

If the staff goofed the last one, don't be afraid to take charge. For example, if a sediment beer is poured half a bottle at a time, rather than down the side of a sloping glass in one go, the yeast will well up and cloud your beer. This is fine if you like it that way but otherwise just assume you know more about the subject that they do!

A few of the really cool dudes from the beer cafés manage to pour ales right into the centre of the glass, sometimes from a height, with perfect results. Don't mess around with these people; their nonchalant squash-player's wrist-flick finish took a decade to learn.

There is a Dutch habit of swilling a glass and leaving it dripping cold water while the barman fills it with beer. This is supposed to cool it and clean off the accumulated tobacco smoke.

UNDERSTANDING YOUR GLASS

You will rarely encounter the British habit of re-using the same glass. When you do, the glass will usually be swilled before use.

Different beers should be served in different types of glass. Nowadays a lot of this is about marketing gimmicks and being able to sell expensive badged glasses but there remains some logic to it.

A highly aromatic beer can best be appreciated in a wide-rimmed glass. An acid, spritzy beer needs to retain its gas, like champagne, and so needs a thin-rimmed tall glass. Potent winter brews benefit from warm hands clutching a broad cup on a stem while a thinner rim helps retain the gentle carbonation. A heavy sediment beer can be similarly warmed but will have so much life that a broad rim works better. Thick glass may keep a summer wheat beer cooler. A long tall glass pampers the vanity of a crystal clear Pils or fine pale ale.

A good café will know exactly which glass to use for serving your beer. They may have a selection of a hundred different types. They are increasingly easy to find in beer shops and warehouses and make appropriate souvenirs.

NIBBLES

One civilised custom which could be exported to Britain is the provision of a small plate of things to nibble with a beer. Usually this will be nuts or cheese. Sometimes it resembles more an Athenian mezze.

In the Netherlands, nostalgia merchants will love the bar-top nut machines in the more traditional cafés. Many are old "gob-stopper" dispensers, essential to the youth of any baby boomer. They dispense portions of salted almonds and roasted peanuts into small plastic bowls.

PAYING THE BILL

Most Dutch and Belgian cafés will run a tab for you unless you make it clear that you would like to pay for each round as it comes. It is often a matter of what you prefer. The exceptions come if they are busy, if the owner has a different custom or if he judges that you might leave without paying.

They will never indulge in the appalling British habit of charging you for food before it arrives. People are not as dishonest in continental Europe.

LEAVING A TIP

Generally, don't. Service is included in meal prices. If the bar staff have been exceptionally helpful – and this is not uncommon in the specialist beer cafés, a small token of appreciation is reasonable, though this need be no more than five per cent.

FOOD

BELGIAN CUISINE is an unexpected treat for many first time visitors. Regulars will talk about "French cooking in German portions" but this is simplistic and understates the love the Belgians have for what they term the Burgundian way of life. This involves fine eating and hearty drinking with affable company in comfortable surroundings.

One Belgian restaurateur put the importance of this national expression of good taste into perspective, when he said: "Our cuisine is perhaps the only aspect of Belgian life which unites us and makes us a nation". It is the single biggest issue on which the French south and Flemish north are at one.

The Dutch remain noticeably more "northern European" in the kitchen. As in Britain and Scandinavia, cooking tends to be simple and the ingredients plainer. Their culinary high-spots are mainly imported.

To understand how these different traditions came about you need to appreciate the region's history. The influence of the Mediterranean powers never really reached the area which is the modern Netherlands. However, much of Belgium was occupied for centuries by the Romans, the Byzantines, the Spanish and most recently the French. All shaped the area's view of food.

Perhaps the best illustration of this north-south divide is the differing traditions about fish and seafood. Where the Belgians have elevated the cooking of shell-on mussels into an art form, the Dutch concentrate on raw and cured fish, preferring their shellfish unshelled and deep-fried in batter.

Fast food is available throughout the two countries, though Bruges remains the only town in the world where MacDonalds had to leave because trade was bad. You can survive on Eurosnax such as pasta, pizza, omelettes and burgers if you really want but it seems a waste of a good opportunity. Even the most conservative tastes should find something to suit and to astonish.

BREAKFAST

Visitors to England always mention the breakfasts. So it is with the Netherlands, where breakfast is completely different but equally distinctive. The stock version offers a glass of fresh juice, four types of bread, butter, jam, chocolate nut paste, slices of cold meat and cheese plus a warm hard-boiled egg. Optional extras might include fruit cake, cheese spread, liver sausage, preserved dried fruit, date paste and chocolate drops. All is washed down with the obligatory rich coffee and optional condensed milk.

This feast is available all over Belgium too, usually in a

scaled down version. There is no tradition of cereal products or a fry-up, though hotels may offer these.

SNACKS

In bars or restaurants, you will routinely be offered nuts or pieces of cheese with a beer. The latter often come with mustard and celery salt. Sausages hanging to dry over the bar are called bierwurst and are best when dry and crunchy.

A typical Belgian snack lunch might consist of an omelette, a hash of smoked pork and vegetables or else a plate of charcuterie. They sometimes serve a plate of cooked vegetable, such as chicory (Flemish: witloof) prepared in the traditional local way, often baked with some cheese, or bacon pieces.

In the Flemish north you will find varieties of brawn, sometimes set in aspic and mixed with lightly cooked vegetables. These are typically served on rye bread with salad and pickles. In Brussels try to find kip-kap, a mixed meat terrine, or tête pressée, a brawn of pork or mixed meats.

In the French south, an assiette of various raw wet-cured, or baked dry-cured Ardennes ham is frequently on the menu, supplemented by a wide variety of sausages from leverwurst via black pudding to salami.

The pâtés of the Ardennes region are world famous. Their hallmark is their coarseness, though some do come in the smoother style of a foie gras and it is also possible to find Breton style rillettes.

Cannibaal and Americain are pulverised raw minced beef, the latter often accompanied by an egg yolk. This is typically served with salad and pickles on a piece of toast. The traditional accompaniment is "Worcestershire Sauce" from a familiar bottle.

The Dutch pannekoekhuis is similar to the French crêperie. Here the house specialty is pancakes, though many will also serve omelettes. The major difference from the British pancake is the array of sweet and/or savoury fillings.

The Dutch are also great fish eaters, particularly favouring herring (maatjes). British tourists seem to assume that these are cooked. They may be cured or pickled but more often are eaten filleted and raw. They can be taken with onion or pickled dill, sometimes on pappy white bread.

In Belgium, especially along the Flemish coast, the penchant is for mussels (mosseln) and eel (paling). All varieties of shellfish are appreciated and the array on sale in a typical open market will generally outstrip the average British supermarket's range.

The classic Flemish presentation of mussels is cooked in great pots, shell on, bathed in a soup of celery, onion and black pepper. Provençale implies additional tomatoes, red peppers and garlic. Served with an unending supply of chips, they can become a major blow-out.

Eel is generally conger. It is sometimes found smoked but more frequently is braised and served with one of a number of traditional sauces, such as "green" sauce, based on spinach but full of chevril and other herbs. That one is an acquired taste.

All over Europe, cheese production is burgeoning in a way that is similar to beer production. Artisanal cheese makers often set up as a response to the EC milk quota rules and the variety available is increasing so fast that it is impossible to keep up.

Edam and Gouda are familiar to most Europeans and are found all over the Netherlands. Edam is nearly all for a mass-market taste but Gouda comes in various forms depending on its degree of maturity and the production method. The older, drier versions are quite challenging.

The Dutch also like heavy, sweet, fudge-like cheeses in the Scandinavian style and holed smoky ones in the Swiss Emmental style. It is not uncommon to find herbs in the cheese.

In Belgium, cheeses in the Port Salut style abound. Try Damme or one of the Abdijkaas cheeses. These are like the trappist beers in that they are made by monks but they too have imitators. Other popular local varieties are softer, with chalk skins like Brie and Camembert. Try also Passendael – Gouda with raggedy holes and more flavour. Goats milk cheese is found in the Ardennes.

DINING OUT

Typical Belgian haute cuisine consists of a cleanly filleted piece of fish, meat or poultry, undercooked by British standards (i.e. just right), served with a meticulously prepared butter or cream sauce and the minimum of vegetables. Be prepared for chips with everything, even in the finest restaurants.

In the fish line, salmon and monkfish are prized whilst cod and plaice are not. Trout is usually farmed but is nonetheless popular, especially away from the North Sea coast.

Beef is held in high regard in restaurants but often strikes British diners as lacking full-blooded flavour. Its preparation makes up for much of this and non-vegetarians really should treat themselves to a proper Belgian steak and chips in one of the five national sauces (hollandaise, bearnaise, provençale, roquefort or archiduc). Cooking times are down one notch from Britain, so saignant (bloody) means practically raw, à point (spot on) means rare and bien cuit (well cooked) means medium. The phrase for well cooked is "Sorry, I'm English".

Lamb and plain pork meat are less common on menus and

where they appear are often marked at quite a low price. The quality is usually good, however. Offal is rarely found though there are some classic Walloon ways of cooking it.

Belgian chips (frites) are the best in the world. This is because they are parboiled before frying. The traditional way to eat them is with mayonnaise, though the roadside chip bars (frituurs/friteries) sell loads of different sauces nowadays. In a restaurant, if you finish your chips the waiter will often fill up the bowl without even asking.

Cooked vegetables are better than in France but still do not reach up-market British standards; they are too often over-cooked. The Brussels sprout really did originate in Brabant but is rarely seen out of season. Like fennel, asparagus, artichokes and other heartier vegetables, the Belgians may feature it as a meal in itself, braised in nutmeg or served in a cheese sauce.

Salad vegetables abound in the Netherlands throughout the year, grown in heated greenhouses by artificial light. The white super-radish variety, mouli, with the shape and texture of an inflated carrot, is frequently found shredded as a side dish.

Despite the wealth of vegetables and cheeses, proper vegetarian dishes are quite hard to find, compared to British and American restaurants. If you are vegetarian, be aware that even where you find vegetable-based dishes, all too often they are laced with small pieces of ham or cooked in animal fat.

As a rule, the further south you travel, the hauter the cuisine. However, across the whole of Belgium you will also find a lower but equally enjoyable type of cooking, sometimes called "peasant" or "grandmother" style. Its commonest form is the slow casserole. The Belgians gave the British the phrase "hotpot" from the southern Flemish dish hutschpot – which comes with as many spellings as there are recipes, but is basically a meat and vegetable stew. Stoovlees is a heavy, rich stew of beef or horse. Waterzooi puts chicken or fish with vegetables. Vlaamse carbonnade is beef cooked in brown ale. There are other dishes featuring rabbit, pigeon, venison and duck breast, often stewed with fruit and sometimes using beer in the recipe.

The Belgians are increasingly using high quality beers for cooking in the same way that the French use wine. There are now restaurants devoted to "Cuisine à la Bière".

The Dutch tend to adapt foreign cooking styles, rather than inventing their own. For many years they have had a liking for Swiss-style fondue cooking. This involves cooking your meal in a pot on the table. In Switzerland the pot traditionally contains melted cheese into which vegetables and pieces of cured or cooked meat are dipped on skewers. In the Netherlands, it is more common to see raw meat on the skewers and hot oil in the pot.

Two variations on this theme are the stone grill, in which the cooking of raw meat and vegetables happens on a super-heated stone at the table, and the pyramid, where the cooking surface is made from four triangular sheets of metal. None of these makes for great cuisine but they are good fun.

SWEET TREATS

Belgian chocolates are superb. Put this observation alongside those about frites, butter sauces, heavy stews and beer and you may understand why, as one native put it: "Many Belgians have a lower centre of gravity than the British.". Console yourself that they also have a lower rate of heart disease, somehow!

Chocolate is made in several strengths, from the ebony-black cocoa blends to the sweetened, white buttery ones. Inside you may find soft whisked fillings made with real fresh cream or the more traditional pralines, quarried from a mix of nuts and candy.

In the Netherlands, custard doughnuts make regular appearances on the counters of streetside vendors and in snack bars. Both countries offer delicious pastries with lashings of cream. Perhaps surprisingly this affinity with confections does not reach the dessert menu, which is rarely a major feature in a Dutch or Belgian restaurant.

TYPES OF RESTAURANT

As in France and Italy, the choice of restaurants and other eating places is huge in both Belgium and the Netherlands. The difference most British people notice is the far greater variety of relatively inexpensive, quality cooking.

The one disadvantage of having a strong national cuisine is that it tends to stifle the growth of ethnic restaurants. Outside Brussels and Antwerp, there are relatively few such places in Belgium and where they do exist, they often have distinct Belgian overtones. The Netherlands is different.

When the Dutch had an empire they used to control a large chunk of what is now Indonesia. Our first edition was quite rude about Indonesian restaurants and an apology is in order. Confusingly billed as "Indo-Chinees", the majority of these places err on the side of safety when it comes to spices and flavourings. In Java and Sumatra spicing is assertive, in the Netherlands it is timid. Nonetheless in the last ten years a substantial minority have taken Dutch-style Indonesian cookery into the serious league, as some superb feasts have confirmed, particularly in Amsterdam.

Proper satay (barbecued marinated pork with a spicy peanut sauce) sets the palate alight. Soups, taken at any time in the meal, should be fragrant but powerful. Sauces should be distinctively different from each other and not taste like a mild home-made curry. Take advice from the locals about the best places to try.

Argentinian restaurants, which are found with increasing ease, also took some stick in the first edition. Our experience of their tenderised low grade beef, sprayed with monosodium glutamate has not improved.

With the other nationalities of restaurant, generally the quality of the ingredients is better than in the country or region of origin but often the added flavourings have been under-emphasised. The one style which does seem to benefit is Greek food in Belgium, which takes on a different dimension when high quality meat meets the old-fashioned cooking methods.

OTHER DRINKS

BOTH BELGIUM AND THE NETHERLANDS have plentiful varieties of non-alcoholic beer. These are every bit as dire as their British and American equivalents. The ones which do not contain noxious preservatives taste foul. The others also taste foul but frequently manage to impart a hangover without any of the usual pleasure.

Dutch coffee is invariably strong by British standards, usually freshly brewed and generally brilliant. Belgian coffee is good but not great. Drinking chocolate comes in sachets from France and is tolerable. Tea comes in bags from Britain and is not.

The only distinctive soft drinks are the flavoured milk drinks, of which Chocomel (chocolate-flavoured) and Fristi (strawberry-flavoured) are the leading brands. Neither is as bad as it sounds. Both appease hangovers and small children equally effectively.

The usual fizzy, international-brand tooth solvents are available widely, though the low-calorie versions are not prominent and the caffeine-free varieties practically unobtainable in cafés.

G E N E V E R

The typical spirit of the Low Countries is what the Flemish call "genever", the Dutch "jenever" and the Walloons "genièvre". Like whisky, it is distilled from grain but usually without the colour or aroma. English gin was based on it.

In Belgium, there are only four distillers remaining. The largest is Smeets of Hasselt in Limburg. The others are Filliers of Bachte-Maria-Leerne and Van Damme of Oosterzele, both near Ghent, and St. Pol of Kortrijk. The fact that you can find many hundreds of Belgian genevers on the market is accounted for by the activities of the blenders, of whom up to a hundred appear still to be functioning.

The best genever is distilled from pure fermented grain.

The Vieux Système of distillation in Belgium uses tall copper cylinders which are steel-lined nowadays. Its flavour and bouquet derive from the inclusion of only the tiniest amounts of grainy esters in otherwise pure spirit so any short-cuts crucially affect the character of the drink. It varies in strength from 30–50 per cent abv. Many experts like to drink it ice cold, like Russian vodka, from a glass shaped like an hourglass and filled to the brim.

The sale of genever in Belgian cafés was outlawed in 1880 by an act of parliament called "De Wet van der Velder". This was not rescinded until the early 1980s and even now a spirits licence for a café can be an expensive luxury. The Guide lists two genever cafés in Ghent and Antwerp and mentions a third in Bruges.

In the Netherlands, production is concentrated on a few large companies. Cynics say that there is an alcohol factory in Bergen op Zoon and a flavour manufacturer in Hilversum. Put the two together and you have most modern Dutch spirits. This may be true for some jenevers but certainly not for corenwijn and moutenwijn, the pure grain spirits sold in the same stone jars as Belgian genever. Regardless of quality, Dutch jenever is universally 40 per cent abv.

Some producers market "oud" genever. The age of the spirit is largely irrelevant to quality unless the time is used to steep it in oak casks for a few years. However, colouring it light brown improves the sale price most agreeably.

Some old Dutch jenevers come in glass bottles in which a pod or sprig of aromatic herb is suspended. You can also find some fruit brandies made by sousing whole fruit (delicious) or mixing the spirit with fruit syrup (cacky). We have a special piece on spirits houses in our section on Amsterdam cafés.

It almost goes without saying that the Belgians dislike Dutch jenevers because of the commercial production methods and "foul taste". Equally, the Dutch dislike Belgian genevers because of their low alcohol content and "foul taste". Only British tourists think that tonic water should be added to either.

Beware beer drinkers: apparently we have a tendency to gulp genever, especially after we have a few beers on board. This is a serious error and can have dire consequences. Heed the lesson of history. Mishandling strong drink can lead to the kind of hangovers that make Calvanism look like a good idea.

If you want to know more, seek out the extraordinary Museum of Genever in Hasselt, where the café stocks nearly 400 different brands.

Beer Tourism

IN RECENT YEARS Belgium has become well aware of its popularity with beer lovers throughout the world. It is not surprising that tourist attractions have been created which reflect the importance of beer and brewing.

This interest has rubbed off on the Netherlands and at one stage both countries were promoting themselves as "Het Bierland" (the Beer Country).

Those who know the two museums of brewing in Burton-on-Trent, the great brewing town of the English East Midlands, may not be too impressed by the smaller scale, low key Belgian museums. However, the ones we list are nearly all labours of love and worth a peek.

BELGIAN MUSEUMS

ANTHISNES

Avouerie d'Anthisnes
19 Avenue de l'Abbaye
In southern Liège province. Described as a museum of mediaeval beers and brewing. Open from 1st April to 31st October from 10.00 to 12.00 and 14.00 to 19.00. Closed on Monday.

BEERSEL

Oud Beersel 1882 Museum
250 Laarheidestraat
Tel: 02 380 3396
The museum at Henri Vandervelden's Oud Beersel brewery is an idiosyncratic collection of objects, generally related to lambic brewing. It is only open on the first Sunday of the month from April to September, starting at 16.00.

BRUGES

Brugs Brouwerij-Mouterij Museum
10 Verbrand Nieuweland
Tel: 050 330699

The brewery museum is set in the old malthouse of the Gouden Boum brewery, parallel with Langestraat, off Molenmeers. The building was built in 1902 and was fully functional until 1976. It displays the history of the thirty-one breweries that were in Bruges before World War One and remains remarkably intact. There is a pleasant café selling all the Gouden Boum brews. Groups can pre-book a visit with a brewery tour. Open from 1st June to 30th September, from Thursday to Sunday between 14.00 and 17.00.

BRUSSELS

Confederation of Belgian Brewers Museum
10 Grand'Place
Tel: 02 512 2696
The Belgian brewers' official museum is appropriately based in the Brewers' Guildhouse on the world famous and beautiful Grand' Place in the heart of the capital. It is tiny and entrance costs BFr 100, for which you get a reasonable video and display board introduction to mass production brewing and a glass of what tastes like Vieux Temps, in the attractive small sampling room. It is open from 10.00 to 12.00 and 14.00 to 17.00, Monday to Friday all year round. Between April and September it also opens from 10.00 to 12.00 on Saturday mornings.

Musée Bruxellois de la Gueuze
56 Rue Gheude (Gheudestraat)
Tel: 02 520 2891
Cantillon brewery declares itself a museum. You can walk round at any time during business hours (Monday to Friday 09.00 to 16.00) on payment of BFr 60 entrance fee. There are guided tours every Saturday at 11.00, 14.00 and 15.30 for BFr 90. Groups tours of 20 or more can be arranged at other times. If you want a real treat, on the first

Saturdays in March and November, they have an open brewing day, but be warned that they kick off at 06.00 and it can be pretty crowded. It is all part of Jean-Pierre Roy's effort to teach the world to appreciate lambic beers.

HASSELT

Nationaal Genevermuseum
19 Witte Nonnenenstraat
Tel: 011 241144
Nothing really to do with beer but a well-presented collection of genevriana in the home town of Belgium's largest distiller, Smeets. There are around 400 different genevers on sale in the museum's café, representing a unique collection covering every known style and variation. Open Tuesday to Friday from 10.00 to 17.00 and Saturday and Sunday from 14.00 to 18.00. Closed in January.

HOUTHALEN-HELCHTEREN

Bier-o-Rama
Domein Kelchterhoef
9 Kelchterhoefstraat
Eight kilometres north of Hasselt is this "recreation hall" which now houses an exhibition about Flemish beers. There is a collection of glasses and bottles plus a video montage of the brewing process. In July and August it is open every day except Monday from 10.00 to 13.00 and 14.00 to 17.00. For the rest of the year it is only open on Wednesdays, Saturdays and Sunday morning.

LEUVEN

Stedelijk Brouwerijmuseum
Stadhuis
1 Naamsestraat
This small museum of brewing in the town which boasts Belgium's largest and smallest lager breweries, is found in the cellars of the Town Hall. It is open Thursday to Saturday from 10.00 to 12.00 and 14.00 – 16.00.

POPERINGE

Nationaal Hopmuseum
71 Gasthuisstraat
In the middle of the West Flanders hop growing region is the ultimate museum in praise of the bitter berry. A 1936 black-and-white movie leads you through hop cultivation before the era of mechanisation. There are over 300 implements on show. Admission is BFr 80 and includes a glass of the local Hommelbier from the Van Eecke brewery. Parties may book at any time between March and October. Individuals can visit between 14.30 and 17.30 on Sundays and Public Holidays between May and September, and daily in July and August.

TOMBERG-RODT

Biermuseum
Ski-Centrum am Tomberg Rodt
In the German district of Eastern Liège, near the village of Roth, near Sankt-Vith, in the unlikely setting of a ski centre, this museum is said to contain 2,000 bottles and glasses from 62 countries plus some old brewing equipment. It is open on Saturday and Sunday 10.00 to 18.00.

DUTCH MUSEUMS

ALKMAAR

Biermuseum de Boom
1 Houttil
Tel: 072 113801
The longest established Dutch beer museum, now heavily sponsored by Heineken. Housed in a former brewery. It gives a good idea of how artisan beers are brewed, including displays about malting, brewing and cooperage. It has a canalside café in the basement (see Dutch Cafés: North Holland). It is open Tuesday to Saturday from 10.00 to 18.00 and Sunday from 13.00 to 17.00.

HILVARENBEEK

Museumbrouwerij De Roos
20 Vrijthof

The building that was North Brabant's De Roos brewery from 1850 until 1940 was opened as a museum in September 1992, when there was free admission to the exhibition of the brewing process for two days. It is not yet clear what their future plans are.

MOLENBEEK

Brouwerijmuseum Raaf
232 Rijksweg
Tel: 080 5811787
Directions appear under the café entry (see Dutch Cafés: Gelderland). A three-storey display of old brewing equipment plus a video of the brewing process in the 1950s give a rough idea of how brewing is done. Most of the time you are allowed around the current day brewery to get an even better idea. Hours are limited but you can hire the site for private functions and it is particularly popular as a venue for wedding receptions! Given that Raaf is brewing to capacity, it will be interesting to see what they do with the dismantled factory in the brewery forecourt. It opens from 12.00 to 17.00 every Sunday and, in July and August, daily except Monday.

Visitors are welcome at Cantillon Brewery

BREWERY VISITS

THE MAJORITY OF BREWERIES in Belgium and the Netherlands will be happy to arrange visits by tour parties, with advance notice. A few will open their doors to casual visitors. They will often sell their products by the bottle or case and sometimes this is the object of the exercise, so use discretion. The thoroughness of the tour and the standard of English spoken, varies.

BELGIUM

Visitors to Bruges can see inside the Straffe Hendrik brewery on a guided tour March to September, daily except Sunday, at 11.00 and 15.00 provided numbers warrant it. Tours of the modern brewery cost BFr 50 and include one drink. If the old brewery is included the cost rises to BFr 100 but includes a panoramic view of old Bruges.

In the brewers' town of Watou the new brewery, De Bie, welcomes visitors every Sunday between 10.00 and 18.00 and again on Friday evening between 15.00 and 18.00. De Dolle Brouwers is another West Flanders brewery that opens its doors on a Sunday, at 15.00 sharp. And if mother conducts the tour, you are in for a treat!

In East Flanders the Crombé brewery, just off the main square of Zottegem opens its doors on Thursday and Friday from 08.00 to 17.00 with a break for lunch and then again on Saturday mornings from 09.00 to 12.00.

The Cantillon brewery in Brussels has practically an open door policy, as described above in the section on Beer Museums. It will also sell direct to the public. The other lambic brewery described there, Oud Beersel of Beersel, is much more limited in its opening times but equally appealing.

Down the road in Leuven, Domus has its small lager plant on show and a short conducted tour is not difficult to arrange if the brewer is not busy. You turn up and take your chances.

The Kerkom brewery opens its doors on Sundays and public holidays for you to try Bink in its attractive proeflokaal. A much larger Limburg brewery, Martens of Bocholt, only accepts groups but has a museum on site, exactly the same arrangement that occurs at the Bosteels brewery in West Flanders.

We have less information about Wallonian breweries but we do know that Blaugies brewery in Hainaut has a surprisingly open door. Visitors are welcome on Wednesdays and Saturdays from 17.00 to 18.30 and on other weekdays from 09.00 to 13.00.

Vapeur in northern Hainaut opens the doors of its rambling brick-built Wallonian pile for public brewing days on the last Saturday of the month, commencing 09.00.

La Ferme au Chêne at Durbuy in Luxembourg province must have the smallest functioning brewery in Belgium. The conducted brewery tour takes about thirty seconds so they include a video of the brewing process to extend the visit!

NETHERLANDS

Drie Ringen brewery in Amersfoort has a brewery café actually inside the brewery which is often staffed by the brewer himself. The Utrecht wheat beer brewery at the Oudaen in Utrecht conducts regular brewery visits to its cellars on Wednesdays, Saturdays and Sundays involving a small fee for a small beer.

At the Amsterdams Brouwhuis at the Café Maximiliaan, part of the brewery is actually in the bar area. For more details see the entry under Dutch Cafés: North Holland.

Arcen brewery in the northern part of Dutch Limburg is now part of Allied-Carlsberg but they still encourage customers to come to the brewery tap, called De Proeverij (see Dutch Cafés: Limburg) and trips around the brewery are often possible.

The Gans brewery in the Hollandsche Hoeve craft park in Goes, Zeeland is a real craft brewery and opens to the public for sales and visits every Saturday from 13.00 to 17.00. There is an artisanal cheese maker on the same site. Parties can book in for an evening by arrangement.

At Raaf brewery in Gelderland, brewery trips are strictly for parties only but party bookings are pretty regular and they let stragglers tag along.

BEER FESTIVALS & CARNIVALS

SOME BELGIAN TOWNS used to have beer festivals like miniature versions of the Munich Oktoberfest. However, these drifted towards being unpleasant single-sponsor piss-ups and so most have faded away.

The modern day beer festival is similar to its British counterpart, often mounted by one of the Belgian or Dutch beer consumer organisations and with that marvellous mix of surprising professionalism, undoubted enthusiasm and endearingly amateurish edges.

Belgium and the Netherlands each has one national festival, details of which appear below. However, there is also an array of mini festivals organised by regional groups of beer lovers, chains of cafés or entrepreneurial bar owners. The easiest way to find details of these is to take a subscription to either OBP or PINT (see Beer Organisations).

THE 24 HOURS FESTIVAL

Organised by OBP and usually held on the second weekend

in September, at the Stadsfeestzaal in Antwerp, a huge hall on the street called Meir that is on the main road from Antwerp Centraal Station to the city centre. An excellent place to sample draught Belgian beers and some bottled brews. Between 40 and 50 breweries take stands and there is a system of purchasing 15 cl glasses of beer so it really is a tasting session. There is a small entrance fee, entertainments and some snacks.

BOKBIER FESTIVAL

The Dutch group, PINT, holds a festival of bokbiers in Amsterdam on the first or second weekend of November. In 1993 this was at the old Olympic stadium but may move in future years. Of the consumer-run beer exhibitions only CAMRA's Great British Beer Festival has a longer pedigree. The event has now spawned imitators all over the Netherlands and chains of cafés such as ABT offer wide ranges of bokbiers at the same time.

CARNIVAL

Although town beer festivals are a thing of the past, many Belgian and Dutch communities continue a long tradition of "Carnival". These tend to be impressively boozy affairs, often built around an ancient pageant celebrating some long-forgotten event in national or civic history. Some can last up to three days. The most popular dates are between February and June. They are far too numerous to list but a few deserve special mention.

At Binche, between Charleroi and Mons, on Shrove Tuesday, it becomes politically correct to throw oranges at people during the procession of the Gilles (or clowns). On the third Sunday before Easter at Stavelot in the northern Ardennes the grotesque and bizarre Blancs Moussis dance through the streets like extras in a Peter Greenaway movie. Traditionally more sober, but equally unnerving, is the Procession of the Penitents at Veurne in West Flanders on the final Sunday of July.

POPERINGE HOP FESTIVAL

The beeriest carnival is held in Poperinge, the capital of the hop growing region of West Flanders, once every three years on the third weekend of September. The next one will be in 1996. In the other years they make over the Festival Hall to 15 breweries and have a mini beer festival with tasting competitions and quizzes.

To give an idea of the scale of some of these events, the pageant at the Poperinge show, at 15.00 on the Sunday, has 1,400 participants in all, including seven marching bands and 12 themed floats. The week-long bash culminates on the Sunday evening with a practical celebration of beer and brewing in which the town entertains, among others, representatives from the hop towns with which it is twinned

(Zatec in the Czech Republic, Wolnzach in Bavaria and Hythe in Kent).

TOURS

POPERINGE
The Hop Route

The tourist office in Poperinge will supply a map with a bicycle route around the hop growing areas. You can work the route to include visits to some of the World War One battlefields, the café by St Sixtus Abbey near Westvleteren and the famous Hommelhof restaurant in Watou.

HALLE
The Breughel Route and the Gueuze Route

From the tourist office in Halle you can acquire suggested routes around the Senne Valley area where gueuze beers are produced. Surprisingly, no suggestions are made about where to sample the beers, so you will need to use the route in combination with our listings under Belgian Cafés: Brabant. The essential stopping off point is Beersel but other gems can be found.

Beer Styles

THOSE WHO UNDERSTAND WINE realise how diverse are its many different forms. Those who prefer beer generally do not, though there are far more variations of style open to the brewer than the wine-maker.

For too many people, beer is a straw-coloured, weakly alcoholic, canned or cannistered, bitter-sweet fluid, code-named "pils" or "lager". Some have heard of other beers, like bitter and mild, or stout, which is Irish and brown ale which is not.

These are the people who have never been to Belgium or, if they have, were ill-prepared. They may die believing that the difference between a good beer and a bad one is in the size of the glass.

In the next few pages we outline 60 completely separate, definable styles of beer found in Belgium and the Netherlands and discuss some of the variations within each style. We then go on to give details of nearly 800 different brews and where you can find them.

The common link is that all are brewed from a mash containing at least seventy per cent grain, that all contain hops and all are fermented by yeast at some stage in their maturation.

To make the rest of the story understandable, perhaps it would be best to start with the bare essentials.

HOW BEER IS MADE

THE INGREDIENTS

WATER is for cleaning the brewery floor. Liquor is what you brew beer with and its mineral content is important, though nowadays this can be doctored. It makes up over 90 per cent of most beers.

Grain is the source of the sugars which are fermented to make beer. Most beers use mainly MALT, an abbreviated term for malted barley. This is barley which has been soaked and warmed to help it germinate, then cooked to capture its sugars.

HOPS are herbal weeds, with leafy berries called cones, which through careful cultivation over the centuries have developed flowery aromas, bitter flavours and strong preservative qualities.

YEAST is a living micro-organism which ferments various types of sugar into alcohol and carbon dioxide gas.

THE METHOD

1. To extract the sugars, the grain is crushed in a mill to make GRIST and then boiled in the water to form a runny

porridge called the MASH.

2. When filtered, the mash becomes SWEET WORT, to which are added hops. When this is boiled (or BREWED) the mixture becomes HOPPED WORT.

3. When the brewing is finished, the wort is pumped into tanks, where it cools before the yeast is added to start the PRIMARY FERMENTATION, in which the grain's sugars are converted to alcohol and carbon dioxide gas.

4. Once fermented, some beers undergo further CONDI-TIONING. Whether or not this occurs, they will eventually be partially or completely FILTERED to remove yeast and other solids and might be PASTEURISED to kill off remaining yeast, before being RACKED into bottles, cans or barrels.

THE VARIATIONS

A skilled brewer can alter almost every part of the process described above. Historically, the ability of brewing scientists and artisan beermakers to do just that, has left us with a huge range of different beer styles. The major variations happen because of changes to the ingredients, the method of fermentation and/or the preparations made before sale.

CHANGES TO THE INGREDIENTS

Malt

Malted barley comes in different qualities depending on the species and how it is grown. It then takes on numerous characteristics depending on how it is prepared. Darker, richer malts add colour and caramel flavours to a beer. Pale "crystal" malts leave a lighter colour and grainier character.

In lager brewing, great play is made of limiting the amount of protein from the grain which gets into the sweet wort. Decoction is a process of running clear wort off a sediment. (If you want to take the upper hand in a conversation with a beer bore, floor him – it is always a him – by singing the praises of triple decoction mashing.)

Although the use of barley malt is the best established, the brewer is at liberty to use many other sources of sugar. Using sugar itself will increase the alcohol content but add no flavour and thus may detract from the character of the beer. On the other hand, using other cereals such as unmalted wheat may give the beer a distinctively different grain character from standard beers.

As well as unmalted wheat we are aware of Belgian and Dutch brewers using unmalted barley, malted wheat, malted and unmalted oats, rye, buckwheat and, in one case, malted millet! In some new beers from Wallonia, honey is added to the mash.

Belgian brewers have a long tradition of adding fruit to fermented beer to spark re-fermentation. In some cases whole fruit is used and in others juice works better. This practice should be distinguished from the habit at some breweries of adding fruit syrup to a completed brew before bottling or kegging, as a British adolescent adds lime cordial to lager.

Hops

The Flemish probably had hops in the 9th century, 400 years before the British. Originally, hops were used as a preservative but their bitter and flowery qualities also appealed to drinkers. Apothecaries swore they were medicinal. Different hop varieties have different degrees of bitterness, mixes of aromas and preservative strength.

Nothing preserves beer better than hops. If a brewer wants to avoid bitterness or flowery esters altogether, for example in the production of lambic beers, he can use old hops, as the preservative effect outlives their other qualities. However, many other substances can add flavour to a beer.

As well as the fruits and honey already mentioned, fig juice, dates, dried orange peel and juniper berries appear in popular and well-known Belgian ales. Spices such as coriander, cinnamon, cumin, aniseed, vanilla and ginger have been spotted as have mint, woodruff, ginseng and horseradish!

Strength

British and American beers are weak and large quantities may be drunk in a single session. The European standard beer contains five per cent abv (alcohol by volume) and is drunk in judicious quantities. Some Belgian and Dutch beers top ten per cent abv so the brewer has considerably greater room for altering the recipe without heavily slanting the flavour. At the higher strengths, the alcohol lends a taste in its own right.

CHANGES TO THE FERMENTATION PROCESS

Yeast

Yeast is often seen as a brewer's thumbprint. Although all brewers' yeasts are similar, no two strains are identical and two beers of the same recipe, made by identical methods with different yeasts will have different flavours. Every commercial brewery would prefer to possess its own reliable yeast(s).

Primary fermentation

At this stage in the process a critical distinction is made. A beer is either "top-fermented" or "bottom-fermented". Top-fermented beers are known correctly as "ales". Bottom-fermented beers are becoming collectively known as "lagers".

The distinction is not complicated in its origins. Lagers are fermented more slowly at lower temperatures, causing the yeast to sink to the bottom of the tank – hence bottom fermentation. It is an altogether more organised process than ale fermentation, which occurs at higher temperatures, causing volatility which makes the yeast rise to the top of the tank – hence top fermentation.

As well as making alcohol, fermentation results in the production of small amounts of hundreds of different organic chemicals which can be picked up by human tastebuds. Especially in ale fermentation, these create a wide variety of subtle flavours found also in the taste of hundreds of other items. Hence the emergence in recent years of a more vivid and colourful language to describe the flavour of beers. It is not just that beer writers are trying to sell their books to wine buffs!

Yeast being vital to beer production, you would have thought that it would pay the brewer to be very careful what strain he adds to his brew. So it is in every form of brewing, except that found at the lambic breweries around Brussels and nearby Pajottenland. Here the brewer relies on natural micro-organisms falling from the night sky onto his cooling wort to bring about his fermentation. This uniquely chaotic process has been going since the days of the Breughels and we hope will continue long into the future. We give a fuller description of this later.

CHANGES IN PREPARATION FOR SALE
Conditioning at the brewery

Some beers do not condition at all. As soon as primary fermentation has subsided, they are filtered and racked off into casks or bottles, or else they are killed off by pasteurisation and bottled, kegged or canned.

It is a simple general rule that the best beers will not have been pasteurised but will have undergone some form of further conditioning.

Proper lagers condition as a result of prolonged storage at low temperatures. This stage is actually called "lagering", after the German word meaning to store. The fermented brew is filtered into tanks in the brewery cellar where it remains for weeks or months, gently developing character.

British cask-conditioned ales condition in the barrel (or cask), thanks to residual yeasts which extend the fermentation period. If you store a beer in a wooden cask for longer than a few weeks, not only will most of the sugars ferment out but sour lactic and acetic tastes will evolve. This is exactly what some Flemish brewers do to brown ale and in a slightly different way, what a lambic brewer does to age the ales in his cellars.

The final trick allowed to the brewer is to breathe life back into the flat old ales by blending them with younger ales which still contain sugars. This mix produces a beer which shows all the maturity of age but appears to retain the liveliness of youth.

Conditioning in the container

Although you will sometimes find young lambic sold straight from the barrel, there is no great tradition of cask-conditioned beers in modern Belgium or the Netherlands. What does survive frequently, however, is the practice of bottling beers with a yeast sediment (Flemish: op gist; French: sur lie). This is usually achieved by filtering the beer, bottling it and reseeding with yeast before capping the bottle. Either way it allows the beer to continue developing its character.

Beers which have been pasteurised contain no active yeast. Filtered beers contain a little. Sediment beers contain a lot.

Sediment beers cannot be canned or kegged as the containers would explode. In casks they have a shelf life of about three weeks. In bottles the initial shelf life is six months though stronger brews may weather considerably better. On the other hand, sediment beers in good condition taste the best.

Pasteurised beers do not develop flavours beyond pasteurisation so unless they were brewed to spectacular recipes, they can taste dull. Their advantage is a shelf life which may be measured in years.

Filtered beers are an attempt at compromise which often fails to satisfy either the demands of the shop or café owner for a longer shelf life or the desires of customers for a top-rate beer.

Ageing in the cellar

Combine the high gravity of specialist Belgian beers with the yeast content of the bottle and it is not too surprising that many beers continue to age nicely in the cellar, in the case of some gueuze beers for up to 20 years.

A recent fad has developed among Belgian beer lovers for beers which have been aged in the cellar for so long that they taste sherried. This is an attractive quality in small quantities. Whether the appreciation of "vintage ales" will catch the public taste remains to be seen.

THE CLASSIFICATION OF BEERS

THE CLASSIFICATION OF DIFFERENT beer styles is a recent art. Historically, even common beer descriptions are coined loosely and are often confused. It does not help that they are grossly misused by brewers and marketing men, especially when trying to boost the profile of a drab product.

To appreciate the artisanal Belgian and Dutch beers, even the plainest of speakers needs to have some understanding of what he or she is drinking. What is attempted here is not a definitive classification, as such a thing does not exist. See it more as a considered opinion, which is developing gently with years of experience but has not yet reached full maturity.

When most people think of European beer they think of lager. So do Belgians, who drink large quantities of the stuff. Perhaps ironically, given the huge storehouse of excellent ales in the country, Belgian lager is remarkably dull. The Dutch produce a broader range of styles and have a few which are outstanding but have little to compare to the lagers of Bavaria and the Czech Republic. So if you are reading this on the ferry and are determined not to chance your arm on some of the grown-up beer styles to which this book has dedicated most of its efforts, we suggest you find Ostend or Rotterdam station and take the through train to Munich or Prague.

That is not to say that lager is inherently duller than ale; far from it. Lagers have cleaner tastes because of their slower fermentation which is preferred by brewers because it is more predictable. Indeed the best lager breweries keep things even tighter by meticulously removing potential sources of cloudiness from the beer at every opportunity. This degree of control means that in order to make a classic lager, the recipe must be tip-top, and to create a new style, the variation to ingredients or production method has to be greater.

Where the Germans and Czechs manage a widely varying range of lagers, light and dark, weak and strong, dry and sweet, gentle and bitter, fresh and matured, the Belgians and Dutch stick most of the time to the safer Pilseners and even then fail to make them to the highest standards.

PALE LAGER

Pilsener

The world's favourite beer style. It is often spelt "Pilsner" or shortened to "Pils", which is the term used in the Guide's brewery sections. It is named after the Czech town of Plzen, which used to be Pilsen when it was part of German-speaking Bohemia.

Pilsener makes up 70 per cent of all the beer sold in Belgium and 90 per cent of that sold in the Netherlands. Despite this, there is virtually no market for top quality Pilseners and most Belgian and Dutch beer experts steer clear.

Because very few Pilseners reach above five per cent abv, there is very little body in which to hide a substandard recipe. So any Pilsener brewed from a mash which is not 100 per cent barley malt is likely to be shown up. Equally the hop count needs to be high or else the brew will lose its bite. Finally, to develop all its flavours, Pilsener needs to be lagered for at least eight and preferably 12 weeks.

Most Belgian and Dutch Pilseners contain a significant percentage of non-malt sugars, have lowish hop contents and are lagered for six weeks. Their only saving grace is that they are not quite as awful as the most popular British, American,

42

Canadian, Australian, Mexican, New Zealand, Indian, Thai, Italian, Norwegian or Danish brands which increasingly clog up the shelves of European supermarkets.

Not everything is bad news. One Dutch Pilsener, Christoffel Bier from the St. Christoffel brewery near Roermond, would hold its own in a Munich bierkeller and comes close to gaining a five star rating. None of its Dutch fellows earns a fourth star, not even Grolsch, which now shares three, along with the recently elevated Heineken Pils. Several Belgian Pilseners reach a three star rating and one or two, such as Strubbe's Super Pils, scrape four stars.

To the residents of Plzen: the Guide agrees that Pilsener has become a catch-all phrase to describe any light-coloured lager which cannot be defined as anything else, but will continue to join in this abuse of your town, at least until Northamptoner becomes an internationally recognised term.

Wiener

The brewers of Vienna have traditionally used a darker, richer malt which imparts a faint toffee aroma to the brew and gives a fuller, orange-copper colouring. It is generally a less bitter form of lager than Pils and for reasons which are not entirely clear, it has been popular for some years in the Netherlands. The typical strength is five per cent abv. One Belgian brewer, St. Jozef, brews a slightly stronger example called Bokkereyer.

Dortmunder

Dortmund is arguably the least famous of the great German brewing towns but in fact produces the greatest quantity of beer. Its typical style is similar to proper Pilsener but with a more robust, slightly drier, hoppier, more aromatic character. When this is translated into Dutch, it also implies, though not invariably, one or two extra per cent of alcohol. Gulpen, Kroon and Leeuw have passable ones but Alfa Superdortmunder seems the best.

Münchener

Munich (München) is the city where lager fermentation was discovered and although most of its production nowadays is of Pilsener-style beers, a darker, spicier local style remains. In the Netherlands, St. Christoffel played about with quite a nice one a few years ago and Us Heit claim to make one currently.

Pale Bok

The story of bokbier is outlined below. Whether its spring equivalent, meibok, ever existed in the annals of Dutch brewing before 1988 is questionable. Ironically, the ruddy-amber, sweetish and complex pale bok beers that make the spine of this new style share more of the characteristics of a German Bockbier than do those of the darker October boks.

Oranjeboom call their fine example Lentebock, while Alfa

drop the "c". Lindeboom, Kroon and Gulpen prefer Meibock, leaving Grolsch with the only Meibok. As a rule all these beers are appealingly rounded and sweet but with enough maturity to make them interesting. Many smaller brewers make an ale style in imitation and so may some larger producers in the near future.

DARK LAGER
Dark Bok

Every Dutch beer enthusiast has heard of bokbier, not because it is a great style but because it stamped out a principle. Bokbiers are Dutch, they are different and no brewery big or small has the right to order their destruction.

The earliest traditions of lager brewing involved using the cold Alpine caves in Bavaria to store beers over the hot summer for consumption in the Autumn before fresh beers were available. In the Netherlands it seems more likely to have been a tax dodge than the long hot summers but the principle was the same. Hence came bokbier, a dark, strongish, bitter beer style, released on the first Monday of October every year since the Dutch had an empire and PSV Eindhoven played barefoot.

Possibly because the Dutch dislike the idea of being brewing innovators, they say that the style is based on German Bockbier. While the colour is similar to one of the styles of German bocks and the billy-goat logo has come too, and while nobody can deny the similar spelling, there the likeness ends. Where the German brews are fullsome and warming, Dutch bokbiers are simple and direct. Distant cousins maybe, sisters never.

By 1975 bokbier had all but died out. However, it was adopted as the cause célèbre of the Dutch beer revival and in 1991 nearly 30 different varieties were produced. By 1993 the gilt was off the gingerbread and several famous beer cafés stocked only a small range. However, some brewers enlivened the choice by introducing wheaty versions called tarweboks (below). It remains to be seen whether the tradition of a single, annual brew will hold. There is no technical reason why it should; one of the attractions of the move towards tarweboks must be to remove the restrictions on marketing imposed by a seasonal product.

Almost all bokbiers are of 6.5 per cent abv. They vary a little from year to year. The offerings from Grolsch, Amstel and Ridder have impressed the most. There is a modern tendency for smaller ale brewers to imitate the style in ale form, though these can be equally, if not more successful.

Wheat Bok

In 1992 Heineken caught the beer world by surprise by producing a bok made from a recipe with 30 per cent wheat. It was lighter in colour than typical October bokbiers, sweeter, grainier and most appealing. They called it Tarwebock and to our knowledge it was unique at the time. For 1993 a few other Dutch breweries imitated the idea and Heineken had a second go with a different, many would say inferior, brew. A style was born. This is probably the only instance in history of a multinational brewery corporation inventing a new variety of specialist beer.

Stout Lager

One or two Dutch stouts are bottom-fermented. The most popular is Heineken's Van Vollenhoven's Stout. Whether this is bottom-fermented for convenience or by tradition we do not know. In the third world there are numerous examples of local breweries producing a Pilsener type beer and adding company X's stout mixture to it. We know of no equivalents in Europe, so discount this theory.

STRONG LAGER

Bock

If only on the principle that it is no use holding an opinion unless you are willing to be guided by it, the Guide has categorised separately that small number of Dutch beers which are brewed more in the mould of a German Bock than Dutch bokbier. These include the excellent Brand Imperator. In Belgium, Eupener's Klosterbier gets bockier as the years go by.

Dubbelbock

And as if to clarify by confusing things further, we have also classified a few stronger lagers as being in the German Dubbelbock style. Brand Dubbelbock is in this small, elite group, as is Belgium's strongest lager, the surprisingly impressive Bugel from Domus.

WEAK LAGERS

Oud Bruin

As the Belgians have table ales, so the Dutch have table lagers. These are collectively known as oud bruin beers and tend to be cloyingly sweet, to contain less than 3.5 per cent abv and to be drunk by the oppressed. Many Dutch beer lovers express a nostalgic regard for these beers but none is strong enough to be included in the Guide.

HOLY ALES

In Britain the connection between beer, brewing and the church has largely faded into history. In the Roman Catholic parts of Europe, however, a more complex relationship survives and in Belgium and the Netherlands, six abbeys survive which continue to operate commercial breweries. Furthermore, in a world where romantic facts are all too frequently contrived, it is comforting to know that they are all largely staffed by real monks, known as fathers.

In addition to the Little Six, a number of non-brewing abbeys either commission secular brewery companies to produce ales bearing their name or else license the use of their names for marketing ales of particular styles. The proceeds in either case will go to finance the activities of the Order. Less scrupulous brewers and wholesalers exploit the name of a ruined abbey or just pick a holy name out of a hat to do likewise, to finance the activities of the beer seller.

Finding a linking theme between all the beers which claim to be abbey beers is not easy. All are ales and the majority are sedimented. Many feature the residual sweetness of unfermented sugars due to the heavy use of crude "candy sugar" in the mash. About half can be classified as a "dubbel" or a "tripel", after the styles developed by the Westmalle abbey. However, many more fall outside these rules and yet can claim a genuine heritage. We will deal with the general rules first, before returning to look at some exceptions.

Trappist

The term "trappist" should be used to describe only the ales of the six surviving abbey breweries. These are listed under Chimay, Orval, Rochefort, Westmalle and Westvleteren in the Belgian Independent Breweries section and under Koningshoeven in Dutch Independent Breweries.

All monastic brewing stopped soon after the French Revolution. The first abbey to take up the craft once more was Westmalle in Antwerp province in 1836. None was seriously commercial until after World War One. Even now, Westvleteren runs a fairly small operation, though since it stopped engaging the St. Bernardus brewery in Watou to brew and distribute imitations of its beers, production has expanded.

Brewing remains under the strict control of the fathers. Lay "brothers" are sometimes employed to assist with the marketing operations and the degree of commercialisation varies.

At one stage the Cistercian Order formed a marketing company to promote the beers, cheeses and other products made by their abbeys and beguinages, copyrighting the Trappiste brand name. Koningshoeven is even more commercially minded, to the extent that it operates, in effect, as a contract brewer, producing its Koningshoeven brands for Allied-Carlsberg (VBBR) and most of its La Trappe brands for John Martin of Antwerp and for a Dutch wholesaler. It even undertakes extra work for secular breweries which run out of capacity or are trying to test brew ales.

Abbey

The term "abbey" (Flemish: abdij; French: abbaye) should be applied to those ales brewed by commercial breweries in imitation of the trappist style. As everywhere in the brewing industry, the term is frequently misused. Secular abbey beers are sometimes mis-labelled as trappist, usually by ignorant or duped café owners. In turn, some very ordinary beers are given names with religious connotations to imply abbey qualities or connections, where there are none. The religious places named on some labels are either ruins or else figments of the wholesaler's imagination.

The quality of the beer appears unrelated to the integrity of its holy connections. One or two abbeys order abyssmal brews to be made in their name, whilst two of the best quality and longest established ranges of abbey beers are Het Kapittel from Van Eecke and Witkap from Slaghmuylder, neither of which profess any monastic connections.

The varying standard of abbey beers can make sampling them a precarious pleasure. Be warned that while some of the pretty labels on these saintly brews herald divine pleasure, others can hide unholy awfulness.

Dubbel

Westmalle abbey spearheaded the two styles most associated with monastic beers. "Dubbel" and "Tripel" are said to refer to the custom of mediaeval brewers across Europe to define the quality and strength of a beer by marking the cask with up to four "X"s. Ordinary beer scored a single "X", the better brew was "XX", top of the range was "XXX" and special brews were "XXXX".

Whether or not this is true, "dubbel" has come to imply a dark beer of six or seven per cent alcohol, with a candy sweetness and variable degree of sourness. Unfortunately, in the Netherlands the same word implies a dark ale with precisely 6.5 per cent abv, though not necessarily in the abbey style. Also, in some parts of Belgium, the word "dubbel" is a perfectly legitimate way of saying "the stronger version of" and has no bearing on the alcoholic strength or style. Be prepared to get it wrong sometimes.

Tripel

The same general comments apply to the term "tripel" as apply to "dubbel" (above). In this case the Westmalle precedent is a dark golden brew of nine per cent abv with distinct candied sweetness. Where the hop content is high, abbey tripel almost merges with the strong golden ales like Duvel (below), which is ironic when you make the translation.

Once again, the Dutch see things differently and apply the term to ales of any style in the 7.5 to 9.5 per cent abv range, while some Belgian brewers append the word "tripel" to all manner of brews.

Other Holy Ales

Arguably the very best of the trappist beers are neither dubbels nor tripels. Orval, the single beer produced from the southernmost abbey brewery, is a 6.2 per cent abv sediment pale ale with an exceptional hop character, in any terms. At the other end of the scale, the massive Rochefort 10° and the complex Chimay Bleue are both heavyweight black beers more in the style of a strong porter. Westvleteren Abt 12° is more of a barley wine.

In Autumn 1991 Koningshoeven produced a medium pale trappist beer of ten per cent abv and called it Quadrupel. They went on to expand the theory in a downwards direction by pruducing a rather flabby, blond beer, which they called Enkel (implying one "X").

While we have yet to discover a pale dubbel, there exist several very respectable dark tripels. Rochefort 8° is in this style, though not as sweet as its blond northern counterparts. Westvleteren Extra 8° is drier but almost as dark. The most untypical of all is Damy brewery's St. Idesbald Tripel, which is not just dark but also bitter and sour, yet in his defence, the brewer can show that this was typically the West Flanders style of strong abbey beers a century ago.

We have sub-classified the beers of all the above styles into "Pale", "Dubbel", "Tripel" and "Strong" and appended the terms "Trappist" or "Abbey" where the characteristics of the brew appear to justify the positioning of the beer legitimately within the overall style. We have no doubt that further refinements will need to be made in our next edition.

WILD ALE

The only beer style which is absolutely unique to Belgium is lambic, the group of ales produced by "spontaneous fermentation". Although recent legislation to approve an appellation contrôlée for these beers failed in the Belgian parliament, there are nonetheless strict laws applying to the use of the term lambic.

All lambic must contain at least 30 per cent unmalted wheat in the mash, which must contain at least five per cent grain. No yeast is allowed to be added to the beer at any stage, other than by falling from the air while the wort cools at the brewery.

Old hops are used. For 1993 most lambic was brewed with 1984 hops. At this age they have very little bitterness and practically no aroma but retain all their powers as a preservative.

The unmalted wheat and unmalted barley may be mashed separately but come together before the hops are added. Apart from this, the actual brewing part of the process is pretty normal. The unique bit is what happens next.

The hot filtered wort is run into a large, shallow fermentation tray, where it is left overnight to cool. Although the precise method varies from brewer to brewer, the aim of this period is to expose the cooling sweet liquid to all the microbes in the night sky for long enough for a representative quantity to take root in the mixture. At Cantillon the roof has thousands of vents between the tiles; at Belle Vue (Molenbeek) the huge, shallow cooling tank is housed under a suspended pavilion roof.

Lambic fermentation is an enormously complex biological

process but essentially has four parts to it.

First there is a period when enterobacteria work on the beer. These are the unpleasant bugs which give normal beers unwelcome infections. While all brewing scientists agree that some of the toxins deriving from these are unwelcome, there is debate about any useful contribution they may make. Most breweries kill them off by sulphuring the casks into which the cooled wort is poured, which makes the beer too acid for the enterobacteria to survive.

Second comes the phase of action of the naturally occurring saccharomyces. These yeasts are very similar to those used to ferment normal beer and are responsible for making most of the alcohol. This phase is vigorous for four weeks then tails off. By this stage you have a very young lambic, not enormously different from British real ale.

Third comes the period of the lactic and acetic bacteria. These spend about a year giving the beer its acid character and make the difference between the sweetish, neutral young lambic and the noticeably drier and sourish old lambic. Young lambic is beery, old lambic is winy.

Finally comes the effect of Brettanomyces, the slow motion yeasts which do remarkably little in the way of alcohol production but create the sherry and Madeira flavours of a classic five- or six-year old lambic.

The brewer has only three controls over this process. He can determine the ingredients within legal limits, he can alter the acidity to inhibit certain micro-organisms and he can alter the temperature of fermentation. Other than that he must trust in God – and his skills as a blender.

Draught lambic can be found in some cafés, particularly in Pajottenland, to the west of Brussels. Some café owners prefer young lambic and others an aged one. A few even get the brewery to mix old and new lambics in the same cask. This creates some refermentation as described later. However, the vast majority of lambic beers are set aside for refermentation and blending, the second major part of the lambic brewer's art.

Lambic
Most lambic sold in cafés is found on draught and will tend to contain around five per cent alcohol. The differences in character between young and old are unmistakable. Cantillon has tried bottling one of its older lambics with some success as Bruocsella 1900 Grand Cru but there are drawbacks due to the low carbonation making it flatter than the flattest real ale.

Lambic Doux
Particularly in Brussels, some cafés sell a clear filtered lambic sweetened with brown sugar. This is called soft lambic (Fr. lambic doux). It tends to be flat and is an acquired taste.

Faro
Faro is the traditional name for a draught lambic to which

sugar is added for refermentation. The principle is that if the yeast gets a second wind and a vigorous refermentation, it produces a sweetish beer with a sparkle.

In recent years the term has been corrupted and is applied to bottled, pasteurised, sweetened lambics, generally of little character. Cantillon sometimes supply the real thing to some Brussels cafés.

Cherry Lambic

Adding fruit to beer is an old habit in Belgium. It has probably been going on for 400 years or more, with cherries and raspberries always the most popular choices.

Anyway, if you take the cherry crop in July and add selected fruit to lambic beer, it does three things. There is a refermentation because of the sugars in the cherries, their fruit flavours are absorbed into the beer and there is a major effect on colour.

The most popular varieties of cherry are firm and juicy but without much sweetness. Schaerbeek cherries used to be popular but varieties like Gorsem and Du Nord are used more nowadays. There is no doubting the different fruit character in the cherry lambics produced, though all are pleasant.

Some producers use cherry juice to balance the cherry lambic and one blender, Hanssens, admits to using all juice. Our impression is that the greater the proportion of juice to fruit, the more perfumed the beer.

Cherry lambic can occasionally be found on draught. Drie Fonteinen has a sweetened version of theirs on handpull at their café. We have a strong impression, but no factual evidence that some smaller producers and one not-so-small producer pasteurise their cherry lambic at an early stage and bottle it as "cherry lambic", rather than blending it with another lambic to make cherry gueuze as described below.

Raspberry Lambic

Raspberry lambic is made in exactly the same way as cherry lambic. Raspberries are the other fruit traditionally added to lambic beers. Their only drawback is that when whole fruit is added, being less robust than the cherry, it tends to break up in the brew and the mass of seeds and mush can bung up every pipe and outlet in the brewery. Mainly for this reason, many brewers prefer to use raspberry juice. Draught raspberry lambic is extremely rare. We have the same reservations about its fate at some breweries as are noted above for cherry lambic.

White Lambic

In 1993 Timmermans pioneered a strange new hybrid style of beer which seems to involve blending old lambic with young wheat beer, with or without fruit essence. Whether such a style survives has yet to be seen but we have included it because of rumours that other brewers will soon follow suit.

Gueuze

Let us start at the end. Perfect traditional gueuze (pro-nounced "Gurrs") is served from a champagne bottle covered by the dust and cobwebs of several years in the cellar. Although some brands now carry a label, many of the best older varieties have simply a sash mark in whitewash, with the maker's name stamped on the cork.

Traditional gueuze should be opened gently and poured carefully if you do not wish to disturb the sediment, though some people prefer to drink it cloudy. It should be sour and spritzy, with only a hint of bitterness. The first encounter can be astonishingly awful. It may make you want to send it back immediately, but persuade you to hold on for just another mouthful. Having soldiered through the bottle and awarded yourself a gold rosette for adding painfully to your knowl-edge of the world's great beer styles, it should make you vow never to try anything like it again. Then order another bottle while you think about it.

Gueuze is made by taking old lambic, blending it with young and then bottling it. The remaining sugar from the young lambic sparks some refermentation in the bottle. If the blend is right, the characterful old lambic is enlivened by the natural gas of the fermentation and made slightly less sour and fuller bodied by the younger beer.

At its best, gueuze is the champagne of ales. At its worst it makes Lambrusco look like finest claret.

The brewers say that after the World War Two, Belgian drinkers turned away from dry lambics and gueuze, to demand sweet beers. That may be true but surely not to the exclusion of the type which had survived four centuries. Either way, the past 40 years have seen the emergence of fil-tered gueuze, made from young lambic blended with youth-ful old lambic and pasteurised at a pretty early stage. Despite denials from brewers, some still taste sweetened. While these commercial beers may be easy to drink, they are not what you could call authentic.

Cantillon and Oud Beersel are the only breweries which refuse to produce anything but traditional gueuze. Two blenders which do not brew, Hanssens and Drie Fonteinen, also are exclusively traditional. Of the rest, the companies which definitely produce one traditional gueuze are Lindemans (Fond Gueuze), De Troch (Gueuze Ongefilterd), Van Honsebrouck (Gueuze Tradition Fond) and Interbrew's Belle Vue (Sélection Lambic). Alken-Maes' De Keersmaeker is rumoured to have stopped its production recently.

The next rung down is partially filtered gueuze. This is definitely produced by Interbrew's De Neve plant (Gueuze Refermentatie) and Boon (Gueuze Mariage Parfait). It may be produced by Girardin (Gueuze 1882), Vander Linden (Vieux Foudre Gueuze) and Timmermans (Gueuze Caveau) but these three were called into doubt by a recent laboratory analysis commissioned by OBP. This looked at the micro-organism content of ten different gueuzes and certified these three brands dead.

Of the pasteurised and filtered versions the range runs from dryish to disgustingly sweet. Our tasting notes should help you plot your course.

Cherry Gueuze

In Belgium no distinction is made between any of the beer styles featuring cherries. All are lumped together as "kriek". This is not helpful to the consumer and so the Guide has proposed distinctions between "cherry lambic", "cherry gueuze" and the "old cherry" beers based on the aged beers found in East Flanders.

"Cherry gueuze" refers to those lambic-based cherry beers where some blending of cherry lambic with another lambic beer has occurred.

The degrees of tradition are as broad here as with gueuze. Of the beers which are definitely blended, Belle Vue Kriek is probably the most commercial. At the traditional end you will find Cantillon, Drie Fonteinen, Oud Beersel, Hanssens and the unfiltered version of De Troch. In between are partly filtered beers from Boon (Mariage Parfait), Girardin (possibly) and Vander Linden (possibly), via sharpish filtered brands to the increasingly sweet. Some allegedly lambic-based cherry beers are claimed by non-lambic brewers but we think these are probably fraudulent, though no doubt perfectly legal.

Raspberry Gueuze

Lambic-based raspberry beer, often called framboos or framboise, is rare in traditional form. Drie Fonteinen still sell a fiercely traditional product and Cantillon have a mixed raspberry-cherry variety. Boon, Girardin, Belle Vue and Vander Linden have heavily compromised brews and Timmermans, Van Honsebrouck and De Troch produce purely commercial ones.

Other lambic fruit beers

Somewhere in the market-led minds of some Belgian brewers is an evil jester called the Fruit Fairy. This malignant elf has of late brought his country a strange selection of new beers which are made by adding fruit juice or diluted fruit syrup to lambic beers and others. You can hardly miss the bottles. They tend to have orange, pink or purple foil tops and labels featuring gawdy cartoons of this or that juicy fruit. The beer inside is often like a Vimto Grand Cru. Some contain as little as 2.5 per cent abv.

There are a few pleasant surprises. Cantillon have produced two beers based on grape lambic, with the effect that the disciplined palate feels distinctly uncomfortable. De Troch's adventures of the mid-Eighties included an extraordinary, cloudy, sour, banana lambic but alas this is now a filtered beer tasting of bubble gum and sweeties.

One or two of the fruit adjuncts seem to show some promise, notably peach, plum and damson. Maybe somebody will get round to refermenting lambic with the whole fruits and even going on to blend it. Who knows, one day perhaps.

WHEAT ALE

Lambic is not the only beer style to utilise wheat in its mash. Belgium and the Netherlands have several different styles of wheat beer brewed by ordinary brewing methods. These are all made by including between 30 and 50 per cent malted or unmalted wheat in a mash with malted barley, sometimes with small quantities of malted or unmalted oats.

Wheat beers have undergone an extraordinary revival all over northern Europe in the past 20 years, even in places where no consumer campaign or pioneering brewers are at work. For example, in southern Germany the old Weizenbiers, especially in their unfiltered forms, have increased their production by over a third. Berlin's light, dry, slightly sour Weissbier is equally successful.

In Belgium and the Netherlands, wheat beers had practically disappeared by the mid 1950s. Then in 1966, a beer enthusiast called Pierre Celis re-opened a tiny brewery in the Brabant town of Hoegaarden and started to produce a cloudy, sweet, lightly spiced, old-fashioned wheat ale which he called Oud Hoegaards.

It is a long story, but by 1993 his somewhat expanded De Kluis brewery, taken over by Artois in 1989 and merged into Interbrew by 1991, was producing 800,000 hectolitres (2.2 million pints) of Hoegaarden wheat beer per year. Furthermore, at the last count, 22 other Belgian breweries had followed suit.

Across the border in the Netherlands the imported style went down so well that new small breweries like Arcen and Raaf started to imitate it. The style took root in 1991 when Heineken paid it the honour of making it their first new specialist beer style for 20 years. Fourteen Dutch breweries currently produce wheat beers and three more are committed to do so in the near future.

To bring the Celis story up to date, Pierre retired on the profits of the Artois buy-out and took up residence in Austin, Texas. Unable to resist the temptation to brew again, in 1991 he set up the Celis Brewing Company to produce wheat beer for America. The latest twist in the tale is that he has signed an agreement allowing De Smedt brewery to produce Celis White under licence in Belgium.

The Guide has classified all wheat ales simply as "wheat beer" (unfiltered or filtered) or "wheat bok ale". This is not a fair reflection of the diversity of styles but will have to do for now!

The commonest Dutch (Flemish) word for wheat beer is

"witbier". This causes some confusion as it sounds like "wheatbeer" but actually means "white beer", translated into French (Walloon) as "Bière Blanche". The Dutch word for wheat beer is "tarwebier".

Unfiltered Wheat Beer

The reason the Belgians and Dutch called wheat ales "white beer" is that in their natural, unfiltered form, wheat beers have a milky haze. Beer is not strictly a liquid, it is a suspension of solid particles in liquid. Most wheat protein particles are too light to sediment out and so unless the beer is finely filtered they remain in suspension, denying the beer a "polished" look.

Wheat, especially when unmalted, also gives beer a stronger grainy flavour, like freshly baked local bread. Many brewers like to balance this by leaving the beer sweetish. Some also add spices and other flavourings.

Wieckse Witte from Heineken defines nicely a Dutch style, which has definite toffee flavours to it. These are also found in Raaf Witbier and Leeuw's Valkenburgs Witbier. The other Dutch style which is developing among the smaller breweries is a much drier, livelier, unspiced version which drops bright in the bottle. Maybe there is a smaller proportion of wheat in the mash. Gans, Moerenburg and Maasland produce good examples.

In Belgium, Hoegaarden is the front runner and yardstick for all others. Riva's Dentergems Wit and Palm's Steendonk are also very popular, respectively harsher and gentler than their great rival. Gouden Boum Tarwebier used to verge on sour but has now lurched back to a softer sweetness. Fellow West Flanders brewer, Van Eecke, seems to have tugged Watou's Witbier in the opposite direction. Lefèbvre's Student is probably the best from a Walloon brewer, though Silly's Titje and Du Bocq's Blanche de Namur are also contenders,

Finally, it is worth mentioning the style being developed by Houten Kop, the brewery company without a brewery, who borrow the Strubbe plant in Ichtegem to brew their two beers, Vlaskop and Houten Kop. These contain 30 per cent wheat. Most of the others mentioned here have 50 per cent. The difference in recipe shows markedly in the palate.

Filtered Wheat Beer

Despite its contribution to the flavour of wheat beers, the milky haze in unfiltered brews makes them unacceptable to some drinkers. Some of the more commercial brewers, like Bavik and Clarysse, remove most or all of the protein suspension. At the Oudaen in Utrecht, you can taste what happens when this is done, as they sell their home-brewed wheat beer filtered and unfiltered.

Wheat Bok Ale

The Amsterdams Brouwhuis was the first producer of a wheat-based bokbier in the Dutch style, beating Heineken to it by about a fortnight in October 1992. For the 1993 bokbier season, tarwebok (described previously) was all the rage and inevitably the smaller brewers produced these as ales, arguably as an imitation. However, the contorted irony of this is that while bokbier may have derived originally from the German lager style known as Bock, the only equivalents to wheat bok are the dark wheat beers produced in Franconia and Bavaria, all of which are ales. So who mimicks whom is a matter of opinion.

FLAVOURED ALE

Brewers have been adding flavourings to their beers for centuries. So have customers, for example, in the winter tradition of mulling with fruit and spices.

From the brewer's perspective, the reasons vary from altering a pH balance, to colouring the brew, complementing the flavour characteristics, or trying to drown out unpleasant tastes. There is no ethical reason why herbs, spices and other flavourings should not be added to beer. After all, what are the hops doing there?

Many Belgian beer experts despise these beers because of the use of spicy flavours to hide poor brewing practice. They have a point and the Guide agrees that such dubious procedures are unwelcome. Nonetheless, some brewers use flavourings deliberately and with great aplomb and we believe their efforts should be recognised. Some of these beers can appeal greatly to the bored beer palate.

Spiced Ale

We have already alluded to the use of spices in the production of traditional wheat beers. Coriander is a great favourite for these and also appears in many a Flemish spiced ale (or "kruidenbier"). Cinnamon and even ginger, albeit in small quantities, is commonly used in beers brewed for Christmas. The beers where spicing works best seem to be stronger pale and brown ales.

In Flanders, breweries like Huyghe and Van Steenberge, both with reputations for highly organised brewhouses, experiment freely and produce commissioned beers with unique spice combinations.

In Wallonia, brewers add spices to beers which have been fermented through to a striking dryness. The exception is the king of the spiced beer producers, Achouffe, from Luxembourg province. To gauge the quality of Achouffe's brewing, try their La Chouffe with only the faintest hint of spice in a highly aromatic beer deriving its flavours and nuances almost entirely from its hops and malt sugars. Then contrast this with the other beers in their range, which now list their flavourings on the label.

Honeyed Ale

A great fad, especially of Walloon brewers, in the last couple of years is honeyed ales. Obviously honey acts as a sugar for fermentation. However, it also leaves lots of residual flavours in the brew which have marked effects on the palate. The maximum allowable in the mash is 30 per cent of solids. The best we have found is Le Pavé de l'Ours from Binchoise. The ultimate example is said to be Cuvée d'Aristée from Praile.

Other flavourings

Not all flavour additives are successful. The Guide's nomination for the worst beer in Christendom remains Huyghe's Minty, a bright green, filtered peppermint-flavoured liquid claimed to contain beer. We are not entirely sure how much help the apple juice is in Achouffe's Vielle Salm or the alleged nine per cent white wine in Slaghmuylder's Witkap Tripel. Our favourite remains the juice of boiled figs in Blaugies' Darbyste.

In cases where we think a flavouring has been added to a completed beer at, or close to, the time of bottling we have designated the beer a "flavoured ale" or in the case of one brewer, "flavoured lager".

A G E D A L E

It should go without saying that provided a beer contains living micro-organisms its flavour will continue to develop. As a rule of thumb, if the organism is a yeast the news is good, if it is a bacterium it is bad. However, as our notes above on lambic fermentation should make clear, it is not as simple as that, as any producer of fine wines could tell you.

Where ordinary fermentation (i.e. non-lambic) takes place the brewer aims to inject his wort with a pure strain of one or more chosen yeasts in conditions clean enough to ensure no infection spoils things. The yeast works away, turning sugar into alcohol and when that process peaks the brewer prepares his beer for sale. But what happens if it carries on maturing?

At some breweries, a proportion of the fresh beer is set aside for prolonged maturation, usually in oak casks. Such a process introduces a sourness and maturity of flavour not too dissimilar from a young adult lambic. This is then either pasteurised, lightly carbonated and bottled or else mixed with a small amount of sweeter, fresher beer to spark refermentation in ther bottle. Either way, a classic sour style of ale, usually though not invariably dark, is born.

These styles of beer have been given various names including "the Burgundies of Flanders", "Flemish reds", "sour browns" and others. The Guide had chosen the more prosaic "old red", "old brown" and "old pale", which not only hint at the colour but also acknowledges the distinction made by beer writer Michael Jackson between the West Flanders Rodenbach style and those found in the southern part of East Flanders, around the town of Oudenaard and elsewhere. We have also defined an "old cherry" style for those beers to which cherries are added which have never seen a cask of lambic in their lives.

Old Red

These highly distinctive beers come almost exclusively from West Flanders. Cynics might divide the style into Rodenbach Grand Cru and "beers which would like to be Rodenbach Grand Cru".

The red colour comes from using Vienna malt, an ingredient of some of the prettier Dutch lagers. At Rodenbach the maturing beer is stored in hundreds of massive oak tuns for a minimum of 18 months before bottling. This length of maturation gives the beer a delicious sourness backed by a great complexity of flavours.

Neat mature beer is filtered and bottled as Grand Cru. When cherry essence is added it makes Alexander. The ordinary Rodenbach is a three to one blend of fresh and aged beer. Blending lowers the acidity at the expense of character.

There are many pretenders to the Rodenbach crown but none is consistently excellent. The best of the rest is Bavik's Petrus. The other company whose products are worth trying and seem to improve with every tasting is Verhaege.

Old Brown

Old brown ales come mainly from East Flanders and the classic beer of the style was Liefmans Goudenband. This is currently being brewed at Riva, who now own Liefmans, and shipped to Liefmans for maturation, so its future is unclear.

Goudenband was made from a mash which was simmered overnight, as opposed to the usual practice of being boiled for a few hours. It was then fermented in open vats for six weeks before being stored in oak casks for a further nine months before bottling. It reached its peak after about two years in the cellar.

While we have fewer details about their brewing methods, the single, extraordinary product of the Cnudde brewery is worth seeking out. The generally commercial Clarysse brewery sometimes release a sediment version of its Felix Oudenaards Oude Bruin with a similar vintage character.

Old Pale

The Contreras brewery brews a beer in March which has much of the character of an old brown but which is brewed from much paler malt. The Block brewery make an old pale ale but blend it with fresh ale and some lambic to create a unique and delicious concoction called Block Special 6°.

Old Cherry

Liefmans make a cherry beer which has very little in common with cherry lambic, except in so far as the cherries are used to spark refermentation in an ageing ale. It is, like Goudenband, in a transitional phase but we hope will return to a five star rating soon. At the Crombé brewery in Zottegem they referment pale ale with cherries to amazing effect in their Oud Kriekenbier.

Old Raspberry

Liefmans raspberry beer is probably unique in involving the addition of raspberry juice to old brown ale before bottling. The more commercial brands either add fruit juice or fruit essence at the time of bottling and have been categorised as "flavoured".

SEASONAL ALE

Most beer-producing nations have a tradition of seasonal beers. Sometimes these derive from the need to supply an annual celebration with a special beer, as in Christmas ales. Other traditions started because farmers needed to clear their excess grain supply or brewers had difficulty keeping their beers cool enough to avoid easy contamination in the hot summer.

Whatever the origin, seasonal ales have traditionally developed particular characteristics which marked them out as distinct beer styles. While in recent years the linking characteristic of most styles is their ability to make money for the brewery, some of these qualities survive.

Saison

Saison beers are Wallonian. They originated because Walloon brewers found that fermenting beer in the high summer could be a precarious business, So to avoid a shortage of beer from July to September, they brewed in the spring a beer which was packed to the gunnels with hops and in which most of the sugar was fermented through to alcohol. Such a style had the advantage of being thirst-quenching, as well as resilient to warm storage.

Traditional saison beers have all but disappeared but Dupont still produces Vieille Provision Saison in the classic mould. The commonest is Saison Regal from Du Bocq, typical of the modern style not only in the front-loading of its hop character but also in being largely filtered and available most of the year.

Many Wallonian beers, especially those produced by newer breweries anxious to revive traditional brewing methods, owe something to the saison style without being true saisons.

Winter Ale

The least consistent of the seasonal styles is winter ale, often marketed as Christmas beer. In the past these beers were typically dark, mature, dryish strong ales with Madeira in their palate. More recently the concept has been corrupted to mean "something different for Christmas". The Dutch go more for eindejaarsbier (New Year's ale).

Brewers of spiced ales tend to add cinnamon. Palm make a premium pale ale, Du Bocq produce an orange-coloured wheat ale and Haacht try a Christmas Pilsener. Dolle

Brouwers' Stille Nacht (Silent Night) is typical of the rich, sweet variety which is often much better once vinous after two or three years in the cellar. The Interbrew beer Campbell's Christmas and the John Martin's import, Gordons Christmas, illustrate the dry, sharp, deep brew style well. De Smedt's Super Noël Abbaye d'Aulne impressed with its depth in 1993.

Dark Bok Ale

The Dutch style, bokbier, is described earlier. Although these were all traditionally dark, heavy lagers, in 1983 the Arcen brewery imitated the style with a top-fermented brew. By 1993 nearly half the brands on the market were ales, including most of those from the smaller breweries. Some beer drinkers prefer these. We refer to this style as "dark bok ale" to distinguish it from the smoother, cleaner lagers of the same tribe. With the exception of Arcen's Oerbock, which is available all year round, they appear on the first Monday in October and are generally sold out by early December.

Pale Bok Ale

As dark bok ales mimick the bokbiers of October, so pale bok ales copy the meiboks of spring. Those appearing later are sometimes called zomerbocks. Brewing these beers as ales is gaining respectability with the news that some larger brewers may do the same.

Other seasonal ales

Some breweries such as Dolle Brouwers in West Flanders, the Domus home brewery in Leuven and the Prignon brewery in Luxembourg province, produce a cycle of beers designed for each of the seasons. Each has their own logic for this but there is no consistent pattern.

There was a fad for paasbiers (or Easter beers) a few years ago but this was strongest in the Netherlands and has largely merged with the meibok phenomenon.

Some Dutch breweries have taken to producing an anniversary ale or verjaardagsbier to celebrate the brewery's birthday. You would be amazed how many were born in the first three months of the year. We preferred the honesty of the brewer at St. Martinus who explained his St. Valentijnsbier by saying: "You try thinking of anything else to celebrate in the middle of February".

WALLOON ALE

One does not talk about Flemish ale or Dutch ale or even French ale, so whether it is legitimate to talk of Walloon ale is a moot point. However, in the French-speaking southern part of Belgium there exist numerous small breweries producing in their product range a variety of beers of a style not found elsewhere. Once one has excluded the regular beers, the spiced ales, the brews of the French styles bière brune and bière blonde, the pepped-up table beers and the saisons, there remains a small but distinct cluster of remarkable beers.

The linking characteristic is a champagne dryness, presumably the result of fermenting the sugars through to alcohol. There is often evidence of mixed grains, most vividly demonstrated in beers like Abbaye des Rocs' Montagnarde. Blaugie's Moneuse is another good example, as is Prignon's controversial Fantôme. (Is it really supposed to taste like that? We think so.)

Some examples are clearly the base beer for honeyed or spiced ales and there is a common allegation that these beers are not the result of good styling but bad brewing. However, excellent brewers like Dupont, especially in their Biologique brands, seem to be producing something of the same basic character but heavily hopped. Their Moinette brands, along with Binchoise's Marie d'Hongrie and, arguably, Du Bocq's Gauloise and Triple Moine are just aromatic versions of something remarkably similar.

For better, for worse, the Guide has created the categories of "Walloon ale" and "Walloon strong" to mark out those beers which are not strictly saisons but which stand out from regular pale and brown ales and are not a feature of the Flemish north.

LIGHT ALE

At the tail end of any attempt to classify beers into various categories, there come a variety of classes which are effective buckets for the rest. The Belgians especially have a broad-ranging tradition of lighter coloured ales of all strengths and styles, from cooking bitter to rocket fuel, from bière blonde to yeast-packed hop stews. The sub-styles overlap and the rules become murkier than some of the beers. The Guide has highlighted some styles which stand out from the crowd but thus far has kept an unreasonably large number classified simply as "pale ale".

Pale Ale

It is a matter of opinion whether the Belgians invented pale ales and exported the idea to Britain, or vice versa. It depends how far you go back in history and you could point out that as it was the Flemish who introduced the hop plant to England, they must claim first shot. Over the years, however, there has been a trading of tastes.

There is definitely a difference between a Belgian pale ale, typically dominated by a roasted, slightly caramelised backtaste and hopped with Northern Brewer, and the English style, with lighter malts and hopped by Goldings.

Belgian brewers try hard to achieve a mix of flavours from energetic fermentation. The French and the Dutch much prefer smoother, gentler flavours in pale ales with a polished finish. French bière blonde will be light in colour, sweetish and rounded. The Dutch style is without a name but is distinctively clean, of darker hue and if judged on taste alone could be mistaken for a lager.

The best examples of the Belgian style are De Koninck from Antwerp and Straffe Hendrik from Bruges. The English style is well demonstrated by the Belgian version of Whitbread Pale Ale. The best bière blonde is probably the one from Brunehaut, whilst Grolsch Amber and Drie Ringen Hoppenbier illustrate the Dutch style.

Of the properly sedimented pale ales, two which are outstanding are Esenaar from Dolle Brouwers and, from the unlikely direction of Friesland, Us Heit's Frysk Bier – one of the finest beers produced in the Netherlands.

Kölsch

In the industrial north east of Germany, there are a number of centres of ale brewing. In Köln (Cologne) they make a drinkable, lightly coloured ale called Kölsch. While it would be nice to think that the emergence of Kölsch beers in the Netherlands has something to do with European accord, the truth of the matter is that smaller Dutch brewers do not want to invest in lager plant but do want to produce a Pilsener. So they brew ale in the Kölsch style and make everybody think it is Pilsener. Naughty, but no more so than putting maize in Pilsener.

Altbier

Just down the autobahn in Düsseldorf, several breweries make "Düsseldorfer Altbier", a darkish ale of low-medium strength. One or two examples of the style have crossed the border, such as Leeuw's Venloosch Alt and Arcen's Altforster Alt. Neither sets the Rhine on fire.

Strong Golden

Not many beer styles can trace their origins more precisely than Belgian strong golden ales. In 1968 the Moortgat brewery changed the colour of Duvel, from deep brown to light straw. When they did so they liberated a classic style that had been waiting to happen. These heavyweight ales look like lagers and tend to be appallingly drinkable. They should be awash with hop character which lasts to the final swallow. Their paleness is achieved by using the most lightly kilned of malts. The pungent, almost spicy bouquet comes from using highly aromatic hops.

Duvel is the classic but other notable examples of the style include Van Steenberge's Piraat, Louwaege's Hapkin, Crombé's Zottegemse Tripel, Hoegaarden Grand Cru from Interbrew's De Kluis plant and Judas from Alken-Maes' Union brewery. Gouden Boum's Steenbrugge Tripel thinks it is an abbey tripel but veers over into this style.

DARK ALE

The variety of darker ales in Belgium is as great, if not greater, than of pale ales. Some overlap with British styles such as stout, porter and the now defunct Scotch ale. There are many examples of beers which could be classified as pale or brown depending on personal preference.

Brown Ale

As with the category of "pale ale" above, we have used the term "brown ale" as a bucket into which to put a large number of beers of divergent character.

In Flanders, for example, the towns of Diest, Oudenaard and Mechelen were all famous for producing a particular type of dark brew. It is doubtful whether any beers of the original styles continue to exist but even if Haacht's Gildenbier, Anker's Mechelsen Bruynen and Liefman's Odnar are faithful replicas, it is difficult to see which characteristics make them stand out from the crowd.

Stout

Stout is a style of dark, bitter beer made from highly kilned black malt varieties. We have sub-divided the group into "sweet stout", "dry stout" and "strong stout" depending on their secondary characteristics. Sweet stouts are particularly common in West Flanders. Drier and stronger stouts are found more randomly.

The best examples of the sweet version include those from Leroy, Louwaege and Van Steenberge's Wilson Mild Stout. Facon makes a pleasant dry stout. The best known of the strong stouts is the one which John Martin of Antwerp has been importing from Guinness since 1912 and which the Irish can no longer find at home, though the Nigerians can. In the Netherlands, the even stronger Hertog Jan Grand Prestige is impressive.

Scotch Ale

It is thought that Scotch ale began to be brewed in Belgium during World War One, for British servicemen. Ales brewed on mainland Britain used to have a smaller ratio of hops to malt as one moved north, away from the hop-growing areas of Kent and Herefordshire. It followed that in Scotland, ales were lightly hopped and closer to the true all-malt brews of mediaeval times.

Ironically, the style has faded from legitimacy in Britain but continues in Belgium, where it remains a dark, sweetish, strongish beer with a low hop count. One, Gordon's, is imported from Scotland by Martin's of Antwerp, who have recently taken to re-exporting it back home. Douglas's too is imported. Of the Belgian brewed variety, Campbell's is the most widely available but the best we have found so far is Scotch de Silly, with the seasonal Scotch-Christmas from Facon also impressing.

STRONG ALE

Some beers are just plain strong and should be categorised as such. It is not invariable that strong beers have to be characterful or even interesting but most are, if only because of the potential for brewers to play with the recipes. Yeast tends to die of alcohol poisoning above ten per cent abv so bottling with a sediment is often a waste of time. Some yeasts are specialists above that strength, hence their ability to put the finishing touches to brews like Dubuisson's Bush Beer, the strongest beer in Belgium.

OTHER ALE

Table Beer

As the French raise children on diluted wines, so the Belgians raise children on sweet, low-alcohol ales called "table beer" (Flemish: tafelbier; French: bière de table). These can be pale or dark. The principle is similar to Dutch oud bruins. Just as some British beer lovers hate to see mild ales disappearing, so some Belgians are disgusted at the demise of table beers in favour of high-profile, high-profit NABLABs (No Alcohol / Low Alcohol Beers).

Most tafelbiers have not been included here as they do not reach our threshold of 3.5 per cent abv. However, one or two of the beers of the style do contain as much alcohol as a British ordinary bitter and Gigi's Unic Bier squeezed in for its unusual character despite being below our normal cut-off point. One normal strength brew which can trace its origins to the table beer tradition is Devaux's extraordinary Schwendi.

The Rest

There are five alleged beer styles which the Guide has ruled out of order and will not use. These are "Cuvée", "Grand Cru", "Speciaal", "Export" and "Luxe". In our experience, the first two usually mean "more expensive", the next two mean "weak version" and the last means "ten per cent stronger, 20 per cent dearer". None are useful for the consumer and until there are restrictions on their use we will ignore them.

Examples of the brewers' art

Belgian Independents

BELGIUM'S INDEPENDENT BREWERIES are supreme in the craft of producing beers of great character. Despite the hard-won reputation, few are more than a century old and practically none have the sort of folksy brewhouses that legend or image would have you believe.

In 1900, there were over 3,200 working breweries in Belgium. By 1986 this figure had fallen to 125 and closures were still occurring. Then, as had happened in Britain a decade earlier it was as though the Belgians re-discovered their beer culture and new brews began to appear, followed inevitably by some new breweries.

With the re-organisation of the larger combines, the number of operating breweries in the country in 1993 is, depending on your definitions, between 103 and 108. It is hoped that this will represent an all-time low figure, as the trends seem to indicate that the creation of new breweries now outnumbers planned closures.

Three quarters of Belgium's beer consumption is rather dull Pils, not a patch on the products of German or Czech breweries. Unlike their colleagues in the Netherlands, few Belgian brewers produce other lager styles, perhaps because the lager market is not yet a discriminating one. As in Britain, anything will do for most lager drinkers, provided the label is familiar and the advertising appeals.

Since our first edition, the trends within the specialist beer market have been fascinating. Lambic brewing took a nose-dive in 1991. Brewing stopped at De Neve and Eylenbosch in Schepdaal and there was to be no more blending at Belgor, De Koninck of Dworp, Moriau and Wets. However, Interbrew then re-entered the market with a traditional gueuze and Van Honsebrouck, long regarded by serious beer drinkers as commercially obsessed, stunned everyone by coming out with a serious gueuze too. With De Troch restarting production of sour beers and several producers experimenting with "wheat lambics", the future looks interesting.

Considerable concern remains about other brewing styles. Most recently it is the Wallonian style, saison, which appears under threat. The authentic versions of this heavily hopped ale style, brewed in the cool spring for consumption in the hot summer, seem to have slipped quietly off the nation's beer menu. In part, this is through brewers wanting year-round product ranges but is also a reflection of the hopelessly disorganised nature of the beer retailing business in the French-speaking south of the country.

Every beer café in southern Belgium seems to operate in ignorant isolation from its peers and wholesalers exploit this by commissioning relabelled brews, often Flemish, for an increasingly uninformed clientèle apparently incapable of forming a consumer organisation. In the middle of that, Wallonia is losing large parts of its brewing heritage to a welter of spicy nonsense with names which sound misleadingly local.

Ironically, Wallonia has three of Belgium's five remaining monastery breweries; these are listed under their brand names – Chimay, Orval, Rochefort, Westmalle and Westvleteren. The sixth member of the brotherhood is the abbey of Koningshoeven, listed under Dutch Independent Breweries.

Smaller breweries are less likely nowadays to produce lagers, more frequently specialising in one or more types of palate-challenging ales. The larger independents often piece together a portfolio of the principle styles and tend to go for blander brews, acceptable to the common palate.

The increasing commercialisation of the "regional beers" market has led to some famous brands being acquired by mass-market brewers. However, overall there has been an increase in the total number of beers brewed. Although the consumer has undoubtedly benefitted from this, there is a downside through the epidemic of "label beers", made to satisfy the demand from some cafés, beer shops, drinks distributors, tourist attractions and other places for a "house" beer unobtainable elsewhere.

There are two ways of labelling. Some breweries simply take an existing beer and stick a new label on the bottle. Others, conscious that this (misleading but legal) activity annoys beer lovers, prefer to doctor it in small ways so that the seller can claim that their house beer is genuinely new. Typical ploys involve dilution, sweetening, spiking with spice or herbs or else altering the usual degree of filtration.

To put the problem of labelling in perspective, 1990 saw 696 brews in regular production in Belgium, under 1,193 names. Of the 162 which appeared for the first time during that year, only 73 (46 per cent) were new brews; all the rest were label jobs.

Even where a brewer genuinely tries to create a new beer for every customer, it is doubtful that the practice of producing 30 different brews from the same brewhouse does anything to improve consistency or quality.

The Guide's policy is to try to list only the principle beer brand of each recipe with a full listing given to commissioned beers only when they are genuinely different from other products. We have listed many of the better known label beers in the Beers Index. We apologise for any errors which have occurred. It is not our intention to mislead our readers. We wish that the same could be said of the people who commission and supply the things.

For every listing we have included the strength of the beer (in percentage alcohol by volume), the style (as previously described) and have given a star rating. An asterisk (*) denotes a seasonal beer.

✪✪✪✪✪ = a world classic
✪✪✪✪ = a fine example of the style
✪✪✪ = enjoyable and well-produced
✪✪ = a standard brew
✪ = lacking something

The star ratings should not be taken as anything other than the editor's considered opinion and inevitably may in some cases, be based on a sample kept in below average condition.

The breweries are listed in alphabetical order, by their commonly used names, followed by the full company title and address.

ABBAYE DES ROCS

BRASSERIE DE L'ABBAYE DES ROCS
Chaussée Brunehaut 37
7383 Montignies-sur-Roc
Tel: 065 759976

Hainaut micro-brewery set up in 1984 near the French border, south west of Mons. Despite its name, this is not a monastic brewery but a producer of classic Wallonian strong ales. The abbaye in question is a ruin, near the owners' farmhouse, its beautiful setting in rocky terrain gave the brewery its name. Production is limited to 500 hectolitres (hl) a year and many brews appear only occasionally. Despite this, they export a little to Canada, USA, Australia and Europe. Possibly unique in using malted oats in some beers, such as Blanche des Honnelles. Some of the unsampled brands may be similar beers with different labels.

LA MONTAGNARDE
9% abv ✪✪✪✪ Walloon Strong
Extraordinary ale brewed from five cereals. Starts like paint-stripper but grows on you. Will improve with ageing.

ABBAYE DES ROCS
9% abv ✪✪✪✪✪ Abbey Tripel (dark)
Dark brown brew of enormous character, with overtones of butterscotch.

BLANCHE DES HONNELLES
6% abv ✪✪✪✪ Wheat Beer
(unfiltered)
Typically Wallonian, light and spritzy, with a Champagne dryness.

Other brands include: Abbaye des Rocs Spéciale Noël* (9% abv; winter ale); La Bière de Jumelage, Cuvée Jean d'Avesnes Ambrée, Cuvée Jean d'Avesnes Blanche, La Perverse, St. Hubert, St. Lenderik and Thulin (all 9% abv; spiced ales) and Regain Blanche (6% abv; wheat beer).

ACHOUFFE

BRASSERIE D'ACHOUFFE
Route du Village 32
6666 Achouffe-Houffalize
Tel: 061 288147
Fax: 061 288264

Set up in 1982 in the outhouse of a farm in the hamlet of Achouffe near Houffalize, a few miles from the border of Luxembourg province with the Grand Duchy. Capacity is now 10,000 hl a year but the company remains a "small country living" with a family atmosphere. Enjoys a well-justified reputation for its impressive and challenging, high quality ales, which have tended to be sweetish and spiced. In recent years some of the beers have started to derive their spiced flavour from a clever malt and hop recipe.

Adopts a progressive marketing approach. Its beers can be found throughout Belgium and the Netherlands, as well as Italy, France, Denmark, Canada and Japan. Tours of the brewery can be arranged easily and a sampling café on the site is open daily in summer and at weekends throughout the year from 09.00 to 20.00. In 1991 they dared to produce a dark bok for the Dutch market. Lowie Kators is sold in Wallonia as La Malmédy Blonde. They advise the Dutch brewery, Maasland, and occasionally brew for them.

McCHOUFFE
8.5% abv ✪✪✪✪✪ Spiced Ale
Excellent, sweet, spicy, medium brown, sediment ale which is supposed to resemble the scotch ale style.

MILLENEIR
8.5% abv ✪✪✪✪ Spiced Ale
Strong pale ale flavoured with woodruff, ginseng and horseradish.

NE JANNEMAN
8.5% abv ✪✪✪✪ Spiced Ale

Strong sediment pale ale flavoured
with woodruff.

VIELLE SALME
8.5% abv ✪✪✪✪ Spiced Ale
Almost perfumed with spices and
fruit, including apple. Crude
aftertastes.

LOWIE KATORS
8% abv ✪✪✪✪✪ Pale Ale
Usually excellent amber ale, packed
with herby hoppy flavours.

MALMEDY BRUNE
8% abv ✪✪✪✪ Spiced Ale
Dark, spicy and delicious.

LA CHOUFFE
8% abv ✪✪✪✪✪ Spiced Ale
Recently upgraded, deep amber
brew, full of hops and a little spice.

CHOUFFE BOKBIER*
6.7% abv ✪✪✪ Brown Ale
Thin, dry brown ale.

Other regular beers include:
Lilliput (9.5% abv; spiced ale).

ANKER (RIVA GROUP)
BROUWERIJ HET ANKER
Guido Gezellelaan 49
2800 Mechelen
Tel: 015 203880
The brewery in Mechelen, between
Brussels and Antwerp, was
established in 1873, though there
has been brewing on or near the site
since the 15th century. In 1990 they
"came to an arrangement with" the
Riva group, but retain an option to
regain independence. The town of
Mechelen has specialised in
producing brown ales for over 600
years. Since the Riva involvement,
the marketing of all the Anker beers
has improved markedly both at
home and abroad. Consistency has
improved too but at the price of
some distinctiveness. Production
remains at around 4,000 hl per year
and consumer groups remain
concerned about the brewery's long
term future.

GOUDEN CAROLUS
7% abv ✪✪✪✪ Brown Ale
Dark, sweetish, caramelled,
sediment ale with a burnt bitterness.
Formerly a great ale, now just
reasonably good.

TOISON D'OR TRIPEL
7% abv ✪✪✪ Pale Ale
Blond and grainy, with a suggestion
of adjuncts.

MECHELSEN BRUYNEN
5.5% abv ✪✪✪ Brown Ale
Medium dark, sedimented, bitter-
sweet ale; less demanding than
Gouden Carolus.

BAVIK
BAVIK-DE BRABANDERE
Rijksweg 16a
8531 Bavikhove
Tel: 056 711379
Large independent regional brewery
founded in 1894 in the village of
Bavikhove, north east of Kortrijk.
Despite the relatively high output,
110,000 hl per annum, Bavik's
middle-of-the-road brews are found
mainly in its home province of West
Flanders. The Petrus brands are
found further afield. The brewery
enjoys good working relations with
Van Honsebrouck (see below), who
actually brewed some of their beers
for them in 1991.

PETRUS TRIPEL
7.5% abv ✪✪ Tripel
Unimpressive filtered pale ale.

BAVIK SUPER PILS
5.5% abv ✪✪ Pils
Slightly stronger than average,
neutral Pils.

PETRUS
5.5% abv ✪✪✪✪ Old Red
Matured in oak for 18 months, unlike
most imitators of Rodenbach Grand
Cru. Seems to improve further with
age.

PETRUS SPECIALE STOP
5.5% abv ✪✪ Pale Ale
Ordinary, rather sweet pale ale.

BAVIK WITBIER
5% abv ✪✪✪ Wheat Beer
(unfiltered)
Simple, sweetish, unspiced witbier.

GOLDEN HOP
5% abv ✪✪ Pils
Another standard Pils.

Other regular beers include:
Pony Stout (5.5% abv; stout) and
Bavik Export (5% abv; Pils). There
are also five table beers.

BIE
BROUWERIJ DE BIE
Stoppelweg 26
8978 Watou
Tel: 057 388666

The Bee microbrewery set up in 1992 in the village of Watou, at the heart of hop country, near the French border in West Flanders. Opens its doors to the public on Sundays and on Friday afternoons. Production is tiny – just 75 hl in its first year – but this has not stopped them being taken to the Netherlands. Cultured beers for one so small. An excuse to claim that you might be amused by their prententiousness.

ZATTE BIE
9% abv ✪✪✪✪ Spiced Ale
Big, black stout with rich burnt flavours dominating. Car tyres grand cru.

HELLEKETELBIER
7% abv ✪✪✪✪ Spiced Ale
Delicious, brandy coloured ale with wheat and spices.

BIERTOREN
BROUWERIJ BIERTOREN
Brouwerijstraat 23
1910 Kampenhout

Shortly before going to press we heard that Biertoren brewery had been acquired and closed by Huyghe (below). This seems peculiar as it is only a few years since considerable investment was made in the plant to buy equipment for which Huyghe would have little use. The senior member of the family which owned it was apparently not in full agreement with the sale and will try to raise money to re-open the plant. Quite what is in the deal for Huyghe is anyone's guess. It had been an independent family brewery, north east of Brussels, since 1845.

CAMPUS
7% abv ✪✪✪ Pale Ale
Copper-coloured, balanced, candied ale with a light sediment.

AARSCHOTSE BRUINE
4% abv ✪✪✪ Unclassifiable
Mix of light ale and lambic; dry as a bone and slightly sour.

Other regular beers included: Campus Gold (6% abv; pale ale), Curtenberg 1095 (6% abv) and Kerstbier* (winter ale).

BINCHOISE
BRASSERIE LA BINCHOISE
Faubourg St. Paul 38
7130 Binche
Tel & Fax: 064 336186

Hainaut micro-brewery, founded in 1987 at Binche, between Mons and Charleroi. Although production is limited to 700 hl per year, some of its beers are developing excellent reputations for both originality and quality. There are at least a dozen label brands based on the five basic brews. There have been times when the 33 cl bottles of Fakir and Réserve Marie de Hongrie have been brewed by Du Bocq. Brewery tours by arrangement.

RESERVE MARIE DE HONGRIE SPECIALE NOEL*
9% abv ✪✪✪✪ Spiced Ale
Dark walnut coloured brew with more yuletide spices than a Christmas cake.

LE PAVE DE L'OURS
8.5% abv ✪✪✪✪ Honeyed Ale
Superbly different, sediment ale with honey, spice and a sense of humour.

RESERVE MARIE DE HONGRIE
8.5% abv ✪✪✪ Spiced Ale
Dark, sweetish spiced saison-style beer with burnt sugar flavours.

FAKIR
6.8% abv ✪✪✪✪ Walloon Ale
Distinctively dry Wallonian pale ale with wheat beer qualities.

Other regular beers include: La Malognarde Blonde (7.5% abv; pale ale) and Bière de Pâques* (7% abv; Easter ale).

BLAUGIES
BRASSERIE DE BLAUGIES
Rue de la Frontière 435
7370 Blaugies
Tel: 065 650360

Micro-brewery started in 1987 at Blaugies, south west of Mons in western Hainaut. Small, even by micro standards, its annual production is around 280 hl. This does not stop its brewer experimenting, though. Darbyste is said to be derived from the days when a Staffordshire preacher dominated the parish of Blaugies with his ideas on abstinence. The locals invented a "soft drink", which they said was fig juice, but bore a remarkable resemblance in smell, flavour and effect to the local ale. The first brews were said to have come from the 1920 edition of the Larousse Household Encyclopedia! Visits by arrangement.

LA MONEUSE
8% abv ✪✪✪✪ Walloon Strong
Big, spritzy saison beer. Hazy amber brew, like a huge best bitter.

DARBYSTE
5.8% abv ✪✪✪✪ Walloon Ale
Hazy, vinuous, dry but malty amber brew with added figs.

Other regular beers include: La Moneuse Spéciale Noël* (8% abv: spiced ale) and Cuvée du Belvedere (6.8% abv).

BLOCK
BROUWERIJ DE BLOCK
Nieuwbaan 92
1785 Peizegem
Tel: 052 372159
Established in 1887 at Peizegem, north west of Brussels, in the province of Brabant. Produces both ales and lagers, the product range tending to vary over recent years. Annual production is 7,500 hl per annum but this does not stop them exporting, especially to the Netherlands.

SATAN GOLD
8% abv ✪✪✪ Strong Golden
Lightly sedimented straw-coloured ale, lacking the panache of a Duvel.

SATAN RED
8% abv ✪✪ Pale Ale
Filtered, candied, sweet clear ale.

KASTAAR
6.3% abv ✪✪✪ Brown Ale
Unimpressive dark copper ale with brown ale character.

BLOCK SPECIAL 6°
6% abv ✪✪✪✪ Unclassifiable
Blend of pale ale, lambic and aged pale ale. Sour and splendidly different.

Other regular beers include:
Satan Dark (8% abv; brown ale), Block Pils (4.5% abv; Pils) and Block Export (4.3% abv; Pils).

BOCKOR
BROUWERIJ BOCKOR
Kwabrugstraat 5
8510 Bellegem
Tel: 056 216571
Fax: 056 227683
Regional brewery, founded in 1892 south of Kortrijk in West Flanders, 300 metres up the road from the Facon brewery (below). Produces 42,000 hl of beer a year, most of the ales being distributed by the much larger Haacht brewery (below). They deny being a subsidiary, but do share Haacht's propensity to go for the blander end of the ale market. The lambic-based beers do not manage to taste of their alleged beers of origin.

KORTRIJK 800
6.9% abv ✪✪✪ Pale Ale
Filtered, well-attenuated pale ale with additional sweetness. Scotchy.

JACOBINS GUEUZE LAMBIC
5.5% abv ✪✪ Pale Ale
Strangely fruity, like alcoholic Vimto.

JACOBINS FRAMBOZEN LAMBIC
5.5% abv ✪✪ Flavoured Ale
Curious, sweet and sour brew with a lot of fruit but not much beer.

JACOBINS KRIEK LAMBIC
5.5% abv ✪✪ Flavoured Ale
Sweet and dark without much sourness. Not a cherry lambic.

Other regular beers include:
Bockor Ouden Tripel (5.5% abv; old brown) and Bockor Pils (5.2% abv; Pils). There are also two table beers.

BOELENS
BROUWERIJ BOELENS
Kerkstraat 7
9111 Belsele
Tel: 03 772 3200
Brand new microbrewery, near Sint Niklaas in the north eastern part of East Flanders. Experimental brew runs began in August 1993, with a view to going fully commercial in March 1994. Two ales are planned, a tripel and a honeyed ale. One of these may be called Reynaert.

BOON

BROUWERIJ FRANK BOON N.V.

Fonteinstraat 65
1502 Lembeek
Tel: 02 356 6644
Fax: 02 356 3399

A pioneering lambic brewer and gueuze blender, based in Lembeek, south of Brussels. When he set up in 1975, Frank Boon was looked on as an eccentric who misunderstood the beer market. Next he went through a phase of being regarded as a daring traditionalist, then a time as a pragmatist who took a middle course between traditional and commercial lines. Nowadays he works for Sainsbury's, among others, for whom he brews a quite awful "Belgian Ale" and a cleverly fruity and tangy new cherry beer. In Belgium, the standard brews are becoming steadily sweeter while the Mariage Parfait brands are more or less holding true. A sour gueuze is rumoured to be in the making but Frank himself is worrying Belgian beer buffs with statements about traditional gueuze being far too acid. The brewery produces 1500 hl of lambic a year.

BOON KRIEK MARIAGE PARFAIT
6.5% abv ✪✪✪✪ Cherry Gueuze
Partially filtered, fruity, sourish cherry beer, leaning towards traditional.

BOON FRAMBOZENBIER
6.2% abv ✪✪✪ Raspberry Gueuze
Originally a fine acid framboise, nowadays drowned in sweet fruitiness.

BOON GUEUZE
6% abv ✪✪✪ Gueuze (filtered)
Clean, acid gueuze, slightly sweetened; not traditional but pleasant.

BOON GUEUZE MARIAGE PARFAIT
6% abv ✪✪✪✪ Gueuze
Smooth, partially filtered, fuller bodied gueuze; not quite traditional.

PERTOTALE FARO
6% abv ✪✪ Unclassifiable
Unimpressive cocktail of lambic, pale ale and sugar.

BOON KRIEK
5% abv ✪✪✪✪ Cherry Gueuze (filtered)
The best of the sweet krieks. Bags of fruity flavours saved by background character.

Other beers include: Boon Lambik (6% abv; lambic). There is also a low alcohol beer.

BOSTEELS

BROUWERIJ BOSTEELS
Kerkstraat 92
9255 Buggenhout
Tel: 052 332282
Fax: 052 335956

East Flanders brewery, equidistant from Antwerp, Brussels and Ghent. In the same family for six generations since its founding in 1791. Produces one standard Pils and one tasty piece of marketing, to a total of 50,000 hl a year, in the old tower brewery at the manor which was once the family home. Kwak is served in a sort of foot of ale (as opposed to a yard); a tall glass with a ballooned end, held vertically on a wooden stand. It is exported this way to many European countries. The business is helped by its soft drinks company. Tours of the brewery are for groups only but include a view of the private museum of breweriana and its proeflokaal.

PAUWELS KWAK
8% abv ✪✪✪✪ Brown Ale
Big, darkish, sweetish ale which fails to drink to its alleged strength.

Also produces: Prosit Pils (4.8% abv; Pils).

BRUNEHAUT

BRASSERIE DE BRUNEHAUT
Rue de la Pannery 17
7623 Brunehaut
Tel & Fax: 069 346412

Set up south of Tournai, a kilometre from the French border in Hainaut province, during 1992. It has rapidly found a foothold in the highly competitive artisan ale market and its interesting and consistent products are widely available, especially in East Flanders.

BRUNEHAUT AMBREE
6.5% abv ●●●● Pale Ale
Sweetish and burnt, copper brown
sediment ale with blunt bitterness.

BRUNEHAUT BLONDE
6.5% abv ●●● Pale Ale
Sweet, hoppy, copper coloured
sediment pale ale with a touch of
class.

CANTILLON
BROUWERIJ CANTILLON
Gheudestraat 56
1070 Brussel (Anderlecht)
Tel: 02 521 4928
Fax: 02 520 2891
Jean-Pierre Van Roy's family firm is a
splendid anachronism in the modern
world of brewing. The supreme
lambic brewery and gueuze blender,
founded in 1900 but plonked at the
city end of Anderlecht, the Everton
of urban Brussels. Annual production
is only around 700 hl a year. Nearly
all his lambic-based brews are
uncompromisingly sour but delicate
beers. These are about the only
brews currently on the market about
which it is acceptable to say that
they are sometimes perhaps too dry
or too acid – say it about anybody
else's brews and you do not yet
understand Belgian ale.

Cantillon produce all the
traditional lambic-based styles,
blended and unblended. They also
make a few beers in new styles but
to savagely traditional methods.
Bruocsella Grand Cru illustrates what
happens if you bottle old lambic
without blending in young, sweet
lambic – it lacks life. Rosé de
Gambrinus and Vigneronne
demonstrate what happens when
you throw away the rule book; they
are extraordinary drinks.

Van Roy campaigns vigorously
and sometimes rudely for gueuze,
"the champagne of ales", to be
produced in a traditional manner to
the very highest standards and
champions the idea of an appellation
contrôlée. His products do not fail
him. In 1992 he was awarded OBP's
first golden trophy, their equivalent
to a Man of the Year award. The
brewery exports to the Netherlands,
Switzerland and Japan.

BRUOCSELLA 1900 GRAND CRU
5% abv ●●●● Lambic
Darkish old lambic in a bottle.
Livelier than draught but flatter than
gueuze.

CANTILLON BRABANTIAE
5% abv ●●●●● Gueuze (unfiltered)
Deliciously dry; blended from one-,
two- and three-year-old lambics.

CANTILLON FARO
5% abv ●●● Faro
Dark, sweet and sour draught ale. A
sugared, refermented Lambic.

CANTILLON KRIEK LAMBIK
5% abv ●●●●● Cherry Gueuze
(unfiltered)
Superb, rose coloured, dry, aromatic
bottled Kriek.

CANTILLON LAMBIK
5% abv ●●●● Lambic
Sharpish, cleanish draught lambic
with more acidity than many.

**CANTILLON ROSE DE
GAMBRINUS**
5% abv ●●●●● Fruit Gueuze
(unfiltered)
Flowery, extra dry, delicate, wine-
like lambic made with cherry and
raspberry.

CANTILLON SUPER GUEUZE
5% abv ●●●●● Gueuze (unfiltered)
Lightly sedimented, sour, very dry
and slightly bitter. Highly
accomplished.

GUEUZE VIGNERONNE
5% abv ●●●●● Fruit Gueuze
(unfiltered)
Unique dry champagne gueuze,
made from green grapes and mixed
lambics.

Other regular beers include:
Cantillon Druivenlambik (5% abv;
fruit lambic).

CARACOLE
BRASSERIE LA CARACOLE
Rue de la Halle 6
5000 Namur
Tel: 081 220683
Micro-brewery set up in 1990 in
Namur town by the owners of an off-
licence at the above address. The
beers are not yet settled in range,
recipe or consistency but some
interesting brews have emerged.

LA CARACOLE BRUNE
6% abv ✪✪✪✪ Brown Ale
Well constructed, dryish French-style brown ale; bottle-conditioned.

Other regular beers include: La Caracole Ambrée (6.5% abv; pale ale) and La Caracole Cuvée Reservée (6.5% abv).

CHIMAY
BRASSERIE DE CHIMAY
Route du Rond Point 294
6464 Forges-les-Chimay
Tel: 060 213063
Fax: 060 213422

Trappist brewery, situated on the French border at the southernmost tip of Hainaut province. The abbey was founded in 1850 and its brewery was founded in 1862 to operate on a fully commercial scale. The brewery remains at the abbey but bottling is done at a modern plant in nearby Baileux. With an annual production of 130,000 hl, it remains the largest of the monastic producers. Its internationally renowned ales are known simply as Chimay, the name of the small town 10 km north of the abbey. They export to Britain, the Netherlands, France, Germany, Spain, Denmark, Greece, USA, Canada, Japan and Australia.

Three regular ales are produced, distinguished by the blue, white or red colour of their caps. Three presentation brews called Grand Réserve, Cinq Cents and Première also appear but are believed to be the same beers in 75 cl corked bottles. The abbey is also responsible for producing a range of cheeses with the brand name Chimay, the best known of which is in the Camembert style.

CHIMAY BLEUE
9% abv ✪✪✪✪✪ Trappist Strong
Big, dark, strong trappist ale of great complexity.

CHIMAY BLANCHE
8% abv ✪✪✪✪✪ Trappist Tripel
Firm, strong, sweetish, amber-coloured ale with burnt malt flavours.

CHIMAY ROUGE
7% abv ✪✪✪✪✪ Trappist Dubbel
Dark and slightly sour. Just as interesting but not so overwhelmimg.

CLARYSSE
BROUWERIJ CLARYSSE
Krekelput 16-18
9700 Oudenaarde
Tel: 055 311721
Fax: 055 319476

East Flanders brewery, founded in 1946, producing mainly brown ales under the brand name of Felix. The standard beers are filtered and sweet but you may find matured sediment versions of far greater character. The company do not appear to believe in sourness, which is a shame. Total production is around 15,000 hl a year.

ST. HERMES
8% abv ✪✪✪ Abbey Tripel
Amber brew with minimal sediment, lacking the subtlety of great tripels.

FELIX OUDENAARDS KRIEKBIER
6% abv ✪✪ Old Cherry
Very sweet, filtered and dull, despite two years' alleged ageing.

FELIX OUDENAARDS OUD BRUIN (Unfiltered)
5.5% abv ✪✪✪✪ Old Brown
Delightfully fruity, sourish, sweet brown ale, verging on a 5✪ rating.

FELIX OUDENAARDS OUD BRUIN (Filtered)
5.5% abv ✪✪✪ Old Brown
Surprisingly sweet and lacking the quality of the unfiltered version.

FELIX KRIEKBIER
5% abv ✪✪ Old Cherry
Syrupy, brown, very slight acidity but unpleasant back taste.

FELIX SPECIAAL OUDENAARDS
4.8% abv ✪✪✪ Old Brown
Slightly sour and sweetish filtered brown ale.

OUDENAARDS WIT TARWEBIER
4.8% abv ✪✪✪ Wheat Beer (filtered)
Clear, subtle and unmistakably wheaty but lacks the complexity of a "mucky" brew.

CNUDDE
BROUWERIJ CNUDDE
Fabriekstraat 8
9700 Eine
Tel: 055 311834

East Flanders brewery founded in 1919, just north of Oudenaarde. It produces a singular ale, which deserves to be better known, plus an occasional kriek for special events. Nearly closed in 1992 but the owner's three sons have banded together to try to keep things rolling. We have never found their beer outside the town. Try the Café Casino at 6 Eineplein, 50 metres from the brewery.

CNUDDE BRUIN
4.7% abv ❍❍❍❍ Old Brown
Distinctive, slightly fruity, sourish, grainy brew with lactose overtones.

CONTRERAS
BROUWERIJ CONTRERAS
Molenstraat 111
9890 Gavere
Tel: 091 842706
Small East Flanders artisan brewery, tracing its origins to 1818. It produces 2,000 hl of its three beers per year. The brews are found in painted brown bottles distinguishable only by their tops. Cream is Pils, white is Tonneke and blue is Marzenbier. The last of these is brewed in March because the brewer reckons his brewing water to be best then! It is fermented for two months in the brewery and has similarities with the aged brown beers of nearby Oudenaarde.

MARZENBIER
5.8% abv ❍❍❍❍ Old Pale
Unfiltered, sourish, dry, amber-coloured pale ale.

TONNEKE
5% abv ❍❍❍❍ Pale Ale
Sweetish, copper coloured, filtered ale with a surprising mix of malt flavours.

Other regular beers include: Contra Pils (4.8% abv; Pils).

CROMBE
BROUWERIJ CROMBÉ
Hospitaalstraat 10
9620 Zottegem
Tel: 091 600240
Established in 1798 at the village of Zottegem, south of Ghent. Always run by the same family. A tiny concern employing just the brewer

and a helper, it still manages to produce 1,650 hl of beer a year. The brewery enjoys growing affection and respect from Belgian beer lovers for its slightly unusual ales. Oud Kriekenbier is the only cherry beer not based on lambic to be made with 100 per cent whole cherries. New brews seem to be appearing with great regularity and production is expanding. It is open to visitors every week (see Beer Tourism: Breweries). The Pee Klak brands are brewed for a wholesaler.

ZOTTEGEMSE GRAND CRU
8.4% abv ❍❍❍❍ Pale Ale
Surprisingly full, copper-coloured, bitter-sweet ale with saccharin backtaste.

CHRISTMAS BEER*
8% abv ❍❍❍ Winter Ale
Disappointing amber sediment ale tasting of fermented molasses.

EGMONT ZOTTEGEMSE TRIPEL
7% abv ❍❍❍ Strong Golden
Billed as an abbey style tripel but more of a spicy, hazy, golden beer.

OUD KRIEKENBIER
6.5% abv ❍❍❍❍❍ Old Cherry
Pale ale refermented with whole cherries. Largely filtered but sour, with excellent fruit flavour.

OUD ZOTTEGEMS
6.5% abv ❍❍❍ Pale Ale
Ricy, but otherwise acceptable amber ale.

CEZARKEN
5.5% abv ❍❍ Pale Ale
Not the best of the Crombé beers.

PEE KLAK
5.4% abv ❍❍❍ Pale Ale
Unusual, slightly bitter, straw coloured sediment ale with wheaty leanings.

Other regular beers include: Cleopaterken (5.6% abv), Crom Pils (5% abv; Pils) and Zottegems Bruin (5% abv; brown ale).

DAMY
BROUWERIJ DAMY
Heirweg 6
9870 Olsene
Tel: 091 888707
East Flanders brewery, reputed to have been founded in 1540 in a

village between Ghent and Kortrijk. They have links with the Roman brewery (below). Their beers are named after an old religious institution known as the Abbey of the Dunes. The tripel is said to be the only beer in Belgium brewed in the old style favoured by West Flanders abbeys years ago. Some of the sourness comes from fermentation by a yeast used for brewing old red beers. Part of the sweetness is saccharin, more obvious in the lighter brews. Annual production is 8,500 hl.

ST. IDESBALD TRIPEL
8% abv ✪✪✪✪ Abbey Tripel (dark)
Strong and sour, sedimented brown ale, like a beefy old Flemish red beer.

ST. IDESBALD DUBBEL
6% abv ✪✪✪ Old Brown
Also known as St. Idesbald Brune. The Licht, darkened with Wayland syrup.

ST. IDESBALD LICHT
6% abv ✪✪✪ Old Pale
Sweet and sour light ale. An acquired taste.

DECA

DECA SERVICES
Elverdingestraat 4
8640 Woesten
Tel: 057 423412
Fax: 057 423686

North west of Ieper (Ypres) in West Flanders. Formerly the Isebaert brewery, taken over in 1991 by the former owners of Van Assche (below) in a version of musical chairs for breweries. Set up to be a major small brewery for local wholesalers. It is hoped that production will eventually reach 10,000 hl a year. St. Amandus Blonde is subtitled "Kortenbergs Abdijbier" but has no abbey qualities.

VLETEREN ALT
8% abv ✪✪✪✪ Brown Ale
Medium dark sediment ale; full of malt and alcohol but lacking bitterness.

VLETEREN SUPER 8
8% abv ✪✪✪✪ Pale Ale
Similar to the Alt, with a less complex flavour. Grows on you.

ST. AMANDUS BLONDE
5% abv ✪✪✪ Pale Ale
Bitter but plain sediment pale ale.

DE ES

BROUWERIJ DE ES
Schalkhovenstraat 38
3732 Schalkhoven

Old brewery, established in 1835, between Hasselt and Tongeren in the south of Belgian Limburg. It specialises in brown table beers but brews only rarely. It is still deciding whether to close or go into serious brewing.

There are two table beers called De Es Gersten and De Es Dubbel Gersten.

DE KONINCK

BROUWERIJ DE KONINCK
Mechelsesteenweg 291
2018 Antwerpen
Tel: 03 218 4048
Fax: 03 230 8519

Independently owned brewery in the city of Antwerp, founded in 1833 and since 1989 rumoured to have business connections with Heineken, Interbrew, VBBR, Old Uncle Tom Cobley and all. Its single regular brew is the classic Belgian pale ale against which all the others are judged. It is found filtered on draught or pasteurised in the bottle. It seems to be available in every café in Antwerp, where you ask simply for a "bolleke", described by Antwerpers as a 33 cl glass with 25 cl of beer in it! In 1990 they made a contract with the Vjena brewery of Leningrad and now export to Russia as well as the Netherlands and Spain. Try the Russian version next time you are in what is now St. Petersburg, at the Café Antwerpen above Gorkovskaya metro station!

Production stands at around 130,000 hl per year. For Easter 1991 the company brewed a one-off stronger pale ale called Trio. Later that year came a low-alcohol brew called Duo. 1993 saw a 7.5% abv pale ale, Cuvée Antwerpen 93 to celebrate the city's year as European city of culture. A regular, higher gravity beer would certainly be a welcome innovation.

DE KONINCK (bottled)
5% abv ❍❍❍❍ Pale Ale
Well-rounded, beautifully balanced, plain but firm.

DE KONINCK (draught)
5% abv ❍❍❍❍ Pale Ale
A slightly softer, smoother version of the bottled ale.

DELBECCHA

RELAIS DELBECCHA
Bodegemsestraat 158
1700 Dilbeek
Tel: 02 569 4430
Home brewery on the western outskirts of Brussels, started in 1991. Its equipment was bought from the microbrewery run for a time by the Hopduvel café and warehouse in Ghent. Brews around 250 hl a year of ales in 75 cl bottles, for sale at the hotel and restaurant complex (see Belgian Cafés: Brabant) and in the free trade. They sometimes add coriander and orange peel to their brews. A cherry beer and a Christmas ale have also appeared during its brief history. Shortly before going to press they lost the brewer, prompting rumours that brewing may cease.

DELBECCHA BLOND
7% abv ❍❍❍ Pale Ale
Slightly sour, yeasty, pale home brew.

Other regular beers include: Delbeccha Bruin (7.5% abv; brown ale).

DE RYCK

BROUWERIJ DE RYCK
Kerkstraat 28
9550 Herzele
Tel: 053 622302
Small family ale brewery based between Ghent and Brussels. Established in 1886, it produces 6,000 hl a year of reliable but plainish ales. Rochus and Special were introduced to celebrate the company's centenary but proved so popular that they stayed in the range.

DE RYCK CHRISTMAS PALE ALE*
4.7% abv ❍❍❍❍ Pale Ale
Available from mid-September. Characterful and well-rounded.

ROCHUS
4.7% abv ❍❍❍ Brown Ale
Dark and sweet with overtones of aniseed and vanilla.

DE RYCK SPECIAL
4.2% abv ❍❍ Pale Ale
Not that special. Surprisingly weak for Belgium.

The other regular beers is: Molenbier (5.3% abv).

DE SMEDT

BROUWERIJ DE SMEDT
Ringlaan 18
1890 Opwijk
Tel: 052 359911
Commercially adept, family owned brewery from Opwijk, north west of Brussels. It was founded in 1790 and production has now reached 40,000 hl a year. Produces mainly ales with abbey style flavours with character and authenticity present to varying degrees. Tends to make slight adaptations to basic brews in order to create an array of additional brands with the labels Abbaye d'Aulne, Abbaye de Brogne, Affligem and Postel. Dikkenek ("thick neck") is a juniper flavoured beer, inspired by the genever-making town of Hasselt, whose residents suffer this collective nickname. Affligem Rood and Wit refer to the colours of the caps. Recently acquired a licence to brew Celis White, the wheat beer produced in Austin, Texas by ex-pat Hoegaarden pioneer, Pierre Celis.

ABBAYE D'AULNE 10° DIVINE
10.5% abv ❍❍❍ Abbey Strong
Strong, clear, roasted, dark ruby ale without individual character.

ABBAYE D'AULNE 8°
SELECTION
9% abv ❍❍❍❍ Strong Stout
Filtered, deep chestnut, sharply bitter, heavily caramelised distinctive brew.

SUPER NOEL ABBAYE D'AULNE*
9% abv ❍❍❍❍ Winter Ale
Deep, dark and mature with a rocky head and a light sediment.

AFFLIGEM TRIPEL
8% abv ❍❍❍ Abbey Tripel
Full of abbey character (❍❍❍❍) when with a sediment. Sweet and dull without.

NAPOLEON
7.5% abv ❸❸❸ Brown Ale
Sienna coloured, crystal clear,
lacking distinctive characteristics.

POSTEL DUBBEL
7% abv ❹❹❹❹ Abbey Dubbel
Bitter-sweet, rich brown ale.

AFFLIGEM ROOD
7% abv ❸❸❸ Abbey Dubbel
Sometimes sold as Dubbel or Bruin.
Light sediment, wrong sugar
balance.

AFFLIGEM VAN'T PATERS VAT
7% abv ❹❹❹❹ Abbey Tripel
Delicately balanced weak tripel with
a light sediment.

AFFLIGEM WIT
7% abv ❸❸❸ Pale Ale
Also sold as Blonde. Possibly the
previous beer in filtered form.

ABBAYE D'AULNE BLONDE DES
PERES
7% abv ❸❸❸ Pale Ale
Plausible blond abbey style brew but
not in the big league.

DIKKENEK
6% abv ❸❸❸ Spiced Ale
Filtered garnet brown ale, sweet and
juniper flavoured.

OP ALE
4.8% abv ❸❸❸ Pale Ale
Pleasant drinking ale with slight
saccharin flavours.

Other regular beers include:
Postel Tripel (7.5% abv; abbey
tripel), Christmas Ale* (7% abv;
winter ale) and Celis White.

DE TROCH
BROUWERIJ DE TROCH
Langestraat 20
1741 Wambeek
Tel: 02 582 1027
De Troch is one of the oldest
surviving lambic breweries, dating
from 1820. The company, based at
the western edge of the Senne
Valley, always used to brew darker,
fuller bodied lambics than other
producers. In the mid 1980s they
decided to go commercial with a
vengeance, such that they
specialised almost exclusively in low
strength "fruit beers", produced
under the brand names of Chapeau
(3% abv) and Abondance (3.5% abv).

These are made by adding diluted
fruit syrups to young lambic. This
increased annual production to
3,500 hl but ended their excellent
reputation for sour and delicious
traditional lambic-based beers. Then
history turned upside-down and
traditional De Troch Kriek and
Gueuze started to re-appear. This
was quickly followed by an
extraordinary ersatz product which
appears to be a pressurised, kegged
lambic. What happens next is
anyone's guess. When the traditional
corked products are available, they
are amongst the best on the market,
improving in the cellar for at least
five years.

DE TROCH GUEUZE
5.5% abv ❺❺❺❺❺ Gueuze
(unfiltered)
Dark, sour, full-flavoured, proper
gueuze, only rarely found.

DE TROCH KRIEK
5.5% abv ❺❺❺❺❺ Cherry Gueuze
(unfiltered)
Dark, sour and deliciously fruity
traditional gueuze-based kriek. Best
when heavily sedimented after two
years in the cellar.

CHAPEAU GUEUZE
5.5% abv ❸❸❸ Gueuze (filtered)
Seriously compromised version of
their traditional gueuze.

DE TROCH CHAPEAU LAMBIK
(draught)
4.5% abv ❹❹❹❹ Lambic
Experimental kegged lambic. Sour,
bitter and pleasantly quaffable
concoction.

Other regular beers include:
Chapeau Faro (4.5% abv; faro) and
De Troch Lambic (5% abv; lambic).
There is a range of weak,
commercial fruit beers (see above).

DEVAUX
BRASSERIE DEVAUX
Rue de l'Eglise St Phillippe 1
5600 Phillippeville
Tel: 071 666347
Small brewery in the south west of
Namur province, dating from 1900.
They have traditionally concentrated
on table beers. The production of
Schwendi and the takeover of the
Février table beer brewery may

indicate that they are thinking of staying in business by doing some serious brewing. Current production is limited to 700 hl a year. Schwendi comes in swing-top stoppered bottles and is fermented with Rodenbach yeast. This is not a marketing decision, they just don't have any others!

SCHWENDI

6.5% abv ✪✪✪✪ Pale Ale
Superbly refreshing, copper coloured, sweet and sour ale with a unique tang.

There are also two table beers called Blonde and Brune.

DOLLE BROUWERS
DE DOLLE BROUWERS
Roeselaerestraat 12b
8600 Esen-Diksmuide
Tel: 051 502781

The Mad Brewers brewery. Founded in 1980 in the village of Esen, near Diksmuide in West Flanders, by three brothers and their formidable mother. After winning a national home brewing competition, they entered the commercial market by buying up an old brewing plant. One of the brothers is now a doctor and another an architect. The unusually old-fashioned equipment produces 1,000 hl a year of regular, seasonal and experimental ales of unusually high quality, even by Belgian standards. Brewery visits are possible every Sunday at 15.00 (sharp). They now export to the Netherlands. One of their original beers, Oeral, re-appeared once in 1993 and may alternate in the range with Esenaar, which has some similarities.

STILLE NACHT*

8% abv ✪✪✪✪✪ Winter Ale
Silent Night, strong and sweet in November. Powerful amber nectar by April. Vinous and special after two or three years.

ARABIER*

8% abv ✪✪✪✪✪ Summer Ale
Strong, subtle, complex and delightfully bitter amber ale.

BOSKEUN*

8% abv ✪✪✪✪ Easter Ale
Strong, honeyed, spicy ale. Literally, Wood Rabbit, the brewer's nickname!

LICHTERVELDS BLOND

8% abv ✪✪✪✪ Strong Golden
The Mad Brewers' atttempt at a Duvel-style beer.

OERBIER

7.5% abv ✪✪✪✪✪ Brown Ale
Strong, dark, slightly sour and distinctive. The original Dolle Brouwers ale.

VLOTBIER

6.9% abv ✪✪✪✪ Pale Ale
Cloudy, honeyed, spiced, straw coloured ale.

ESENAAR

6% abv ✪✪✪✪✪ Pale Ale
Secular version of Orval, aromatically bitter and delicious.

Other regular beers include: Special Reserva (11% abv), Dulle Teve (10% abv) and Zwarte Molenbier.

DOMUS
BROUWERIJ DOMUS
Tiensestraat 8
3000 Leuven
Tel: 016 201449
Fax: 016 206436

The first of only three home-brew houses in Belgium, established at Leuven in August 1985 by a former brewer of the Alken Cristal brewery. Two or three draught beers are available at the pub at any one time. Domus, a unique lager probably closest to the Wiener style, is available all year round, the others appearing in rotation. The brewery plant is English, designed by Peter Austin, the Hampshire-based originator of much of the British small brewery revolution of the 1980s. The brewhouse, which produces 1,000 hl of beer a year, is visible through picture windows behind the pub. Its portfolio is unique for Belgium in that most of the beers are bottom fermented. Our classification of its beer styles has had to be approximate for this reason.

BUGEL*

8% abv ✪✪✪✪ Dubbelbock
Medium brown heavy Christmas lager with a sweetish lace of molasses. The strongest bottom fermented brew produced in Belgium.

DUBBEL DOMUS HONINGBIER
7% abv ✪✪✪✪ Dortmunder
From January to Easter. Honeyed
lager which develops a meibok
character.

DUBBEL PAASKRIEK*
7% abv ✪✪✪✪ Unclassifiable
Around Easter. Honingbier
refermented with cherry juice.

DOMUS MEIBOK*
7% abv ✪✪✪ Meibok
May to June. The only real Belgian
meibok. Like unhoneyed
Honingbier.

DOMUS
5% abv ✪✪✪✪ Wiener
Fresh-tasting, slightly sweet amber
coloured lager of character.

FONSKE*
5% abv ✪✪✪ Pils
October to December. Unusual
variant of Pils, aimed at new
students.

LEUVENS WITBIER*
5% abv ✪✪✪✪ Wheat Beer
(unfiltered)
June to September. Deliciously
balanced ale with honeyed
overtones.

The other seasonal beers include:
B-4 Lusbier* (6.5% abv; wheat beer).

DRIE FONTEINEN
GUEUZESTEKERIJ DRIE FONTEINEN
Hermann Teirlinckplein 3
1650 Beersel
Tel: 02 376 2652
Fax: 02 376 0703
The nearest thing in the world of
gueuze to a home-brew house. A
home-blender, based alongside an
excellent café-restaurant of the same
name in the main square at Beersel,
south of Brussels. Armand and Guido
Debelder are the second generation
to run the Three Fountains. Most of
the time Armand is in charge of the
kitchen and Guido runs the bar.
They buy lambics from Girardin and
Lindemans and may keep them in
the cellar for up to three years. The
small black cherries required for the
Kriek come from nearby St Genesius
Rode. All the bottled beers improve
with ageing up to five years. The

best continue to be drunk for 20
years. Despite the small scale (only
80 hl a year), these beers are world
classics. The sweetened draught
cherry lambic is a great rarity and an
acquired taste. The raspberry gueuze
has not been produced since 1989
but stocks lasted nearly four years
and the Debelders may produce it
again in 1993. For more details about
the café, see Belgian Cafés: Brabant.

DRIE FONTEINEN FRAMBOISE
5% abv ✪✪✪✪✪ Raspberry Gueuze
(unfiltered)
Harshly sour, uncompromisingly dry
but yet delicate, salmon coloured
raspberry beer. The best of its kind
on the market today.

DRIE FONTEINEN GUEUZE
5% abv ✪✪✪✪✪ Gueuze (unfiltered)
Superb, dry, lemony gueuze with
slight bitterness. Ages well.

DRIE FONTEINEN KRIEK
(Bottled)
5% abv ✪✪✪✪✪ Cherry Gueuze
(unfiltered)
Fuller fruit than the framboise,
darker and slightly more bitter.

DRIE FONTEINEN KRIEK
(Draught)
5% abv ✪✪✪✪ Cherry Lambic
Like fine, light, oaky lambic that has
drowned in Ribena! Too sweet for
many tastes. Served by handpump at
the restaurant.

DU BOCQ
BRASSERIE DU BOCQ
Rue de la Brasserie 4
5530 Purnode
Tel: 082 613737
Fax: 082 611780
Active independent brewery from
just north of Dinant in Namur
province. Founded in 1858. Brews
60,000 hl a year of an impressive
range of ales, many of high quality.
Notorious for producing label beers
under contract to a wide array of
distributors. There have been dozens
of these, based closely on the
brewery's standard products. They
also brew beers for other breweries
and used to brew Leffe Tripel for
Interbrew. Blanche de Namur was
the name of a noted beauty who
became the Queen of Sweden in the
14th century.

CHRISTMAS REGAL*
9% abv ✪✪✪✪ Winter Ale
Similar to Triple Moine but darker.

LA GAULOISE
8.8% abv ✪✪✪✪✪ Walloon Strong
Strong, surprisingly delicate,
medium brown sediment ale, spicy
but not spiced, and not too bitter.

TRIPLE MOINE
8% abv ✪✪✪✪ Walloon Strong
Strong and crisp, herbal and hoppy;
with all the flavours of a strong
saison.

ST. BENOIT BLONDE
7% abv ✪✪✪✪ Pale Ale
Strong hop nose and a subtle mix of
malty backtastes.

ST. BENOIT BRUNE
7% abv ✪✪✪✪ Brown Ale
Similar to St. Benoit Blonde. So many
hops in a brown beer is unusual.

SAISON REGAL
6.1% abv ✪✪✪ Saison
Pleasant, light brown ale with a huge
hop punch which does not last.

BLANCHE DE NAMUR
4.5% abv ✪✪✪✪ Wheat Beer
(unfiltered)
Unspiced bière blanche with a
pronounced grainy flavour.

BLANCHE DE NOEL
4% abv ✪✪✪ Wheat Beer
(unfiltered)
Medium orange-brown, thin, spicy
sediment wheat beer for the
Christmas market.
   Other brands include: La
Bosquetia (7.5% abv).

DUBUISSON
BRASSERIE DUBUISSON
Chaussée de Mons 28
7904 Pipaix
Tel: 069 662085
Fax: 069 661727
Smallish brewery at Pipaix, east of
Tournai in the artisan ale belt of
western Hainaut. It traces its roots to
1769. Essentially produces nearly
16,000 hl a year of a single mighty
ale which is one of the strongest in
the world. At this strength it barely
matters that the beer is filtered as
most yeasts would die from alcohol
poisoning anyway. A beer for
sipping not quaffing. Called Bush

Beer (buisson is French for bush), it
is marketed in the US as "Scaldis".
This is to ensure nobody mistakes it
for Budweiser, which is brewed by
Anheuser Busch. Would that they
were so lucky. Christmas 1991 saw
the launch of a seasonal version.

BUSH BEER
12.2% abv ✪✪✪✪✪ Strong Ale
Huge and impressive amber nectar,
full of character. Billows excellence.

BUSH NOEL*
12% abv ✪✪✪ Winter Ale
Deep copper coloured barley wine
that rasps the palate like British
sherry.

DUPONT
BRASSERIE DUPONT
Rue Basse 5
7904 Tourpes-Leuze
Tel: 069 662201
Brewing since 1850 in that part of
Hainaut traditionally associated with
the production of saison ales. One of
the best artisan breweries in
Belgium, its annual production is
surprisingly small, at 5,500 hl. "Made
by Nature and Progress" reads the
label. Vielle Provision Saison Dupont
is arguably the finest of the style and
some say the last saison beer made
by the traditional method. The full
name of its other classic beer is Avec
Les Bons Voeux de la Brasserie (With
the Best Wishes of the Brewery).
Dupont is gaining a good reputation,
both for the quality of its recipes and
the adventurous range of its
products. Its Biologique products are
claimed to be 100 per cent organic.
On the downside, it is one of the
most prodigious producers of label
beers. At the last count there were
over 30 rejigged versions of
Moinette Blonde alone.

BONS VOEUX*
9.5% abv ✪✪✪✪✪ Winter Ale
Delightfully hop-packed sediment
Christmas brew, which holds its
bitterness and flowery flavours well.

MOINETTE BLONDE
8.5% abv ✪✪✪✪ Walloon Strong
Highly aromatic spicy pale ale with
saison-ish leanings.

MOINETTE BRUNE
8.5% abv ✪✪✪✪ Walloon Strong

Sour, brown and strong. Like a mighty old brown with saison overtones.

MOINETTE BIOLOGIQUE
7.5% abv ✪✪✪✪ Walloon Ale
Light bistre coloured sediment ale with a huge hop character. Would be 5✪ but for a sharp bitter backtaste.

VIEILLE PROVISION SAISON DUPONT
6.5% abv ✪✪✪✪✪ Saison
Golden oak colour, dry, herbal and hoppy with lingering aromatic aftertastes.

REDOR PILS
6% abv ✪✪ Pils
Tastes like a lager fermented by ale yeast.

Other regular beers include: Cervesia (8.5% abv; spiced ale), Dupont Biologique (5.5% abv; saison) and Moinette Scotch (5.5% abv; Scotch ale).

EUPENER

EUPENER BIERBRAUEREI
Paveestrasse 12-14
4700 Eupen
Tel: 087 554731

The only German style bierbrauerei in Belgium, situated on the high street in Eupen, the market town at the heart of the small German-speaking cantonment in eastern Liège. After World War One this part of Germany was subsumed into Belgium and two breweries, the older of which was founded in 1834, merged to form the present company. It produces 20,000 hl of beer a year, mainly Pils, for sale in the locality. Klosterbier is really a German Bock, the matured lager style which the Dutch adapted to their bokbier style but which is significantly different. A third beer, Eupener Extra, tastes as if it is a dilute version of the Pils.

EUPENER KLOSTERBIER
5.5% abv ✪✪✪ Bockbier
Light brown, sweetish and smooth. Fails to reach taste potential.

EUPENER PILS
4.7% abv ✪✪✪ Pils
Pleasant and quite accomplished. There is also a low alcohol lager and

two dark table beers in the German malzbier style.

FACON

BROUWERIJ FACON
Kwabrugstraat 23
8540 Bellegem
Tel: 056 220769
Fax: 056 259347

Family run brewery established in 1874 at Bellegem, south of Kortrijk, in West Flanders. Determined to remain an independent company. It has made major investments in the old plant recently, increasing potential capacity six-fold to 100 hl per day. Eighty per cent of the production is Pils, mainly supplied to the area between Mons, Tournai and Mouscron. Until recently the rest was table beer but since the fourth generation of the Facon family have joined the company, an interesting array of specialist ales are emerging, accounting for the expanding output. It is only 300 metres down the road from Bockor brewery (see above).

FACON SCOTCH-CHRISTMAS*
6.1% abv ✪✪✪✪ Scotch Ale
Sweet, dark, filtered brew tasting of demerara, pear drops and autumn evenings.

FACON EXTRA STOUT
5.4% abv ✪✪✪ Dry Stout
Dark, dry, filtered stout in the Guinness mould.

Other regular beers include: Bière du Château de Ramègnies-Chin (12% abv; strong ale), Facon Tripel (8% abv; tripel), L'Obigeoise (8% abv; pale ale), Facon Oud Bruin (4.5% abv), Facon Pils (4.5% abv; Pils) and Facon Export (4.3% abv; Pils). There are also two table beers.

FERME AU CHENE

LA FERME AU CHENE
Rue Comte d'Ursel 115
6940 Durbuy
Tel: 086 211067

Oak Tree Farm is a home brew house opened in 1989 at Durbuy in the north of Luxembourg province. The single house beer, named after an old brewery once active in the village, is occasionally supplemented by other one-off brews. Annual production is 100 hl. For further details about the pub see Belgian Cafés: Luxembourg.

MARCKLOFF
6.5% abv ❍❍❍ Walloon Ale
Distinctively Wallonian, hazy pale ale.

Other beers include: Louisiana Blonde (7% abv; Walloon ale).

FRIART

BRASSERIE FRIART
Rue d'Houdeng 20
7070 Le Roeulx
Tel: 064 662151

A long established brewery which closed in 1977 and then re-opened in 1988 at Le Roeulx, between Charleroi and Mons, initially to brew abbey beers for the Abbaye de St. Feuillien. They are taking on some contract brewing and have produced some of the Abdij van Dieleghem brews. Production thus far has reached 15,000 hl per year. The beers sometimes have an unpleasant bitter backtaste suggesting they balance the sweetness with saccharin. They are masters of the art of bottle design, from the deliberately plain 25 cl stubbies to the imposing six litre Methuselahs.

ST. FEUILLIEN CUVEE DE NOEL*
9% abv ❍❍❍❍ Winter Ale
Umber coloured, heavy sediment ale with aged and burnt character.

ST. FEUILLIEN BLOND
7.5% abv ❍❍❍❍ Pale Ale
Light coloured sediment pale ale with a massive hop aroma and fine flavour.

ST. FEUILLIEN BRUNE
7.5% abv ❍❍❍❍ Brown Ale
Very dark and sweetish sediment ale with caramel and liquorice flavours.

GRISETTE
5% abv ❍❍❍ Pale Ale
Sweetish, gentle, filtered, distinctively Belgian pale ale.

GIGI

BRASSERIE GIGI
Grand Rue 96
6769 Gerouville
Tel: 063 577515

Small brewery at Gerouville in the deep south of Luxembourg province, right on the French border. Previously known as the Brasserie de l'Etoile, it was founded in 1888. Traditionally it has specialised in table beers but went into serious brewing in 1991 when it took over the production of the Gaumaise beers from the nearby Maire brewery, which closed. Prior to that it was already earning four stars for Unic Bier. Such a rating for a beer as strong as a Welsh valley mild denotes real class.

LA GAUMAISE BLONDE
5% abv ❍❍❍ Pale Ale
Straight forward, dryish, sediment pale ale.

LA GAUMAISE BRUNE
5% abv ❍❍❍ Brown Ale
Light, sweet and fruity in the French bière brune style.

UNIC BIER
3.2% abv ❍❍❍❍ Table Beer
Slightly sour light ale with a touch of class.

Three other table beers are produced.

GIRARDIN

BROUWERIJ GIRARDIN
Lindenberg 10
1700 Sint-Ulriks-Kapelle
Tel: 02 452 6419

Senne Valley lambic brewer and gueuze blender, with an annual output of 3,200 hl; family firm who still brew on the farm. They produce clean, gentle, bitterish beers and also sell their lambic to other blenders. In 1990 they took over the blending of the gueuze and cherry gueuze for De Koninck, the beer wholesaler and former gueuze blender of Dworp. However, these did not appear in 1992. That year saw the blending of gueuze and kriek for Wets, the drinks wholesalers and former gueuze blenders of St Genesius Rode. Whether these survive has yet to be seen. Nowadays some beers appear filtered and others lightly sedimented. In 1993 their collective nose was put out of joint by the findings of an OBP microbiological analysis which found no live cells in their gueuze. [Editor's note: This contrasts with the observation that their 1990 bottled gueuze and kriek both improved when laid down in my cellar for two years.]

GIRARDIN GUEUZE 1882
5% abv ✪✪✪✪ Gueuze
Partially filtered, semi-traditional gueuze, with a grapefruit tang.

GIRARDIN FRAMBOOS
5% abv ✪✪✪ Raspberry Gueuze (filtered)
Highly perfumed and sweetish. Must be juice-based with youngish lambics.

GIRARDIN KRIEK 1882
5% abv ✪✪✪✪ Cherry Gueuze
Like the gueuze with a delicate cherry flavour. Highly quaffable.

GIRARDIN LAMBIC
5% abv ✪✪✪✪ Lambic
Pleasantly sour and lemony. One of the commoner traditional lambics.

WETS GUEUZE
5% abv ✪✪✪✪ Gueuze
Partially filtered and not too dry but yet with a typical traditional flavour.

WETS KRIEK
5% abv ✪✪✪✪ Cherry Gueuze
Sweeter than other traditional krieks but full of sharp and fruity flavours.

The other regular beers are: Girardin Kriekenlambic (5% abv; cherry lambic) and Ulricher Lager (5% abv; Pils).

GOUDEN BOOM
BROUWERIJ DE GOUDEN BOOM
Langestraat 45
8000 Brugge
Tel: 050 330699
Fax: 050 334644

A small brewery in old Bruges, founded in 1889 and taken over in 1983, when it changed its name from 't Hamerken. It had its own maltings until 1976, now converted into a museum (see Beer Tourism). Produces 20,000 hl of distinctive ales per year, exporting to France, the Netherlands, Italy, Germany, Spain, Canada, USA and Japan. Even found in the Canary Isles! In 1993 it was taken over by Rodenbach. Brewery trips are easy to arrange and there is

now a fully equipped sampling room.

BRUGSE TRIPEL
9.5% abv ✪✪✪✪ Abbey Tripel
Strong, sweetish, dark straw coloured sediment ale with rather coarse hopping.

STEENBRUGGE TRIPEL
9% abv ✪✪✪ Strong Golden
Thinner than the Brugse, more saccharin flavour and less rounded.

ABDIJ VAN STEENBRUGGE
6.5% abv ✪✪✪✪ Abbey Dubbel
Chestnut coloured, caramelised, abbey beer also known as Steenbrugge Dubbel.

BRUGS TARWEBIER
5% abv ✪✪✪✪ Wheat Beer (unfiltered)
Sweet, summery wheat beer with a very slight sharpness.

HAACHT
BROUWERIJ HAACHT
Provinciesteenweg 28
3190 Boortmeerbeek
Tel: 016 601501
Fax: 016 608384

Established in 1890 at Boortmeerbeek, north of Leuven in the province of Brabant. The largest independent brewery in Belgium, its annual production reaches 1,100,000 hl, mainly of mass-market Pils and a varying range of reliable but unadventurous ales. They have a trading agreement with Bockor to supply their Jacobins range. Gildenbier was inherited from the Cerckel brewery in Diest and is said to be the only remaining beer in the Diest style of firm brown ales. The brewery can be visited on Monday to Thursday afternoons between April and September. Telephone for details. The trip includes a video and tasting. A café near the brewery, called the Brouwershuis, serves Haacht Primus straight from the lager tank, unfiltered. This is one of the few examples of this custom outside Bavaria, where it is called Zwickelbier.

TONGERLO 8°
8% abv ✪✪✪ Abbey Tripel
Light amber coloured sediment ale. Palate too thin to be all malt.

ADLER
6.3% abv ❸❸❸ Dortmunder
Strongish, sweetish lager.
Approximately Dortmund.

GILDENBIER
6.3% abv ❸❸❸ Brown Ale
Sweetish, caramelised, clean, walnut
coloured ale.

CHARLES QUINT
6.1% abv ❸❸ Brown Ale
Sucrose sweet brown ale of little
character.

TONGERLO 6°
6% abv ❸❸❸ Abbey Dubbel
Ruddy chestnut ale, finely
sedimented with burnt sugars.

PRIMUS
5% abv ❸❸ Pils
Ordinary Belgian Pils.

HAECHT TARWEBIER
5% abv ❸❸❸ Wheat Beer
(unfiltered)
Plain, dryish, unaromatic witbier.

Other regular beers include: Coq
Hardi Spéciale (5.5% abv; Pils),
Primus Christmas* (5.2% abv; Pils),
Coq Hardi Bière Blonde De Luxe
(4.8% abv; Pils) and Haacht Export
(4.7% abv; Pils). There are also four
low alcohol beers and four table
beers.

HANSSENS
GUEUZESTEKERIJ HANSSENS
Vroenenbosstraat 8
1512 Dworp
Tel: 02 380 3133
Tiny gueuze blender from Dworp,
just south of Brussels, producing just
two beers in sash-marked, cork
bottles. White sash for gueuze, pink
for kriek. One of best of the few
remaining artisanal gueuze blenders.
The gueuze is fully traditional.
Despite the fact that it is made with
cherry juice rather than whole
cherries, the kriek is also one of the
very best. Well worth seeking out.
The beers improve with age for at
least five years.

HANSSENS GUEUZE
5% abv ❺❺❺❺❺ Gueuze (unfiltered)
Superbly traditional gueuze. Sour,
bitter and pleasantly dry.

HANSSENS KRIEK
5% abv ❺❺❺❺❺ Cherry Gueuze
(unfiltered)

The fruit flavours balance a sour and
characterful background gueuze
taste superbly.

HOUTEN KOP
HOUTEN KOP
Oude Kouterdreef 166
9140 Zele
Tel: 052 445570
Not strictly a brewery but then
neither is Hanssens (above). These
guys actually hire out the Strubbe
brewery a couple of times a
fortnight to brew. Presumably, when
they have saved enough centimes
they will set up their own plant, but
the arrangement has suited both
sides of the deal since 1989 so
progress towards that goal must be
of limited appeal.

HOUTEN KOP
6.5% abv ❹❹❹❹ Spiced Ale
Pleasant, slightly spiced pale ale.

VLASKOP
5.5% abv ❸❸❸ Wheat Beer
(unfiltered)
Brewed with 30% unmalted wheat.
Dry and light with a tendency to
sediment out.

HUYGHE
BROUWERIJ HUYGHE
Brusselsesteenweg 282
9090 Melle
Tel: 091 521501
Fax: 091 522931
Interesting brewery on the outskirts
of Ghent. Founded in 1906 and
rebuilt in 1938. Production has
expanded in recent years to 50,000
hl a year and it has been
experimenting with a huge range of
bottom fermented and top
fermented beers in numerous styles.
Some are more successful than
others. If they stuck with a smaller
range of distinctively labelled brands
they might settle down in the
market. Some beers of identical
recipe appear to fare very differently
after brewing. Others are brewed to
slightly different recipes but
marketed separately with
unconnected French and Dutch
names. Still more appear in several
different forms with similar names.
The La Poiluchette brands are

brewed for Italy and Blanche des Neiges for the USA. They have recently started exporting to the Netherlands. Their latest effort is a bière de malt au whisky in the style of the French brew, Adelscott, sold in identical plain bottles. Despite the ridiculous size of the product range – a Guide editor's nightmare – they are seen by Belgian beer lovers as being on the side of the angels.

LA GUILLOTINE
9.1% abv ✪✪✪✪ Spiced Ale
Despite the silly name and painted stone-effect bottle, an effective, spicy, strong amber ale. The paint obscures the sediment when pouring.

DELIRIUM TREMENS
9% abv ✪✪✪✪ Spiced Ale
Remarkably similar to Guillotine but Flemish. Served in a glass spattered with pink elephants.

ABBAYE DE DIELEGHEM
7.5% abv ✪✪ Pale Ale
Sediment pale ale with problems.

LA POILUCHETTE BLONDE
7.5% abv ✪✪✪ Spiced Ale
Probably a spiced version of a pale ale. Typically Huyghe.

LA POILUCHETTE BRUNE
7.5% abv ✪✪✪✪ Spiced Ale
These things work better in brown.

ARTEVELDE GRAND CRU
7.4% abv ✪✪✪✪ Brown Ale
Chestnut coloured sediment ale, sweetish like over-roasted parsnips.

ARTEVELDE OP GIST
6.9% abv ✪✪✪ Pale Ale
Dark, sweetish, fruity sediment pale ale, brewed with 100 per cent malt and hops.

MacGREGOR
6.5% abv ✪✪✪ Unclassifiable
Sweet and burnt. No great peaty taste but maple syrup, surely.

ARTEVELDE
5% abv ✪✪ Pale Ale
Dull, neutral pale ale.

MINTY
4.7% abv ✪ Flavoured Ale
Bright green peppermint-flavoured fluid. Possibly the worst beer in the world.

BLANCHE DES NEIGES
4.5% abv ✪✪✪✪ Wheat Beer (unfiltered)
Sweetish, soft, hazy wheat beer with strong elderflower flavour.

LA POILUCHETTE BLANCHE DE THY
4.5% abv ✪✪✪✪ Wheat Beer (unfiltered)
Slightly sour, spritzy and very refreshing.

Other regular beers include: Corsaire (9% abv; spiced ale), Bobelier (8.5% abv; spiced ale), Cuvée de Namur Blonde (7.3% abv; pale ale), Cuvée de Namur Brune (7% abv; brown ale), San Michael Triple (6.8% abv; pale ale), 'n Balens Kruierke (6.2% abv), Golden Kenia (5% abv; Pils), Karibik Pils (4.8% abv; Pils), Huyghe Export (4.2% abv; Pils) and Mell's Bock (4.1% abv; table beer).

JAWADDE
BROUWERIJ JAWADDE
Karel van den Doorenstraat 18
9600 Ronse
Tel: 055 456440
Micro-brewery founded in 1993 in Ronse, one of the towns of the Flemish Ardennes, in the south of East Flanders. The first beer, a tripel, contained camomile. A cherry beer is planned and perhaps one using sloes. Even a ginger beer has been contemplated. Now there's a thought.
Regular beers include: Jawadde Tripel (7% abv; spiced ale) and Jawadde Kriek.

KERKOM
BROUWERIJ KERKOM
Naamsesteenweg 469
3800 Kerkom-Sint Truiden
Tel: 011 682087
Micro-brewery founded in 1987 at the village of Kerkom in the south west of Belgian Limburg. Produces 400 hl a year of a single, pretty accomplished pale ale in a blue-green stoppered bottle. The brewery and its sampling room can be visited (see Beer Tourism: Breweries).

BINK
5.5% abv ✪✪✪✪ Pale Ale

Light oak coloured sediment ale. Spritzy, bitter and characterful.

KOO

BRASSERIE DE KOO
Verviers

Founded in 1992 at Verviers in Liège province. Very little known at the time of going to press.

Regular beers include: Kelottes (8% abv; tripel).

KROON

BROUWERIJ DE KROON
Beekstraat 8
3040 Neerijse
Tel: 016 477104

The Crown Brewery. Tiny company based south west of Leuven. Founded in 1898, it is in the process of revamping its brewhouse. To date it has concentrated on producing a single unusual wheat beer in the local style plus a table beer version of the same thing. No relation to the Dutch company of the same name. Production halted in 1992 but is due to restart at the end of 1993.

Regular beers include: De Kroon Dubbel Wit (5% abv; wheat beer). There is also a table wheat beer.

LEFEBVRE

BRASSERIE LEFEBVRE S.A.
Rue de Croly 52
1430 Quenast
Tel: 067 670766

Brabant brewery established in 1876 at Quenast, south west of Brussels, just beyond gueuze country. Produces a large number of brands of ale plus a few lagers. Markets some of its beers under many names. One of the better brewers of abbey beers. Total annual production is 15,000 hl a year. For more details of the café at Floreffe Abbey, see Belgian Cafés: Namur.

FLOREFFE LA MEILLEURE
9% abv ✪✪✪✪ Abbey Strong
Sweetish, strong, dark and spicy beer with the aroma of mint humbugs!

FLOREFFE TRIPEL
8% abv ✪✪✪✪ Abbey Tripel
Characterful, strong, sediment ale, spoilt only by a harsh bitterness.

ABBAYE DE BONNE ESPERANCE
8% abv ✪✪✪✪ Abbey Tripel
Slightly darker version of Floreffe Tripel.

MOEDER OVERSTE
8% abv ✪✪✪✪ Brown Ale
Strong, medium brown ale with a forceful, unsubtle aroma and backtaste.

FLOREFFE DOUBLE
7% abv ✪✪✪✪ Abbey Dubbel
Spicy, pale brown ale just about warranting the dubbel designation.

FLOREFFE BLONDE 7°
7% abv ✪✪ Pale Ale
Lacking the class of the other Floreffe brews.

1900 SAISON
5% abv ✪✪ Pale Ale
Plain pale ale lacking saison characteristics.

STUDENT
4.5% abv ✪✪✪✪ Wheat Beer (unfiltered)
Light, fruity, spiced bière blanche. A quaffing ale.

Other regular beers include: Lefèbvre Extra Stout (6.5% abv; stout), Zafke (6.2% abv), Dorée (5% abv) and Lefèbvre Pils (5% abv; Pils). There are also three table beers.

LEROY

BROUWERIJ LEROY
Diksmuideseweg 406
8904 Boezinge
Tel: 057 422005

Long established brewery near Ieper, founded in 1720 but concentrating on bottom fermented beers for some years until recently. It has now developed a strong range of ales. There are family connections with Van Eecke of Watou (below) and since 1967 the two breweries have worked in close co-operation but remain separate businesses. They export to the Netherlands and Italy. Annual production stands at 32,000 hl.

OLD MUSKETEER
7% abv ✪✪✪ Pale Ale
Sweetish, firm, well hopped and distinctly Belgian filtered pale ale.

CHRISTMAS*
6.8% abv ✪✪✪ Winter Ale

Clear, walnut-coloured ale with old flavours but little bitterness.

SASBRAU
6% abv ❸❸❸ Dortmunder
Enjoyable premium lager, sometimes found as Kerelsbier Licht.

YPERMAN
6% abv ❹❹❹❹ Pale Ale
Fiercely Belgian, ginger coloured, caramel flavoured, sediment pale ale.

KATJE SPECIAL
5% abv ❸❸❸ Pale Ale
Darker than most pale ales. Surprisingly unimpressive for its gravity.

LEROY STOUT
5% abv ❷❷ Sweet Stout
Ridiculously sweet, chewy, burnt umber, filtered ale.

PAULUS
5% abv ❸❸❸ Old Red
Rodenbach-like but with more bitter, burnt flavours and a clinical sourness.

Other regular beers include: Christmas Leroy* (7.5% abv; winter ale), De Pompeschitter (5.3% abv; Pils), Sas Pils (4.7% abv; Pils) and Suma Pils (4% abv; Pils). There are also three table beers and a low-alcohol brew.

LIEFMANS (RIVA GROUP)
BROUWERIJ LIEFMANS
Aalststraat 200
9700 Oudenaarde
Tel: 055 311392
Liefmans is a lovely old East Flanders brewery, dating back to 1679. When it was taken over in April 1990 by Riva, European beer lovers got nervous. When, in 1992, the beers started to be brewed at Riva HQ in Dentergem and sent on to Liefmans only for fermentation and storage, they developed a pronounced tic. Riva assure everyone that production will return to Oudenaarde once the brewery is upgraded. It is to be hoped that the same improvements in brewing consistency that have occurred at Het Anker and Straffe Hendrik will happen at the 13,000 hl a year Liefmans site, without having to pay the current price of a loss of panache. The three strongest beers are usually sold in individually

wrapped corked bottles. All three, especially Goudenband, improve further with ageing for a couple of years in the cellar. The weaker beers are more for the local market.

LIEFMANS KRIEK
6.5% abv ❹❹❹❹ Old Cherry
Dark, fruity and deceptively strong classic cherry beer. Available on draught.

LIEFMANS FRAMBOZENBIER
5.7% abv ❸❸❸ Old Raspberry
Goudenband with raspberry juice. Sweeter than the Kriek but pleasantly fruity.

LIEFMANS GOUDENBAND
5.1% abv ❹❹❹❹ Old Brown
Accomplished, sweet and sour brown ale, typical of its style.

LIEFMANS
4.9% abv ❸❸❸ Old Brown
Lighter sourish brown ale. Blend of Goudenband with younger beer.

ODNAR
4.6% abv ❸❸❸ Old Brown
Indistinguishable from Liefmans but said to be 10 per cent weaker.

LINDEMANS
BROUWERIJ LINDEMANS
Lenniksebaan 257
1602 Vlezenbeek
Tel: 02 569 0390
Lambic brewer and gueuze blender at Vlezenbeek, on the outskirts of Brussels. Although still producing traditional lambic and selling it to traditional gueuze blenders, the Lindemans products are nearly all refined beers, including some fruit beers of the modern genre with strengths as low as 2.5 per cent abv. A shame for a blender which has been around since 1869 and produces 18,000 hl a year. If you want to demonstrate the difference in style and quality between commercial gueuze and the traditional form you can do no better that take a glass of the two Lindemans examples alongside each other. The traditional form is exceptionally fine and very difficult to find. The much commoner commercial version is frankly unpleasant. It is to be hoped that Lindemans pick up the same vibes

about the lambic market as Belle Vue, Van Honsebrouck and De Troch have. They have an ideal product with which to supply the quality market.

LINDEMANS FOND GUEUZE
5% abv ✪✪✪✪✪ Gueuze (unfiltered)
Superb, lemony gueuze in the finest artisanal tradition. Demonstrates well the unbitter, unaromatic hop taste.

LINDEMANS GUEUZE GEFILTERD
5% abv ✪ Gueuze (filtered)
Disgustingly sweet and tasting of canned fruit. Better when spiked with the juice of a whole lemon.

LINDEMANS FARO LAMBIC
4.8% abv ✪✪ Faro
Darkish, filtered, sweet but harmless when reasonably priced.

LINDEMANS KRIEKENLAMBIK
4% abv ✪✪✪ Cherry Lambic (filtered)
Sweet and commercial but salvaged by good fruitiness and minimal sourness.

Other regular beers include: Lindemans Cassis (4% abv; fruit lambic) and Lindemans Lambik (4% abv; lambic). There are also low gravity fruit beers flavoured with blackcurrant, raspberry and peach.

LOUWAEGE
BROUWERIJ LOUWAEGE
Markt 14
8610 Kortemark
Tel: 051 566067
West Flanders regional brewery founded in 1877 at Kortemark, north of Roeselare. Concentrates on Pils and a slowly increasing range of ales.

HAPKIN
8.5% abv ✪✪✪ Strong Golden
Strong, dry, unfiltered, straw-coloured ale with wheaty undertones.

FLANDRIEN
5% abv ✪✪✪✪ Pale Ale
Pleasant, pale, lightish, bitter beer with a light sediment.

LOUWAEGE STOUT
4.8% abv ✪✪✪ Sweet Stout
Almost sickly sweet and dark as hell.
Other regular beers include:

Akila Pilsener (5% abv; Pils), Louwaege Export (4.6% abv; Pils) and Louwaege Pils (4.5% abv; Pils). There are also two table beers.

MARTENS
BROUWERIJ MARTENS N.V.
Reppelerweg 1
3950 Bocholt
Tel: 011 472980
Fax: 011 472700
Large Limburg brewery near the Dutch border, currently producing Pils and two ales. Founded in 1758 it remains strongly under the family's influence despite being one of the largest independents in Belgium, at 600,000 hl a year production. Seizoens is sold widely across Belgium and Quattro may follow. The company earns a lot of business from brewing foreign Pilseners under licence.

SEIZOENS QUATTRO
8% abv ✪✪✪✪ Pale Ale
Sweet, potent, dark amber brew with honeyed backtastes.

MARTENS SEIZOENS
6% abv ✪✪✪ Pale Ale
Clean and pale, with a big hop bouquet and dry saison type back flavours.

MARTENS SEIZOENS EUROPE
6% abv ✪✪✪ Pale Ale
Lightly sedimented version of normal Seizoens. Not dramatically different.

MARTENS PILS
5% abv ✪✪✪ Pils
Dryish, with a coarse bitterness.
Other regular beers include: Kwik Pils (4.8% abv; Pils). There is also a table beer.

MIROIR
BRASSERIE LE MIROIR
Place Reine Astrid 24-26
1090 Bruxelles (Jette)
Tel: 02 424 0478
New home brewery, opened in 1992 at a famous suburban Bruxellois beer café of the same name (see Belgian Cafés: Brabant).
Regular beers include: Spéciale Miroir (5% abv; wheat beer), Spéciale Dark Miroir (Scotch ale) and Spéciale Brune Miroir (brown ale).

MOORTGAT
BROUWERIJ MOORTGAT
Breendonkdorp 58
2870 Breendonk-Puurs
Tel: 03 886 7121
Fax: 03 886 4622

Large, well respected, independent brewery, founded in 1871 and producing 250,000 hl a year of Duvel and other beers. Found at Breendonk, between Antwerp and Brussels. Unusually, it retains its own maltings. Its most famous beer, Duvel, started life in 1918 as "Victory Ale", to celebrate the defeat of Kaiser Wilhelm. It changed its name in 1923 and its colour, from brown to the current, distinctive light straw, in 1968. This spawned a whole new style of strong golden, bottle-conditioned ales. The darker brews are produced for the Abbaye de Maredsous in Anhée-Denée (see Belgian Cafés: Namur). Steendonk was a joint venture with Palm, dating from 1989. Extra Pils became Bel Pils in 1991, while Silver Label is brewed for the Delhaize chain of supermarkets. The company exports to Britain, the Netherlands, France, Italy, Spain, Switzerland, Canada, USA and Japan. Brewery trips are available on application but for groups only. Moortgat's owner died in March 1992, sparking worries about the future of the brewery but nothing untoward had been spotted by the time we went to press.

MAREDSOUS 10°
9.5% abv ✪✪✪✪ Abbey Strong
Black, abbey style beer in the manner of a strong, slightly sour stout.

MAREDSOUS 9°
8.7% abv ✪✪✪✪ Abbey Tripel (dark)
Dark, abbey style beer with porter overtones.

DUVEL ROOD
8.5% abv ✪✪✪✪✪ Strong Golden
Deceptively strong, delicious, straw coloured ale with hop aromas billowing out of the glass. This is the proper sediment version in the red-lettered bottle.

MAREDSOUS 8°
8% abv ✪✪✪ Abbey Dubbel

Dark and mellow but unmemorable.

DUVEL GROEN
8% abv ✪✪✪ Pale Ale
Filtered, emasculated version of Duvel found in green-lettered bottles.

MAREDSOUS 6° (Bottled)
6.8% abv ✪✪✪ Pale Ale
Nicely balanced, sweetish pale ale. Not really in the abbey style.

SANCTUS
6.8% abv ✪✪✪✪ Brown Ale
Medium dark dilute Duvel without the hop rate.

MAREDSOUS 6° (Draught)
6.4% abv ✪✪✪ Pale Ale
Similar to, but weaker than, the bottled version.

GODEFROY (Bottled)
6.1% abv ✪✪✪ Pale Ale
Balanced pale ale with little outstanding character.

GODEFROY (Draught)
5.6% abv ✪✪ Pale Ale
Like the bottled version, only less of it.

BEL PILS
5.3% abv ✪✪✪✪ Pilsener
Serious Bavarian style Pilsener with great hop character throughout.

Other regular beers include: Silver Label (5.2% abv; Pils). There are also two low alcohol beers.

ORVAL
BRASSERIE DE L'ABBAYE NOTRE DAME D'ORVAL
6823 Villers-devant-Orval
Tel: 061 311261
Fax: 061 312927

Orval Abbey in the far south west of Luxembourg province was founded in 1132 but sacked in 1793 following the French Revolution. It was reconstructed in 1926 and a brewery was added in 1931 to help meet the costs of reconstruction and maintainence. A single ale is produced, different from all other trappist brews and held in the highest regard by every beer connoisseur worthy of the name. It is marketed in a delightfully simple, distinctive bottle. In 1993 its declared strength rose from 5.2% abv without any noticeable difference in flavour or impact. This followed a failed attempt to import it to Sweden, where beers over 5.6% abv are banned. The fathers explained that it was the extra fermentation in the bottle which must have done it, a fact which added to the knowledge of brewery chemists across the world who, prior to that, had never credited secondary fermentaion with adding more than 0.2% abv at most. Despite these difficulties, the abbey produces 34,000 hl of it each year. They also make two cheeses and some excellent bread. The old ruins may be visited by tourists but brewery trips require considerable advance notice.

ORVAL
6.2% abv ✪✪✪✪✪ Trappist Pale
Distinctive and delightful amber ale. Stupendously bitter with slight candy overtones and marvellous hop aromas.

OUD BEERSEL

HENRI VANDERVELDEN
Laarheidestraat 230
1650 Beersel
Tel: 02 380 3396
Listed in our first edition as Vandervelden but known universally as Oud Beersel. Tiny lambic brewery and gueuze blender at Beersel, south of Brussels. It dates from 1882 but is still effectively a one-man affair, with annual production limited to 500 hl a year. There is a small museum (see Beer Tourism) and an extraordinary pub (see Belgian Cafés: Brabant) next door to the brewery.

OUD BEERSEL KRIEK
7% abv ✪✪✪✪✪ Cherry Gueuze (unfiltered)
Strongly acid and quite bitter with a cherry aroma and faint fruitiness. One of the best dry, sour krieks. Also known as Sherry Poësy.

OUD BEERSEL GUEUZE
6% abv ✪✪✪✪✪ Gueuze (unfiltered)
Traditional gueuze in unlabelled bottles. Naturally sour with a faint musty sweetness, it improves for at least five years in the cellar.

OUD BEERSEL LAMBIK
5.7% abv ✪✪✪✪ Lambic
Like flat real ale with added

mushrooms! Grows on you. And in you, perhaps.

PALM

BROUWERIJ PALM
Steenhuffeldorp 3
1840 Steenhuffel
Tel: 052 309481
Fax: 052 304167
Another of the largest independent breweries in Belgium, producing 530,000 hl of beer a year. Based north west of Brussels, they produce Pils, lighter ales and a few heavyweight products. Reputed to be the only brewery in Belgium to have rejected a takeover bid from Interbrew. They were founded in 1747 and are good friends with Moortgat brewery but only at the holding hands stage. Palm Speciale on draught has made quite an impression in the Netherlands. They now brew the famous English style pale ale for John Martins of Antwerp, which used to be relabelled Bulldog Pale Ale from Courage (UK).

AERTS 1900
7% abv ✪✪✪✪ Pale Ale
Unusual copper coloured ale with Scotch overtones, fermented twice then bottled with a sediment.

JOHN MARTIN'S SPECIAL
5.8% abv ✪✪✪ Pale Ale
Not as English as it used to be. Rather plain.

PALM DOBBEL*
5.5% abv ✪✪✪ Pale Ale
Brewed for the winter. Darker and sharper than the Speciale.

PALM SPECIALE
5.2% abv ✪✪✪ Pale Ale
Well brewed, with strong hop aroma but rather too clean to be impressive.

STEENDONK
4.5% abv ✪✪✪✪ Wheat Beer (unfiltered)
The sweetest and most mellow of the witbiers.

Other regular beers include: Bock Premium Pils (5% abv; Pils). There are also two table beers and an alcohol-free beer.

PIESSENS
BROUWERIJ PIESSENS
Oostberg 52
9140 Temse
Tel: 03 771 0353
Microbrewery founded in 1988, at
Temse, south west of Antwerp by a
home brew fanatic who thought he
would put his hobby to work.
Despite the small scale he still
produces 250 hl per year. The two
Sublim beers and Promesse are
regular brews. Others are produced
to order. All except Sublim Light are
bottle-conditioned.

SUBLIM
8.2% abv ❸❸❸ Pale Ale
Dry, straw coloured ale with a home
brew character.

PROMESSE
7.5% abv ❷❷ Dubbel
Dry, dark, sedimented home brew,
developing unpleasant backtastes
with keeping.

Other regular beers include: 't
Meeuwken (6.5% abv; dubbel),
Sublim Light (5% abv; pale ale),
Sublim Kriek and Witbier Van Temse
(wheat beer).

PIRON
BRASSERIE PIRON
Rue Battice
4880 Aubel
Tel: 087 687020
The newest brewery in Liège
province, set up in August 1993 at
Aubel, a market town which is
equidistant from Liège, Maastricht
and Aachen. Like one or two Flemish
operations which have emerged
recently, it was based on an old
brewing operation, which in this
case closed in 1969. It was founded
with the expectation is that it will
reach 10,000 hl annual production
with its four bottled sediment ales.

TRIPLE DE VAL-DIEU
9% abv ❹❹❹❹ Abbey Tripel
Delightfully balanced, bitter,
chestnut sediment ale in a tightly
corked bottle.
Other regular beers include: Val-Dieu
Brune (8% abv; spiced ale), Legende
d'Aubel (7% abv; spiced ale) and Val-
Dieu Blonde (6.5% abv; pale ale).

PRAILE
BRASSERIE DE LA PRAILE
3 Rue de la Praile
7120 Peissant
Tel: 064 771643
Founded in October 1991 by Jules
and Frederic Navez, at Peissant,
south east of Mons, in Hainaut
province. Output is tiny at present
but the owners have hopes for
expansion. Thirty per cent of the
mash for Cuvée d'Artistée derives
from honey, the owner's excuse
being that he used to keep bees.

Regular beers include: Cuvée
d'Aristée (9.5% abv; honeyed ale),
Blonde de la Praile (8% abv) and La
Campagnarde Brune.

PRIGNON
BRASSERIE PRIGNON
Rue Préal 8
6997 Soy
Tel: 086 477586
Microbrewery, founded in 1988 at
Soy, near Erezée, in the northern
Ardennes. Fantôme is produced all
year round. There are five seasonal
beers and numerous other one-off
products. Total output is around
900 hl a year.

FANTOME
8% abv ❹❹❹❹ Walloon Strong
Unusual, dry, summery. spritzy ale
with strong hints of apple and pear.

Other regular beers include: The
Best of Fantôme Brewery (12% abv;
spiced ale), Fantôme de Noël (10%
abv; spiced ale), Saison d'Erezée
Hiver* (8% abv; spiced ale), Saison
d'Erezée Automne* (7% abv; spiced
ale), Saison d'Erezée Eté* (7% abv;
spiced ale) and Saison d'Erezée
Printemps* (6.2% abv; spiced ale).

RIVA
BROUWERIJ RIVA
Wontergemstraat 42
8720 Dentergem
Tel: 051 633681
Originally established in 1880 at
Dentergem on the border of East and
West Flanders. The main plant
produces a range of Pils, plus a
number of specialist ales. In the past
five years, the company has shown a
hawkish attitude to other small

breweries, having taken over Straffe Hendrik in 1988, Liefmans in 1990 and then reached an arrangement with Het Anker. In 1991 they bought the pubs of the Verhaege brewery but did not buy the brewery. They have started producing several of these breweries' beers at their main plant but have the odd habit of returning them to the original brewery once the recipes and production methods have been "tidied up". In the case of Liefmans beers the return is more literal. They are brewed at Dentergem and the wort is transported to Oudenaarde for fermentation. If Riva was originally intent upon decimating the range of beers from their four breweries, they are certainly proceeding in an odd way. Vondel was discarded in 1991 only to return in 1993. The Dentergem brewery's production is 115,000 hl per year. There are exports to Britain, the Netherlands, France, Greece and Taiwan.

LUCIFER
8% abv ✪✪✪✪ Strong Golden
Same colour and bouquet as Moortgat's Duvel but less flowery and sweeter.

VONDEL
8% abv ✪✪✪✪ Brown Ale
Clear, sweet, aromatic, chestnut ale with a light sediment.

RIVA CHRISTMAS*
7.5% abv ✪✪✪ Christmas Ale
Pleasant but unexceptional, sweet, mature brown beer.

DENTERGEMS WITBIER
5% abv ✪✪✪ Wheat Beer
Popular witbier, drier and thinner in flavour that its main rivals.

Other regular beers include: La Vieille Bon Secours (7.5% abv), Riva Abdij Tripel (7.2% abv), Cardor (7% abv; strong pale), Riva 2000 (6% abv) and Riva Pils (5% abv; Pils). There are also three table beers.

ROBERG

BROUWERIJ ROBERG
Rodebergstraat 46
8954 Westouter
Tel: 057 446214
Fax: 057 446745

Small brewery opened in 1991 at Westouter, south west of Ieper (Ypres), in West Flanders. Brews its ales with identical labels! Output is currently 500 hl a year.

ROBERG BLOND
8% abv ✪✪✪✪ Pale Ale
Very much a home brewed ale, fermented out, but interesting.

ROBERG BRUIN
8% abv ✪✪✪✪ Brown Ale
Slightly acid and more complex sugars than the blond.

Other regular beers include: Roberg Junior (5% abv; Pils).

ROCHEFORT

BRASSERIE DE L'ABBAYE NOTRE DAME DE ST. RÉMY
Rue de l'Abbaye 8
5580 Rochefort
Tel: 084 213181

Trappist brewery, deep in the Ardennes on the southern boundary of Namur province. The abbey was founded in 1230 as a convent and converted to a monastery in 1464. The brothers founded a brewery in the 16th century but this closed along with the abbey in 1794. It was re-occupied in 1887 and the current brewery opened in 1899. Its three ales are sold under the name Trappistes Rochefort and distinguished by the colour of the caps on their bottles. They are known colloquially as Noire (10°), Verte (8°) and Rouge (6°). Production runs to 15,000 hl per year.

ROCHEFORT 10°
11.3% abv ✪✪✪✪✪ Trappist Strong
Deep, dark and potent, filled with complex flavours. A contemplative brew. Perhaps the finest of all the trappist beers.

ROCHEFORT 8°
9.2% abv ✪✪✪✪✪ Trappist Tripel (dark)
Firm and enjoyable, strong dark ale. A cross between the heavy complexities of the 10° and the simpler character of the 6°.

ROCHEFORT 6°
7.5% abv ✪✪✪✪ Trappist Dubbel
Dark and dry ale, surprisingly plain for a trappist beer.

RODENBACH
BROUWERIJ RODENBACH
Spanjestraat 133
8800 Roeselare
Tel: 051 223400
Fax: 051 229248

One of the world's most extraordinary breweries, at Roeselare in the south of West Flanders. Founded in 1836, its current production is 150,000 hl a year. They start by brewing a reddish brown ale and transferring it into modern conical fermenters. At the end of normal fermentation some of this is set aside for blending and the rest is racked into row upon row of massive oak tuns for further fermentation for up to two years, involving micro-organisms which produce characteristic sourness. The raw version of this is filtered to become Rodenbach Grand Cru, one of the world's greatest and most unusual beers. Some is blended 3:1 with fresh beer to make a smoother, more docile version called simply Rodenbach. The remainder is blended with cherry juice and some essence to make Alexander. Opinion is divided as to whether this last process is a travesty or a legitimate variation on a theme.

The brewery received a significant injection of "technical support" from Interbrew in 1991 but a cash stake was denied by both companies. Since then, Rodenbach itself has lent technical assistance to a number of smaller independent breweries and in 1993 took over, or should it be "completely assisted" Gouden Boum of Bruges. Rodenbach beers can be found in the Netherlands and also in Britain.

RODENBACH GRAND CRU
6.5% abv ✪✪✪✪✪ Old Red
Supremely sour red-brown beer, fermented in oak for at least 18 months. One of the world's classic beers and the finest example of an old or Flemish red ale.

RODENBACH ALEXANDER
6.5% abv ✪✪✪✪✪ Old Red
Grand Cru which has been "krieked" by the addition of cherry essence. Ruins the authenticity but avoids spasm of the salivary glands.

RODENBACH
5% abv ✪✪✪✪ Old Red
25% matured beer, 75% fresh beer. Blander and less acid than the Grand Cru but indicative of the style.

ROMAN
BROUWERIJ ROMAN
Hauwaert 61
9700 Oudenaarde-Mater
Tel: 055 455401
Fax: 055 455600

Large, family run brewery in East Flanders. The Romans can trace their history back to 1545. It is now one of four breweries around Oudenaarde and has the greatest tendency to go for middle-of-the-road flavours. It is also by far the largest, with an annual production of 100,000 hl. It produces a good balance of brews, the most recent being the two Ename abbey beers. As well as running a well managed brewery, the company also produces mineral waters and soft drinks.

TRIPEL ENAME
9% abv ✪✪✪✪ Abbey Tripel
Powerful, filtered, blond beer, lacking the complexity of a sediment brew.

ROMAN DOBBELEN BRUINEN
8% abv ✪✪✪ Dry Stout
Strong filtered brown ale. Full, medium brown, mellow and bitter.

SLOEBER
7.5% abv ✪✪✪ Pale Ale
Strong pale ale of nondescript character, despite being bottle-conditioned.

DUBBEL ENAME
6.5% abv ✪✪✪ Abbey Dubbel
Dark and sweet, filtered ale drinking beyond its strength.

ROMAN SPECIAL
5.5% abv ✪✪ Brown Ale
Pasteurised dark brew. Fermentation killed just as it was getting interesting.

ROMAN OUDENAARDS
5% abv ✪✪ Brown Ale
Medium brown ale.

Other regular beers include: Hotteuse Grand Cru (8% abv), Bell Christmas* (7.3% abv; Christmas old brown), Romy Luxe (5.6% abv; Pils),

Romy Pils (5.1% abv; Pils), Hotteuse 5° (5% abv; Pils) and Roman Export (4.6% abv; Pils). There are also three table beers and a low alcohol beer.

ST. BERNARDUS
BROUWERIJ SINT BERNARDUS
Trappistenweg 23
8978 Watou
Tel: 057 388021
Fax: 057 388071

A relative newcomer to the West Flanders world of brewing. Founded in an old dairy in the "brewers' town" of Watou, near the French border and a few kilometres from the brewing abbey of St. Sixtus in Westvleteren in 1946. It was created in order to produce and distribute, for commercial sale, licensed imitations of the abbey's beers, under the brand name St. Sixtus. For a while in the 1980s they had a connection with Whitbread. In 1992 the licence came to an end and although the beers continue with slightly different names, other products are being introduced into its range. They export to the Netherlands, France, Switzerland and the USA. Total production is around 13,000 hl a year.

SIXTUS ABT 12°
9.5% abv ❂❂❂❂ Abbey Strong
Dark flavour-filled ale with a tendency to cloy.

ST. BERNARDUS TRIPEL
7.5% abv ❂❂❂❂ Abbey Tripel
Slightly temperamental, sometimes superb, classic mellow-bitter tripel.

SIXTUS PRIOR 8°
7.5% abv ❂❂❂❂ Abbey Tripel (dark)
Dark, sweet and unbitter but fuller flavoured than its strength suggests.

SIXTUS PATER 6°
6% abv ❂❂❂❂ Abbey Dubbel
Surprisingly well-rounded, black, sweetish, roasted beer.

Other regular beers include: Sixtus Blond (6% abv; pale ale).

ST. JOZEF
BROUWERIJ SINT JOZEF
Itterplein 19
3690 Opitter
Tel: 011 864711
Fax: 011 867419

Family brewery at Opitter, in the far north eastern corner of Belgian Limburg, near the Dutch border. Believed to have started production in 1874. Since the latest generation of the Cornelissen family took over, in 1981, production has increased five-fold to 65,000 hl per year. Unusually for a Belgian brewer, it does not yet produce any ales but is experimenting with different styles of lager.

BOKKEREYER
5.8% abv ❂❂❂ Wiener
Rare Belgian example of the Vienna-style beers produced in the Netherlands.

OPS-ALE
5.5% abv ❂❂❂ Pils
Not an ale but a tasty, bitter Pils, above the usual Belgian standard.

BOSBIER
5% abv ❂ Flavoured Lager
Pils infused with bilberry juice. Nice idea, shame about the taste.

KRIEKEN BIER
5% abv ❂ Flavoured Lager
Ordinary lager with cherry syrup. Not even a nice idea.

Other regular beers include: Limburgse Witte (5% abv; wheat beer) and Pax Pils (5% abv; Pils).

SILENRIEUX
BRASSERIE DE SILENRIEUX
Rue de Naupre
5630 Silenrieux
Tel: 071 667634
Fax: 071 668204

Set up in 1991 at Silenrieux, 20 km south of Charleroi, bang on the French border in Namur province. Was originally called Agripur. Its purpose is to experiment with making beer from odd grains. Sara features buckwheat. Its annual output is currently 250 hl.

Regular beers include: Joseph Bière à l'Epeautre (6.5% abv) and Sara Bière au Sarrasère (6.5% abv).

SILLY
BRASSERIE DE SILLY
Ville Basse A 141
7830 Silly
Tel: 068 551351
Fax: 068 568436

A perfectly serious brewery which happens to be based in the town of Silly, north of Mons. Brews a broad selection of ales and lagers, probably marketing several of them under more than one name. Founded in 1854 and sometimes still referred to as the Mynsbrugen brewery. Its current annual production is 12,000 hl. The mark of most of the brewery's pale ales is an intense fruitiness. Some of the darker beers are classics.

LA DIVINE
9.5% abv ✪✪✪✪ Strong Ale
Medium dark, powerful ale, with abbey pretensions.

DOUBLE D'ENGHIEN SPECIALE
8% abv ✪✪✪ Walloon Strong
Copper coloured beer with unsubtle flavours, possibly with saccharin.

SCOTCH DE SILLY
8% abv ✪✪✪✪✪ Scotch Ale
Superbly rounded, warming, sweet, filtered, chestnut coloured, classic Scotch.

DOUBLE ENGHIEN BLONDE
7.5% abv ✪✪✪✪ Spiced Ale
Mellow, pleasantly sweet pale ale with spice and possibly honey.

SAISON DE SILLY
5% abv ✪✪ Saison
Fruit flavoured ale, not convincingly in the saison tradition.

CERVOISE DE L'AVOUERIE D'ANTHISNES
5.3% abv ✪✪✪ Pale Ale
Filtered ale with little bitterness and loads of fruitiness.

BRUG-ALE
5% abv ✪✪✪✪ Pale Ale
Fine, filtered pale ale. Sweet without compromising proper hop bitterness.

SUPER 64
5% abv ✪✪✪ Pale Ale
Said to be based on Brug-Ale but much less Belgian and rather ordinary.

TITJE
5% abv ✪✪✪✪ Wheat Beer
Fresh tasting, fruity wheat beer of character.

Other regular beers include: Villers St. Ghislain (8% abv), Silbrau Dort (6% abv; Dortmunder), La Petite Follie (6% abv), Myn's Pils (4.8% abv; Pils) and Silly Triple Bock (4% abv; table beer).

SLAGHMUYLDER
BROUWERIJ SLAGHMUYLDER
Denderhoutembaan 2
9400 Ninove
Tel: 054 331831
Fax: 054 338445
Enterprising artisan brewery dating from 1860, based in Ninove on the Flanders-Brabant border. Annual output is 6,500 hl. Its abbey beers rate among the best. In the era of marketing gimmickry, if it ever decides to export to Britain, Slag Lager can surely be expected to take the country by storm.

AMBIORIX DUBBEL
8% abv ✪✪✪✪ Strong Stout
Dark brown, dryish sediment beer with a rasping bitter middle and burnt edges.

WITKAP TRIPEL
7.5% abv ✪✪✪✪ Strong Golden
Unusual, straw coloured sediment ale with nine per cent white wine in the mash.

WITKAP DUBBELE PATER
7% abv ✪✪✪✪ Abbey Dubbel
Medium rich, burnt and bitter sediment beer said to be bottom fermented.

STROPKEN GRAND CRU
6% abv ✪✪✪✪ Spiced Ale
Sweet, copper coloured and delicious, with added aniseed.

WITKAP STIMULO
6% abv ✪✪✪✪✪ Abbey Pale
Superbly aromatic, light coloured ale with great hop character.

SLAG LAGER
4.8% abv ✪✪✪ Pils
Light and enticingly bitter beer. The name means Cream Lager.

Other regular beers include: Slaghmuylder Kerstbier* (5.5% abv; Pils), Slaghmuylder Paasbier* (5.5% abv; Pils), Helles Export (4% abv; Pils). There are also two table beers.

STEEDJE
BROUWERIJ STEEDJE
Schoolstraat 45b
8460 Ettelgem
Tel: 059 267739
Small brewery, founded in 1986 at
Ettelgem, between Ostend and
Bruges. The owner runs it as his
weekend job. Specialises in strong
ales, frequently one-off brews. Even
the regular ones tend to vary from
brew to brew and ingredients can be
a tad unusual. The mash for
Pontonnierke includes malted millet!
Engeltjesbier is produced for the
Brouwershuis in Baarle-Hertog.
Annual production is 1,000 hl.

ENGELTJESBIER
10% abv ✪✪✪✪ Strong Ale
Winy, bitter, copper coloured
sediment ale with dangerous
tendencies.

OUDENBURGS ABDIJBIER
8% abv ✪✪✪✪ Brown Ale
Dark, sweet, fruity and interesting
beer with abbey pretensions.

PAASCHE*
8% abv ✪✪✪ Easter Ale
Perfumed and lightly spiced red-
brown ale with a home brew
character.

PONTONNIERKE
7% abv ✪✪✪ Spiced Ale
Unusual, sharp, winy brown brew
with a heavy sediment.

SPECIAL KERSTBIER*
7% abv ✪✪✪✪ Christmas Ale
Loaded with hops, dark and slightly
sour.

Other regular beers include:
Nonnenbier (8% abv), Oudenbergs
Bruin (8% abv; spiced ale),
Polderbier Bitter (8% abv; pale ale),
Polderbier Fruitig (8% abv),
Snellegemsen (8% abv), Steedje
Special (7.9% abv) and Steedje
Trippel (7.9% abv; spiced ale).

STERKENS
BROUWERIJ STERKENS
Meerdorp 20
2321 Meer
Tel: 03 315 7145
Fax: 03 315 9420
Established brewery at Meer, on the
Dutch border at the northern tip of

Antwerp province, currently
undergoing radical changes. Claims
to have been brewing since 1650. In
the past five years it has expanded
its range of ales considerably and in
1993 sold all its pubs to Haacht
(above). Its pale ales are in the
classic Antwerp mould. The St
Sebastiaan range is sold in 50 cl,
stoppered, stone-effect, non-
returnable bottles, sometimes at
astronomical prices. Annual output
is over 8,500 hl.

ST. SEBASTIAAN GRAND CRU
7.6% abv ✪✪✪✪ Abbey Tripel
Amber tripel, lightly sedimented and
clean, sweetish, well-rounded
flavour.

ST. SEBASTIAAN DARK
6.9% abv ✪✪✪ Abbey Dubbel
Dark, clean tasting, burnt brown ale,
apparently filtered.

DE SOLDAAT EXTRA DUBBEL
5.6% abv ✪✪✪ Pale Ale
Firm pale ale, more bitter and
caramel flavoured than most.

Other regular beers include: St.
Paul Tripel (7.2% abv; abbey tripel),
Bokrijks Kruikenbier (7.2% abv),
Poorter (6.5% abv), Flanders Farmers
Ale (6% abv; pale ale) and Ster Ale
(4.7% abv; pale ale). There are also
two table beers.

STRAFFE HENDRIK (RIVA GROUP)
STRAFFE HENDRIK
Walplein 26
8000 Brugge
Tel: 050 332697
Small brewery and home brew
house in old Bruges, producing a
single pale ale, available in bottle and
on draught. Formerly De Halve Maan
brewery of Henri Maes (no relation
to Alken of that ilk). Founded in
1856, it was acquired by Riva in
1988. Since the takeover, the
character of the beer has changed
for the better, and its quality is far
more consistent. The strength has
also increased. It remains better in
the bottle.

BRUGSE STRAFFE HENDRIK
(bottled)
6.5% abv ✪✪✪✪✪ Pale Ale
Blonde pale ale with pungent

bitterness from heavy hopping.

BRUGSE STRAFFE HENDRIK (draught)
6.5% abv ✪✪✪✪ Pale Ale
Softer, less pungent version of the bottled beer.

STRUBBE
BROUWERIJ STRUBBE
Markt 1
8480 Ichtegem
Tel: 051 588116
Small, family brewery founded in 1830 at Ichtegem, south of Ostend, producing all types of beer but majors in medium strength ales. They lease out their brewery to the brewers of Houten Kop (see above) on a couple of days a fortnight. Strubbe's own production is around 15,000 hl a year.

COUCKELAERSCHEN DOEDEL
6% abv ✪✪✪ Spiced Ale
Spicy, hazy, brown brew with a light sediment but saccharin bitterness.

DIKKE MATHILE
6% abv ✪✪✪ Pale Ale
Plain but pleasant ale originally aimed at the Ostend area.

STRUBBE SUPER PILS
5.5% abv ✪✪✪✪ Pils
Exceptionally well hopped. One of the best Belgian Pils.

'N SEULE
5.4% abv ✪✪✪ Pale Ale
Plainish amber ale brewed for the area around Ostend.

ICHTEGEMS OUD BRUIN
4.9% abv ✪✪✪✪ Old Red
Passable Flemish red. Not too sour but highly quaffable.

Other regular beers include: Strubbe Stout (5% abv; stout), Natuurbier Speciaal (4.9% abv; pale ale), Dobbelken (4.3% abv; brown ale) and Strubbe Export (4.2% abv; Pils). There are also three table beers and an alcohol-free beer.

TEUT
BIERBROUWERIJ DE TEUT
Stationstraat 97
3910 Neerpelt
Tel: 011 649187
This Limburg microbrewery was founded in 1985 as the Rik Gielen

brewery and sold in 1990 to new owners. De Teut has two meanings; "the dawdler" or else "the spout". The beer range is not yet settled. 't Paterken is brewed for the fathers of the hermitage at Achel, just north of the town. Breda's Begijntje Dubbel and Tripel are brewed for a beer wholesaler in Breda which is aiming to brew for itself in due course, under the name Loonbrouw. In 1992 they teamed up with several Dutch brewers to form BAB, the Broederschap van Ambachtelijke Brouwerijen (Brotherhood of Craft Breweries), a sort of collective to promote the mutual interests of microbreweries trading in the Netherlands. Total output is 800 hl a year and rising.

TEUTENBIER
7.5% abv ✪✪✪ Pale Ale
Sediment pale ale with a strong flavour of Hallertau hops.

Other regular beers include: Breda's Begijntje Tripel (abbey tripel), Breda's Begijntje Dubbel (8% abv; abbey dubbel), De Teut Meibok* (7.5% abv; pale bok ale), Teutenbok* (7.5% abv; dark bok ale), Zure Lomeleir (7.5% abv), 't Paterken (6.4% abv), Pruver (5.2% abv; pale ale) and Witte Van De Teut Tarwebier (wheat beer).

TIMMERMANS
TIMMERMANS N.V.
Kerkstraat 11
1701 Itterbeek
Tel: 02 569 0358
Fax: 02 569 0198
Fairly large lambic brewer and gueuze blender founded in 1850 at Itterbeek on the outskirts of Brussels. Annual production is 10,000 hl. Taken over in 1993 by John Martin of Antwerp, a large wholesaler and import-export agency. Since that time there has been a move towards producing low gravity fruit beers of the modern genre, too weak to be listed here. Conical fermenters have been spotted at the brewery so we assume that they take the same view of young lambic fermentation as Belle Vue. Although the brewery had

already introduced filtration when it was under family control, Timmermans had enjoyed the reputation of being the best of the commercialised lambic breweries and its fruit beers were the best of the sweet style. Like some other lambic brewers they were embarassed by the finding of the OBP laboratory analysis which showed that both their Gueuze Lambic (unsurprisingly) and Gueuze Caveau (surprisingly) brands contained no detectable yeasts or bacteria at work.

Our descriptions are based on beers of the old strength. The introduction of the first lambic wheat beer surprised everybody but is an interesting development. Bourgogne des Flandres is a lambic-based imitation of the Flemish old red style. Timmermans Lambic on draught is an extremely rare commodity but we list a couple of outlets in our tour of Pajottenland.

BOURGOGNE DES FLANDRES
6.5% abv ❸❸❸ Old Red
Pleasantly sour, with a true Burgundy colour. Not strictly an old red.

TIMMERMANS GUEUZE CAVEAU
5% abv ❸❸❸ Gueuze
Recently altered, formerly semi-traditional, sourish gueuze.

TIMMERMANS GUEUZE LAMBIC
5% abv ❸❸ Gueuze (filtered)
Commercial, filtered, presumably pasteurised and sweet.

TIMMERMANS KRIEK LAMBIC
4.5% abv ❸❸❸❸ Cherry Geuze (filtered)
A good commercial kriek with balanced acidity.

TIMMERMANS FRAMBOISE LAMBIC
4.5% abv ❸❸❸ Raspberry Gueuze (filtered)
One of the better commercial raspberry beers. Not too sweet or fruity.

TIMMERMANS PECHE LAMBIC
4% abv ❸❸❸ Peach Lambic
A pretty good joke beer. Really peachy!

TIMMERMANS BLANCHE WIT LAMBIC
4% abv ❸❸❸❸ Wheat Lambic
Successful and refreshing meld of lambic, wheat beer and fruit essence.

Other regular beers include: Timmermans Lambic (5% abv), Timmermans Cassis Lambic (4% abv; blackberry lambic) and Agenoise (plum lambic).

VAN ASSCHE
BROUWERIJ VAN ASSCHE
Liezeledorp 37
2870 Liezele-Puurs
Tel: 03 889 0044
After the owners of the Vieille Villers brewery took over Isebaert and called it Deca (above), Mark Knops, a brewer who was planning to open a new brewery called Gouden Vleghel, changed his plans and took over the Vieille Villers plant, returning its name to the original of Van Assche. Founded in the village of Liezele, between Antwerp and Brussels, in 1727, in recent years its trade depended on a strange range of mainly commissioned beers. Annual production was 3,000 hl. The new product range is not clear yet but may be adventurous. A recent test brew resulted in Antwerpen Rookbier, Belgium's first ever smoked beer!

Regular beers include: Antwerps Rookbier, Loteling Bruin, Villers Dubbel Amber and Villers Tripel.

VAN DEN BOSSCHE
BROUWERIJ VAN DEN BOSSCHE
Sint-Lievensplein 16
9560 Sint-Lievens-Esse
Tel: 054 500411
Small East Flanders brewery at St. Lievens-Esse, to the south of Ghent. Annual production is limited to 1,700 hl but in recent years it has enjoyed an increasing reputation as an artisan ale brewer, especially following the introduction of Lamoral Degmont in 1986 and Bumke in 1988. Although the revival is recent, the brewery dates from 1879.

LAMORAL DEGMONT
8% abv ✪✪✪✪ Pale Ale
Clear, light copper, aromatic ale.

PATER LIEVEN
5.7% abv ✪✪✪✪ Pale Ale
Full, deep orange sediment pale ale of character.

BUFFALO
5.5% abv ✪✪✪ Sweet Stout
Sweet, black sediment beer tasting of liquorice, molasses and glucose.

VAN DEN BOSSCHE KERSTBIER*
5% abv ✪✪✪ Winter Ale
Dark, sweet and bitter, without the usual punch of a Christmas beer.

Other regular beers include: Bumke (5.5% abv), S-Pils (5% abv; Pils) and Zwarte Flesch.

VANDER LINDEN
BROUWERIJ VANDER LINDEN
Brouwerijstraat 2
1500 Halle
Tel: 02 356 5059

A small lambic brewer and gueuze blender in Halle, south of Brussels. It has been operating since 1893. Duivelsbier is a traditional local variant on the lambic/gueuze theme in which lambic is mixed with pale ale and candy sugar. Our classification of it as bottled faro is slightly inaccurate. The Vieux Foudre brands are more traditional and sour but OBP's microbiological analysis revealed no active organisms in it. All the Vander Linden brands are becoming increasingly sweet, against the trend. Let us hope this is just a phase. Total brewery production is limited to 2,000 hl a year.

VANDER LINDEN FRAMBOZENBIER
7% abv ✪✪✪ Raspberry Gueuze
Sweet and increasingly commercial but still hazy. Strong for a raspberry beer.

VIEUX FOUDRE GUEUZE
6% abv ✪✪✪✪ Gueuze
Dry, lightly sedimented and quite sour.

DUIVELSBIER (bottled)
6% abv ✪✪✪✪ Faro
Like a strong version of the draught faro.

DUIVELSBIER (draught)
6% abv ✪✪✪✪ Faro
Intentionally acidic, dark and slightly sweet. Very unusual for a draught beer.

VANDER LINDEN DOBBEL FARO
6% abv ✪✪✪✪ Faro
Dark amber beer. Presumably gueuze with a little caramel or sugar, bottled with a light yeasting. Sourish but sweet.

VIEUX FOUDRE KRIEK
6% abv ✪✪✪✪ Cherry Gueuze
Full pink colour and slightly refined. Pleasant acid-fruit balance.

VANDER LINDEN FARO (draught)
4% abv ✪✪✪✪ Sweet Lambic
Deliciously fruity, medium-brown beer. Slightly acid and surprisingly bitter.

Other regular beers include: Vander Linden Lambik (6% abv; lambic).

VAN EECKE
BROUWERIJ VAN EECKE
Douvieweg 2
8978 Watou
Tel: 057 422005
Fax: 057 423970

West Flanders ale producer from Watou in the hop growing area near Poperinge. Founded in 1852, it has a long reputation for brewing good ales in a variety of styles. The Kapittel range of abbey beers is one of the longest established and best of the secular brewers. It works hand-in-hand with the nearby Leroy brewery and the production of individual beers seems to be transferred frequently between the two. There are a few label beers. Total annual production is around 9,000 hl. Brewery tours are possible (see Beer Tourism: Breweries).

HET KAPITTEL ABT
10% abv ✪✪✪✪ Abbey Strong
Light oak in colour. Strong, slightly aromatic, sweetish Tripel in character.

HET KAPITTEL PRIOR
9% abv ✪✪✪✪✪ Abbey Tripel (dark)
Full, medium dark, complex and delicious sediment ale. Pear drops, rich caramel and alcohol. Best after laying down for a year.

POPERINGES HOMMELBIER
7.5% abv ✪✪✪✪ Pale Ale
Deceptively strong, lightly sediment
amber ale with extra hopping.

HET KAPITTEL DUBBEL
7% abv ✪✪✪✪ Abbey Dubbel
Medium dark, complex, but slightly
coarse.

HET KAPITTEL PATER
6.5% abv ✪✪✪✪ Abbey Dubbel
Full and fresh, slightly sour, medium
dark, fruity beer.

WATOU'S WITBIER
5% abv ✪✪✪✪ Wheat Beer
(unfiltered)
Excellent, slightly cloudy, really
refreshing witbier with a lemony
tang.

VAN HONSEBROUCK

BROUWERIJ VAN
HONSEBROUCK
Oostrozebekestraat 43
8770 Ingelmunster
Tel: 051 303414
Fax: 051 313839
Commercially successful West
Flanders brewery, at Ingelmunster
near Roeselare. Founded in 1900.
Produces 80,000 hl a year. The St.
Louis brands were accused some
years ago of not being lambic-based.
To stem the criticism in 1993 the
brewery went on the offensive by
brewing and blending the first
traditional gueuze beer to be made
outside Brussels or Pajottenland for a
generation and thus dare critics to
repeat the allegation. Tastings
suggested that it may be a little
young and will reach five stars after
laying down. The fruit beers are
definitely less sweet and soppy than
they were and the future of the
brewery's products will be watched
with great interest, especially if they
continue to head down a less overtly
"industrial" path.

KASTEELBIER INGELMUNSTER
11.5% abv ✪✪✪✪ Strong Ale
Medium dark, clean but mighty
brew; uncompromising and
unsubtle.

BRIGAND
9% abv ✪✪✪ Strong Ale
Ruddy brown, lightly sedimented

strong ale, lacking complexity.

BACCHUS
5% abv ✪✪✪ Old Red
Sweeter than most of the imitation
Rodenbachs.

ST. LOUIS CASSIS KIR ROYAL
5% abv ✪✪✪ Fruit Lambic
Annoyingly pleasant, as if they
crushed the stalk in the Ribena
before adding.

ST. LOUIS FRAMBOISEE
5% abv ✪✪ Raspberry Lambic
The same in raspberry.

ST. LOUIS GUEUZE FOND
TRADITION
5% abv ✪✪✪✪ Gueuze (unfiltered)
Lightly sedimented, but otherwise
traditional gueuze with grapefruit
overtones.

ST. LOUIS GUEUZE LAMBIC
5% abv ✪✪ Gueuze (filtered)
Sweet pale beer with a hint of
mushrooms.

ST. LOUIS KRIEK LAMBIC
5% abv ✪✪ Cherry Lambic
Becoming less sugary sweet but a
way to go yet.

VLAAMSCH WIT
4.7% abv ✪✪✪ Wheat Beer (filtered)
Light coloured, smoky, soapy, sweet
wheat beer.

Other regular beers include: St
Louis Aardbeien Lambic (5% abv;
strawberry lambic). There is also a
low strength, peach flavoured beer.

VAN ROY

BROUWERIJ VAN ROY
Nieuwstraat 1
9280 Wieze
Tel: 053 215201
Fax: 053 775840
Large independent East Flanders
brewery between Ghent and
Brussels. Traditionally a Pils brewer
but more recently developing a
broad range of ales, regettably on the
bland, commercial side. Annual
production is around 275,000 hl. It
organises the Wieze Beer Festival.

ROYAL TYPE
5.2% abv ✪✪✪ Pale Ale
Reasonable Belgian style pale,
lacking individuality.

WIEZE FARO EXTRA
5% abv ✪✪ Brown Ale
Sourish light brown ale with little resemblance to a lambic-based ale.

WIEZE KRIEK LAMBIC
5% abv ✪✪ Flavoured Ale
Sweet and cloying, bright pink beer without much lambic taste.

Other regular beers include: Upper 19 (7.5% abv), Salvator (7.5% abv; Abbey), Wieze Christmas* (7.5% abv; Christmas ale), Wieze Pils (5% abv; Pils), Royal Pils (4.6% abv; Pils) and Wieze Export (4.3% abv; Pils). There are also three table beers and a low alcohol brew.

VAN STEENBERGE

BROUWERIJ VAN STEENBERGE
Lindenlaan 25
9940 Ertvelde
Tel: 091 445071

East Flanders brewery, in business since 1784, based at Ertevelde, north of Ghent. The company used to be known as Bios but in recent years has been referring to itself by its official name. Produces a wide range of beers, including some impressive contenders in the classic ale styles. Surprisingly, annual production is limited to 30,000 hl a year, though there are exports to Britain, the Netherlands, France and Italy. Numerous beers are produced to contract for wholesalers, particularly De Hopduvel warehouse in Ghent. These tend not to be the same old beers under different labels, though this occurs sometimes. In 1993 they snapped up the Neyt brewery in Evergem and closed it down almost immediately. Criticism was muted by the fact that the first brew of imitation Neyt Ever was at least as good, if not better than the original.

GULDEN DRAAK
11.5% abv ✪✪✪✪ Strong Ale
Powerful herbal medicine in a white gloss bottle which hides the sediment.

PIRAAT
9.7% abv ✪✪✪✪ Strong Ale
Well brewed sediment ale, vaguely in the strong golden style but less flowery.

AUGUSTIJN GRAND CRU
9% abv ✪✪✪✪ Abbey Tripel
Dry, sedimented tripel spoiled only by cardboardy backtastes.

BLONDINE
9% abv ✪✪✪ Pale Ale
Sweet, blond sediment ale with a silly label and an unpleasant bitter backtaste.

BRUNETTE
9% abv ✪✪✪ Brown Ale
Blondine in a brown wig.

GENTSE TRIPEL (bottled)
8.5% abv ✪✪✪✪ Abbey Tripel
Amber sediment ale, bitter-sweet and honeyed with wheat beer back flavours.

AUGUSTIJN
8% abv ✪✪✪✪ Abbey Tripel
Big amber coloured beer with coarse bitterness.

BORNEM TRIPPEL
8% abv ✪✪✪✪ Abbey Tripel
Powerful, golden ale with spicy undertones but sugary backtaste.

CUVEE CHATEAU DES FLANDRES
8% abv ✪✪✪ Strong Stout
Dark and dry, bitter, sediment beer with little bouquet.

BORNEM DUBBEL
7% abv ✪✪✪ Abbey Dubbel
Dark, dryish and burnt. Stronger and less characterful than it was.

REINAERT
7% abv ✪✪✪ Pale Ale
Ruddy-copper filtered ale of simplistic sweetness.

STOEREN BONK
6.2% abv ✪✪✪✪ Old Brown
Astringent, sour brown beer with a highly marketable name.

WILSON MILD STOUT
5.2% abv ✪✪ Sweet Stout
Ridiculously sweet, dark brown ale with the bitterness of a British stout.

BIOS VLAAMSE BOURGOGNE
5.1% abv ✪✪✪✪ Old Red
Surprisingly bitter for a sourish ale in the Old Red style.

EVER
5% abv ✪✪✪✪ Pale Ale
Clean, unpretentious, light straw coloured beer with firm flavour.

SPARTA PILS
5% abv ❸❸❸ Pils
Sweetish, balanced and moderately
bitter.
    Other regular beers include:
Gentse Tripel (draught) (7% abv;
pale ale). There are also two table
beers.

VAPEUR
BRASSERIE À VAPEUR
Rue de Maréchal 1
7904 Pipaix-Leuze
Tel: 069 662047
Active little brewery, founded in
1984 at Pipaix in western Hainaut.
Three basic ales and over 40 label
beers derived from these. The beers
may vary quite a lot, which can be
both charming and precarious.
Annual production is around
1,000 hl.

L'A VAPEUR EN FOLIE
8% abv ❸❸❸❸ Spiced Ale
Dry, sourish, spiced pale ale.

SAISON DE PIPAIX
6.5% abv ❸❸❸❸ Spiced Saison
Highly aromatic intitially,
disappointing half way through.
    Other regular beers include: L'à
Vapeur Rousse (8% abv; spiced ale)
and Vapeur Légère (4.5% abv; pale
ale).

VERHAEGHE
BROUWERIJ VERHAEGHE
Beukenhofstraat 96
8570 Vichte
Tel: 056 777032
Small West Flanders brewer founded
in 1892 at Vichte near Kortrijk.
Specialises in low-medium strength
ales, including a strange collection of
similar tasting variants on the old red
theme. In 1991 it sold its pubs to
Riva and since then has been
concentrating on brewing, which
has improved. Annual production is
said to be 7,200 hl.

NOEL CHRISTMAS
WEIHNACHT*
7.2% abv ❸❸❸❸ Christmas Ale
Aroma-free, light golden, deliciously
sweet, filtered ale, much like a
meibok.

ECHTE KRIEK
5.8% abv ❸❸❸ Cherry Brown

Pasteurised cherry-laden dark ale
with an indefinable distinctive
backtaste.

DUCHESSE DE BOURGOGNE
5.5% abv ❸❸❸❸ Old Red
Improving, increasingly sour and
mature, filtered Flemish red.

CAVES
5.3% abv ❸❸❸ Brown Ale
Quaintly odd, ruddy amber brew
with fruity undertones.

GAPERSBIER
5.3% abv ❸❸❸❸ Pale Ale
Filtered but accomplished pale ale in
the De Koninck style.

QUEUE DE CHARRUE
5.2% abv ❸❸❸ Old Red
Like a rather soppy version of
ordinary Rodenbach.

CAMBRINUS
5.1% abv ❸❸❸ Pale Ale
Typical, slightly candied, filtered
Belgian pale ale.

VICHTENAAR (draught)
5% abv ❸❸❸❸ Old Red
Cleaner than the bottled version.
Sour, bitter, sweet and fruity. Rocky
head.

VICHTENAAR (bottled)
4.9% abv ❸❸❸ Old Red
Revised old brown ale with a bit
more revision to do.
    Other regular beers include: 't
Vlaskapelleke Vlassersbier (6% abv;
old red), Vera Pils (4.7% abv; Pils)
and Vera Export (4.3% abv; Pils).
There are also four table beers.

WALRAVE
BROUWERIJ WALRAVE
Lepelstraat 36
9270 Laarne
Tel: 091 690134
Small pils brewery at Laarne, east of
Ghent, producing 2,800 hl a year.
Founded in 1862. Unusually for such
a small brewery, it has its own
maltings. Despite this they tend to
brew with malt flour. Their beers are
rarely found beyond a five km radius
of the brewery.

PICK-UP PILS
4.8% abv ❸❸❸ Pils
Gently bitter, easy-drinking Pils with
lingering grainy flavours.
    Other regular beers include:

Walrave Export (4.8% abv; Pils).
There is also a table beer.

WELDEBROEC
BROUWERIJ WELDEBROEC
Mechelsesteenweg 53
2830 Willebroek
Tel & Fax: 03 886 1244
Vaartlander arrived in 1992, despite
the absence of a brewery. When
brewed at Huyghe in 25 cl bottles it
clocked up 7.5 per cent abv, while
from Van Eecke in 75 cl bottles it
declared nine per cent abv. The
weaker version must have gone
down better, for when the brewer
finally got his brewery rolling, this is
the strength he chose. Originally to
be called St. Niklaas, we understand
that he finally plumped for the name
Weldebroec; the tasting notes refer
to a brew labelled as coming from
the new brewery in Willebroek,
between Antwerp and Brussels.

VAARTLANDER
7.5% abv ✪✪✪✪ Spiced Ale
Sweet and spicy sediment amber ale,
with a slight haze.

WESTMALLE
ABDIJ DER TRAPPISTEN VAN WESTMALLE
Antwerpsesteenweg 496
2390 Malle
Tel: 03 312 0535
Fax: 03 311 7735
The second largest of the Trappist
breweries, close to the Dutch border
near Malle in the eastern part of
Antwerp province. Its proper name
is the "Abbey of Our Lady of the
Sacred Heart" but it is known
universally as Westmalle. It was
founded in 1794, soon after the
French Revolution had led to the
closure of many Abbeys in Wallonia.
Its brewery commenced operations
around 1836 and became more
commercial in 1920. The "Dubbel"
and "Tripel" styles of Trappist beers
originated here and the Westmalle
brews have become the archetypes
of each classification. Total
production is around 125,000 hl per
year. A third brew, called Extra (4%
abv) is brewed for the brothers and
only rarely makes a public
appearance. The abbey also

produces a cheese. There is an
official tasting café near Westmalle
(see Belgian Cafés: Antwerp).

WESTMALLE TRIPEL (bottled)
9% abv ✪✪✪✪✪ Trappist Tripel
Smooth, deep straw coloured, finely
balanced and delicious. Develops
mellow, honeyed backtastes when
properly stored.

WESTMALLE TRIPEL (draught)
9% abv ✪✪✪✪ Trappist Tripel
Smoother and more predictable but
lacking vivacity.

WESTMALLE DUBBEL (bottled)
6.5% abv ✪✪✪✪✪ Trappist Dubbel
Dark, complex, slightly spicy brew.
When properly stored, it should
have a roasted sweetness in the
background.

WESTMALLE DUBBEL (draught)
6.5% abv ✪✪✪✪ Trappist Dubbel
Less of a challenge, more one of the
crowd.

WESTVLETEREN
SINT SIXTUS ABDIJ
Donkerstraat 12
8640 Westvleteren
Tel: 057 400376
The smallest of the five Belgian
abbey breweries, situated near the
French border just outside the
village of Westvleteren in West
Flanders. Founded in 1831, its
brewery followed eight years later. It
has never produced beer on a
heavily commercial scale but still
manages 4,000 hl per year, much of
it sold through the abbey gates or at
the In de Vrede and its off-licence
opposite (see Belgian Cafés: West
Flanders). Some owners of specialist
beer houses come regularly to
collect crates for their cafés. The
brews were imitated under licence
at the nearby St. Bernardus brewery
(above) until 1992 and some cafés
still sell these unwittingly or
dishonestly as Westvleteren trappist
ales. A fourth beer called Dubbel (4%
abv) is now brewed almost entirely
for consumption by the brothers.
The abbey also produces a cheese in
the Port Salut style.

WESTVLETEREN ABT 12°
11.5% abv ✪✪✪✪✪ Trappist Strong
Dark, interesting, vinuous brew in

the tradition of an aged barley wine.

WESTVLETEREN EXTRA 8°
8% abv ✪✪✪✪ Trappist Tripel
(dark)
Dark, sour and challenging,
sometimes with overtones of home-
brew.

WESTVLETEREN SPECIAL 6°
6.2% abv ✪✪✪✪ Trappist Dubbel
Dark and dry, lacking the candy
sugar flavours of other trappist
beers.

The waterfront at Bruges

Belgian Cafés

THE NINE PROVINCES of Belgium are listed in alphabetical order. Within these provinces, the names of the town or village appear, also in alphabetical order. Suburbs appear bracketed after the name of their city.

This edition of the Guide has omitted the definite and indefinite articles and, in most cases, the designation of the type of café from its name. So for the purposes of the listing, In de Wildeman becomes "Wildeman", Café de la Paix becomes "Paix", Hôtel aux Ardennes becomes "Ardennes" and so on.

We have also introduced for the first time star ratings to the café sections. The quality of the café and its beer range have been rated separately. The café quality has been judged to similar standards across the two countries. In rating the beer list we have taken into account the regional availability of beers and the café's skill in choosing, keeping and serving their beers.

Star ratings are confined to those cafés visited personally by the Guide's accredited inspectors. No star rating means no view. As with the ratings given by the Guide to individual beers, these judgements must be taken only as the individual inspector's opinion and not that of the publisher or any other organisation.

A † by the café name denotes we only have limited information or have been notified of an impending change. The categories used denote:

CAFÉ RATING:

✪✪✪✪✪ = a classic of its kind

✪✪✪✪ = well worth seeking out

✪✪✪ = above average

✪✪ = ordinary but pleasant

✪ = lacking something

BEER RATING:

✪✪✪✪✪ = exceptional range of well-kept beers

✪✪✪✪ = well above average range and/or quality

✪✪✪ = interesting or above average list

✪✪ = typical list

✪ = not really a beer café

[Note: "Proeflokaals" limited to one company's products generally score a ✪✪✪ beer rating. Single star beer ranges are limited to a few spirits houses and other cafés included for their historic or cultural interest alone.]

As well as giving the locations of towns and villages and their relation to major roads, we have also noted where they are on a railway line.

[IC] denotes a mainline or Inter City station.

[IR] denotes a branch line or Inter Regional station.

Opening times are listed wherever possible. Cafés are not obliged to display these and café owners do not have to reveal them to Guide inspectors. In our Belgian section many cafés are shown as closing "late", which can mean any time from 22.00 to 06.00 depending on how trade and the bar staff's eyelids are holding up. Where a closing time is stated, this usually represents a policy, rather than a rule. The owner's discretion is far greater than in countries which retain the tradition of licensed hours of opening.

Closed periods are listed where known. Commonly cafés will close on particular days of the week. In Belgium there remains a tradition for some cafés to close when the owner goes on holiday.

Public holidays lead cafés to operate very unpredictable hours of opening in our experience and may result in complete closure, reduced, normal or even additional hours.

Keeping track of all developments over such a wide area is extremely difficult. The Guide does its best to be alert to changes but cannot be held responsible for inaccuracies. Contributions in the form of corrections or additional information from readers are an essential part of our continuing success and are always warmly received (even when you are putting us right!).

BELGIAN CAFÉS – ANTWERP

Antwerp

ANTWERP PROVINCE (Flemish: Antwerpen) makes up the western half of Belgium's border with the Netherlands. Most of its population is based in or around the old cities of Antwerp and Mechelen in the south west. Antwerp is often referred to as the capital of Flanders.

The rural north and east of the province is made up mainly of traditionally barren flatlands called the Kempen. These used to consist of heath and sandy areas but in more recent times have been extensively planted with pine forests, transforming large parts of the landscape.

Outside the eastern industrial area, the largest community is the historic town of Turnhout, the northernmost town of significance in Belgium.

There are ten breweries in the province. Traditionally Mechelen was associated with the production of dark, dryish, brown ales. In more recent years the most famous products have come from the trappist brewery at Westmalle, De Koninck of Antwerp and Moortgat of Breendonk.

ANTWERP

Major town [IC]

Amsterdam and Bruges are top destinations for visitors to the Low Countries. Brussels and Ghent are popular too. The best kept secret is Antwerp. For lovers of unusual cafés and superb ales, this is a great city to explore.

The place known to the Flemish as Antwerpen and to the French as Anvers is the capital of Antwerp province and is Belgium's second largest city, after Brussels. Despite being over 80 km from the sea up the slowly silting River Schelde, it remains a massive merchant port and one of the gateways of European trade.

The best way to come here, even if you are on a driving holiday, is by train. Taking the car is difficult because of the chaotic drivers and chronic lack of parking.

Centraal Station is architecturally one of the most beautiful in Europe, its foyer is straight out of the Golden Age of Steam with lashings of Art Deco. It lies at the centre of the newer part of the city. The diamond

industry is based around here, as are the cheaper tourist hotels and the world famous Zoo. Unfortunately, we know of no good cafés in this area. For those you need to find the Old Town, ten minutes away on foot, five by tram.

The simplest route to the massive Gothic cathedral at the centre of old Antwerp is a single road which begins life at the station as De Keyserlei and becomes successively Leystraat, Meir and Schoenmarkt. The 400-foot spire of the Cathedral of Our Lady is now to the right. Behind it is Grote Markt where the tourist information office is based. Be sure to get one of their maps to guide you around the maze of ancient streets.

The Cathedral is worth a visit if only for its three paintings by Rubens. The Royal Museum of Fine Arts in Leopold De Waelplats contains around 1,000 paintings by Dutch and Flemish masters and even more from the past 150 years. Those seeking less elevated pleasures will love the zoo, which is one of the few able to claim to have saved species from extinction and successfully re-introduce them into the wild.

Antwerp is one of the world centres for precious stones but there are few bargains to be had. It was the diamond market which helped to attract the largest Jewish population anywhere in Europe, including a high proportion of Orthodox families. Ironically, you can sample restaurants in Antwerp from every style of cuisine in the world - except Jewish!

If your timetable allows, try to visit the docklands to the north of the town centre. Despite the rise of Zeebrugge, the merchant shipping continues unabated. To get a better idea of the scale of operations you should try taking a cruise down the river from the quay by the National Maritime Museum.

This is a rugged, active town which gets on with its business. But don't let this put you off visiting. Antwerpers enjoy life. With guide in hand, despite the closure of one or two of the best beer cafés in the past two years, we promise you an enjoyable time too.

BERENBAK
17 Minderbroedersstraat
Tel: 03 231 1173
Café: ✪✪✪✪ *Beer:* ✪✪✪
Minderbroedersstraat runs from the side of university's school of fine arts to hit Minderbroedersrui on the way to the Grote Markt and Cathedral. Berenbak is a pleasant café serving the locality. It sports a splendid collection of ties and some delightfully simple early 20th century ornaments. The café is well managed but its atmosphere is unstrained and friendly. The affable landlord will be delighted to accept your donation of a club tie. There are around 50 beers and a small but adequate menu of high quality snacks and single plate meals. Food is available from 12.00 to 14.00 and 18.00 to 21.00.
Opening hours 11.00 – late
CLOSED SUNDAY

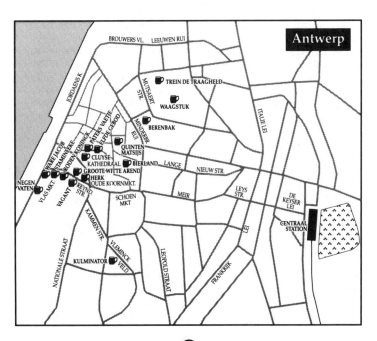

BIERLAND

28 Korte Nieuwstraat
Tel: 03 231 2340

In an unattractive street just off the north east corner of the cathedral square. You can watch the trams pass by, directly outside the panoramic windows of this former newspaper office. The sparsely decorated, high-ceilinged and airy but comfortable café was until recently the unofficial headquarters of Antwerp's organisation of beer lovers, De Dolle Proevers (The Mad Drinkers). Then came new owners, "yoof", loud house music and only vague promises about the old range of 400 beers. Included more in hope than expectation. The beer and café ratings are suspended.
Opening hours 12.00 – 02.00
CLOSED SUNDAY

CLUYSE

26 Oude Koornmarkt
Tel: 03 232 3516
Café: ✪✪✪✪ *Beer:* ✪✪✪
Oude Koornmarkt runs parallel to the back of the cathedral at the heart of the Old Town. The Vault is a remarkable cellar café dating from the 13th century, though the building on top is mere 15th century. Expensive and clearly aiming for the romantic end of the market, there is nonetheless a good range of 80 or so beers served in generally good condition. Candle-lit and highly atmospheric; classical music, of course. It is one of many cellar cafés in Antwerp, but one of the least likely to be swamped by coach parties. Ironically, it can become unpleasantly full on Friday and Saturday nights.
Tuesday to Friday 19.00 – late
Saturday & Sunday 15.00 – late
CLOSED MONDAY

ELFDE GEBOD

10 Torfbrug
Tel: 03 232 3611
Café: ✪✪✪✪✪ *Beer:* ✪✪
Directly opposite the cathedral on the corner of Blauwmoezelstraat, The Eleventh Commandment is the first of the essential visits. It is perfectly in order just to drink here, though most customers in the

evenings prefer to dine as well. There is a terrace outside by the creeper-clad stone walls but if you sit here you will miss the point. For inside the café is a awash with religious paraphernalia. Statues and ikons, altars and a pulpit. The whole lot is bathed in classical or church music. From your ancient bench and table on the ground floor you can count your way around 500 ornamental pieces, all of them religious art rather than kitsch. Is it serious? Judge from the angry paintings and perhaps from the statuette called "Madonna with the Head of a Dog". Is this just a vogue collection of curios or is it an attempt to use café decor as a political, or at least religious, statement? The ground floor is high-ceilinged and the spiral staircase leads up to a second eating area in the gallery. The food is reasonable Flemish fare. The beer list barely passes 30 but ale is only a sideshow while you take time to absorb the absurdity of it all. The Eleventh Commandment in question is "Remember to eat and drink well".
Opening hours 10.00 – late

GROOTE WITTE AREND

18 Reyndersstraat
Tel: 03 232 0880
Café: ✪✪✪✪ *Beer:* ✪✪✪
Reyndersstraat is the extension of Schoenmarkt down towards the Schelde and we list a number of cafés in this area. The Great White Eagle is the most special. Its courtyard entrance opposite De Vagant makes up a significant part of the pub in the summer. It has no bar as such. Waiter service comes from the kitchen. The courtyard has a huge piece of modern ceramic sculpture which ought to be called "Cement Mixer Hit by Meteorite". This tranquil, often windless area makes a splendid auditorium for classical music. This should be accompanied by one of the 40 or so beers, which could be one of those from Cantillon. A range of snacks and single plate meals includes some superb cheeses, chicory wrapped in ham, ragout of lamb and game plus trout. In winter, only the three inside rooms are used. These

resemble some of the sparse chapel-like rooms of a Bohemian beer hall, with chunky straight-backed seating around solid wooden tables. They hold concerts here on occasion. On the other side of the yard is a chapel.
Opening hours 11.00 – 01.00

HERK
33 Reyndersstraat
Tel: 03 232 2157
Café: ✪✪✪ *Beer:* ✪✪✪

Just down the way from our last entry is another multi-roomed café which in any other town would probably get star billing but in Antwerp is just another in a long list of quality places. The division of space is clever. You can sit in a pleasant courtyard, stand around the bar, venture left into a comfortable and attractive lounge with music or file right and find the quiet room. Food is limited to nibbles. There are about 50 beers. They occasionally host jazz or blues nights. It opens at 12.00 in high summer.
Monday to Saturday 18.00 – late
Sunday 14.00 – late

KULMINATOR
32 Vleminckveld
Tel: 03 232 4538
Café: ✪✪✪✪ *Beer:* ✪✪✪✪✪

Opposite the corner of Reyndersstraat and Oude Koornmarkt there is a small street called Kammenstraat. Follow this across Kleine Markt and it becomes Vleminckveld. This is the edge of the old town but is well worth locating for this elegant café and its superb collection of beers, Antwerp's essential visit. The layout is intelligent and allows both for quiet conversation and noisier gatherings. There is an open fire in winter and candle light all year round. The range of beers tops 500, which is huge even by Belgian standards. The beer menu is informative and owners Dirk and Leen are exceptionally knowledgeable. The illuminated beer cellar is on view at the back of the room, along with a collection of old glasses and ephemera. Try the interesting range of over 200 vintage ales, up to ten years old. The music is classical. The tables have flowers. The furnishings are comfortable and well chosen.

There is no food. The customers do occasionally get out of hand. Rumours that Dirk's moustache hides a beaming smile are without foundation. The unofficial headquarters of OBP.
Monday 20.30 – 23.30
Tuesday to Thursday 12.00 – 23.30
Friday 12.00 – 01.00
Saturday 17.00 – 01.00
CLOSED SUNDAY; CHRISTMAS TO NEW YEAR and TWO WEEKS IN JULY/AUGUST

NEGEN VATEN
3 Zand
Tel: 03 226 3983
Café: ✪✪✪✪ *Beer:* ✪

Even our most hop-encrusted, malt-sodden, beerophiliac readers may weary of good ale in Antwerp and so, by means of light relief, we have included this Spanish bodega. When Vlasmarkt hits the ring road on the banks of the Schelde, off to the left is a small street called Zand. The Nine Barrels is entered through a small courtyard on the left a few yards from the corner. Spain and Antwerp go back a long way together. In 1556 King Phillip II of Spain (as in Francis Drake and the Armada) inherited Antwerp, along with much of the rest of the Low Countries, from Charles V following his resignation as Hapsburg Emperor. Some form of trading arrangement has existed ever since, so do not mistake this place as one of a chain of ethnic cafés from a recent fad. Rather, it is a piece of drinking heritage. The nine barrels in question contain large quantities of delicious red and white port, fino, amontillado and cream sherries, Muscat, Tarragona and Malaga wines and sangria. If you insist on beer they can offer five, including Westmalle, Duvel and Hoegaarden. Food is limited to some superb nibbles - try the chorizo. The café itself is small, wooden and delightfully cosy. Mellow punters start singing by candlelight. The old chap in his hammock hanging from the ceiling has been known to join them.
Monday to Saturday 19.00 – late
Sunday 15.00 – late

PATERS' VAETJE
1 Blauwmoezelstraat
Tel: 03 231 8476
Café: ✪✪✪ *Beer:* ✪✪✪✪

The Priests' Little Barrel is a smallish, atmospheric café found within incense-whiffing range of the north wall of the cathedral. It has a pleasant design and probably the best beer list in the square, now expanded to around a hundred. It has a small gallery up a wooden staircase and zinc-topped tables in the back room. Outside is a terrace, drowned by the free carillon concerts on Monday evenings and Friday lunchtimes in summer. The beer list includes Van Eecke's Kapittel range. A selection of Eurosnax is available throughout opening hours. In the summer and at weekends it has been known to remain open until seven in the morning!
Opening hours 11.00 – late

QUINTEN MATSIJS
17 Moriaanstraat
Tel: 03 225 0170
Café: ✪✪✪ *Beer:* ✪✪

In the pedestrian area off Koepoortstraat, just north of the Cathedral, on the corner of Hoofdstraat. Built as a pub in 1565 and said to be Antwerp's oldest café. Don't expect much authenticity, although the food and professional service are truly Belgian. Try the rabbit with plums or the black pudding with apple sauce. The decor is mainly modern with the exception of a few items such as the pianola and the splendid model yacht. The beer list is pretty limited but the bolleke of De Koninck is famously consistent. You get 11 beers for the price of ten!
Opening hours 12.00 – 02.00
CLOSED MONDAY

ROODEN CONINCK
33 Vlasmarkt
Tel: 03 232 4812
Café: ✪✪✪ *Beer:* ✪✪✪

Vlasmarkt is the extension of Reynderstraat to the banks of the Schelde. At street level, The Red King looks like and is an ordinary café. Its hidden face is downstairs, where it hides one of the city's few small cellar vaults, a splendidly atmospheric place to drink. It was formerly a cloister for Beguine nuns and dates from the 13th century. There are tiny snacks and a beer list of around 40.

STAMINEEKE
23 Vlasmarkt
Tel: 03 231 9652
Café: ✪✪✪✪ *Beer:* ✪✪✪✪

New beer cafés are few and far between in Antwerp. The Little Tavern started in 1992, a few doors down from Rooden Coninck (above) and was an immediate hit. The brick-fronted bar, tiled floor and white light give a modern air to it. The beams and atmosphere lend it a lived-in feel. Upstairs is an overspill bar. The beer list is limited to 60, with one or two of the beers in stone-effect bottles at outrageous prices but others good value. Its range is imaginative enough to earn the fourth star. Food includes sandwiches, Eurosnax and a dish of the day.
Saturday & Sunday 14.00 – late
Other days 17.00 – late
CLOSED MONDAY (October to Easter)

TREIN DE TRAAGHELD
33 Lange Noordstraat
Tel: 03 232 2111
Café: ✪✪✪ *Beer:* ✪✪✪

Off the corner of Stadswaag, the Slow Train used to be one of the highlights of Antwerp beer drinking. Awash with 1930s railway nostalgia, including a bar area built in the style of a train, it attracted bucolic beer lovers from all over the country with some very unusual beer choices. More recently, as if to prove that the British need not be alone in their quest for embarrassing mediocrity, it has become a karaoke bar! The beer range has shrunk to around 30. You may wish to shrink, too, unless you are in that precise stage of intoxication where making a complete prat of yourself feels like a good idea at the time.
Thursday to Saturday 20.30 – 05.00
CLOSED SUNDAY to WEDNESDAY

VAGANT
21 Reyndersstraat
Tel: 03 233 1538
Café: ❍❍❍ *Beer:* ❍❍❍
Opposite De Groote Witte Arend
(above) and a genever off-licence of
the same name, on the corner of
Pelgrimsstraat. A vagant was a
travelling student priest of the
Middle Ages who earned his living
by singing. This one has large
rectangular tables and a pleasant,
sophisticated saloon bar atmosphere.
It is no longer owned by the same
people as the off-licence but retains
a strong list of Belgian genevers and
likeurs ranging in strength from that
of fortified wine to industrial
solvent. At the last count these came
from 62 different Belgian blenders.
Unlike the other two genever cafés
mentioned in Bruges and Ghent, the
spirits here are served at room
temperature. There are around 40
beers, including Duvel which has
been deliberately aged in the cellar,
plus Cantillon Gueuze and Kriek.
Monday to Friday 11.00 – late
Saturday & Sunday 01.00 – late

WAAGSTUK
20 Stadswaag
Tel: 03 233 1979
Café: ❍❍❍ *Beer:* ❍❍❍
Small, old courtyard café in a square
behind the school of fine arts. The
name refers to the city's weigh
station but is also slang for Risky
Business. Under new ownership, the
old café area has been closed down
and new rooms opened. The beer
list of 60 is more consistent and the
standards of service are more reliably
courteous. The ratings may be
unkind but were made in the early
days of the new regime, so are
cautious.
Opening hours 18.00 – 01.00

WARE JACOB
19 Vlasmarkt
Café: ❍❍❍❍ *Beer:* ❍❍
Another one on the road which links
Reyndersstraat to the Schelde. A
pleasant, gritty, old brown café with
a paraffin stove and wood-panelled
walls. Typical of the style of cosy
saloon bar which used to abound in
Antwerp. A small kitchen at the back
produces a brief list of high quality
snacks and single plate meals.
Strongly atmospheric with a basic
beer list featuring many of the best
"standard" brews plus Dublin-
brewed Guinness.
Opening hours 12.00 – late
CLOSED SUNDAY

---

*TRY ALSO: CAMRA Brussels'
frequently updated guide to the
cafés of the capital now regularly
lists the results of field trips to
Antwerp. For further details see
Consumer Organisations.*

ANTWERP (BERCHEM)
Southern suburb [IC]
Berchem straddles the Kleine Ring
dual carriageway which encloses
most of Antwerp. It has its own
railway station. The simplest way to
get here is to hop on a train for the
two-minute ride from the Centraal
Station. Most routes stop here.

CAMARGUE
34 Statiestraat
Tel: 03 230 0100
The back of Berchem Station is
bordered by the road called
Posthoflei. Statiestraat is on the
other side of this. Do not confuse it
with Stationsplein, which is at the
front of the station. This bistro-cum-
brown-café serves environmentally
friendly snacks and single plate
meals as well as over 150 ales. A
good wine list includes some
unusual fruit wines, there are
numerous herbal teas and an
impressive cheese board with an
array of raw vegetables.
Opening hours 11.30 – late
*CLOSED SUNDAY and MID-
JULY TO MID-AUGUST*

ANTWERP (HOBOKEN)
South western suburb
Hoboken is part of New Antwerp, a
suburban area to the south west of
the city, reachable by tram or bus.
Much of it is not what the rest of us
might call new. The name is
probably more familiar to American
readers, as it was given to the town
in New York state where Frank
Sinatra was born.

GOUDEN LEEUW
180 Kapelstraat
Tel: 03 827 0779
Kapelstraat lies between New Antwerp South railway station and the banks of the Schelde. The Golden Lion has been in the same family for four generations, so the antique feel has been nurtured, not sprayed on. There is candlelight, an open fire and classical music indoors and a spacious beer garden outside. Enjoy a list of around 100 beers. The owner has been threatening to close it down for at least the last ten years but to date nothing untoward has occurred.
Opening hours 20.00 – late
CLOSED SUNDAY and SECOND HALF JULY

BAARLE-HERTOG
12 km N of Turnhout on N119
Baarle-Hertog is an enclave of Belgian territory surrounded by Dutch North Brabant. It has been that way since a dispute over settlement of a Ducal will in the late 15th century. There are no customs posts and both Belgian Francs and Dutch Guilders are acceptable in the shops. There are parts of town where to make a telephone call across the street involves using an international line at the full rate.

BROUWERSHUIS
42 Molenstraat
Tel: 014 699403
Café: ✪✪ *Beer:* ✪✪✪✪✪
50 metres from the centre of this typical small town, on the road towards Turnhout, you will find The Brewers House off-licence (see Beer Shops & Warehouses). Although most people come here to stock up with their favourite beers for home consumption, there is also an excellent facility for casual tasting and for groups to undergo an education in the basics of beer. Various "programmes" are available, which offer a video film about beer, a few samples of classic beer styles and suitable accompanying snacks. These range from a 45 minute quickie to a five-hour beer spectacular with barbecue, buffet and live music. The shop can cater for parties of up to 50. Alternatively, pop in on your own, especially if you are heading north to the Netherlands – Belgian prices are lower than Dutch and the range of beers on offer is impressive by any standard. They also commission a number of original beers.
Friday 10.00 – 20.00
Other days 10.00 – 18.00
CLOSED MONDAY

ESSEN
28 km N of Antwerp on N133
Bang on the Dutch border. Home to three major beer wholesalers (see Beer Shops & Warehouses).

BOSRUST
10 Kleine Horendonk
Tel: 03 677 0124
Tavern style café in a rural setting. Hidden away down a heathland path. Home-made snacks and ice creams. Over 100 beers. Large outside drinking area with a playground for children. A Belgian country pub for all the family.
Sunday and feast days 10.00 – 24.00
Other days 11.00 – 22.00
CLOSED THURSDAY (winter)

ITEGEM
20 km SE of Antwerp between A13 (E313) & N10
Small village off the old road from Antwerp to Diest.

SPINNEWIEL†
36 Hooiweg
Tel: 015 244828
You will find The Spinning Wheel on the way out of town in the direction of Berlaar. There has been an impressive beer range for many years but shortly before going to press we discovered that it had changed hands with no guarantee of a continued interest in special beers. Opening hours refer to the old regime. Reports please.
Sunday to Wednesday 12.00 – 02.00
Friday 18.00 – 02.00
Saturday 18.00 – 03.00
CLOSED THURSDAY

MECHELEN

Halfway between Antwerp &
Brussels off A1 (E313) [IC]
Mechelen (French: Malines) is a right
old mix. It shares an Archbishop
with Brussels and is a major railway
junction. It is an industrial sprawl
which is the centre of the asparagus-
growing trade. It is the province's
second city, with a population of
80,000.

Because of its marshalling yards it
was heavily damaged in both world
wars but its religious importance
saved much of the Cathedral of St.
Rumbault and the old town around
the Grote Markt. The damage in this
area was carefully restored in the
post-war years and you should try to
glimpse, even on a whistle-stop tour,
the Renaissance-style Law Courts.
The newer of the cathedral's two
marvellous 49-bell carillon offers free
concerts every Monday from 20.30
to 21.30 in summer.

STILLEN GENIETER

9 Nauwstraat
Tel: 015 219504
Nauwstraat is near the Fish Market
(Vismarkt) – follow your nose. De
Stillen Genieter is renowned as one
of Belgium's best beer houses. The
split-level layout, tiled floor and
clever arrangement create a good
atmosphere. The range of beers is
huge, stretching to at least 330, and
is well chosen. Where else in
Flanders will you find the four Saison
d'Erezée beers of the Prignon
brewery? They also stock a wide
range of teas and coffees. Food is
limited to Eurosnax with a few
traditional dishes like uitsmijter. The
background music is popular
classical. There is a terrace outside.
The building on the opposite side of
the canal is the Lamot brewery, for
the moment at least.
Monday to Friday 11.30 – 15.00
Monday to Saturday 19.00 – late
Sunday and feast days 18.00 –
late

NIEUWMOER

18 km N of Antwerp on N133
Village on the Dutch border
between Essen and Wunstwezel.

MAATJES†

4 Spreeuwstraat
Tel: 03 667 6098
The Herring is one of those
institutions you could only find in
the Low Countries, a café-cum-
pancake-house, selling waffles,
pancakes and ice creams alongside a
range of 100 beers.
Opening hours 13.00 – 23.00
CLOSED JANUARY &
FEBRUARY

OELEGEM

12 km E of Antwerp off A21 (E34)
Commuter village, east of Antwerp.

TORENHOF†

21 Torenplein
Tel: 03 383 0326
A traditional Belgian tavern with a
large dining room. In the square by
the church at the village centre.
There are 80 beers.
Opening hours 11.00 – late
CLOSED MONDAY

POEDERLEE

12 km SW of Turnhout on N153
Village in a wooded area of the
Kempen.

HEIDE

42 Zittaartstraat
Tel: 014 554914
Café: ✪✪✪✪ *Beer:* ✪✪✪✪
Driving into Poederlee from the
direction of Herentals this rural pub
is signposted on your left down
Zittart, a lane through a wood, just
before the town boundary sign. This
crosses Zittartstraat after two
kilometres. Turn right to find the
tavern on your left. This is excellent
walking and cycling country. There
is a spacious ancient-and-modern
interior, a large garden and play area
and swings. The beer range tops a
hundred. There is a typically
generous range of snacks, meals and
ice creams, served from 11.30.
Monday & Tuesday (summer)
11.00 – 20.00
Friday (October to Easter) 18.00
– late
Other days 11.00 – late
CLOSED MONDAY to
THURSDAY (October to Easter)

TURNHOUT
Major town [IR]

Belgium's northern most town of any size (pop. 40,000) is an industrial community surrounded by the flatlands of the Kempen. Its surprising array of 16th century buildings comes from its glory years when it was the seat of government for first the Burgundian, and then the Austrian, administrations of the region. The present law court was once a palace of the Dukes of Brabant. Students of the obscure might like to locate the Museum of Playing Cards, in one of the baroque church houses near the gothic Church of St. Pieter.

SPYTIGHEN DUVEL
99 Otterstraat
Tel: 014 423500
Café: ✪✪✪✪ *Beer:* ✪✪✪✪✪

The Spiteful Devil is a gem, tucked away off the tourist's beaten track but well worth including in any tour. Found just off the Grote Markt, at the centre of town, it was the first beer café in Belgium seriously to buck the chauvinistic tendency to stock only Belgian ales. That is not to say that native beers are ignored but rather that they only make up half the beerlist of 200. With the rest, you can travel the world on your bar stool. They also have a stock of specially aged beers. Their range of genevers and likeurs is unusually adventurous too. The hot and cold bar food is well above average, served from 17.00 to 24.00. Try the winter stew called Hechtelse Stoverij or find out what Breughel did to filleted chicken. A lovely old café too and not overrun by tourists.
Opening hours 14.00 – 01.00
CLOSED MONDAY & TUESDAY

VIERSEL
15 km ESE of Antwerp off A13 (E313)

Commuter village for Antwerp, straddling the A13 motorway and Albert Canal. Good walking country.

KROON
12 Dijkstraat
Tel: 03 484 3466

Just out of the village, across the Albert Canal you will find The Crown. One wag translated its Flemish name as The Crooner, after the café's penchant for employing a pub chanteuse, Cecile van Dijck, in the evenings. Ninety bottled beers will either aid your enjoyment or help drown out the noise, depending on your tastes.
Opening hours 11.00 – late
CLOSED MID JANUARY to MID FEBRUARY

WESTMALLE
24 km ENE of Antwerp on N12

Westmalle, Malle and Oostmalle practically run into one nowadays. Blessed is the Abbey of Westmalle for it bringeth the town a fame which its other attractions would not manage.

TRAPPISTEN
478 Antwerpsesteenweg
Tel: 03 312 0502
Café: ✪✪✪ *Beer:* ✪✪✪

Two kilometres out of town in the direction of Antwerp on the N12 is this roadside tavern, opposite the lane which leads up to the door of Westmalle abbey, an easy walk once you have crossed the busy road. The no. 41 bus stops outside. There used to be three cafés along this road, all presenting themselves as the original and authentic place to try Westmalle beers. Perhaps it is a sign of the times that one is now the Gypsy Tavern and the other the Laser Karaoke Disco Lounge. Here in the original is a huge saloon, an equally huge terrace, 12 beers including the draught and bottled versions of each Westmalle brew, plus a helpful range of smallish snacks.
Opening hours 09.00 – late

ZOERSEL
20 km ENE of Antwerp on N14

Small town off the old Antwerp to Turnhout road.

BOSHUISJE
1 Boshuisweg
Tel: 03 324 1137
Café: ✪✪✪✪✪ *Beer:* ✪✪✪

Getting to Zoerselbos (Zoersel wood) is fun. For a start, do not try it from Zoersel town which is five kilometres by road. Rather, start from junction 20 of the A21 [E34] and head away from Zoersel. After 600 metres, turn right into Hooidonck. After a kilometre, at a café called Den Hunck, turn right again and cross the motorway to enter a large public park. The Little Wood House is 150 metres from the car park up a bridlepath. The trek is rewarded by a most unusual café which comes into its own at quiet times. While the enormous garden is fine for families and soaking up the sun, inside this small, converted Kepish farmhouse is a delightful rustic simplicity. There is a single, long room without a bar as such, just an open wood fire, a few tables and chairs, candlelight and a stove. The food is less simple, featuring giant prawns, bouillabaisse, frogs legs, steaks and lamb fillet Dijonnais, as well as Eurosnax, pancakes and ice creams. They usually have around 60 beers in stock. Afterwards, a walk in the woods is compulsory. Although winter opening is restricted, parties may book for special occasions.

Friday (October to Easter) 17.00 – 22.00
Saturday 12.00 – 01.00
Other days 11.00 – 23.00
CLOSED MONDAY to THURSDAY (October to Easter)

Brabant
including Brussels

THE PROVINCE OF BRABANT makes up central Belgium and encloses the provincial, national and European capital, Brussels. The area to the south and west of Brussels is known as Pajottenland and includes the Senne Valley, the centre in recent years of lambic beer production. A few miles further south is Waterloo, the place where Napoleon's plan for a single Europe finally ended.

Brabant is the only province in Belgium to be divided into French and Flemish speaking parts. Flemish and Wallonian Brabant were officially divided into two separate provinces on 1st August 1993 but this has escaped the notice of most Belgians, which is reason enough for the Guide to ignore the fact too.

The linguistic divide runs about ten miles south of Brussels. The capital itself is officially bilingual, though in practice French tends to predominate. Many locals speak a form of mangled dialectic French caused Bruxellois. The Guide's policy is to list in the official language of the locality. In Brussels we have prioritised French and bracketed Flemish.

For the beer tourist, the suburban town of Beersel is a compulsory visit, with its two gueuze blenders and fine selection of simple cafés. To complete your education in spontaneously fermented beers, be sure to take in Cantillon's Museum of Gueuze in the capital.

Brabant has more breweries than any other province, with 11 standard breweries, three home brew houses, 10 or 11 lambic brewers and the two remaining non-brewing blenders of gueuze beers.

ALSEMBERG

10 km S of Brussels between N5 & A7 (E19)
Small town in the Brussels commuter belt. Within easy reach of the country park at Huizingen, just off the E10 motorway.

ARTEVELDE
1 Windericxplein
Tel: 02 380 1150
Café: ❍❍❍ Beer: ❍❍❍
Formerly the Café Hof, a famous beer café, the new owners of this old corner house have transformed it into an excellent small restaurant with attached café. The beer list is reduced but still interesting. The live oysters and occasional lobster in the dining room's aquarium are more eye-catching that the Wets Geuze and Kriek on the beer menu but to gain maximum enjoyment try these

in combination. In winter they go Dutch and offer both stone grills and fondues. For the less hungry there are simpler bar snacks. The restaurant operates from 11.00 to 23.00.
Opening hours 10.00 – 24.00

ASSE

15 km NW of Brussels on N8
Small village in northern Pajottenland, at the eastern end of Belgium's smaller hop growing region, which stretches as far as Aalst. In the town square is the statue of the Hopduvel (hop devil).

KILO
46 Snassersweg
Tel: 02 452 7422
Café: ❍❍❍❍ Beer: ❍❍❍
One of the great little lambic cafés, off the beaten track. Travelling by bus from Brussels North Station or

Aalst, the stop is called Wijndruif (wine grape) and is 50 metres off the main Ghent highway near Kobbegem. From there it is first right, first left and down to the end of the lane! The excellent Girardin young lambic is also available half-and-half with gueuze ("kilowatt"), with cherry gueuze ("kiloboy") or with old lambic as "weg en weer", which is Flemish for "coming and going". Superb, totally unspoilt, old village café; a classic of its type, which well rewards the visitor. Nice outside drinking area. Snacks include the Brabantine speciality, "pottekaas", a soft white cheese served with spring onions and radishes. Prices are low for lambic. There are a few other beers.
Sunday to Wednesday 16.30 – 24.00
Friday & Saturday 10.00 – 24.00
CLOSED THURSDAY

BEERSEL
8 km SSW of Brussels off A7 (E19) [IR]
The only "official" tourism to be had in the small town of Beersel is its well-preserved 14th-century castle, so heavily moated that it could almost claim to be an island in a lake. For the beer tourist, the town is the most important shrine on the pilgrim's trail around the lands of the gueuze blenders. Here are the smallest two of the remaining "stekerij", as well as a collection of pleasant and varying cafés in which to try other blenders' products. On weekdays there are trains throughout the day to Brussels and into the evening. At weekends, the bus service to Calevoet links Beersel hourly with the no. 55 tram into Brussels centre. Staying in Beersel and travelling into Brussels is worth considering if you are trying to avoid Brussels prices.

BIERHUIS OUD BEERSEL
232 Laarheidestraat
Tel: 02 380 3396
Café: ❍❍❍ *Beer:* ❍❍❍
Beersel's larger gueuze blender, Oud Beersel, also brews the lambic ales from which its beers are blended (see Belgian Independent

Breweries). Next door is one of those cafés which is quietly extraordinary. The contrast with Drie Fonteinen (below) could not be greater. To get here from the village centre, follow the signs to Oud Beersel 1882 until you reach the edge of town, a distance of 2.5 km. This is a typical local Pajottenland café where both young and old lambic are available on draught, the latter served by handpump. Oud Beersel Gueuze and Kriek are also available. A handful of locals swap gossip and natter about the latest performance of Anderlecht FC. A peculiar variant on snooker and table football takes centre stage in the front bar. The gem which marks it out from other cafés lurks in the back room; it is a 1932 Dutch mortierpijp fairground organ of the whistling and whooping variety. If this does not appeal, there is also a new terrace at the back.
Opening hours 10.00 – 20.00
CLOSED TUESDAY

CENTRUM
11 Ukkelsesteenweg
Tel: 02 378 0157
Café: ●●●● *Beer:* ●●●
Hilltop hotel near the centre of Beersel with a pleasant view from its sheltered garden over the Senne Valley. They do not speak English or much French here and la patronne is German Swiss. The pleasantly old-fashioned, tiled front bar has a selection of just over 30 beers, including Hanssens gueuze and kriek. The main attraction is the fact that it offers good value accommodation if you want to make a night of it in Beersel. There are 12 rooms from BFr 1200 single and BFr 1500 double. In the tradition of a continental auberge, these vary considerably and offer facilities which, like the opening hours and the method of communication, can be scatty at times. Brussels is commutable on weekdays. There is a broad menu of traditional snacks and more elaborate cooking - try the tournedos with cheese or the sausage made with faro.
Monday 10.00 – 14.00
Wednesday to Sunday 10.00 –

24.00
CLOSED TUESDAY and TWO
WEEKS MID-JUNE

DRIE BRONNEN
13 Hoogstraat
Tel: 02 331 0720
Café: ❍❍❍ Beer: ❍❍❍

The Three Springs could not be
more typical of a middle market
Pajottenland village café. Open to all,
well-managed, comfortable but
neither flashy nor engrained with
history. There is a front bar for
drinking and eating, a side room for
overflow and a sheltered terrace at
the back. The range of 44 beers
includes draught lambic from
Girardin and bottled gueuze and
kriek from Hanssens. The extensive
menu of snacks and light meals
includes omelettes, "toasts",
croques, pancakes, charcuterie and
ice creams. Thirty years ago it was
owned by the Debelder family
before they moved downstream to
the Three Fountains. Rumour has it
that they are now making their own
cherry lambic.
Monday 10.00 – 12.00
Wednesday to Sunday 10.00 –
24.00
CLOSED TUESDAY

DRIE FONTEINEN
3 Herman Teirlinckplein
Tel: 02 331 0652
Café: ❍❍❍❍ Beer: ❍❍❍❍

The Three Fountains bills itself
nowadays as a brasserie restaurant
and underplays its unique position as
the last remaining home blender of
lambic-based beers. It is the largest
café in the small square at the top of
the hill climbing from the E19
motorway. The tiny station halfway
up still attracts trains once an hour
on weekdays (till 20.30) from
Brussels and Halle. Many customers
come simply to enjoy the delicately
casseroled mussels, the darne of
salmon, the excellent steaks, the
lapin à la gueuze, the guinea fowl in
kriek or the hand-whisked chocolate
mousse. Many stick to wines from
the unusually full list. Fools! For here
they make three of the finest acid-
dry beers in the world. The Gueuze,
Framboise and bottled Kriek are
quite magnificent and make a
wonderful accompaniment to meat,
fish and poultry, respectively. Ignore
the sugar lumps and cocktail stirrer
which arrive on the same tray. These
are for absolute beginners! If you
want a "pudding beer" you can
drown everything in the Ribena-
sweet draught Kriek from the
familiar-looking porcelain handpulls
at the bar. The high-ceilinged, airy
rooms look impersonal at first but
the excellence of all the
consumables overcomes this. The
café is so popular that a second
major salon has been built at the
back. There is a terrace outdoors at
the back in summer, between the
café and the blending room
(stekerij).
Opening hours 10.00 – 24.00
CLOSED TUESDAY &
WEDNESDAY; TWO WEEKS
MID-JUNE and CHRISTMAS TO
NEW YEAR

THE BEERSEL BEER SELECTION

As well as the full entries for Beersel, we are aware of a number of other
cafés where traditional lambics and lambic-based beers may be sampled. At
the **In 't Oude Pruim**, one bus stop down Ukkelsesteenweg from the
Centrum Hotel, you will find Girardin Gueuze and 40 or so other beers. It
has a beer garden and serves good snacks and bar meals. It has been in the
same family for five generations and they have spilled across the road to the
more basic **In De Nieuw Pruim**. Here the attraction is the cheap prices
and the Hanssens Gueuze and Kriek. Next to **Drie Fonteinen** is **Au Grand
Salon**, a friendly open-plan café with Oud Beersel Gueuze and Kriek plus
20 other beers. The **Feestzaal** in Hoogstraat and the nearby **Café
Camping** also sell Hanssens, while the **Gaie Pêcheur** round the corner in
Vijverstraat still stocks De Koninck Geuze and Kriek. Finally, Beersel Castle
has at its main entrance the **Auberge Du Chevalier**, a 17th century tavern
which serves Hanssens.

BRUSSELS

Capital city [IC]

As well as being the national capital of Belgium, Brussels (French: Bruxelles; Flemish: Brussel) is the capital of Brabant province and, on a slightly larger scale, the unofficial capital of the European Community.

If ever there was a city about which to say: "It's great if you know your way around", then Brussels is it. It has enormous potential to bore the pants off weekenders and leave the feeling that it is fit only for bureaucrats. Yet with a little inside knowledge, a fine time can be had.

The centrepiece of the city is the stunning Grand'Place, the old cobbled market place flanked by the imposing Gothic guildhouses of the artisans. Among these, at no. 10 Grand'Place, is the Maison des Brasseurs, which houses a small museum and is still the base for CBB, the Confederation of Belgian Brewers. There used to be some pleasant beer cafés on the square but alas a huge hike in rents late in 1992 put paid to them and a significant premium is now charged for gawping at fellow tourists sipping bland lagers on the terraces of the remaining ones.

Ironically perhaps, Brussels rarely preserves its old buildings and pretty places are few and far between. What abounds is gastronomy, fine ale and obscure tourism.

Do not underestimate the

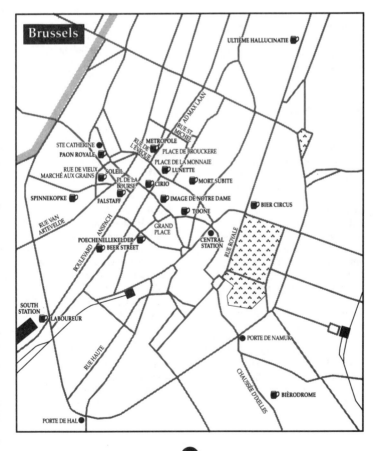

potential for the absurd. Ask yourself whether a city whose most famous monument is a tiny street-corner statue of a little boy urinating is likely to be terminally boring? As its better cafés and restaurants betray, when Brussels wants to turn it on, it does so in style.

Visit the Palace of Justice, the Royal Museum of Fine Arts and the Royal Palace if you must, but be sure to take in the really important bits like one of the dozens of tiny specialist museums, the ridiculous underground-overground metro system and the multifarious street markets that crop up in unlikely places.

The Tourist Information office in the Rue Marché aux Herbes (Grasmarkt) will supply your starter pack and street map.

BRUSSELS CENTRAL

We have defined Brussels Central as the area within the ring of major boulevards that runs from the Porte de Hal, clockwise to the Charleroi Canal, past the Botanical Gardens to the Place Surlet de Chokier, on to the Porte de Namur and back to the start.

BEER STREET
119 Boulevard Anspach
(Anspachlaan)
Café: ❸❸❸ *Beer:* ❸❸❸
The people who created the two Moeder Lambic bars in Ixelles and St. Gilles had been looking for a city centre site for some time. Having found one right at the heart of the city, on the road that runs south from De Brouckère past the Bourse, they have rendered it unique by attempting to stock more draught beers than any other permanent bar in the world. They opened with 74, including six wheat beers, several strange new concoctions from Huyghe and, most interesting of all, the two brews from the Silenrieux brewery, Joseph and Sara, made with experimental grains like buckwheat. Whether they maintain sufficient turnover to keep all the beers in good condition remains to be seen. You will realise as soon as you walk in, from the row of fonts, why they

call it beer street.
Sunday to Thursday 08.00 – 04.00
Friday & Saturday 08.00 – 05.00

BIER CIRCUS
89 Rue de l'Enseignement
(Onderwijsstraat)
Tel: 02 218 0034
Café: ❸❸❸ *Beer:* ❸❸❸❸
CAMRA Brussels' "best discovery of 1993", according to Stephen D'Arcy, bottle-spotter-in-chief; a three-roomed specialist beer café next to the Cirque Royale concert hall, off Rue Royale. One of the most intelligent beer ranges in Belgium, it stretches to a mere 125 choices but includes some classic and unusual brews. Drie Fonteinen Gueuze and Kriek, Vanderlinden's Lambik and Cantillon Vigneronne feature among the lambic-based list; Dolle Brouwers and Van Eecke beers are brought from West Flanders, and there is an excellent selection of Wallonian 75 cl bottles from rarer and smaller breweries like Abbaye des Rocs, Blaugies, Praille and Binchoise. Every trappist beer appears, including all three from Westvleteren. The café will open on Sundays if there is a concert.
Monday to Friday 12.00 – 15.00
Tuesday to Friday 17.00 – 24.00
Saturday 18.00 – 24.00
CLOSED SUNDAY

CIRIO
18-20 Rue de la Bourse
(Beursstraat)
Tel: 02 512 1395
Café: ❸❸❸❸❸ *Beer:* ❸❸❸
A café with something unmistakably different about it. High-ceilinged and ornate early 20th century decor, upholstered bench seating, an ornately carved bar and waiters out of a pre-war Bournemouth hotel. A perfectly powdered octogenarian lady finishes her fourth glass of "half-and-half" (white Alsace with champagne) and staggers with the aid of her walking stick to the ancient porcelain boudoir at the rear. Her usual waiter whisks away the evidence, leaving her change with a nip of "stiff bitters" at her table. On her return she downs it in

one and wanders onto the sunlit street, negotiating the terrace, to greet the watery midday sun. The American postgrad stirs a coffee and adjusts her billowing white dress before passing some nuts to a beige and wrinkled peasant who burps his gueuze. Forty beers including Witkap Tripel and Hapkin. Hot and cold snack meals all day. **Le Fiacre**, a few doors down, is open all day and night for food and drink. Betwen the two is the White House, a shop with a reasonable array of beers, which never closes.

Opening hours 10.00 – 01.00

FALSTAFF
17 Rue Henri Maus (Henri Mausstraat)
Tel: 02 511 8789
Café: ✪✪✪✪ *Beer:* ✪✪✪

By the side of the Bourse, this famous institution is primarily a restaurant with extraordinary opening hours, but as with so many places in Belgium the range of beers, especially trappist brews, is sufficient to attract drinkers too. The decor in the main building is a mix of Art Nouveau, Art Deco and Roccoco with the most eye-catching features being the mirrors and stained glass windows. There is a streetside terrace and an extension on the left side of the building with a simpler bar area. Food is available most of the time, with the menu of full meals served from 12.00 to 02.00.

Opening hours 07.00 – 05.00

IMAIGE DE NOSTRE DAME
3 Impasse des Cadeaux (Geschenkengang)
off 8 Rue Marché aux Herbes (Grasmarkt)
Tel: 02 219 4249
Café: ✪✪✪✪ *Beer:* ✪✪

Up a blind alley off the Rue Marché aux Herbes in the city centre. The shortish beer range is dominated by Timmermans and includes draught Bourgogne des Flandres and the new Witte Lambic. Not a café you will find by accident but well worth seeking out for its old-style interior, tiled fireplaces, stained glass windows and old stove. Surprisingly

quiet for this part of town. In a parallel alleyway off no. 12, is **Au Bon Vieux Temps**, with an equally beautiful interior but very ordinary beer list. Up Impasse St Nicholas (St. Niklaasgang), off no. 11 Rue de Tabora (Taborastraat), is **La Bécasse**, owned by the same company. The bar is not as impressive but they sell sweet, clear lambic doux and cherry lambic in stone jars.

Monday 16.00 – 24.00
Tuesday to Saturday 12.00 – 24.00
CLOSED SUNDAY

LUNETTE
3 Place de la Monnaie (Muntplein)
Tel: 02 218 0378
Café: ✪✪✪ *Beer:* ✪✪✪

Place de la Monnaie is found between the main Post Office and the Opera, off Boulevard Anspach. The type of long café with mirrors and wood panelling that used to be typical of Brussels but is now quite rare. An upstairs saloon has a better view over the square. There are around 45 beers and a food menu ranging from Eurosnax via cold assiettes to steaks and brochettes. Beware that a "large" beer means a litre, served in a glass called a Lunette. Only fools and horses attempt these. Another café in the general vicinity with extraordinary glasses is **Le Corbeau** in Rue St. Michel, just off Boulevard Adolphe Max. On the other side of the Boulevard at 116 Avenue de Laeken is **Le Zageman**, which has a secret list of lambic based beers from most of the surviving producers. It closes at the weekend and in the late evening.

Monday to Thursday 08.00 – 01.00
Friday & Saturday 08.00 – 02.00
Sunday 10.00 – 01.00

METROPOLE
31 Place de Brouckère (De Brouckereplein)
Café: ✪✪✪✪ *Beer:* ✪✪

The Café Metropole is the terraced café of the five-star Hotel Metropole, the ultimate in decadence, Brussels style. Not a place for beer hunters, one for café collectors. Pure fin de siècle elegance. Plush leather furnishings, engraved tinted mirrors, stucco ceiling, stained glass and high ceilings from la belle époque. Waiters to match. The beers, snacks, fruit flans and coffee are expensive but not exorbitant. Nonetheless you do not come here for value per franc. Look on it as a source of future nostalgia.

MORT SUBITE
7 Rue Montagnes aux Herbes Potagères (Warmoesbergstraat)
Tel: 02 513 1318
Café: ✪✪✪✪ *Beer:* ✪✪
From the Grand'Place, the simplest way to reach this classic Art Deco café is via the absurdly elegant Galeries Royale St. Hubert shopping arcade. Try not to be distracted by the sight of the fish restaurants of the Ilot Sacré area. The Sudden Death café actually takes its name from a card game which was played here many years ago. In turn, Alken Maes named their commercial lambic-based brews after it, which is ironic, given that until recently, it was famous for its traditional gueuze. The four-star rating is not due to elaborate style but rather because it is a superb example of a fin de siècle long bar, a cross between a Bohemian beer hall and an old-style Yates's Wine Lodge. Long rows of tables and patched leather seats disappear into the distance, policed by waiters and waitresses in black and white uniforms. The prices are painted on the mirrors. The only compromise with comfort is the hat stand. A small range of bar snacks is available, including tête pressée. The café believes that, to their undying shame, De Keersmaeker have stopped producing their traditional gueuze and at the time of going to press, stocks were running low. If this is true, it would constitute a national scandal.
Monday to Saturday 10.00 – 01.00
Sunday 12.00 – 01.00

PAON ROYAL
6 Rue Vieux Marché aux Grains (Oud Graanmarkt)
Tel: 02 513 0858

Café: ✪✪✪ *Beer:* ✪✪✪
The Old Grain Market is an extension of the square which houses St. Catherine's Church, two blocks to the wrong side of De Brouckère metro station. The Royal Peacock is an excellent place to have an Aberdeen Angus steak lunch and sample from a list of 50 beers. Its hours cater mainly to office workers but on Friday evenings the restaurant stays open (18.30 to 21.30) to serve the other house speciality, skate. The normal restaurant hours are 11.30 to 14.30. Round the corner at 26 Rue Ste. Catherine is **Le Vieux Château d'Or**, a typical old Bruxellois café, that is worth a quick half of lambic.
Friday 11.00 – 22.00
Other days 11.00 – 20.30
CLOSED SUNDAY & MONDAY

POECHENELLEKELDER
5 Rue du Chêne (Eikstraat)
Tel: 02 511 9262
Café: ✪✪✪✪ *Beer:* ✪✪✪
With so many city-centre cafés missing from the second edition of the Guide it is a joy to welcome an excellent new one to our pages, especially in such a prime spot for tourists. Directly opposite the statue of the Mannekin Pis on Rue d'Etuve, this excellent two-storey café opened in 1991 and features almost as many puppets as the Toone (below), a collection of crossbows and many other interesting objects. The puppets' clothes are as distinctive as Scottish tartans and the full listings of those commissioned over the years is also on show. The man who makes them is responsible for many of the murals. There is a menu of 40 beers including lambic-based brews from Vander Linden. Be sure to sample the typical Bruxellois tartines (small snacks) such as a special brawn called Kip Kap and the local version of Tête Pressée. They have on show a bar game called Nijolle, which a sort of cross between toss 'penny and bar billiards. If you are coming in a party and book in advance they can arrange for the puppet theatre downstairs to perform the story of the Mannekin Pis. Alternatively, sit

outside and stare at the strange crowds.
Monday to Thursday 10.00 – 24.00
Friday to Sunday 10.00 – 02.00

SOLEIL
84 Rue du Marché au Charbon (Kolenmarktstraat)
Café: ❉❉❉ *Beer:* ❉❉❉

Rue du Marché au Charbon (coal market street) starts just off Grand'Place and then wanders casually in a far from straight line. The Sun is a quietly chic street corner café in a 17th-century building, populated by twentysomethings, plus graduates of the group. There is plenty of stripped wood and a ceiling fan. Furnishings are simple but packed in. There are about 40 beers of the artisanal but safe variety. Food is ecologically sound snacks. So is the music.
Opening hours 08.00 – 02.00

SPINNEKOPKE
1 Place du Jardin aux Fleurs (Bloemenhofplats)
Tel: 02 511 8695
Café: ❉❉❉❉ *Beer:* ❉❉❉❉

The Place du Jardin aux Fleurs is not that easy to find but the delight of eating and drinking here will repay the effort handsomely. Via the right route it is only five minutes on foot from Grand'Place. Basically three streets west you should find the Rue van Artevelde crossing your path. On the opposite side either Rue Pletinckx or Rue des Six Jetons will bring you to the Little Spider. The specialities here are excellent beers and even better ways of cooking with it. Indeed owner Jean Rodriguez has written a book on the subject, called "Cuisine Facile à la Bière". The seafood, sauces and stews are however far from facile and evening tables may need to be booked. Despite the food emphasis, the list of 70 beers is first rate and includes draught lambic and faro from the Cantillon brewery down the road, as well as a large range of artisanal ales in 75 cl bottles. To come just for a beer is no problem, except perhaps on Friday and Saturday evenings. The restaurant is

open from 12.00 to 15.00 and 18.00 to 23.00. The company's other café-restaurant is **L'Etoile d'Or**, also known as Dit Le Rotte Planchei, 500 metres south of here at 30 Rue des Foulons (Voldersstrat), which limits itself to 30 beers.
Monday to Friday 11.00 – 23.00
Saturday 18.00 – 23.00
CLOSED SUNDAY

TOONE
6 Impasse Schuddevelde (Schulddeveldegang)
off 21 Petit Rue des Bouchers (Korte Beenhouwersstraat)
Tel: 02 511 3711
Café: ❉❉❉❉ *Beer:* ❉❉❉

Opposite the tourist information office on the Rue Marché aux Herbes is a tiny street packed with fish restaurants. About halfway along is the blind alley which leads to the Puppet Theatre and its café, Toone. On entering, the bar is to your right and the famous little theatre to your left. The puppeteers perform a wide variety of productions, mainly in the Bruxellois dialect - so 95 per cent of Belgians can't understand them either! Shows happen at 20.30 on Tuesday to Saturday and there is a Saturday matinée at 16.00 (tel: 02 511 7137 for reservations). Some of the puppets are for sale in the main bar. Even without this added attraction De Toone would warrant a place in the Guide as a centrally situated, all-wooden, heavily traditional brown café with a cosy atmosphere. The second bar can operate as an additional puppet theatre. There are about 40 beers, including several trappist brews and lambic-based beers from Cantillon. For food, step outside.
Opening hours 12.00 – 02.00

BRUSSELS (ANDERLECHT)
South western inner suburb [IC]
Anderlecht is about the only part of suburban Brussels known to the average European, thanks to the antics of its football team. Its far eastern tip is by Brussels' third largest train station, the Gare du Midi or Zuidstation. The Cantillon brewery and Museum of gueuze are only five minutes' walk from here

(see Beer Tourism) and now have a sampling room.

LABOUREUR
3 Place de la Constitution (Grondwetplats)
Tel: 02 512 1859
Café: ❂❂❂ *Beer:* ❂❂❂

Coming out of the Gare du Midi (Zuidstation) there is a massive office block ahead. To its right and 200 metres beyond it along the Boulevard de l'Europe (Europalaan) is Constitution Square. The Worker's café is as basic as its name suggests and has none of the pretences of the surrounding geographical landmarks. Here you will find around 50 beers including Rochefort 10° and sometimes lambic. The walls are adorned with bucolic murals and at the rear there are, perhaps incongruously, some stained glass windows. Table tennis can be played upstairs. Snacks are basic but if you want a real culinary treat come on Sunday morning to the clothes market outside and sample dishes from Italian, Turkish and North African foodstalls, reflecting the ethnic backgrounds of Anderlecht's population.
Opening hours 09.00 – 23.00

BRUSSELS (ETTERBEEK)
Eastern inner suburb [IR]
Many of the offices of the EC are in this attractive suburb, a kilometre or two from the city centre. It is also graced by some of the capital's better small parks.

TERRASSE
11 Avenue de Tervueren (Tervurenlaan)
Tel: 02 733 2296
Café: ❂❂❂ *Beer:* ❂❂❂❂

Adjacent to Merode métro station and close by the Cinquantenaire Park, which houses the Army & Military History Museum, the Art & History Museum, the Air Museum and Autoworld (a collection of 450 rare cars). An old-fashioned café on one of the main roads out of town. A hedge shields the pleasant terrace from the excesses of the traffic. There are around 100 beers in stock, including Frank Boon's Mariage

Parfait brands, La Chouffe and Crombé's Oud Zottegems. Hot and cold food, including stoemp, is always available.
Opening hours 09.00 – 24.00

BRUSSELS (IXELLES / ELSENE)
South western inner suburb
Ixelles (Flemish: Elsene) was once a suburb but is now a continuation of the city centre beyond the Namur Gate. It is easiest to catch the no. 71 bus from De Brouckère metro, Central Station or opposite the Café Mort Subite (above) and get off at St. Boniface. For the far flung entries, nos. 95 or 96 from outside the Bourse are better.

ATELIER
77 Rue d'Elise (Elizastraat)
Tel: 02 649 1953
Café: ❂❂ *Beer:* ❂❂❂❂

The Studio is a Bohemian brown café close to the ULB (Free University of Brussels), so in term time it tends to become a boozy student hang-out. The main attraction here is the selection of 250 or so beers at reasonable prices. The bonuses are occasional live folk or jazz and Tuna, the café manageress who knows her beer. To find it, follow directions to Moeder Lambic Ixelles. Rue d'Elise crosses Chaussée de Boondael after Place de la Petite Suisse.
Sunday to Thursday 16.00 – 03.00
Friday & Saturday 18.00 – 04.00

CHATELAIN
17 Place du Châtelain (Kasteleinplein)
Tel: 02 538 6794
Café: ❂❂❂ *Beer:* ❂❂❂

Technically in the suburb of Ixelles, this pleasant bistro is difficult to reach from our other entries without a map. From the city centre, take tram 93 or 94 from Louisa métro station. Worth finding for its pleasant, lively atmosphere and Bohemian leanings. The floor is tiled and the walls are adorned with artistic posters and movie memorabilia. As well as hot and cold café fare there is a proper restaurant at the rear serving Bruxellois tripe, stoemp and other local dishes which supplement a larger, more typical menu. Around 50 beers are available. Background music is jazz and elderly pop. The restaurant is open from 12.00 to 01.00. There is a Wednesday market in the square outside.

Opening hours 10.30 – 01.00
CLOSED SUNDAY

GEORGE & DRAGON
111 Chaussée de Wavre (Waversesteenweg)
Tel: 02 513 2855
Café: ✪✪✪ *Beer:* ✪✪✪

You may think you are hallucinating when you see the casks of Adnams Bitter, Broadside and/or Greene King Abbot racked at the end of the bar and the handpulls mounted upon it, but you are not. This small, street-corner local in a cosmopolitan area is run with great enthusiasm by the Barrett family, who have left behind the delights of Essex to run a British pub at the crossroads of Europe. We would not include a gimmicky version of le pub Anglais. The George is different. The cask ales are usually in remarkably good condition, the bacon sandwiches and all day breakfast is uncompromisingly British and the usual pathetic attempts at fake beams and brewers tudor are thankfully missing. We reserve judgement on the ceiling decoration, which consists entirely of old copies of the Sun. Around 40 Belgian beers are available, especially from the Haacht brewery.

Opening hours 09.00 – 01.00

MOEDER LAMBIC IXELLES
441 Chaussée de Boondael (Boondaalsesteenweg)
Tel: 02 649 7241
Café: ✪✪ *Beer:* ✪✪✪

Take the no. 95 or 96 bus from the Bourse and ask for Ixelles cemetery (La Cimetière d'Ixelles). Chaussée de Boondael is on the right. The range of draught beers at Mother Lambic's in Ixelles tops 50. The attraction of rare brews like Achouffe's Vieille Salme is outweighed by the unsurprising tendency for some of

the slower moving beers to have seen better days. It does not have the bottled beers selection of its sister café in St. Gilles. Service can leave something to be desired.

Monday to Thursday 11.00 – 03.00
Friday to Sunday 11.00 – 04.00

STOEMELINGS
7 Place de Londres (Londenplaats)
Tel: 02 512 4374
Café: ✪✪✪✪ *Beer:* ✪✪✪

Cosy, wood-panelled café in a busy little square just of Trone Street, four minutes walk from Luxembourg metro station. The beer list of 50 or so includes Blanche des Neiges, the sweeter wheat beer from Huyghe, among many others of interest. Food is limited to snacks but includes stoemp - mashed carrot and potato with bacon and sausage pieces. At no. 4 is a typical, cheery Bruxellois café, **L'Houblonnière**, with a reasonable range of brews. It is linked to the nearby Preservation Hall, which is one of Brussels' best jazz venues.

Monday to Thursday 11.00 – 02.00
Friday to Sunday 17.00 – 02.00

ULTIME ATOME
14 Rue St. Boniface (St. Bonifaasstraat)
Tel: 02 511 1367
Café: ✪✪✪✪ *Beer:* ✪✪✪✪

From the St. Boniface bus stop (route no. 71) on Chaussée d'Ixelles, cross the road and walk two blocks to find this excellent, airy, "light brown" street corner café and bistro. Full of potted plants and white light, it manages to offer nearly a hundred beers including a range of beers from De Dolle Brouwers. There is an interesting and varied menu of good value, high quality snacks and full meals, featuring lots of local and national specialties. Food is served from 12.00 - 14.30; 19.00 - 00.30. Three minutes walk away is another café with a short list of unusual beers, **Les Brassins** at 36 Rue Keyenveld.

Opening hours 11.00 – late

BRUSSELS (JETTE)

North western outer suburb

The best time to visit Jette is on a Sunday morning when the thriving street market is operating in the suburb's main streets. Take the métro to Simonis and either walk or take the tram two stops up the Avenue de Jette (Jettelaan).

MIROIR

24 Place Reine Astrid (Koningin Astridplein)
Tel: 02 424 0478
Café: ✪✪✪✪ *Beer:* ✪✪✪✪

This modern split-level brasserie on Jette's main square has spearheaded artisanal ales in the capital for many years. In the summer of 1992 it went one stage further by becoming Brussels' first microbrewery. You can see it from the cleverly designed bar area. The bottled beer range tops a hundred and is chosen intelligently. It includes a range of trappist beers, usually including brews from Koningshoeven in the Netherlands and real Westvleteren Abt. Unusually they stock the complete range of Dolle Brouwers beers, which might have something to do with the fact that their head brewer is also an architect and is responsible for the redesign of the café. They sell traditional three-litre beer crocks called cruchons, used for serving wheat beer, at a cool BFr 5,000 each! The kitchen is beginning to specialise in cuisine à la bière.
Sunday to Thursday 10.00 – 01.00
Friday & Saturday 10.00 – 02.00

BRUSSELS (SCHAERBEEK / SCHAARBEEK)

Western inner suburb [IC]

In days of yore, Schaarbeek was a fruit-growing area and gave its name to one of the finest varieties of bitter-sweet cherries for the production of cherry lambic and cherry gueuze. Nowadays this is inner suburbia. Its south western tip reaches the Botanical Gardens on the outskirts of the city centre.

ULTIEME HALLUCINATIE

316 Rue Royale (Koningstraat)
Tel: 02 217 0614

Café: ✪✪✪✪✪ *Beer:* ✪✪✪

At the more battered end of Rue Royale, beyond the Botanical Gardens towards Ste. Marie Church. Three separate businesses under one roof. The impressive café is in the Art Nouveau style and opens onto a walled terrace at the back. Très chic among young Bruxellois and the large English-speaking ex-pat community. The range of 35 beers includes three Cantillon brews and several other unusual finds. The bar meals are good quality and good value (12.00 to 14.30 and 18.00 to 24.00). The restaurant at the front is seriously haute cuisine at equally serious prices and they let you play chess, peruse the library or, presumably, tinkle the piano in the lobby before dining. Finally there is a basement disco called Citizen Zeb open on Saturday nights from 22.00. The late opening is unusual for this part of Brussels.
Monday to Thursday 11.00 – 03.00
Friday & Saturday 16.00 – 04.30
Sunday 16.00 – 03.00

BRUSSELS (ST. GILLES / ST. GILLIS)

Southern inner suburb

The area of St. Gilles is due south of the city centre beyond the Halle Gate and is reached by tram no. 55 from Porte de Hal (Hallepoort) métro station. Two of the main reasons to come here are the cafés we list and the oppressive façade of the Maison Communale directly opposite. The third, if you are in the right mood, is the small Horta Museum in the Rue Americaine, dedicated to the man who designed most of the Art Nouveau buildings in Belgium. Edith Cavell, the World War One nurse who assisted Allied troops wishing to escape to Holland was shot at St. Gilles in 1915. The Nursing School she founded was in the street now named Rue Edith Cavell.

BEULEMANS

10 Avenue P. Dejaer (P. Dejaerlaan)
Tel: 02 534 3495
Café: ✪✪✪ *Beer:* ✪✪✪

Avenue P. Dejaer is one of the less important roads off the huge Barrière roundabout, one junction up from the inner ring of boulevards at Porte de Hal. The no. 55 tram, among others, gets you there from the city centre. Le Beulemans is a jolly good all-round small café. The welcome is friendly. The range of ales reaches 70, with the help of the eight draught beers, all detailed on a well-designed beer menu. They serve 20 different single malt scotches and six Irish whiskeys. Food stretches as far as côte à l'os and stoemp served with sausage, pork or steak. Plusher surroundings (and how!) of the Art Nouveau variety accompany a more formidable menu at the nearby **Porteuse de l'Eau**, at 46 Avenue Jean Volders, one of the other roads off Barrière.
Monday to Friday 10.30 – 04.00
Saturday & Sunday 16.00 – 05.00

MOEDER LAMBIC ST. GILLES
68 Rue Savoie (Savoiestraat)
Tel: 02 538 0938
Café: ❍❍❍ *Beer:* ❍❍❍❍❍
Mother Lambic's in St. Gilles claims to sell 1,100 different beers but admits to having a mere 750 or so in stock at any one time. Unlike its sister café in Ixelles (above), draught beers are a minor sideline. Even so, its cellar must be larger than its small, single room. More than half of the regularly produced Belgian beers are available, including rarities like the Drie Fonteinen blends, the Steedje home brews and some Wallonian rarities. The beer menu gives little away except the name, so put it alongside our Beers Index and plot your way. Remarkably, the place is usually staffed by no more than two people, though the regular barman has a memory like St. Peter, which helps. The selection of Belgian brews is bolstered by a large number of imports, including over 120 from Germany. Service is sharp (but never rude) when they are busy, and helpfully chatty when they are not. If you need entertaining while polishing off the last 200 beers in the Guide, browse through the

collection of comic books. Snacks are nibbles only but they often have a fine cheese selection. To find this remarkable institution, continue up Avenue P. Dejaer from Beulemans.
Opening hours 16.00 – 04.00

BRUSSELS (UCCLE / UKKEL)
Southern outer suburb
This suburban community lies between Brussels and the part of Pajottenland at the southern end of the lambic brewing area. The quickest route is from the Halle Gate along the Alsemberg highway. Driving can be a pain. The no. 55 tram which took you to St. Gillis (above) will take you onward to Ukkel and ultimately to Calevoet, for travel on to Beersel. The area is dominated by the enormous Wolvendael Park. The Observatory nearby is worth a peek.

VIEUX SPIJTIGHEN DUIVEL
621 Chaussée d'Alsemberg (Alsembergsesteenweg)
Tel: 02 344 4455
Café: ❍❍❍ *Beer:* ❍❍❍
The Poor Old Devil is strictly one for lovers of incongruous cafés. The list of special beers is not displayed, you have to ask for it. The range is limited to 70 or so, but includes Oud Beersel Gueuze and Kriek. You can even find their draught cherry lambic sometimes. The café dates from the 16th century with distinct overtones of Industrial Revolution, including a tiled floor, pot stove and old weighing machine. Some basic snacks are on offer but the owners seem to prefer you go to the Greek frituur next door and bring back something to eat. They will then set a place for you at a table. Exceptionally friendly and family run, the barmen wear white jackets with braid. Closing time depends on the amount of custom.
Opening hours 12.00 – late
CLOSED SUNDAY

BUKEN
9 km NW of Leuven on N26
Roadside hamlet.

UIL
Steenweg Leuven-Mechelen
Tel: 016 604878
Wayside tavern on the main road
from Leuven to Mechelen. The
official address of Veltem is not
marked on most maps. As well as its
list of around 100 beers, the Owl
Tavern offers carefully prepared
snacks and home-made ice cream.
Families are positively welcomed.
Opening hours 14.00 – late
CLOSED MONDAY & TUESDAY
and FIRST THREE WEEKS
SEPTEMBER

DIEST
30 km ENE of Leuven on N10 [IR]
Market town (pop. 20,000) on the
Limburg border between the fertile
Brabant plain and the woodlands of
the Kempen. Pleasant old town
centre with some impressive
buildings around its Grote Markt.

GRENADIER
2 Allerheiligenberg
Tel: 013 337177
Typical Taverne restaurant, just off
the Markt, with its own art gallery
and 130 beers on the list. Will take
coaches by arrangement.
Opening hours 11.00 – late
CLOSED THURSDAY and TWO
WEEKS IN MARCH

DILBEEK
Western outskirts of Brussels off
N8
Straggling dormitory suburb.

RELAIS DELBECCHA†
158 Bodegemsestraat
Tel: 02 569 4430
A rather splendid hotel off the drab
highway to Ninove. Manicured
gardens, with a swimming pool, a
restaurant and a fully-fledged home
brewery. Top quality dining in the
80-place restaurant will set you back
BFr 1,000 for a proper lunch and
more in the evenings. There are 16
rooms, all de luxe, starting at BFr
3,000 (single) and BFr 4,800
(double). Three large bottles of
home-brewed beer to take away
costs BFr 350. Check the brewery is
still open before you visit.

GALMAARDEN
20 km S of Aalst between N225 &
N495 [IR]
Village in good rambling country.

BALJUWHUIS†
Tel: 054 589511
Only open between Easter and
October. A beer café with a terrace,
in the centre of the village.
Traditional café games are played.
There are 50 beers on the menu and
a variety of food is served. They
sometimes run beer tasting evenings.
The area is off the beaten track, but
popular with tourists, especially of
the hiking variety.
Opening hours 12.00 – late
CLOSED MONDAY and
OCTOBER TO EASTER

HALLE
15 km SSW of Brussels off A8
[IR]
On the banks of the River Senne,
Halle is a bustling market town (pop.
32,000) just north of the linguistic
divide and the capital of the Senne
Valley area. The Basilica of St. Martin
in the main square (Grote Markt) is
14th-century Gothic, said to be
typical of the Brabant style. The
town is the starting point for the
"Breughel Route" and the "Gueuze
Route", the two tours aimed at
introducing visitors to the traditions
of lambic-based ales in the same way
as the Italians display Chianti
Country and the French boost the
Champagne area around Epernay.
The **Hotel des Eléveurs**, across the
river from the railway station, boasts
a superb restaurant and makes a
good base for visiting both
Pajottenland and Brussels. An
interesting out-of-town jaunt can be
made to the old castle at Braine-le-
Château, 6 km south east.

FAZANT
8 Grote Markt
Café: ❍❍❍ *Beer:* ❍❍❍
Opposite the imposing Town Hall
and 100 metres from the Basilica, in
the Grote Markt. One of many cafés
on the square, with possibly the best
beer list. A single, wood-panelled,
brightly lit bar – it sells most of the
beers from the town's own lambic

brewer and gueuze blender, Vander Linden. It serves small snacks only. The square is worthy of a café crawl.
Monday to Thursday 10.00 – 23.30
Friday & Saturday 10.00 – 01.00
CLOSED SUNDAY and SECOND HALF SEPTEMBER

LANDEN
Halfway between Leuven and Liège, off A3 (E40) [IC]
Small town on the Limburg border, five minutes north of the motorway. A major junction on the railway network.

RUFFERDINGE
2 Molenstraat
Tel: 011 832513
In the centre of the town, a quaintly rustic old watermill, with a friendly, peaceful atmosphere. They stock over 100 beers and the menu offers a selection of regional snacks.
Tuesday to Saturday 14.00 – late
Sunday 10.00 – late
CLOSED MONDAY

LEUVEN
Major town [IC]
Large university town (pop. 85,000), 20 km east of Brussels, of great historic importance. It was here that the Counts of Louvain declared themselves the Dukes of Brabant in the 12th century. The University was founded in 1425.

If arriving by train it is simplest to head off down Bondgenotenlaan to the Grote Markt 600 metres away. This area has a number of promising cafés, not including the one with the most symbolic name in modern Europe – the Café Karaoke Beethoven. Both the Town Hall, which houses a small museum of beer, and the massive Church of St. Peter are worth a peek.

The 20th century has seen several disasters; there was considerable damage to the town in both world wars. In the 1960s the long-standing linguistic problems of the university caused a terminal split, with the French speakers leaving to set up in Louvain-la-Neuve. In 1993 Artois Plant No. 2 opened a few hundred metres from the Gotham City tower of the original plant.

DOMUS
8 Tiensestraat
Tel: 016 201449
Café: ✪✪✪✪ *Beer:* ✪✪✪✪
Leuven's other brewery. Domus was Belgium's first home-brew pub in many years when it opened in 1985. It is situated on one of the main roads which branch off the traffic roundabout surrounding St Pieter's church in the town centre. Parking is a lottery and you may have to walk some distance. The brewhouse is at the back in its own building. There is often live music in the courtyard that separates it from the pub. The bars are large, modern, split-level and cleverly furnished to give an ancient feel. They are run with the efficiency of a Swiss railway station, by hordes of uniformed waiters. Despite the long menu of substantial and good quality snacks available throughout opening hours, this is not actually a restaurant and full meals are not available. The beer list of 70, including tripels from St Bernardus and Slaghmuylder, complements the two or three home-brewed lagers. For details of these, see Belgian Independent Breweries.
Opening hours 09.00 – late

UNIVERSUM
26 Herbert Hooverplein
Tel: 016 200750
Café: ✪✪✪ *Beer:* ✪✪✪
Three hundred metres out of town from Domus along Tiensestraat. Parking in or near the square is possible. Although it is an open-plan barn of a place with high ceilings and lots of space, it is broken up sufficiently with furnishings and agricultural memorabilia to create a nice atmosphere. The beer list stretches to 55 choices and the quality is generally good. Bar snacks and simple meals at all times. Music ranges from Wagner to "Stranger in Paradise". Open from breakfast time until the wee small hours. Why do they put prayer mats on the tables?
Monday to Friday 07.30 – late
Saturday & Sunday 08.30 – late

LIEDERKERKE
6 km SSE of Aalst off N405 [IC]

An ordinary but most confusing town. Its railway station is 2 km from its main square, which is only 50 metres from the town boundary of neighbouring Denderleeuw, which is in East Flanders province. In addition, various maps spell the town's name as Liedekerke, Lederkerke or Liederkercke.

HEEREN VAN LIEDEKERCKE
33 Kasteelstraat
Tel: 053 680888
Café: ✪✪✪✪ *Beer:* ✪✪✪✪✪

Technically in Denderleeuw and East Flanders, but little more than 100 metres off the main square of this small Brabant town. A large, modern café and restaurant which succeeds in doing everything well. On the beer side they have a temperature-controlled cellar stocking over 200 beers, including an excellent range of lambic-based beers. You can even find Lindemans traditional gueuze here, possibly because the owner's son was in the army with the brewer's son. If you can follow Flemish, the beerlist is exceptionally helpful. The menu ranges from small snacks to five course haute cuisine. The main features are unusual ingredients, excellent presentation and a willingness to experiment. Examples range from salmon cooked with lychees in honey (!) to veal cooked in gueuze. Upstairs, the brightly lit lounges are spotless but enjoyable. Downstairs, the cellar bar lacks a little of the stylishness of the ground floor but will no doubt weather in time. The background music is classical. There is a no smoking area. Outside is a beer garden and a children's play area. Undoubtedly the best modern café in the Guide, with one of the best menus too.

Monday 10.30 – 23.00
Thursday to Saturday 10.30 – 01.00
Sunday 13.00 – 23.00
CLOSED TUESDAY & WEDNESDAY

LINDEN
4 km ENE of Leuven off N2

Small village just outside Leuven, off the old road to Hasselt.

HOF
17 Gemeentestraat
Tel: 016 620739

The In den Hof, or Garden Inn, is a charming old-fashioned café at the centre of the village. Run by the same family for nearly 150 years, it boasts a beer list of around 50 choices and a small food menu. True to its name, it has a beautiful garden.

Saturday and Sunday 10.00 – late
Other days 16.00 – late
CLOSED WEDNESDAY and FIRST WEEK SEPTEMBER

LOUVAIN-LA-NEUVE
20 km SE of Brussels off N4 & A4 (E411) [IR]

In 1968 the French-speaking half of the famous University of Leuven finally split from their Flemish colleagues and set up campus on a site close to the small industrial town of Ottignies. They called the place Louvain-la-Neuve. Where Leuven is a university town, Louvain-la-Neuve is more a town university, education's answer to Milton Keynes. The residential, teaching and social facilities are clumped together in pseudo-suburbs. A radical concept or horrendous mess, depending on whether or not you are trying to find the shops.

BRETONNE
1a Place des Brabançons
Tel: 010 451585

The only reasons to find the Crêperie Bretonne are if you are seconded to the university for a time or if you are a pathological seeker after fine ale in obscure places. In a part of town called the Biéreau quarter, this Wallonian crêperie serves over 150 different types of pancake, a range of home-made ice creams and milkshakes plus a selection of nearly 180 beers. Our best information is that it stays open all year, though things must go pretty quiet when the 12,000

students go home.
Opening hours 09.00 – 02.00

NIVELLES
Halfway between Brussels &
Charleroi off A7 (E19) [IC]
Historic market town (pop. 22,000)
which was bombed to bits in World
War Two. Its main square symbolises
the integration of church and state -
the town hall is built on to the
enormous Romanesque Church of
St. Gertrude. A few kilometres to the
west is the 1600 metre long sloping
canal lock of Ronquières, a marvel of
civil engineering which carries
shipping down an incline of 70
metres.

PODO
1 Avenue Albert & Elisabeth
Tel: 067 212168
Café: ✪✪ *Beer:* ✪✪✪
Opposite the Town Hall is Place
Albert 1er. From here follow Rue
Ste. Anne for 150 metres to find this
friendly but basic street-corner café.
The beer list of just under 100 ales is
its greatest claim to fame. Note that,
as at its sister café in Mons, they
have converted old Singer sewing
machines to become pub tables.
Monday to Thursday 11.00 –
01.00
Friday & Saturday 11.00 – 03.00
Sunday 18.00 – 01.00

RILLAAR
15 km N6 E of Leuven on N10
Small town on the Diest to Aarschot
road. The village of Scherpenheuvel,
6 km east along the N10 has an
impressive Baroque church and is a
place of pilgrimage.

SNOOKERTAVERNE†
375 Diestsesteenweg
Tel: 016 562312
All we know about this place is that
it is a "snooker palace" which stocks
around 100 beers. If you find out
more, please let us know.
Monday to Wednesday 13.00 –
01.00
Friday to Sunday 10.00 – 02.00
CLOSED THURSDAY

SCHEPDAAL
10 km W of Brussels off N8
Suburban town on the Gueuze
Route. The tram museum at 184
Ninoofsesteenweg is open on
Sundays and public holidays (Easter
to October) and Saturdays (July and
August), from 14.00 to 18.00.

RARE VOS
22 Marktplaats
Tel: 02 569 2086
Café: ✪✪✪✪ *Beer:* ✪✪✪✪
Schepdaal is not big enough to
warrant a Grote Markt so it has a
Marktplaats instead. This wonderful
old tavern could have been
transplanted from the Black Country,
the Potteries or Salford, circa 1935.
It has an excellent public bar at the
front and a number of rooms
without bars used mainly for dining.
The local bevy is draught lambic or
the unusual draught kriek lambic,
both said to be from De Neve. As
well as a range of steaks and mussels
- sometimes cooked in gueuze - the
menu includes stoovlees and dishes
featuring rabbit and pigeon. There
are also simpler dishes such as
cheese tarts and omelettes. The
culinary excellence is celebrated
with regular festivals of food which
tend to happen on the first weekend
of the month, featuring mussels
(November), sausages (October) or
local dishes (March).
Opening hours 10.00 – 24.00
CLOSED TUESDAY &
WEDNESDAY

TERALFENE
10 km SE of Aalst off A10 (E40)
Commuter village just off the
motorway.

LOANTON
103 Bellestraat
Tel: 053 663535
Fax: 053 673535
Café: ✪✪✪✪ *Beer:* ✪✪✪✪
Just of the E40 motorway at junction
19, 20 km west of Brussels, is the
village estate called Teralfene.
Signposted on the southern side of
the exit is this elegant tavern
restaurant, tucked away at the end of
an unpromising road. It was
purpose-built in 1978 to offer a

restaurant, piano bar and cocktail lounge, outside terrace and plainer drinking area. There is an intelligent list of 120 beers featuring all the abbey brews commissioned from the De Smedt brewery by the nearby abbey of Affligem. The wine list is above average, the food is excellent and given its location, it makes an ideal stopping off point.
Opening hours 11.30 – late
CLOSED WEDNESDAY & THURSDAY

TUBIZE
20 km SW of Brussels on N6
Small industrial town in the French speaking part of Brabant. Signposted Tubeke in Flemish.

ARRET DU TEMPS
133 Rue de Mons
Tel: 02 355 5059
Main road café 600 metres south of the town centre, on the road to Mons, opposite the Aral filling station. Bills itself as a beer café and claims to have over a hundred beers. Closing times are approximate.
Tuesday to Thursday 16.00 – 00.45
Friday & Saturday 16.00 – 03.00
Sunday 16.00 – 24.00
CLOSED MONDAY

VILVOORDE
5 km NNE of Brussels on N1
Suburban town on the way to Antwerp.

STRAND VAN VILVOORDE
136 Leuvensesteenweg
Tel: 02 252 0751
Ask for the Levi's factory and you find it is a paintworks, presumably the place where they make those denims that look as if they were painted on. The Beach is next door. A modern beer café with an outdoor terrace. It stocks over a hundred beers and runs a beer of the month. There are bar snacks. The jazz/blues/rock/Sixties music can be a bit intrusive.
Monday to Thursday 11.30 – 02.00
Friday 11.30 – late
Saturday 15.00 – late
CLOSED SUNDAY and CHRISTMAS WEEK

WATERLOO
15 km S of Brussels on N5
The Battle of Waterloo was the turning point in the career of Napoleon Bonaparte. The British think that they won it but in truth an international band of mercenaries, led by an Irishman, held out until the Prussians came to save the day. The battlefield, with the absurd Butte du Lion, erected by the French to thank Wellington for tonking them, is 10 km south of an otherwise dreary town.

BIVOUAC DE L'EMPEREUR
315 Route du Lion
Tel: 02 384 6740
Café: ✪✪✪✪ *Beer:* ✪✪✪
Opposite the Butte du Lion is the Emperor's Tent, a huge tavern restaurant able to cater to the coachloads which visit the site but managing to be enjoyable when empty too. As the name suggests, it is built on the site of Wellington's (!) headquarters in a converted farmhouse. It has about 40 beers including large bottles of Chimay and Napoleon of course. Food stretches to brochettes and charcuterie plus sandwiches and omelettes, with a fuller menu at lunchtime. The best of the group of cafés on or near the battlefield.
Opening hours 09.30 – late

PARIS
199 Brusselsesteenweg
Tel: 02 354 6418
By the time you reach the town end of the Waterloo tourist trail, you have crossed north of the language divide. The Paris is probably the best of the cafés on the workaday high street, worth visiting after clocking the various battle memorabilia found via tourist information. They have around 60 beers. A nice place to contemplate why it was that throughout the Battle of Waterloo, the Prussian leader, Marshall Blucher, was obsessed with the idea that he might be pregnant by an elephant.
Monday to Saturday 10.30 – late
Sunday 15.30 – late

East Flanders
including Ghent

EAST FLANDERS (Flemish: Oost-Vlanderen) lies between Brussels and the coastal provinces of West Flanders and Dutch Flanders in the north. Its eastern border stretches almost to the city of Antwerp and to the south west it borders with French-speaking Hainaut.

The north consists mainly of agricultural flatlands, while south of the provincial capital of Ghent is a hillier area, known as the Flemish Ardennes, which is becoming popular with ramblers. Its eastern strip, around the towns of Aalst, Sint Niklaas and Dendermonde is increasingly seen as the commuter belt for Brussels, Antwerp and Ghent.

Ghent is developing rapidly as a tourist haunt, enjoying as it does a central position on the Belgian motorway and train networks. Antwerp, Brussels and Bruges are an easy half-day trip from here and Liège and Namur can be visited comfortably within a day.

The ancient town of Oudenaarde has four breweries nearby – Cnudde, Contreras, Liefmans and Roman. This area is most closely associated with sour brown ales. The province as a whole now has a total of 19 breweries and is one of the centres of revival of artisan ale brewing, with companies like Huyghe and Van Steenberge enthusiasticly creating beer ranges of several dozen.

DENDERMONDE
12 km NNE of Aalst on N47 [IR]
Small market town (pop. 22,000). The beautiful Town Hall in the Grote Markt was originally 14th century but needed to be substantially rebuilt after a fire in 1914. Several other building in the square are 15th century and there are two Van Dycks in the Gothic Church of Our Lady.

PEREL
6 Franz Courtenstraat
Tel: 052 217389
Café: ✪✪✪✪ *Beer:* ✪✪✪
Dendermonde is a curiously disorganised town, just off the Ghent to Mechelen road. Fortunately it is blessed with plenty of display maps on its streets, which you will need to find the Law Courts, opposite which is the Stamenee De Perel. This slendidly simple brown café was named after the Perel brewery of Antwerp which used to own it and endowed it with a magnificent carved stone bar front. There are 75 beers on the list. Food is limited to variations on ham and cheese sandwiches but if you want to see just how far you can take this, try the raw gammon slice on bread. There is a piano. It often opens earlier - for example, 08.00 on Mondays.
Monday to Thursday 11.00 – 23.00
Friday to Sunday 11.00 – late
CLOSED FIRST TWO WEEKS MARCH and FIRST TWO WEEKS SEPTEMBER

DESTELBERGEN
8 km E of Ghent on N445
Small suburban town just outside the Ghent ring road, on the way to Antwerp.

SCHIPPERSHUIS
19 Scheldekant
Tel: 091 280349
Café: ✪✪✪✪ *Beer:* ✪✪✪✪
From the Bargee's House you can hear the Ghent ring road, see the towers of the city centre and smell the River Schelde, but still feel deep in the countryside. The N445 is Destelbergen high street and comes

off the R4 ring road near the junction with the A14 [E17] Antwerp motorway. Take Reinaertweg off the high street and at a café called 't Pauwken turn right into Scheldekant. Proceed with faith to find this excellent converted farmhouse, which has been an acclaimed beer house since 1960. There is a small terrace outside, while indoors is a larger room wrapped around a small bar, looking out over the fields, plus a small parlour behind the bar. They keep exactly 100 beers and have a helpful and informative list (in Flemish). Food is plentiful and ranges from pancakes and ice creams, Eurosnax and a hot dish of the day, to clever things done with salmon, prawns, seafood and brochettes. If you are staying in Ghent, the cycle path by the Schelde brings you here in 20 minutes on two wheels.

Monday 16.00 – late
Wednesday to Saturday 11.00 – late
Sunday 10.00 – late
CLOSED TUESDAY

ELENE
16 km SSE of Ghent off N42
Small town just north of Zottegem (below) near the train line from Ghent to Geraardsbergen.

OUDE BAREEL
1 Oudenaardsesteenweg
Tel: 091 600304
Postally in Balegem but physically on the N46 just outside Elene. A modern, well-managed, lounge-style roadhouse with a beer range of 60 and the usual accompaniments.
Opening hours 11.00 – late
CLOSED OCTOBER

EREMBODEGEM
3 km SE of Aalst off A10 (E40)
Just off the motorway on the outskirts of Aalst, in the commuter belt for Brussels.

EEKHOORN
155 Brusselbaan
Tel: 053 219857
This unadulterated beer café on the old main road from Brussels to Aalst is where the local beer experts hang out. They hold special tasting evenings. The lone Pils tap is the only concession to popular taste and the only non-liquid entertainments are conversation and the billiards table.
Saturday 16.00 – late
Other days 11.00 – late
CLOSED WEDNESDAY

GERAARDSBERGEN
20 km SSW of Aalst off N42 [IR]
Pleasant small town (pop. 18,000) in the southern Flanders countryside, near the language divide.
Overlooked by the Oudenberg or Old Mountain, a gentle hillock. Features a 14th-century town hall and an impressive Gothic church. The local delicacy is a type of pasty called a mattetaart.

SAF
13 Stationsplein
Tel: 054 412402
Café: ✪✪✪ *Beer:* ✪✪✪✪
You will find the Café Saf amid many other cafés in the square next to the railway station. It has a single, long thin room and an outside terrace. The relaxed and easy-going atmosphere is improved further by a wide range of around 180 beers, including eight on draught. The range of East Flanders brews is strong, as is the list of German imports. The kitchen operates throughout the opening hours and specialises in producing kebab-cooked meat and a wide variety of bar snacks with a good reputation for quality. In nearby Overboelare there is a farmhouse café called the **Ark van Noë** at 7 Kloosterstraat (tel: 054 411327), which is said to stock around 150 beers.
Wednesday 16.00 – 24.00
Other days 11.00 – 24.00
CLOSED TUESDAY and FIRST THREE WEEKS JULY

GHENT
Major town [IC]
Ghent (Flemish: Gent) in its heyday was one of the most powerful cities in Europe. Nowadays, it is the provincial capital and far and way the largest city (pop. 250,000) of East Flanders. Less organised than

Brussels, without the instant charm of Bruges and the spectacular cafés of Antwerp, Ghent is nonetheless becoming a popular weekend venue for tourists from throughout northern Europe.

It is not the sort of city you can do in a day or enjoy easily. Like Liverpool or Dublin, Prague or Boston, just assume it has an indefinable culture that will seep into your bones without ever being pinned down. Unfortunately, expensive beer is one phrase which comes to mind.

Its most annoying aspect is the lack of any town planning. The road and rail links seem designed for people who want to leave. Parking is a mess and routes to the city centre poorly signposted. The main railway station, St. Pieters, is a long way from the centre and tourist-friendly directions for public transport to the hotels and sights are all but absent. The nearest station to the centre is Dampoort but it lacks adequate facilities to leave bags, let alone be directed to a hotel.

The tourist centre is around Vrijdagmarkt, the largest open square in the town centre. The tourist information office is in Belfoortstraat, tucked away beyond the Belfry. Be sure to take time to wander around the Town Hall (Stadhuis) in Botermarkt, the Guildhouses in Koornmarkt, the Castle of 's Gravensteen and the brilliant Folklore Museum in Kraanlei. If you like Gothic architecture, take a week off and

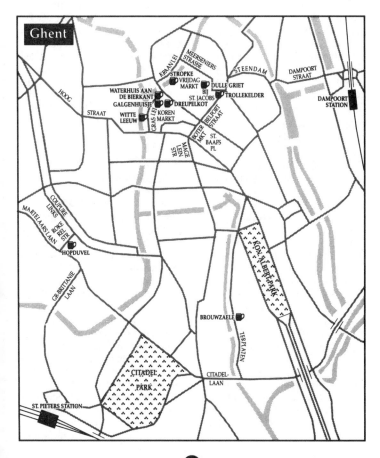

wallow. Ghent's magnificent Cathedral and treasure house of religious art is dedicated to St. Baaf.

BROUWZAELE
17 Ter Plaeten
Tel: 09 224 3392
Café: ✪✪✪✪ *Beer:* ✪✪✪✪

Opposite the Decascoop cinema, on a canal bank 500 metres from the city centre, vaguely on the way to St. Pieters station, which is the other side of the Festival Hall gardens. The Brewhouse features, like its sister café in Kortrijk, the lid of a copper brewing kettle above its bar. It also has the two cellars cooled to different temperatures. The beer list runs to just over 100 and includes some unusual brews like Brunehaut Blonde. The kitchen, open from 11.30 to 13.45 and 18.00 to 22.45, specialises in steaks, scampi and Gentse Stooverij, a beef stew cooked with Rodenbach, brown ale and scotch ale. If you are not that hungry, the bierwurst is excellent and the plate of cheese comes with Tierentyn mustard, the sort you wish they would sell in Sainsbury's. Try to put up with the Max Bygraves tapes in the background.
Opening hours 11.00 – 03.00

DREUPELKOT
10 Groentenmarkt
Tel: 09 224 2120
Café: ✪✪✪✪ *Beer: nil*

Alright, so this is a beer guide and there are no beers sold here. So what. Call it artistic licence. Next door to the Waterhuis (below) and owned by the same people, the Drinking Shack sells only genever and the drinks based upon it. A simple, single room café with candles and wood panelling. Like the Dreupelhuisje in Bruges it favours serving its 100 or so genevers at ice cold temperatures. Late closing here may mean 06.00 at weekends, depending on who is left to enjoy the dawn. There are small snacks only. Turning left out of its back entrance brings you to an unusual café called the **Gepoeierde'n Ezel** or Powdered Ass, which might suit you if you like baseball hats and Tom Waits.

Opening hours 16.00 – late

DULLE GRIET
50 Vrijdagmarkt
Tel: 09 224 2455
Café: ✪✪✪ *Beer:* ✪✪✪

Vrijdagmarkt is one of Ghent's larger squares at the northern end of the old town, near St. Jakobskerk. It used to be the city's centre of political activity. Ons Huis, the grand HQ of the Union of Socialist Workers was the last addition. De Dulle Griet is the Flemish name for Mad Meg, a 16-ton iron cannon seen on Grootkanonplein between the square and the Zuivel bridge. The café of the same name is a deep dark room with raised tables and a long bar. In summer they put tables on the square. Its main attraction ought to be a beer list of well over 200 choices but alas many are usually unavailable, hence the lowish rating. It is unlikely to win prizes for charming service either. Bar snacks are limited to cheese and ham sandwiches. There is a proper restaurant on the first floor, reached via the dizzying spiral staircase that also leads to the toilets but straight questions about opening times were not greeted with helpful answers.
Monday 16.30 – 01.00
Tuesday to Saturday 12.00 – 01.00
Sunday 15.00 – 01.00

GALGENHUISJE
12 Groentenmarkt
Café: ✪✪✪✪ *Beer:* ✪✪✪

The Little Gallows House would be a leading contender for "Smallest Pub in Europe" if it were not for the carefully concealed cellar restaurant, the Galgenkelder, which is the backbone of the business. You will find it on the opposite side of the road from the Dreupelkot (above) and the Waterhuis (below). The café dates from 1748 and has several storeys in its tiny frame, making the interior design exceptionally attractive. Its name comes from the days when the victim took a last drink here before being hanged near the canal. Nowadays the condemned man would have a choice of 70 beers, including many from Huyghe

and Van Steenberge. There is a reasonable range of snacks in the bar. Downstairs is good quality à la carte dining (12.00 to 14.15; 19.00 to 22.00). A side terrace opens in summer.
Opening hours 12.00 – 24.00
CLOSED MONDAY

HOPDUVEL
10 Rokerelstraat
Tel: 09 225 3729
Café: ✪✪✪✪ Beer: ✪✪✪✪

From painful memory we know the Hop Devil is a half-hour walk from the city centre. From St. Pieters station it is around 10 minutes down Koning Albertlaan to Groot Britannielaan, then left on to Martelaarslaan. Rokerelsstraat is the third street on the right. Although they are now separate companies, the café still enjoys close links with the warehouse of the same name, one block away on the river bank (see Beer Shops & Warehouses). Because of this, the range of beers is quite strong though the selection is now down to 120. This includes all the beers commissioned by the warehouse from Van Steenberge brewery. Stephen D'Arcy of CAMRA Brussels calls the café a Tardis, after Dr. Who's time machine which was far larger inside than it appeared from the outside. The many-roomed bar features a lot of old breweriana but the most attractive feature is the extraordinary covered garden at the back, the last thing you expect to find in a row of converted terraced houses in an old suburban street. The fish and meat grill restaurant on the first floor is increasingly popular and booking is wise (Wednesday to Sunday; 18.00 to 23.00). Between 12.00 and 14.00 snacks and bar meals are available in the pub.
Opening hours 11.00 – late

STROPKE
14 Meersenierstraat
Tel: 09 224 3600

Just off Vrigdagmarkt on the far corner from Dulle Griet (above), near the real Dulle Griet cannon. A pleasant, friendly, locals' pub in a street which has several, such as the **Tempelier** which appeared in our

last edition. The beer list of 80 has few surprises but must represent the best value in the city centre. The snacks, such as cannibaal and uitsmijter are good and there is damn fine coffee. An early closer, it may stay open later if there is sufficient trade. They have a copy of the beer list in Braille.
Opening hours 11.00 – 21.00
CLOSED SUNDAY

TROLLEKELDER
17 Bij St. Jacobs
Tel: 09 223 7696
Café: ✪✪✪✪ Beer: ✪✪✪✪

Bij St. Jacobs is the square surrounding St. Jacob's church, just off Vrijdagmarkt. Some of the buildings seem to be numbered at random. The Trolls Cellar is on the city side. Apart from the rather off-putting window display of Einsteinian doe-eyed plastic midgets, the troll connection is unclear. There are two storeys of wooden bar area, draped in hop garlands. The beer list reaches 140 and includes lambic-based brews from Hanssens and Cantillon plus real Westvleteren, all of which are rarities for Ghent. On the first floor is a cheese restaurant boasting 25 types of cheese, 50 wines and four types of bread. Be warned that they close for three weeks in summer, presumably for trolls' hols.
Monday to Saturday 11.00 – 01.00
Sunday 16.00 – 01.00

WATERHUIS AAN DE BIERKANT
9 Groentenmarkt
Tel: 09 225 0680
Café: ✪✪✪✪ Beer: ✪✪✪✪

The last of a cluster of excellent cafés in this part of the city centre. On the bank of the River Leie near 's Gravensteen castle. The name means the Beerside Waterhouse, so it's a joke you see, because actually it is a waterside beerhouse. Who said the Belgians are humourless. Apart from sitting on the terrace outside, you can also stare out over the water from the splendid candle-lit bar with its panoramic windows. Upstairs is the Ghent Puppet Theatre

(Poppentheater), which tends to play in the evening. They also own the Dreupelkot (above) and seem to have some business connection with the Brouwzaele (above). Food is limited to snacks but the spicy sausages are highly recommended. There are around 130 beers to choose from and the café has an ales-only policy - i.e. no lagers. The service is generally friendly, helpful and efficient. A good all-round café.
Opening hours 11.00 – 02.00

WITTE LEEUW
6 Graslei
Tel: 09 223 7983
Café: ✪✪✪ *Beer:* ✪✪✪

Graslei is on the bank of the Leie near the Groentenmarkt, opposite the Castle. It is Ghent's oldest street, bearing several Guild Houses. The White Lion was formerly a famous beer café called Oud Middelhuis. Inside it is now a smooth, wood and stone, ancient but modern tavern, claiming to offer around 100 beers and serving some pretty passable snacks. Outside, a pleasant terrace boasts an above average view of old Ghent. The shrimp croquettes are the house food speciality and bière Normande, a weird concoction of bitter orange, grenadine and old brown ale, is the beer speciality. Approach the latter with a sense of humour.
Opening hours 11.00 – 01.00

TRY ALSO: CAMRA Brussels' frequently updated guide to cafés in the capital often publishes lists of cafés in Ghent with some pretty straight advice about prices. For more details see Beer Organisations.

HUISE
20 km SSW of Ghent off N60
Attractive village just north of Oudenaarde, with an imposing parish church. A good rambling area, it is surprisingly well preserved for this part of Flanders.

GANS
40 Kloosterstraat
Tel: 055 317034
Café: ✪✪✪✪✪ *Beer:* ✪✪✪✪✪

On the outskirts of town in the direction of a village called Nazareth. There is a small cluster of cafés here serving the crossroads of a couple of long-distance footpaths. You could be excused for ignoring the Goose, as its exterior is pretty plain and it only opens at weekends. Indoors is a classic country pub, Belgian style. It is run by an affable and kindly couple, described by one informant as "ideally suited to the profession of pub landlord". Their range of ales is extraordinary, not just covering the usual high quality ales but also stocking many unusual, but rarely found brews, like Block 6 and Contreras Marzenbier, to take two at random. The owner still has a stock of a home-created cherry beer called Ganzenrik, made by adding whole cherries to a commercially available brew. The open log fire and scrub-top tables, unhurried and warm atmoshere and even the forgivable linoleum floors make this a splendidly memorable place. In the food line, they call themselves a pancake house, though the apple tart is recommended too. Sometimes they run barbecues outside. You can also play petanque (boules).
Friday 18.00 – 01.00
Saturday (Sep - Jun) 16.00 – 02.00
Saturday (Jul & Aug) 14.00 – 02.00
Sunday 10.30 – 13.00
15.00 – 23.00
CLOSED MONDAY TO THURSDAY and END JULY & EARLY AUGUST

LEBBEKE
10 km NE of Aalst on N47
Small town that is now nearly continuous with Dendermonde.

SCHUTTERSHOF
79 Dendermondsesteenweg
Tel: 052 220095
On the road from the centre of Lebbeke to the centre of Dendermonde, 800 metres from the main square, the Rifleman's is a pleasant café offering sizeable snacks such as spaghetti or lasagne, plus a range of around a hundred beers. The adventurous closing times

depend on the trade.
Sunday to Tuesday 18.00 – 03.00
Friday & Saturday 18.00 – 05.00
CLOSED WEDNESDAY &
THURSDAY; TWO WEEKS MID-
MARCH and MID-SEPTEMBER
TO MID-OCTOBER

LEDE

5 km NW of Aalst on N442 [IR]
Small town outside of Aalst, on the
slow line to Ghent. Holds carnivals
on the Sunday after Ash Wednesday
and the second Sunday after
Whitsun.

HOF TE PUTTENS
20 Wichselsestraat
Tel: 053 805130

One kilometre out of town on the
Wichelen road is this – wait for it –
art gallery, which happens to have
an up-market snack bar attached,
with a selection of 100 beers. The
exhibitions rotate on a monthly basis
and are no doubt better attended as
a result of the exhibits at the café,
though you should note that this is
another of those cafés which only
opens at weekends and public
holidays. Try the strawberries
steeped in trappist beer, home-made
ice creams, the cheese board with
nut bread and the wide range of
desserts. The range of genevers is
above average and they even stock a
selection of champagnes.
Friday 19.00 – 22.00
Saturday & Sunday 14.00 – 22.00
CLOSED MONDAY TO
THURSDAY

MULLEM

20 km SSW of Ghent off N60
Quiet village, just off the main road
from Ghent to Oudenaarde. On one
of the long-distance rambling routes
that draw tourists to this area.

KROON
15 Dorpsplein
Tel: 091 842820
Café: ✪✪✪✪ *Beer:* ✪✪✪✪

A lovely country pub set in the
village square of an isolated southern
Flanders community. The turning,
off the road which links Huise
(above) to the N60, is easily missed.
The Crown is a low-slung building

which would not be out of place in
rural Britain or Ireland. The front bar
is affable and attracts local farmers
and villagers. There are a couple of
small rooms to expand into if it gets
full and at the back a large, plain
dining room. Outside is a sun-trap
terrace, a lawn and a safe, enclosed
children's play area with slides and
swings and climbing frames. The
beer list just reaches 100 but nearly
rates five stars just on the strength of
its lambic-based brews, which
include Cantillon, Hanssens, Oud
Beersel and even old stocks of
Moriau, among others. The menu
stretches to imaginative large snacks
including special omelettes and
salads, as well as a daily stew in
winter and in summer, bacon and
chicory in cheese sauce.
Friday (Sep - Jun) 19.00 – late
Sunday 10.00 – late
Other days 16.00 – late
CLOSED MONDAY & TUESDAY;
WEDNESDAY & THURSDAY
(Sep - Jun) and
SECOND HALF SEPTEMBER

WANDELAAR
1 Mullemstraat
Café: ✪✪✪ *Beers:* ✪✪✪

In practically any other village in
Belgium, the Rambler would be a
real find. In Mullem it is the "try
also" option but worthy of a full
listing nonetheless. A large, imposing
building on the opposite side of the
small village square to **De Kroon**, it
stocks 60 beers and has a broader
menu of snacks and single plate
meals. Cooking finishes at midnight.
Like its neighbour, it has a safe,
enclosed garden area with facilities
for children.
Friday 19.00 – late
Sunday 10.30 – late
Other days 14.00 – late
CLOSED WEDNESDAY &
THURSDAY; and MONDAY &
TUESDAY (Sep - Jun)

RONSE

25 km WSW of Kortrijk on N48
Near the border with Hainaut, south
of Oudenaarde. A small textiles town
on the edge of the Flemish
Ardennes. It has an 11th century
church with a 47-bell carillon. There
are also museums of textiles and of

folklore. Its French name is Renaix.

BEER TEMPLE
12 Veemarkt
Tel: 055 215855
Café: ✪✪✪ *Beer:* ✪✪✪

Tucked away one block from the Grote Markt, opposite the fire station. Despite its English name, foreign beers are banned. Not as much of a temple as it once was. All but 70 of the beers have been sacrificed on the high altar of restauration. The menu is good quality and features a wide range of charcuterie as well as the house specialities, which are based around Aberdeen Angus beef. A plain layout leaves you with no doubt that this is an eating house but it is still alright to drop in for a beer or a coffee. The weekday lunchtime plat du jour comes in at BFr 200.

Tuesday to Thursday 11.00 – 23.00
Friday to Sunday 11.00 – late
CLOSED MONDAY

ST. LIEVENS ESSE
15 km SW of Aalst off N8
Picturesque small town or large village, as you wish.

TRAMSTATIE
30 Kauwstraat
Tel: 054 502104
Café: ✪✪✪ *Beer:* ✪✪✪✪

The Tram Station is an imposing brick-built roadhouse on the way to St. Antelinks. There are over 120 beers to enjoy in the high-ceilinged, L-shaped bar or out on the terrace. There are snacks to go with them. The town is home to the Van Den Bossche brewery, which can be seen in the main square.

Friday & Saturday 17.00 – late
Sunday 11.30 – late
CLOSED MONDAY TO THURSDAY

ST. LIEVENS HOUTEM
12 km WSW of Aalst off N42
Small town a few kilometres south of the E40 motorway, at the meeting point of three well-known long-distance footpaths.

GOUDEN LEEUW
56 Marktplein
Tel: 053 622594
Café: ✪✪✪ *Beer:* ✪✪✪

The Golden Lion is a cosmopolitan café next to the Pede beer warehouse on the market square in the centre of town. There is a small enclosed terrace on the street. Typical of the sort of town centre café which does not traditionally exist in Britain. Sells around eighty different beers including brews from De Ryck and Wieze. An early starter for the coffee and rolls trade. Market day is Saturday.

Opening hours 08.30 – late
CLOSED MONDAY

PIKARDIJN
6 Cotthem
Tel: 091 605128
Café: ✪✪✪✪✪ *Beer:* ✪✪✪✪✪

Only open at the weekend but no less wonderful for that. From the Grote Markt take the road signposted Zottegem. After 800 metres, just after leaving the town boundary, a lane called Cotthem branches left across the fields. 600 metres down this is a cluster of cafés of which the Picardian is the gem. A rural beerhouse with candles on the tables in the two cosy bar rooms. An array of breweriana includes a notice of sale for a modern brewery and lemonade manufacturer of St. Lievens Houtem, dated 10 weeks after D-Day. At the back is a covered terrace and out front are a terrace, garden and children's play area. The range of nearly 300 beers, including many 75 cl bottles, is possible because the owners also run the Pikardijn Bierwinkel in Zottegem (see Beer Shops & Warehouses). There is a variety of hot and cold snacks plus brochettes in various sauces. Well worth finding. The best rural pub we have discovered thus far in Belgium. They have been known to open on Wednesdays and Thursdays in high summer.

Friday 19.00 – 01.00
Saturday 16.00 – 02.00
Sunday 14.00 – 24.00
CLOSED MONDAY TO THURSDAY

ST. NIKLAAS

16 km WSW of Antwerp on N70 [IC]

The cultural and economic centre for the eastern part of the province (pop. 65,000). It is mainly a modern commercial centre but has some old buildings and the odd museum dotted around the market place.

SCHILDERSVERDRIET

13 Walburgstraat

Tel: 03 777 0019

The name means Saxifrage which, if you are none the wiser, is a genus of rock plant which includes London Pride. This variety is found in a side street off the Grote Markt. The beer list features nearly 80 choices. The music is to the fore, especially on Friday and Saturday nights, when the usual R&B or jazz give way to what our informants call "café dansant".

Opening hours 19.00 – 02.00
CLOSED MONDAY

ST. PAUWELS

20 km W of Antwerp on N403

Village on the main road from St. Niklaas to the Dutch border.

GROUWESTEEN

11 Grouwesteenstraat

Tel: 03 776 6606

This converted farmhouse is an essential port of call for lovers of the Belgian obsession with feeding the palate. On the beer side there are over 150 to choose from and the list includes some more unusual finds. If you drop in on the second Thursday of the month they have a beer tasting conducted by a brewer. The food options vary from full meals to light snacks, including indefinable single plate concoctions such as their legendary panneke spek, a sort of bacon and vegetable hash.

Friday to Sunday 11.30 – 02.00
Other days 11.30 – 24.00
CLOSED TUESDAY

WAASMUNSTER

25 km ENE of Ghent off A14 (E17)

Small town off the motorway, halfway between Ghent and Antwerp.

BELVEDERE

75 Fortenstraat

Tel: 052 461253

Café: ❍❍❍ *Beer:* ❍❍❍❍

In the middle of a popular walking and cycling area 2 km north of the town and south of the A14 [E17] motorway. From town, ask directions! From junction 13 of the motorway turn left off the Waasmunster road after 400 metres down Oude Heerweg-Heide, following signs to the Crystal Palace Hotel and Heidepark. Stick rigidly to this road for 2 km and you will reach the Belvedere. The beer list claims a range of 220 beers, with particular strength in abbey beers. There is also an unusually long wine list, a wide range of steaks, brochettes, satay, pancakes and ice creams. There is a tiny garden at the back and large terrace out the front. The front bar is dominated by an electric organ.

Opening hours 10.00 – late

WETTEREN

10 km ESE of Ghent on N400 [IR]

Almost a suburb of Ghent, on the banks of the Schelde.

RODE DRAAD

5 Kerkstraat

Tel: 091 696581

Café: ❍❍❍❍ *Beer:* ❍❍❍❍

The Red Thread is found 50 metres from the Grote Markt, which can be traced from a great distance thanks to the tower of the massive brick-built parish church. If arriving by train turn right out of the station and Kerkstraat is on your left. This is a thriving café billing itself as a "bierakadamie" and specialising in beers which have been aged in the cellar, as well as its standard list of 120 or so. They run regular beer tastings in the winter months.

Opening hours 09.30 – late
CLOSED MONDAY & TUESDAY

ZOTTEGEM

25 Km S of Ghent off N42 [IC]

Interesting market town in the rural southern part of East Flanders, boasting a splendid artisanal brewery. Known as the gateway to the Flemish Ardennes. The seat of the old Earls of Egmont, whose castle can be visited and whose name lives on in Crombé's strong pale ale. Worthy of a serious saunter.

BROUWERS HOF
8 Hospitaalstraat
Café: ❂❂❂❂ *Beer:* ❂❂❂
Next door to the Crombé brewery, just off the main market square, near the tourist information office. Small old brown café, laced with potted plants and unchanged for 60 years.

MUZE
4 Beisloven
Tel: 091 606904
Café: ❂❂❂❂ *Beer:* ❂❂❂❂❂
To find the Muse, head from the Markt down the rectangular boulevard-cum-car-park that bills itself as a square. Beyond it after 200 metres is the road left to Elene and Oudenaarde. The first domestic street on the left may look unpromising but houses this specialist beer café. Despite the urban setting, it boasts a beer garden, a large covered verandah, a play area for children and even a field for the horses. Indoors, a sprawling tiled lounge bar is broken up into discreet areas. The emphasis is heavily on the list of 250 beers, they run a beer club and sport an excellent collection of specialist glasses. A reasonable range of snacks is served throughout opening times and full meals in the evenings. They

close for a week or two towards the autumn.
Wednesday to Saturday 16.00 – late
Sunday 15.00 – late
CLOSED MONDAY & TUESDAY

ZWIJNAARDE
4 km S of Ghent off A10 (E40)
Satellite town, just to the south of Ghent.

ZWARTE FLES
1 Zandvoortstraat
Tel: 091 215335
Café: ❂❂❂❂ *Beer:* ❂❂❂❂
The Black Bottle is a splendid building with a striking facade. Inside is an attractive bar area broken up into alcoves. It is cleverly designed to use natural light on its terrace and in a winter garden. It often holds small exhibitions of paintings, and at times you can have your portrait drawn while you drink. The beer list is well over 150 and new beers are frequently tried out. The restaurant specialises in eels (cooked in twelve different ways); steaks, lamb cutlets and frogs legs also feature on its menu; open Wednesday to Sunday 12.00 to 14.00 and 19.00 to 23.00.
Tuesday 17.00 – late
Wednesday to Sunday 11.00 – late
CLOSED MONDAY and FIRST HALF SEPTEMBER

Hainaut

HAINAUT is a province with two sharply contrasting parts. The north is built around the coalfields of the Borinage area and the heavy industrial conurbation called the Centre. It accounted for the prosperity of Wallonia up until the collapse of European heavy industry in the 1960s and 70s. The south is virtually unpopulated in comparison and consists mainly of rolling countryside stretching towards France.

Most people visiting the north are there on business but this does not mean it is a dull place. A weekend based in Mons or Tournai with a side-trip to the other is worth considering if you are looking for Belgium without the tourists. Either makes a logical stop-over on the way from the channel ports to the Ardennes. Binche is worth a visit once a year.

In the deep south the landscape is gently rolling downs and forestry, especially around the tourist town of Chimay and its brewing Abbey of Scourmont, a few kilometres from the French border.

The greatest concentration of Wallonian breweries are in Hainaut (with 12). Dupont, producer of classic saison beers and Dubuisson, who make the epic Bush Beer are well established here but there are also excellent new breweries like Blaugies, Binchoise and Abbaye des Rocs, plus revived old companies like Silly, Friart and Vapeur.

BINCHE
16 km ESE of Mons on N90 & N55

A rather dull market town market which goes bananas once a year as it becomes the king of carnival, a tradition which has died out in Britain. The Mardi Gras celebrations on Shrove Tuesday run for 24 hours. The whole population takes to the streets costumed as all manner of unlikely characters with symbolic roles in the glorified street pageant. Severe quantities of ale are imbibed, which assist the surrealist imagery no end.

CHAMADE
44 Grand Place
Tel: 064 369898
Café: ✪✪✪ *Beer:* ✪✪✪
Smart lounge bar café on the main square with a sheltered terrace out front and a well-ordered, single, stripped brick and stone room inside. The beer list of 60 includes most of the better known Walloon beers and 75 cl bottles of ales from the Binchoise brewery. Food is limited to soup, Eurosnax and bacon & eggs (11.30 to 14.00; 17.00 to 22.30). Many of the cafés in the town bill themselves as the Locale des Gilles or Locale des Incorruptibles. This makes them the base for various participants in the carnival.
Opening hours 09.30 – late

CHARLEROI
Major town [IC]

The large industrial city (pop. 220,000) at the centre of the Centre. Old Charleroi was heavy industrial, new Charleroi houses the national exhibition hall. If you are here on business you will not have any problem finding decent restaurants and city bars. We have only been notified of one decent beer café.

BEAU LIEU
3 Rue du Commerce
Tel: 071 328969

The Beau Lieu, off Place Buisset, is a welcome retreat from the industrial shabbiness of this once thriving city. The house specialities are beer (of which there are well over 100 choices) and cheese. The proprietors will be pleased to suggest suitable combinations. At weekends the tone is raised further by a pianist.

Opening hours 11.00 – late

CHIMAY

45 km SSE of Mons on N99 & N53

Pleasant small market town giving its name to the beers brewed by the monks at Scourmont Abbey, eight kilometres south of here.

VIEUX CHIMAY

22 Grand Place
Tel: 060 212432
Café: ❂❂❂ *Beer:* ❂❂❂

Street corner café at the far end of Chimay's main square. There is a streetside terrace in summer. As well as being a typical tavern of the area, the Old Chimay doubles as the town's high class tobacconists and sells a large range of expensive Havana cigars. At the opposite end of the room is a pizza oven. The beer list runs to over 50 and the food menu is longer. The monastery beers are compulsory here. Try them with the town's own up-market brawn, Escavêche Chimacienne, or with something more solid like the fillets of sole or beef in a variety of sauces. Food is served from 12.00 to 15.00 and 18.30 to 22.00.

Opening hours 10.00 – late
CLOSED TUESDAY

MONS

Major town [IC]

The provincial capital (pop. 100,000), referred to as Bergen on Flemish roadsigns. A typically elegant Belgian town in an unlikely setting at the heart of the old Borinage coal-mining area. Unlike Charleroi, heavy industry has not destroyed the town's old cultural centre, much of which is pedestrianised. There are various impressive civic buildings and an appropriate collection of museums

and old churches. Hotels are thin on the ground. Note the Bootle Arms English Pub in Rue de Nimy.

ALAMBIC†

25 Place du Marché aux Herbes
Tel: 065 346007

First left off Rue de la Coupe (below) heading away from the Grand Place is a small square. Fifty metres down on the left is this single room café with a streetside terrace. We visited shortly before going to press and it was closed for major renovations. Prior to this it was a specialist beer café with 80 or more brews, including draught lambic, a rarity in these parts. They also used to offer a wide range of food. Fresh reports welcome.

Monday to Friday 11.00 – 02.00
Saturday & Sunday 15.00 – 02.00

EXCELSIOR

29 Grand Place
Café: ❂❂❂❂ *Beer:* ❂❂❂

The Grand Place in Mons is the town's hub of activity. There are around twenty cafés of varying styles and strengths. The Excelsior's niche is as the most elegant drinks café. On the corner of Rue des Clercs, it has a large terrace outside overlooking the square. Inside is a single long, brightly lit, wood-panelled room with parquet flooring and panoramic windows which open onto the square. The beer list features forty-five regulars and up to a dozen specials, which tend to come from artisan Wallooon breweries. Food is minimal. On Saturday and Sunday in high summer they open at 09.00. The other café on the square with an above average beer list is the **Novada**.

Monday to Friday 09.00 – late
Saturday & Sunday 11.00 – late

PODO

43 Rue de la Coupe
Tel: 065 347077
Café: ❂❂❂ *Beer:* ❂❂❂

Rue de la Coupe is a cobbled pedestrianised street which leaves Grand Place at the corner near the **Excelsior** (above). After 200 metres on the left is this simple, 1970-style café. Like its sister café in Nivelles (see Belgian Cafés: Brabant) it bills itself as Le Musée de la Bière, though the only pretensions of a display appear to be the range of games machines in the room up the stairs at the back. Ninety beers are on the list. Minor snacks only.

Monday to Friday 11.00 – 02.00
Saturday & Sunday 16.00 – 02.00

SCOURMONT

8 km S of Chimay (above)
The Abbey Notre Dame de Scourmont is marked on most road maps, 4 km south of the village of Bourlers, to which it belongs postally. Its grounds and some of its outbuildings may be visited but more tourists go for its beers, cheeses and Pinot aperitif, all of which can be sampled at the two nearby inns.

FERME DES QUATRE SAISONS

8b Rue de Scourmont
Tel: 060 214246
Café: ✪✪✪✪ *Beer:* ✪✪✪

The less obvious of Scourmont's two tavern restaurants is found on the opposite side of the Rue de Poteaupré from the abbey. It is a real brasserie in the French sense serving a broad menu including varieties of mussels, steaks and fish. The beer range nearly reaches 30 and includes all the abbey's regular and special edition beers. The main rooms are large saloons with a lay-out which encourages dining but allows just a drink. There is a large safe children's play area at the back. It is broadly similar to the larger and better known **Auberge de Poteaupré** (closed Monday) back on the main road from Bourlers, where the range of food and drink is slimmer. Both places have an off-sales shop sellig all the beers, glasses, cheeses, aperitifs and farm products which bear the Chimay brand.

Tuesday & Wednesday 11.00 – 17.00
Other days 11.00 – 22.00

SILLY

20 km N of Mons on N57 [IR]
Small town in which the Silly brewery takes pride of place. None of its cafés warrant a full entry here. However, three tied houses are worthy of a look if you are trying to find the beers of this excellent small brewery at their best. Right next to the brewery is the **Café de la Brasserie**, a typical small town café. Up the way, just past the church is **L'Tonne**, the most attractive café in town. In the other direction from the brewery, the road to nowhere takes you past the **Salon de Musique**, a larger, plainer café with an English landlady.

TOURNAI

Major town [IC]
Pleasant town (pop. 70,000) on the banks of the river the French call l'Escaut and the Flemish call the Schelde. To call its Cathedral striking is an understatement. Inside and out it is arguably the grandest in Belgium. Parts date from the 12th century but major reconstructions occurred at regular intervals until 100 years ago. Its many towers dominate the town by day and on cloudy nights the powerful white floodlights used to illuminate its frontage cast an eerie shadow over the town.

CAVE A BIERES

3a Quai Taille Pierres
Tel: 069 212945
Café: ✪✪✪ *Beer:* ✪✪✪✪

In the old cask stores by the banks of the Schelde, on the town side of the tiny pedestrian bridge, downstream from the Pont à Pont. The beer selection of seventy is well-chosen with a suitably Wallonian selection of saison beers from Pipaix, à Vapeur, Dupont and others. Many of the southern beers come in 75 cl bottles for sharing. If you are at a loss as to what to choose, try Dupont's Vieille Provision Saison, rarely found outside its local area but one of the classic Walloon beers. Simple snacks include soupe a l'oignon and quiche. The fuller menu stretches to steaks and a weekend special, such as a cassoulet. Hot food is served between 18.00 and 23.00.

Opening hours 17.00 – late
CLOSED MONDAY & TUESDAY

Liège

THE FRENCH-SPEAKING province of Liège streches from the German border in the west to the Brabant plain in the east. In the north it almost reaches Maastricht in the Netherlands. Its southern border with Luxembourg province covers much of the northern Ardennes and the Hautes Fagnes (high fen) which includes Belgium's highest point above sea level.

The industrial north around the city of Liège has seen better days. Like other parts of Wallonia it was hit badly by the recession. The south is beginning to develop, quite rightly, as a tourist area.

There is a small German-speaking district in the east around Eupen. South of here are nature reserves where excellent long-distance footpaths cross the wild countryside. Where this meets the woodlands of the northern Ardennes there are some beautiful valleys offering first rate accommodation in hotels and pensions.

Apart from the anachronistic presence of the German bierbrauerei in Eupen, the province's only other established brewery is the Interbrew plant at Jupille-sur-Meuse. The presence of a major beer distributor, Sous-Bock & Co, at Vottem near Liège, livens the beer scene.

AVENNES

20 km W of Liège off N69
Long-established rural community on one of the recommended drives through beautiful southern Belgium, called the Route des Blès d'Or.

FONTAINE GAULOISE

7 Rue de la Fontaine
Tel: 019 699938

Delightful, creeper-clad village inn with an attractive enclosed garden. 200 metres out of the village in the direction signposted Moxhe. Interestingly, it advertises itself as a café which is "free from breweries". It stocks over 90 beers – many from small artisan breweries. It also offers 15 varieties of fruit wine and regional cuisine. Note that it is another of those weekend cafés. The owner describes its background music as anything decent from the 11th to the 21st centuries!
Friday & Saturday 20.00 – late
Sunday 15.30 – late
CLOSED MONDAY TO THURSDAY and AUGUST

EUPEN

15 km ENE of Verviers on N67 & N68 [IC]
Eupen is the principle town at the heart of the small German-speaking district of eastern Liège which was part of Germany until after the Treaty of Versailles in 1921. The main street is a splendid confusion of German, French and Flemish road signs, interspersed with an array of shops and restaurants which seem deliberately to offer the national goods and cuisine of a dozen other countries. Within easy distance of the German and Dutch frontiers.

BOSTEN

2 Rue de Verviers
Tel: 087 742209
Café: ✪✪✪✪ *Beer:* ✪✪

This small-town hotel is typically German, with its large saloon bar, partially used restaurant and good value, high quality accommodation. It may well be the only café in town not to serve the beers of the Eupener brewery, Belgium's only German-style bierbrauerei, found 100 metres down the high street.

The beer list is pedestrian by the standards elsewhere in this guide but sampling the full strength imported Guinness from a pewter tankard while listening to Connie Francis singing "If you wish upon a star" and savouring what was said to be jugged hare and dumplings, left a lasting impression! If you do wander out, there is a wide variety of cafés, almost all of which sell Eupen's own Pils and one or two of which also stock the Klosterbock.
Opening hours 08.30 – 22.00

HUY
Halfway between Namur & Liège on N90 [IC]

A pleasant town (pop. 18,000) on the banks of the Meuse, which has seen better days. The main area of tourist interest is the Old Town around the Grand Place. The Church of Notre Dame is an excellent example of High Gothic, the Town Hall is Louis XV. The citadel above the town was blasted out of the rock in the early 19th century. The quickest and most impressive way to see the town is from high above in the cable car from the banks of the Meuse, across the Citadel to the hamlet of La Sarte, a distance of 3.5 km.

BIG BEN
8 Grand Place
Tel: 085 231583
Café: ✪✪ *Beer:* ✪✪✪

Who remembers Watneys Red Barrel? The British brewing industry's answer to Lucozade and the natural accompaniment to flock wallpaper and leatherette seating. Well, here it is. Get off your Vespa Scooter, buy the bird a Snowball wiv a cherry, light up a Woodbine, order your pint of Red and unwind to the sounds of Radio Luxembourg. Well not quite, but the standards of service and presentation are pretty reminiscent of England in the Sixties. The Belgian bits are the omelettes and assiettes (served from 12.00 to 14.00 and 18.00 to 21.00), the list of eighty beers, the attempts at beer-based cocktails and the unfamiliar brand called Watneys Scotch. Not from Brick Lane, Whitechapel,

surely?
Opening hours 10.00 – late

LIEGE
Major town [IC]

The third largest city in Belgium (pop. 440,000) and the provincial capital, Liège has always been synonymous with heavy industry and as such has suffered a decline in recent years. The only good news is that none of the elderly factories looked as if they were friendly to the environment in their heyday. The rusting blast furnaces loom over the River Meuse like Victorian wardrobes with broken hinges.

The city centre has its share of museums and churches but is rather like the mixed late Victorian and postwar centres of British industrial cities. Escape can be found in the parks around the Albert I bridge or in the extraordinary beer cafés which have a tendency never, literally never, to close. The road system is hopelessly chaotic.

At the main railway station, Gare des Guillemins, they seem to have bought a second-hand public announcement system as part of the pickings from the old Soviet Union. It is used to play warped 78s of Richard Clayderman's greatest hits. Enjoy.

FUT
1 Rue Louvrex
Tel: 041 223310
Café: ✪✪✪✪ *Beer:* ✪✪✪✪✪

Coming out of the Gare des Guillemins, the main station, look for Rue des Guillemins on the opposite side of the road. First left is Rue Dartois, which becomes Rue Louvrex. At the far end on the corner of Rue St. Gilles is Au Fût. A friendly, cosy, even cramped, street corner café, it manages to stock nearly 400 beers, which are listed and described on a meticulously compiled beer menu they keep behind the bar. They also sell beer cocktails, such as Super Stout (export Guinness with the yolk of an egg), Romeo & Juliet (Duvel with Gouden Carolus and ruby port). Merveilleuse de Rochefort (Rochefort 10° with genever) might perhaps more aptly be christened Catastrophe de Liège. Food is limited to soups, small snacks, chips and cannibale toast.

Monday to Friday 13.00 – 04.00
Saturday & Sunday 11.00 – 04.00

PIERRE LEVEE
62 Rue de Serbie
Tel: 041 523560

Taking Rue des Guillemins from the station (as above), the first right turn is Rue Sohet. Rue de Serbie is first right again. La Pierre Levée is an ancient cellar café, popular with students, which bills itself as a private club. Relative sobriety and a copy of the Guide should ensure immediate overseas membership. They claim to stock 600 beers but we are sceptical. Our information on opening hours is conflicting. They may open at 09.00 some days.

Monday to Friday 19.00 – late
Saturday 20.00 – late
CLOSED SUNDAY

VAUDREE II
49 Rue St. Gilles
Tel: 041 231880
Café: ❍❍❍ *Beer:* ❍❍❍❍❍

Rue St. Gilles is the extension out of the old town of Rue de la Cathédrale. Alternatively, if you are coming from Gare des Guillemins, follow directions to Au Fût (above) and turn right. Le Vaudrée II is ten metres down on the same side. It is the sister café to the original of the same name in the suburb of Angleur (below). It is a modern long-bar, designed with exactly the same beer list of 1022 beers, 40 on draught. Some are supposed to be very old and appear on a list of extinct beers. Others are just old. At busy times, poor service has been encountered but other staff go out of their way to be helpful and seem to enjoy piling into the maze of shelves which act as the cellar. Among the nine British beers on the list is Greene King's St Edmund Ale, never knowingly exported by the company. Surprisingly it is the menu, which includes steaks, couscous, fast food, Eurosnax, cuisine à la bière (provided you're not hungry try the grenouille in cream Rodenbach sauce), salads and dishes of the

maison, which seems to attract many customers. The food and the beers are available 24 hours a day, all year.

Open all day, every day

LIEGE (ANGLEUR)
South eastern inner suburb [IR]
On the way out towards Chaudefontaine and the south. The easiest way to get here is to peruse the timetables in the Gare des Guillemins and see which trains stop off at Angleur station.

VAUDREE
109 Rue Val Benoit
Tel: 041 671061
Café: ❍❍❍❍ *Beer:* ❍❍❍❍

For those who are used to pub crawls around the duller Edwardian suburbs of Salford or Sheffield, the location of the original Vaudrée will come as no surprise. If you want the quick-in-and-out route, take the train to Angleur station and leave by the back door beyond platform six. Turning right, Le Vaudrée is 200 metres on your left. Honestly. There are the same 1022 beers as at its sister café in central Liège (above) and the menu is identical too. About 20 per cent of the beers may not be in stock and when the more obscure are, they will not necessarily be all that fresh. In fact they might remind you of that mummified sweet sherry you had to endure at Auntie Betty's all those years ago before anyone thought you were old enough for beer. Again, service may be extremely slow at busy times. The most upsetting thing can be watching the local medallion men drinking Corona (you remember, that lemonade that is now a beer) with a slice of lime, straight from the bottle like real beer drinkers do. Don't assume the staff know how to pour a beer, either; but it is open 24 hours a day, every day, and it is extraordinary.

Open all day, every day

SERAING
9km SSW of Liège on N90
Industrial town that is now part of greater Liège, straddling the road out to Dinant and Marche-en-Famenne on the opposite bank to Jemeppe.

CAVES A BIERES
Place Kuborn
Tel: 041 379484
Café: ✪✪✪✪ *Beer:* ✪✪✪✪
On the south bank of the Meuse,
near the end of the Pont de Seraing.
From Liège you can catch bus no. 2
or 3 from Place General Leman, 300
metres from the Gare des
Guillemins. Do not take the buses
from outside the station, which
simply give you a guided tour of
recession-hit hell. The Caves à Bières
is a typical bright and cheerful, well-
managed, airy, street-corner café-
restaurant. It is open from nine in
the morning until well past
midnight. Its sister café next door,
Le Cockerill, is the one that stays
open all night. The food in both is
the usual excellent Wallonian fare,
ranging from snacks to four course
meals. The beer list at Les Caves is
around 140, with 100 from Belgium.
Open all day, every day

SPA
10 km S of Verviers on N62
The name of this small valley town
has entered the English language as
the description of a source of
mineral waters. In Spa's heyday, 200
years ago, the crowned heads of
Europe came hear to drink, bathe
and tend their ills and it gained a
reputation as a sort of aristocratic
Lourdes. Nowadays the tourists who
frequent the baths and casino come
in VW Beetles or on bicycles but
some of the elegance remains.

SANGLIER
2 Place Pierre Le Grand
Tel: 087 877987
Café: ✪✪✪ *Beer:* ✪✪
The best beer café we could find is
in the small square, 100 metres
towards Malmédy from the baths, on
the opposite side of the street. It is
reminiscent of the tavern-tea-rooms
of Flanders. A large multi-purpose
café offering around 40 beers and a
full range of snacks and meals. Like
many towns in the area, Spa has a
"local" beer brewed by a faraway
brewery. In this case it is Bobelier,
an 8.5% abv amber ale from the
Huyghe brewery near Ghent.

STAVELOT
25km SSE of Verviers on N68
Well preserved hillside town
(population 7,000), a few kilometres
from the Grand Prix racing track at
Francorchamps. The cobbled streets
and ancient buildings reflect its
glorious era prior to the French
Revolution, when the Benedictine
Abbey of Malmédy and Stavelot,
founded by St. Remachus, held great
influence. There are one or two
excellent old hotels and several
restaurants. Its most famous event is
the three-day carnival held on the
third weekend before Easter, in
which hundreds of inhabitants dress
in the haunting white capes and
phallic masks of the pot-bellied
Blancs Moussis and act out ancient
folkloric traditions. The most
unusual sight during the rest of the
year is probably the 5 km of Formula
One track and main grandstands,
which are part of the public road
system.

VIEILLES CAVES D'ARTOIS
7 Avenue Ferdinand Nicolay
Tel: 080 862017
Café: ✪✪✪ *Beer:* ✪✪✪✪
A real find for this part of the
northern Ardennes. A specialist beer
café and regional restaurant run by a
pleasant couple. Monsieur tends the
beer cellar and offers 150 choices of
Belgian ale from north and south but
clearly appreciates it if you prefer to
drink the Ardennaise specialities
from Achouffe, Maire and Gigi.
Madame oversees the restaurant and
offers omelettes, assiettes of cold
meats and other snacks throughout
the day, and a selection of
wholesome Ardennaise cooking
from 12.00 to 13.30 and 19.00 to
21.00. Rabbit, guinea fowl and trout
appear in a variety of sauces
alongside brochettes and other
favourites. The house specialities are
the duck breast with shallots and
trout in anise. A lovely café run by
lovely people.
Opening hours 11.00 – late

VYLE-ET-THAROUL

8 km S of Huy off N641

Straggling settlement just off the road from Huy which is known as the Route Jolie vers l'Ardennes – literally, the Pretty Route to the Ardennes.

MERVEILLE DE VYLE

61 Grand Route

Tel: 085 412032

The route would be prettier if it were not for the display of concrete telegraph poles and electricity pylons. 400 metres off the main road is this slightly battered roadside café with its list of over a hundred beers and selection of regional cuisine. There is a covered verandah area out front.

Opening hours 11.00 – 24.00
CLOSED SEPTEMBER

XHOFFRAIX

20 km SE of Verviers off N68

Village in the Hautes Fagnes, a few kilometres from the Signal de Botrange tower, the highest point in Belgium, 694 metres above sea level.

MOULIN DE BAYHON†

13 Long Faye

Tel: 080 330308

Long Faye is a smattering of houses on the winding back road between the villages of Xhoffraix and Ovifat. The Moulin de Bayhon is 150 metres down a track off this road on a heavily wooded hillside. One of the many long distance footpaths which criss-cross this part of the country runs past its front door. You do not have to arrive on foot. It is signposted from the road and they have a small car park next to the chicken run. It is said that this is a family-run auberge-style small hotel with a range of over 200 beers but our efforts to check out either claim have been frustrated. We have got as far as the locked front door on a couple of occasions. Reports please.

CLOSED SECOND HALF JUNE

St Arnold, Patron Saint of Belgian brewers

Limburg

THE BELGIAN BIT of Limburg is not the most interesting part of the country. Traditionally a poor agricultural area with a few mineral deposits, it is only recently that the tourist authorities have been able to come up with reasons to go there. It is the new green province.

It may well become a place of outstanding natural beauty thanks to some terribly sensible initiatives which involve balancing the forestry planted over the last century with the preserved areas of Kempen and Geest. There have also been agricultural developments and one or two exceptional investments in tourism.

It was traditionally a great brewing area like its Dutch counterpart but over the years takeovers rationalised production down to the two big family concerns, Martens and St. Jozef, plus the acquisitive and huge Alken brewery. More recently a couple of new boys have arrived.

HASSELT
Major town [IC]

The provincial capital (pop. 65,000) lies south of the Limburg coalfield and north of the fertile plain. It is home to Smets, the largest genever distillery in Belgium anmd the National Genever Museum (see Beer Tourism: Museums). Five km north west, off the old road to Genk, is one of the bravest tourist investments in the country. The Bokrijk estate consists of 1,400 acres of heathland and woods, in which dozens of lakes have been created, an open-air museum of traditional style buildings has been constructed, the 18th century Manor House has been opened to the public and a Museum of Natural History created. It has good facilities for children.

HEMELRIJK
11 Hemelrijk
Tel: 011 222851

Next to St. Quintus Cathedral in the centre of town. As well as the range of 140 beers, there are over 50 Scotch whiskies. Snacks come big and small from a long list.
Monday to Friday 11.30 – late
Saturday 13.30 – late
Sunday 19.30 – late
CLOSED FIRST HALF JULY

PAAL
18 km NW of Hasselt off A13 (E313)

Small town just off the motorway.

PAALHOF
62 Dalenbergstraat
Tel: 011 428819

You will find this tavern restaurant on the outskirts of town, near the main Antwerp-Hasselt motorway. Its array of beers stretches to 120 choices and they have a menu of snacks and more substantial meals which seems almost to match this. If you are lucky you may catch one of the beer promotion evenings. There is plenty of space inside or on the restaurant terrace.
Wednesday to Friday 18.00 – late (15.00 Apr - Oct)
Saturday 15.00 – late
Sunday 12.00 – late
CLOSED MONDAY & TUESDAY; and SEPTEMBER

ST. TRUIDEN
15 km SW of Hasselt on N3 & N80 [IC]

Interesting market town on the old road from Leuven to Liège. It has numerous small museums and attractive churches. The strangest sight is Festraets Studio at 24 Begijnhof, the display of the world's largest atomic clock and the rest of the life's works of a local physicist.

EGLANTIER
21 Stationstraat
Tel: 011 686029
Conveniently situated between the railway station and the Grote Markt. A temple to the service of Belgian beers. Around 80 are on offer. A beer café with an outside terrace.
Tuesday to Saturday 11.00 – late
Sunday 15.00 – late
CLOSED MONDAY,
CHRISTMAS TO NEW YEAR
and SECOND HALF JULY

TESSENDERLO
20 km NW of Hasselt off A13 [E313]
Small town near the borders with Antwerp and Brabant provinces. Eight km south west is the picturesque Abbey of Averbode, founded in the 12th century, with a famous Baroque church.

EIKELHOF
54 Eikelplein
The Oak Tree House is found in part of the town called Hulst, several hundred metres off the centre, an unusual location for a specialist beer house stocking over 150 different beers. However, the keenness of the owner and his more dedicated customers has put it firmly on the Belgian beer map. Eikelplein is Hulst's main square and the café has a terrace outside for summer. They also have snooker tables.
Opening hours 11.00 – 02.00
CLOSED TUESDAY and JULY

TONGEREN
20 km NNW of Liège on N79 & N20 [IR]
Limburg's best known historic town may be quite small (pop. 30,000) but makes up by being genuinely

ancient. It was founded by Julius Caesar in 57 BC, became a fortress in the 2nd Century and was the seat of a Bishop by the 4th Century. It bills itself as the oldest town in Belgium and, as if to prove the claim, has been razed to the ground on a number of occasions, most recently by Louis XIV of France in 1677. The most important historical sites are the oldest. About a third of the original Roman town walls survive. The best of the smaller finds are preserved in the Gallo-Roman Museum.

TWEE ENGELEN
8 Wijngaardstraat
Tel: 012 237981
Wijngaardstraat runs off the Grote Markt in the centre of town behind the Basilica. The Two Angels is a traditional beer house. It can offer up to three hundred different bottled beers and tries to go out of its way to find unusual draught beers.
Opening hours 17.00 – 02.00
CLOSED MONDAY

ZEPPEREN
15 km SSW of Hasselt off N79 & N80
Small village on the outskirts of St. Truiden.

HASPENGOUW
8 Kerkplein
Old tavern, opposite the church in the village square. Dates from 1740. Good bar snacks and a range of around 130 beers. Keeps a selection of aged beers too.
Sunday and Bank Holidays 15.00 – late
Other days 16.00 – late
CLOSED WEDNESDAY,
CHRISTMAS TO NEW YEAR
and SECOND HALF JULY

Luxembourg

LUXEMBOURG province is one of the least densely populated and most densely beautiful parts of Belgium or the Netherlands, thanks largely in both cases to the forests and valleys of the Ardennes.

The region's recent history is not all sweetness and light. In 1944 the Battle of the Bulge fought in the south of the province was the last German offensive of World War Two. Losses were high on both sides as can be attested by the memorials near Bastogne. Many American tanks remain scattered throughout the area as a reminder of the Ardennes campaign.

Unfortunately for the beer tourist, the ale tradition is poor in this part of Belgium, though things are changing. They would improve a lot more if the Wallonian breweries could be better organised in marketing their distinctive products to interested cafés and wholesalers. There is a fashion in the province for towns to commission the labelling of a pair of ales, one blonde and one brown, as a communal "own brew". Ironically many of these come from Flemish breweries.

Lagers from across the border in the Duchy of Luxembourg appear frequently. Three of the province's six breweries were created in the 1980s, including the hugely successful Achouffe. Of the others, the most famous is the trappist brewery, Orval.

The absence of any organisation of beer lovers in the province makes surveying local cafés very difficult, so if you come across interesting cafés on your travels which we have missed, please let us know.

ACHOUFFE
15 km N of Bastogne off A26 (E25)

Tiny village out in the boondocks of northern Luxembourg, boasting a remarkable farmhouse-style brewery, this small café-restaurant and little else.

GRANGE
Route du Village
Tel: 061 288601

This large, comfortable, high-ceilinged pub-cum-restaurant is very obviously a converted barn. An attractive place, it has its own small fishing lake at the back. It is situated 100 metres down the road from the village's famous brewery and perhaps not surprisingly sells mainly Achouffe beers. Its food has a good reputation. The brewery itself has a rather tatty sampling café in a warehouse-type building at the back, which is open most days in summer and at weekends throughout the year. Brewery tours can be arranged with little difficulty.

ARLON
25 km WNW of Luxembourg on N4

The capital of Luxembourg province. A typical market town (pop. 23,000) with an American World War Two tank in its main square and the Musée Luxembourgeois, which houses some Roman remains from the area. [Editor's note: my own visit to Arlon was cut short by an encounter with la patronne of what appeared to be the only reasonable hotel in town, who refused to allow our three-month-old daughter to sleep in her own cot in our room unless we paid

BFr 1,200 surcharge per night. The only other hotel we found wanted money up front without allowing us to see the room. Is it any surprise that tourism here is at a low ebb?]

ALBY
Grand Place
Café: ❶❷❸ *Beer:* ❶❷

Many of Arlon's cafés offer 20 or so beers but only one appears to offer a larger list. The Alby is a street-corner café just off the old market square, 100 metres from the main square. Lots of light and a modern exterior. The beer list stretches to 40, mainly "standard" artisan ales. No food beyond light snacks is in evidence. More information on Arlon will be welcomed.

BOUILLON
On the far SW border with France, off N89 (E46)

Pleasant small town (population 6,000) on a loop of the River Semois. Dominated by an impressively complete 11th century castle built by the crusader, Godefroy de Bouillon. A good base from which to tour the southern Ardennes.

ROY DE LA BIERE
34 Quai des Remparts
Café: ❶❷ *Beer:* ❶❷❸

A beer house and mussels café on the avenue between the river and the castle on the opposite side to the main part of the town. It is gently moving up-market from the days when it was the hang-out of local "yoof". The beer list of 60 includes brews frim Achouffe and Westmalle. The café is still pretty basic but the restaurant side of the business seems to be doing reasonably.

VIEILLE ARDENNE
9 Grand Rue
Tel: 061 466277
Café: ❶❷❸ *Beer:* ❶❷❸❹

Pleasant, chatty, street-corner café on the castle side of the river, 50 metres from the Pont de Liège. Stocks sixty beers including some from Rochefort, Achouffe and, unusually for this area, Frank Boon. They also sell Belgian cider. The regular menu of bar snacks includes omelettes, assiettes of ham,

sandwiches and speciality ice creams. There is also a fuller restaurant menu at lunchtime and in the evenings featuring fish and game. We asked the landlord when he closed and the rough translation of his reply was "When I'm knackered!"
Opening hours 10.00 – late
CLOSED WEDNESDAY

DURBUY
15 km NNE of Marche-en-Famenne off N86

"The smallest town in the world" (population 400) on the banks of the Ourthe. Packed with small hotels and restaurants. A good touring base for the Ourthe Valley and a pleasant place to boot. La Durbuyse, brown and blonde versions of which are available in just about every café in town, is brewed by Lefèbvre and is remarkably similar to the weaker Floreffe beers.

FERME AU CHENE
115 Rue Comte d'Ursel
Tel: 086 211067
Café: ❶❷❸ *Beer:* ❶❷❸

This modern, airy café and home brew house is practically the first building in Durbuy as you enter from the main road. The Oak Tree Farm brewery is on show in the building next door. It is undoubtedly the smallest in Belgium. On show is the brew kettle they used to produce the first batch of the house beer Marckloff. This historic vessel also held the first vat of Fantôme at the nearby Prignon brewery in Soy and before that the first brews of the Achouffe brewery. Marckloff is available on draught, and a dozen other beers including Fantome are available by the bottle. Marckloff is available for takeaway, as is a locally distilled 40° liqueur. The snack menu includes assiettes of ham and cheese, omelettes and crêpes, a local tarte and the Ardennaise speciality, pommes aux lards. There is a terrace at the back overlooking the river. Opening times are approximate.
Opening hours 12.00 – 20.00
CLOSED WEDNESDAY and FIRST HALF JULY

FLORENVILLE
32 km W of Arlon on N83, N85 and N88

Attractive, small tourist town on the plain above the Semois Valley. The view from its church tower is worth the climb. Beer tourists here are probably on their way to the brewing abbey of Orval, 8 km to the south.

QWARE
1 Rue d'Arlon

No, the name is not a misprint, it is Wallonian and so is the owner, Monsieur Frognet-Sindic. A friendly little café on the main road through the town. Although there are only 37 beers on the list these include Orval, Hotteuse Grand Cru from Roman brewery, the Gaumaise beers from Gigi and a Rochefort brew.

LA ROCHE-EN-ARDENNE
30 km NNW of Bastogne on N89

Small town on the banks of the River Ourthe in the north of the province. Five minor roads converge here at the heart of the Belgian Ardennes. Fierce fighting raged around the town during the Battle of the Ardennes in 1944, commemorated by a museum and the occasional defunct American tank. There are other minor tourist sites in the locality.

VENITIEN
30 Rue de l'Eglise
Café: ❍❍❍ Beer: ❍❍❍

Walking away from the river, The Venetian is 100 metres further down the high street beyond the last entry. Slightly up-market, with superior lighting and a less regimented layout, it too stocks a decent range of

snacks and a selection of around 30 beers, including St Benoit, La Gauloise and six trappist brews. **La Taverne** on the main square has also been recommended.

ST. HUBERT
28 km W of Bastogne off N89 (E46)

Pleasant, friendly little market town just off the majestic but deserted N89 Ardennes highway. The most famous sight is the Gothic Basilica, the church of the ancient abbey of St. Hubert. Its hotels offer adequate, low price accommodation and there are one or two excellent delicatessens and restaurants too. The town has its own beer, Cuvée de Borq on sale in a number of cafés and off-licences; this was originally brewed by the Maire brewery, which was taken over and closed by Gigi in 1991. According to OBP it now comes from Du Bocq and is based on St Benoit Blonde.

SPORTS
25 Place du Marché
Tel: 061 613304
Café: ❍❍ Beer: ❍❍❍

Typical modern street café with a small terrace outside. Gives the impression that the owner likes special beers but does not want to promote these heavily to his (generally) young customers. The beer list is around 40 but includes beers from Chimay, Rochefort, Orval, Westmalle, La Trappe and St Bernardus, as well as the Cuvée de Borq (above). It has an electronic dartboard and pool tables. The only food is small snacks. Deserves encouragement.
Opening hours 10.00 – late

Namur

NAMUR APPEARS TO BE the most prosperous of the French-speaking provinces of Belgium. Its provincial capital has not been too worried by the recession, presumably because heavy industry has little part to play around here.

Tourism is important in the area thanks to the attractions of the upper Meuse Valley that dissects the province. Despite this, it is surprisingly difficult to find pleasure boats for hire on the Meuse; the river is still used quite extensively for industrial traffic.

Although the town itself has few hotels, Dinant is always seen as the centre of the province's tourist industry. The train line, running parallel to the river, has the advantage of stopping near several of our listed cafés as well as allowing you to see something of the region. In the far south, the countryside merges with the southern Ardennes.

Although the province has only four breweries, they include the trappist brewery at Rochefort in the south and the prolific artisanal brewery of Du Bocq in Purnode. The abbeys at Leffe, Maredsous and Floreffe do not brew but commission beers. The abbey at Ciney is a ruin.

ANHEE-DENEE
15 km SSW of Namur off N932
Tiny hamlet with a large abbey.

ABBAYE
Abbaye de Maredsous
13 Rue de Mardesous
Tel: 082 699195
Café: ✪✪ *Beer:* ✪✪✪
The Belgians make a big thing of visiting their abbeys for a beer and a platter of cheese and bread, even if none of the ingredients are made at the abbey any longer. This huge, characterless, modern, bungalow-style self-service kaff sells all the brand name Maredsous goods and fails to mention anywhere that the four beers (6º, 8º, 9º and 10º) come from the Moortgat brewery, just south of Antwerp, makers of the famous Duvel (or Devil!). Food is limited to home-made wholemeal bread, brand name cheese and local ham, served on wooden platters. There is a terrace under the trees near the religious book and souvenir shop. You may prefer the Relais in the village. A bus runs from Namur station.

Monday to Friday 09.00 – 18.00
Saturday & Sunday 09.00 – 20.00

DINANT
20 km S of Namur on A94 & N97
[IC]
Dinant straddles the River Meuse and, despite its lack of decent hotels and car parking, is quite a tourist centre. It does have an above average range of shops but its cafés are pretty boring and it could make more of its impressive setting below the Citadel. It livens up at weekends.

SAX
13 Place Reine Astrid
Café: ✪✪✪ *Beer:* ✪✪✪
The Sax in question is Adolphe, the son of Dinant who invented the saxophone. They have a whole road dedicated to him on the other side of the onion-domed Notre Dame church, which is Dinant's most obvious building and lies opposite this busy café. They stock around ninety beers including Haacht's full range. Food is confined to snacks. A terrace at the front is open in summer. Indoors is a typical busy modern café. For greater comfort,

thirty beers (including Maredsous 8° on draught), excellent cuisine and the best accommodation in town, try the **Hotel de la Couronne**, by the church in Avenue Sax.
Opening hours 08.00 – 23.00

FLOREFFE

7 km WSW of Namur off N90
Small town off the road from Namur to Phillippeville.

MOULIN BRASSERIE
Abbaye de Floreffe
Tel: 081 444057
Café: ✪✪✪ *Beer:* ✪✪
Like many abbeys which license brewers to produce a beer in their name, the Abbey of Floreffe has its own café at which you can enjoy the beers along with home-produced cheese, local charcuterie and home-baked bread. The high-ceilinged café is constructed within the stone walls of the old mill, near the main road which runs past the abbey gates and its school. Tours (one hour) of the abbey and seminary at the top of the hill run four times a day between 13.30 and 17.00 from March to October. In July and August they increase to seven a day from 10.30 to 18.00.
SEPTEMBER to JUNE
Monday to Friday 11.00 – 18.00
Saturday & Sunday 11.00 – 20.00
JULY & AUGUST
Monday to Friday 10.00 – 19.00
Saturday & Sunday 10.00 – 20.00

HAN-SUR-LESSE

6 km SW of Rochefort on N86
Han-sur-Lesse is one of those two-bean towns blessed with a single natural attraction. Les Grottes (the caves) carry the underground rivers of the area and display their stalactites and stalagmites in formations which are magnificent in scale and allow for imaginative presentation. The 90-minute trip includes a ride on the open railway, mastering impossible gradients on its short run from the town centre to the entrance, a guided wander through a mile of caverns and a Son et Lumière show backed by Bach, Vivaldi, Enya and Pink Floyd. The whole thing is designed for ruthless

profiteering but everyone is so charming that you end up hardly minding at all. A half day here is good fun and reasonable value.

HOTEL DES ARDENNES
2 Rue des Grottes
Tel: 084 377220
Café: ✪✪✪ *Beer:* ✪✪
Han-sur-Lesse is awash with cafés and the one we choose seems to be a nose ahead of the rest for beer drinkers, due to its more thoughtful list of beers and high quality food. The trappist beers from Rochefort are de rigeur here as the monastery is only a couple of miles up the road. Similarly the area is awash with the various items of charcuterie including the famous raw cured ham and the coarse pâté. More elaborate cuisine is also available here either inside or on the terrace. Rooms from BFr 1,250 single and BFr 1,650 double.

HASTIERE-LAVAUX

10 km SW of Dinant on N96
Small village in several parts, straddling the Meuse. Here is the first road bridge upstream from Dinant. The basilica is 11th century. There are caves nearby at Pont d'Arcole which can be visited daily from 09.00 to 19.00 between Easter and September.

PICHET
48 Rue M. Lespagne
Tel: 082 645160
Café: ✪✪✪ *Beer:* ✪✪✪✪
Beer cafés obey strange rules in the French-speaking part of Belgium. But if you are touring the Valley of the Meuse at a weekend, The Pitcher is always open for food and ale. They close throughout the week and then stay open, effectively non-stop from early Friday evening until the last customer leaves in the wee small hours of Monday morning. The house beer specialities are its complete range of trappist ales and its unusually broad selection of 50 or so ales in 75 cl bottles. These are usually consumed in the small, cosy café to the right to the right of the entrance. The food specialities are grills, cooked before your eyes over

an open fire in the small restaurant on the left.

Friday 18.00 – late
Saturday & Sunday 08.00 – late
CLOSED MONDAY TO
THURSDAY and SECOND HALF
NOVEMBER

LUSTIN

12 km S of Namur on N947 [IC]
Small village on top of a hill overlooking the Valley of the Meuse. Its railway station and beer café are at the bottom of the hill by the river.

MUSEE DES BIERES BELGES

19 Rue de la Gare
Tel: 081 411102
Café: ✪✪✪ *Beer:* ✪✪✪✪✪

This remarkable place is on the small valley road which runs alongside the railway line at the bottom of the hill, close to the Meuse. Two trains an hour stop on their way between Namur and Dinant at the small halt, 50 metres from the pub. This is not so much a café as a place of homage to the wonders of ale. It stocked around 650 different varieties at the last count, including over 100 rare brews laid down in its cellar. It is a museum of beer where special exhibitions can be arranged out of hours for groups. They will provide cuisine a la bière for these with advance notice. Ordinary imbibers should note the restrictive opening hours, which alter depending on how many parties are visiting. This is allowable in such an eccentric place. The owner is a friendly fanatic. His licence depends on drinkers being classed as visitors to the museum, so don't be surprised if you have to pay a small entrance fee. The decor is a cross between a bottle auction and the sort of simple bench-and-table pubs which were once so popular in the Welsh borders and parts of rural North Yorkshire.

Opening hours 11.00 – 20.00
CLOSED MONDAY TO FRIDAY
(school terms)

NAMUR

Major town [IC]
The provincial capital (pop. 100,000), built at the place where the Sambre joins the Meuse. There is excellent shopping of all kinds to be had in its pedestrianised older areas of town. Its main theatre is famous.

The main tourist attractions of the town are found around the Citadel overlooking the town from the far bank of the Sambre. Set on a hill approached through wooded parkland up a winding road or else directly by cable car, there are a sports stadium, an open-air theatre, a Museum of Forestry, a Museum of Military History, a château and an amusement park. There is also a café at the **Château des Comtes**, a 13th century building, which is worth visiting. Beers currently come from Du Bocq.

EBLOUISSANT

27 Rue Armée Grouchy
Tel: 081 226928
Café: ✪✪✪✪ *Beer:* ✪✪✪✪✪

Whatever you do in Namur, visit The Brilliant One. The easiest way to find it is to turn right coming out of the station, then branch right before the underpass. When you reach the main road, Rue Armée Grouchy is the street opposite, signposted Flawinne. The complete journey is 800 metres. Having praised Alain Mossiat's original café to the hilt in our last edition, he rewarded readers by moving to larger premises, equally off the beaten track. Despite the relocation, the house style is unaltered. Everything in this splendid place reflects the personal taste of le patron. His range of 80 beers is strongly Wallonian. While he respects the sweet and spicy beers of the Flemish north, he prefers the rougher, drier, sparkling beers of the Walloon south, which he says are misunderstood and underrated. You will usually find ales from Abbaye des Rocs, Binchoise, Blaugies, Dupont and Vapeur, as well as Namur's own brewery, La Caracole. He sometimes goes to extraordinary lengths to acquire drinks which he considers worth stocking, such as traditional English cider and perry, authentic Belgian fruit wines, Irish whiskeys and single malt Scotches. The food is all home made and may include some inspired salads or an

exceptional range of cheeses. The decor is an interesting mix of traditional and modern. Even the background music is well chosen. Not the greatest setting and not the most inspiring building but well worth passing a few towns for.
Monday to Friday 12.00 – 24.00
Saturday 19.00 – 24.00
CLOSED SUNDAY

ROCHEFORT

25 km ESE of Dinant on N86
Apart from its famous monastic brewery, Rochefort's greatest attraction is the town itself. A typical, small Ardennaise community going about its business, accommodating a few discerning tourists and enjoying life.

MALLE POSTE

46 Rue de Behogne
Tel: 084 210987
Café: ✪✪✪✪✪ *Beer:* ✪✪✪✪
La Malle Poste is a small town hotel in the finest traditions. Find it on the road into the centre of Rochefort from the motorway. The absence of bright lights or glaring invitations to passing tourists, piniomed to the stone exterior, is the give-away to

seasoned travellers that something special may be found here. The beer list is one of the finest in the French speaking part of Belgium but that is only a start. The accommodation offers smart but homely comfort and represents good value, especially if you take advantage of one of the many gourmet breaks offered throughout the year. There are twelve rooms from BFr 1,750 (single) and BFr 2,050 (double). The food in the attractively appointed restaurant is superb. Try to pick a weekend when the piano bar has a jam session planned and the local jazz aficionados gather. The small, pleasant stone-faced café is open to the public at weekends and daily during the summer. Prices are justifiably higher than in ordinary cafés but then its 120-long beer list includes some extremely unusual choices for the area. For example traditional gueuze from Hanssens and Cantillon and artisan ales from the West Flanders brewery, Van Eecke. There is a French-style garden with tables and umbrellas at the rear.
Opening hours 10.00 – 23.00
CLOSED MONDAY TO FRIDAY
(Sep - Jun)

West Flanders
including Bruges

WEST FLANDERS (Flemish: West-Vlaanderen) is the only Belgian province with a coastline. It should follow, therefore, that as well as containing the country's seaside resorts, it must have the ferry terminals, fishing industry, naval bases and, in any normal part of the world, commercial ports too.

In fact, because of an extensive network of ship canals and major rivers, the province is spared much of the normal commercial trade of a coastal region, leaving most of the 60 km of sandy beaches free for more leisurely pursuits. Aside from the expanding port at Zeebrugge and the central area of Ostend, most of the Belgian coastline is turned over, with aplomb, to the business of accommodating, feeding, watering and generally entertaining tourists from Belgium and further afield.

The inland strip beyond the dunes is called the Polder. Before the construction of the continuous sea dyke from the mouth of the Schelde to beyond the French border, this was boggy fenland and salt marshes. With the draining of the fen came agricultural prosperity, but also silting of the rivers which had allowed the Polder towns to become great trading centres.

In the west, near the French border, are the battlefields of Flanders where a generation of young soldiers died needlessly in the trench battles of what was supposed to be the last Great War; the quiet market town of Ieper (Ypres) displays simple and respectful reminders.

In the south are the towns of Roeselare, home to the remarkable Rodenbach brewery, with its thousands of old oak fermenting casks, and Kortrijk (French: Courtrai), the charming gateway to Wallonia.

The province has 19 other breweries and is second only to Brabant in this respect. In the south, the tradition is of clean, filtered ales from companies like Bavik, Bockor, Facon, Verhaege and Van Honsebrouck. In the West, around the hopfields of Poperinge are brewers who favour more assertive beers, like the three brewers of Watou, Van Eecke, St. Bernardus and the new boy, Bie. North of here at Westvleteren is the tiny brewery at the Abbey of St. Sixtus. Also worthy of mention are Dolle Brouwers of Esen, near Diksmuide, creators of the most unusual range of beers in all of Flanders.

AALBEKE
8 km SSW of Kortrijk on N43
Pleasant village between Kortrijk and the French border.

GROENE WANDELING
32 Talpenhoekstraat
Tel: 056 410808
You will find the Green Man on the outskirts of the village but only if you consult the town plan in the main square first. It is a proper country tavern with seats in the garden and a small holding with geese at the back. At the last visit there remained no draught beers, just a selection of 80 or so bottled ones. If you want to make an

impression, bring a beer book for the library. Note that it is principally a weekend café.

Friday 19.00 – 01.00
Saturday 18.00 – 01.00
Sunday 15.00 – 23.00
Other days 18.00 – 23.00
CLOSED MONDAY TO
THURSDAY (Sep - Jun)

AVELGEM

14 km ESE of Kortrijk on N8
Small town set in delightful countryside near the Wallonian border.

GAREELKE

68 Driesstraat
Tel: 056 648366
Café: ✪✪✪✪ *Beer:* ✪✪✪

The Harness is located in an unpromising setting on the road out of town towards Otegem. A spick and span café-cum-restaurant, with a tiled terrace and large, safe, enclosed garden with all sorts of climbing frames. As well as stocking around 70 beers, there is a wide range of typical Belgian bar food featuring brochettes, seafood and, the specialty of the house, frogs' legs. Note that it only opens at weekends except in high summer.

Saturday & Sunday 11.00 – late
Friday (Sep - Jun) 18.00 – late
Other days 15.00 – late
CLOSED MONDAY TO
THURSDAY (Sep - Jun)

BLANKENBERGE

4 km E of Zeebrugge on coast [IC]

Blankenberge (pop. 15,000) is part of the coastal strip, lying to the east of Zeebrugge. Of the promenade towns it ranks third in size, increasing its population six-fold in the summer. The Zeedijk (sea dyke) stretches for 2.5 km along the dunes and beaches and is lined for most of its length by apartment blocks and hotels, restaurants and brasserie-tea-rooms with their sheltered terraces, tables and parasols. There is also an Aquarama and a casino. The frontage of this stately Victorian resort gives way to a business-like modern town behind. It has been in the holiday business since 1860.

LUXEMBOURG

75 Zeedijk
Tel: 050 419552
Café: ✪✪✪ *Beer:* ✪✪✪✪

Towards the western end of the promenade, the Luxembourg is not the best appointed of the many hundreds of terraced cafés which entice the milling crowds, but it does have the best range of beers – 110 at the last count. If the North Sea is being inhospitable, shelter indoors and take advantage of the panoramic view. Otherwise enjoy the sunshine on the terrace. Food is restricted to basic pub snacks but the coffee and pancakes are recommended.

Opening hours 10.00 – 24.00
CLOSED NOVEMBER 20th TO
DECEMBER 20th

BRUGES

Major town [IC]

The Flemish call their prettiest city Brugge (prounced Brook-her). The hordes of tourists who flock here on every weekend of the year and most other days besides, insist on calling it Bruges.

Spend just a few hours in the authentic and ancient beauty of the old town and you will understand why people love it. Enclosed by an oval canal and dominated by cobbled streets lined with imposing Flemish town houses, it is a strikingly attractive place. It is also the provincial capital and largest town (population 120,000) of West Flanders.

Some years ago the burgers knocked down the old city wall to make way for an encircling dual carriageway, then introduced a one-way system of Mandarin complexity, all to save the beautiful streets from the ravages of traffic.

The most popular pursuit for tourists is simply to wander around enjoying the city. The places worth seeking out include the Memling Museum in Katelijnestraat, dedicated to the best of the painters of the 15th century Flemish school and the nearby Groeninge Museum on the banks of the Dyver Canal, housing a gruesome collection of religious art amongst many treasures. The Begijnhof (nunnery) is worth a peaceful wander too.

Bruges has become an all-year-round tourist haven but thus far has retained a quiet elegance. It is as attractive in February as in July and many British weekenders prefer to visit at this time to exploit the bargain fares on the ferries. The bad news in summer, especially at weekends, is that the town's accommodation is often fully booked. The good news is that the frituur on the Markt sells chips with mayonnaise until 06.00.

The official street map (BFr 10 from Tourist Information in the Berg) is essential. But in a town awash with attractive cafés, only this Guide will direct you to the very best.

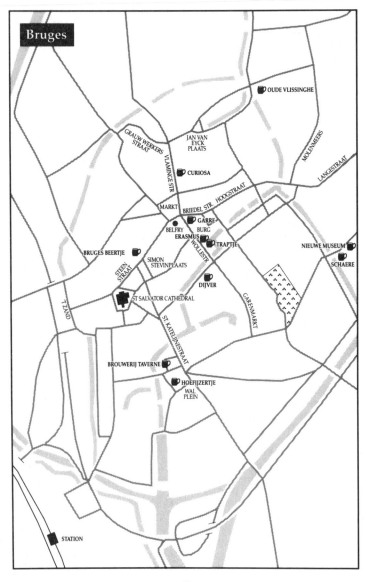

BROUWERIJ TAVERNE
26 Walplein
Tel: 050 332697
Café: ❍❍❍ *Beer:* ❍❍

The Straffe Hendrik brewery is now on most of the guided whistle-stop tours of Bruges, whether you travel on foot, by canal boat or in a horse-drawn trap. It is conveniently close to the Begijnhof. There used to be 31 breweries in Bruges; now there are just two and each welcomes the public. You can tour the brewery at 11.00 or 15.00 on most days. You do not have to tour the brewery to drink in its café. Big and basic with some wickerwork seating around plain tables, it will not win any design awards. Outside is a courtyard, off which is a small art gallery. Straffe Hendrik's pungent, bitter pale ale is the only brew available and there is a small range of snacks. Large parties can be catered for easily with advance notice.
Opening hours 09.00 – 18.30

BRUGS BEERTJE
5 Kemelstraat
Tel: 050 339616
Café: ❍❍❍❍❍ *Beer:* ❍❍❍❍❍

Steenstraat runs from the Markt to the modern square called 't Zand. Halfway along is Simon Stevinplein and opposite this is Kemelstraat, home to one of the finest beer cafés in the world. The Little Bruges Bear is run by the irrepressible Jan de Bruyne and his partner, the unflappable Daisy Claeys. It has two rooms, a few candles, rickety chairs and tables and a wall covered in brewery adverts. There is classical music on the CD and classical Belgian ales on the beer list of 200. Jan and Daisy have been promoting artisan ales since the very beginning of the Belgian beer revival and their café is held in great affection by knowledgeable beer drinkers from Antwerp to Antarctica. You cannot buy Pils here, it is considered an ersatz foreign beer style which has no place in a proper Belgian café. They stick to the ales of their own country and stock examples of almost every style and variation in the land. Jan's greatest regret is the inexorable disappearance of proper traditional gueuze, which he calls "Belgium's only truly unique beer style". Daisy does not exactly approve of imitations or label beers. They both have a soft spot for De Dolle Brouwers. Food is limited to basic snacks like cheese with mustard and celery salt, or a plate of pasta. The bar staff know their business and will make helpful suggestions, especially if you make it clear that you are after a fine brew. Jan is called upon increasing to do radio broadcasts and hold seminars for bar owners but if you want to hear him in full flow, book a party of a dozen or more friends on a weekday evening into a session of the Bieracademie. There is nothing more absorbing than watching a virtuoso play to a class of willing students. For a nightcap, you could consider dropping in to the **Dreupelhuisje**, just down the street, which has a well above average range of genevers.
Friday & Saturday 16.00 – 02.00
Other days 16.00 – 01.00
CLOSED WEDNESDAY

CURIOSA
22 Vlamingstraat
Tel: 050 342334
Café: ❍❍❍ *Beer:* ❍❍❍

Vlamingstraat runs off Markt to the north. The Taverne Curiosa is a popular candle-lit 16th century cellar café. You will find its entrance 100 metres along it on the right. As well as the 60 or so choices on the beer list there is an ambitious all-day range of snacks plus lunch and evening bar meals which stretch as far as steaks and fish (12.00 - 14.30; 18.00 - 01.00), but no chips - unique in Flanders? The staff dress in uniforms which seem to say "I am efficient" and on Saturday evenings especially they need to be, as the fire limits are strictly adhered to and they do not like people standing around. Help them by pouring your own beer - they are not trained to do so! The only major downer is background muzak that features the Shadows' "Apache" as a highspot.
Tuesday to Friday 10.00 – 01.00
Saturday 10.00 – 02.00

Sunday 12.00 – 24.00
CLOSED MONDAY

DYVER
5 Dyver
Tel: 050 330604
Café: ✪✪✪✪ *Beer:* ✪✪✪

The owners of the Staminee de Garre (below) have opened a second business just along from the Groeninge Museum, a few hundred metres from the old town centre. This is not so much a beer café as a restaurant specialising in cooking with beer. Lunch is served from 12.00 to 14.30 and dinner from 18.00 to 22.00. It is allowable to come here just for a beer before 18.00, though if it is full for lunch, you may be asked to drink on the terrace and if that gets full they may prefer you to withdraw. There are around 50 beers including a house blonde beer from Van Steenberge. In the cooking line they will try anything tasty and Flemish. Recommended dishes include quail in Westmalle Tripel, monkfish in Brugse Tripel and snails in bacon, mushroom and Rodenbach sauce. There is the same attention to historic detail in the layout of the restaurant as at their original place and the same polite, efficient service. In the evening, especially at weekends, it is essential to book.
Opening hours 11.00 – 22.00
CLOSED WEDNESDAY

ERASMUS
35 Wollestraat
Tel: 050 335781
Café: ✪✪✪ *Beers:* ✪✪✪✪

Welcome the return of the prodigal. Beer trippers to Bruges in the early eighties considered there to be three compulsory visits - Brugs Beertje, Staminee de Garre and the Hotel Erasmus. Then the management at Erasmus changed and things went downhill. Now they are back and Erasmus is once more offering around a hundred Belgian ales in the lobby bar of this small hotel, which also sets chairs and tables on a terrace round the side in summer. It is found on the main street running south off the Markt. You can drink in the fairly posh lounge at the front or

the small terrace at the back. The menu is typically Flemish and reasonably good value, with regional dishes and cuisine à la bière creeping in noticeably. Accommodation is as expensive as ever (singles from BFr 2,750, doubles from BFr 4,250).
Friday & Saturday 12.00 – 02.00
Other days 12.00 – 01.00
CLOSED MONDAY

GARRE
1 De Garre
Tel: 050 341029
Café: ✪✪✪✪✪ *Beer:* ✪✪✪✪

If you appreciate unpretentious elegance you will enjoy this place enormously. The cobbled street which runs from the Markt to the Burg is called Breidalstraat. It is easy to miss the tiny entrance on an alley way, usually signposted by a barrel. Find it! The Staminee de Garre is perhaps the most charming of all the cafés in Bruges. Simple and brightly lit, its small ground floor bar is used for tasting beers from the beer list of 130, perhaps accompanied by some cheese or bierwurst. There is an overflow room up the tight staircase, by the gallery. The establishment looks as if it ought to be a select restaurant or perhaps the finest of patisseries but it is first and foremost a specialist beer café where excellent coffee and a selection of wines enhance the menu. The object is not to quaff ale but to dabble in it a little, as a few, but not all, of the prices suggest. They have a unique, spiced tripel on draught from Van Steenberge. There is polite table service, classical music and magazines. A thoroughly civilised place. In high summer they may even be open on Wednesdays, their traditional closing day.
Saturday & Sunday 11.00 – 01.00
Other days 12.00 – 24.00
CLOSED WEDNESDAY

HOEFIJZERTJE
12 Walplein
Tel: 050 330604
Café: ✪✪ *Beer:* ✪✪✪✪

Fifty metres along Walplein from the Brouwerij Taverne (above) is this easily missed beer café and restaurant. You may spot its shop window more instinctively as there are numerous artisanal beers on sale with their correct glasses. Tucked away at the side is the entrance to a plain but tidy, sun-filled room which houses a small Flemish tavern – the meals are good but you are equally welcome to drop in for a beer or a coffee. There are over 100 brews on the list covering most of the specialist styles, though there is no proper traditional gueuze or kriek yet. The range of food covers light snacks through to a full selection of heavy regional cooking (12.00 - 14.30; 17.30 - 20.00). Despite the tablecloths, it is primarily a beer house.

Opening hours 11.00 – late
CLOSED MONDAY & TUESDAY (Nov - Mar)

NIEUWE MUSEUM
42 Hooistraat
Café: ○○○○ *Beer:* ○○

Just because you have to move on from your old café doesn't mean that you have to change the name, or even the fittings, as the friendly crew from the New Museum have proved. Their new location is 100 metres from the Schaere (below). The move out of the centre has given them much more room and a chance to install a grill over the open fireplace and a substantial food menu. The piano came, of course, but then so did the huge drinks cabinet and, unless memory fails us, so did the bar top! The beer list remains down around 30 with a couple of Dolle Brouwers beers, so come here for the old style atmosphere.

OUDE VLISSINGHE
2a Blekerstraat
Café: ○○○○○ *Beer:* ○○

In one of the quieter parts of the old town; take Vlamingstraat off Markt until you reach Academiestraat on your right. Walk down this to Jan Van Eyckplein, then take the right bank of the canal at the opposite end. Blekerstraat is fifth on your right. Bruges has several exceptionally attractive cafés where the beer was almost an afterthought. This is probably the best, a splendid 16th century tavern, carefully and

cleverly renovated in 1991. You won't see the join! At the Herberghe Oude Vlissinghe, friends play cards on the antique tables. The clever lighting turns modern faces into caricatures of the portraits in the Groeningen Museum. The ancient fireplace is laid out like the centre-piece of a set from an 18th century costume drama. There is a table for the football-style pool players. You are supposed to sit down, rather than wander around gawping at the oil paintings and the curios. The toilets are at the back, off the sheltered courtyard. It has a quiet magnificence. The beer list is surprisingly dull.

Sunday to Thursday 12.00 – 01.00
Friday & Saturday 12.00 – 02.00

SCHAERE
2 Hooistraat
Tel: 050 332067
Café: ○○○ *Beer:* ○○○○

Off the well-worn tourist track. From Berg, find Langestraat and after the canal bridge head right, down Predikherenrei. The Shears is on a corner after 200 metres. It is a pleasantly revamped corner house dating from 1614 with some old stone carving outside. Worth finding in its own right, the journey there will offer the traveller a sight of the old residential areas of this superbly preserved town. The owners like to encourage conversation, art, tea and beer. The paintings and prints on the wall are for sale. The range of teas stood at 56 when we last checked, coming from as far away as Paraguay, Morocco and Russia. The beer list of 115 is large for Bruges and features a few from as far away as the Limburg microbrewery, De Teut. Decor is bare brick and old-fashioned tables. Background music, when it is played, tends to be classical and they have a CD request list. A small range of hot and cold snacks is available but for serious cooking move on to the Nieuwe Museum (above).

Wednesday to Friday 17.00 – 01.00
Saturday 15.00 – 02.00
Sunday 15.00 – 22.00

CLOSED MONDAY & TUESDAY

TRAPTJE
39 Wollestraat
Tel: 050 338918
Café: ✪✪✪ *Beer:* ✪✪

There is a paved yard by the side of the Erasmus Hotel (above). Below it, at the canal end, is the Bistro 't Traptje. Not really a beer café but a pleasantly situated canalside eating house offering a wide range of excellent quality light meals. In summer they have a street level terrace by the canal, next to that of the Erasmus. In winter you have to stick with the organised Burgundian interior and the window view across the water to some of the oldest parts of the town. There are around 40 beers but many of the old faithfuls are there. Opening times are different every day and are too complicated to list!

DAMME
7 km NE of Bruges off N374

Damme used to be the outer harbour of Bruges and for 200 years enjoyed the status of one of the leading merchant ports, specialising in the wine trade. Then some idiot built the sea dykes, the River Zwin silted up and the prosperity came to a rapid end, leaving Damme to become a quiet village with a pleasant selection of Burgundian architecture. Many tourists like to get here by bicycle or tandem from one of the hire shops in Bruges. What they do not tell you is that the wind is almost invariably behind you coming that way. Going back you realise how strong it is. If you want to put Flanders in proportion, climb to the top of the Church of Our Lady. The view of the surrounding countryside on a clear day is stunning.

UYLENSPIEGHEL
44 Kerkstraat
Tel: 050 372609
Café: ✪✪✪✪ *Beer:* ✪✪✪

A cynical way of looking at Damme is to see it as a collection of old buildings interspersed with pubs and restaurants (or vice versa). Certainly there are more of each per head of

population here than anywhere else in Belgium. Choosing a single one as the most appealing is a random effort but we were impressed at the all-round excellence of the Silly Pranks. There are around 60 beers on the list. There is also high quality and interesting café food as well as full meals of typical Flemish excellence. If you are only after a snack, try the local cheeses and the selection of pastries. They welcome families by providing a variety of table games indoors and a terrace with a children's play area at the back. There has been a recent name change, implying new owners.
Opening hours 10.00 – 24.00
CLOSED THURSDAY; and FRIDAY (Oct - Mar)

DE PANNE
30 km SW of Ostend on coast [IR]

A modern seaside resort, the third largest in Belgium and the nearest to the French border, at the western terminal of the coastal tramway. At low tide the beach here is the largest on the Belgian coast. The sport of sand yachting was invented here. Makes allowances for the fact that the French border is only 2 km away.

ROBINSON
169 Zeelaan
Café: ✪✪ *Beer:* ✪✪✪

Like every other town on the Belgian coast, De Panne is soggy with cafés. The one which comes closest to being a specialist beer café is the Café au Robinson, which stocks around 55. It is at the crossroads of the coastal road with Duinkerkelaan, the main drag into town from the middle of the pleasure beach, behind the Hotel Terlinck. Food is limited to bar snacks.
Opening hours 09.00 – late

EERNEGEM
15 km S of Ostend on N368

Typical small Flemish town, five minutes from junction 5 on the A18 [E40], off the Ostend-Torhout road.

BUUZESTOVE
174 Stationstraat
Tel: 059 290342
Café: ❍❍❍ *Beer:* ❍❍❍

The Buuzestove is the impressive piece of ironmongery that blazes away in the middle of the front bar in winter and warms the cubicles and small tables of this pleasant small-town café. The beer list is now limited to around 70, with the Strubbe brewery contributing several of these, probably including the dark, sweet bitterish house brew, Buuzestoveke. Some of the stronger beers are excellent value. More impressive is the cooking, which is well above average for a beer café off the beaten track. As well as frogs' legs, steaks and eel, they muster impressive ideas about what to do to giant prawns, scampi and scallops. There are also Eurosnax and smaller dishes. The café is found on the road into town from the N368. There is a public car park at the back. It can get busy on nights when the many local societies meet in the function room and overspill for a beer or three.
Saturday 11.00 – 04.00
Other days 11.00 – 02.00
CLOSED MONDAY

GULLEGEM
NW outskirts of Kortrijk, off A19
Small town on the outskirts of Kortrijk. If you want an insight into the untypically opulent world of the Belgian family brewer, visit the castle at Ingelmunster, 6 km north of here. It is the home of the Van Honsebroucks and is open throughout the summer and every weekend of the year.

RUSTEEL
168 Heulestraat
Tel: 056 356564

On the road to Heule at the outskirts of the town, adjacent to the bus stop for the no. 748 Kortrijk to Roeselare service. A huge converted farm in a suburban setting with a massive dining room and cobbled courtyard. There is also a veranda and outside terrace, as well as an attractive garden. It stocks over 300 beers and

its kitchen serves a wide range of regional food, from simple snacks to elaborate meals. They run a Friday night barbecue in summer. The huge car park on the opposite side of the road is not immediately obvious.
Sunday 14.00 – 24.00
Other days 16.00 – late
CLOSED TUESDAY &
WEDNESDAY (Oct - Easter) and
FEBRUARY

IEPER
25 km W of Kortrijk off N38 (E19)
[IR]

Ypres, the French name of this quiet market town (population 35,000), was engrained in the memory of a generation. "Wipers", as the English-speaking troops called it, was at the centre of some of the fiercest fighting of World War One. The Menin Gate (Menenpoort), which spans the eastern entrance to the town centre, lists the names of 55,000 soldiers who died in the vicinity during three years of fighting for control of a few square miles of drained fen and the odd hillock or two. The Last Post is sounded there at 20.00 on every night of the year. Tyne Cot Cemetry, just off the Menen road a kilometre beyond Nieuwe Molden, is the final resting place of just 60,000 of those who died - over half the graves are unnamed. The tour route of the war graves is humbling. If the purpose of travel is to feed the mind, the fields in this part of Flanders are rich pastures.

POSTERIE
57 Rijselstraat
Tel: 057 200580
Café: ❍❍❍❍ *Beer:* ❍❍❍❍❍

The simple excellence of the Post Office comes either as a welcome relief from, or solid preparation for a tour of the military monuments. Opposite the real post office, in one of the main streets off the Grote Markt, it typifies everything which is good in Belgian café life. There is a terrace outside and cellar café indoors. The menu includes all the Flemish favourites, including pots of mussels and steaks with sauces cooked to perfection. The beer

menu of 140 options is strong on West Flanders ales and contains some rarities, especially from smaller local breweries. The service is friendly and helpful and the owner speaks good English. His daughter is in charge of the beer cellar. They serve until the wee small hours and the kitchen carries on much later than is usual. Thoroughly recommended.
Easter to mid-October 11.00 – 02.00
Mid-October to Easter 17.00 – 02.00
CLOSED WEDNESDAY

KNOKKE-HEIST

3 km E of Zeebrugge on coast [IC]

The second most popular resort on the Belgian coast and probably the most expensive. Tucked up against the Dutch border it was originally four villages, Heist in the west, then Duinbergen to the east, Knokke beyond that and Het Zoute nearest to the Dutch border.

The coastal tramway ends at Knokke, 400 metres short of the Royal Golf Club at Het Zoute. The official population of the town is 30,000 but this rises to over 180,000 in the summer. Every form of modern holiday amenity is here but we could only find one specialist beer café.

SCHILDIA
250 Zeedijk
Tel: 050 515058
Café: ❂❂❂ *Beer:* ❂❂❂❂

The coastal promenade is called Zeedijk and is numbered consecutively. You will find no. 250 at the eastern end of Heist to the west of Knokke and Duinbergen. We did not count what percentage of the other numbers are café-tavernes but it may well be half. The café is larger than most, which may be how it manages to stock 160 beers. The food is pretty good too, ranging from omelettes and single plate meals to steaks and mussels. The terraced area across the road allows tanning in summer as well as a chance to watch the kids careering up and down the pedestrianised part of the

promenade on all manner of pedal- and electric-powered people mowers.
Easter to mid-November 09.00 – late
Christmas to Easter "limited"
CLOSED MID-NOVEMBER TO CHRISTMAS

KORTRIJK

Major town [IC]

Kortrijk (French: Courtrai) has been a centre of the textiles industry for over 500 years. It is the largest town in southern Flanders (pop. 77,000) and is the least Flemish. An elegant town with a number of memorable monuments, of which the most striking are the Broeltorens, twin tours on the bridge by the Broelkaai. The Grote Markt has a picturespue old belfry with a war memorial built on. It took a heavy pounding in both world wars but some older parts survive and its 17th century nunnery (Begijnhof), at the back of the Church of Our Lady, is one of the most picturesque in Belgium. Worth considering for a weekend.

BROUWZAELE
19 Kapucijnenstraat
Tel: 056 456451
Café: ❂❂❂❂ *Beer:* ❂❂❂❂

Take Leiestraat from the Grote Markt, across the canal, turn right and Kapucinenstraat is first on your left, a street of cafés opposite the Pentascoop cinema, just off the canal in the old part of Kortrijk. The canopy above the bar is the lid of an old brewing copper, the same design feature as at its sister café in Ghent (see Belgian Cafés: East Flanders). Potted plants create a cool atmosphere. The beer range tops 90, with draught beers coming from two cellars which are kept at different temperatures. Food is limited to snacks and single plate meals, including salade Niçoise, omelettes and zakouskis, a type of Russian snack. Outside is a pretty terrace, sporting flower boxes and umbrellas in summer.
Opening hours 11.00 – 03.00

ENGEL
6 Rogier Saverijstraat
Tel: 056 201976

Café: ✪✪✪✪✪ *Beer:* ✪✪✪
Take Rijselsestraat from the Hotel
Belvedere in Grote Markt. When you
reach Louis Robbeplein, hook round
to the left and turn immediately right
to find this superb Art Deco café run
by, and for, the artistically inclined.
There is no pub sign. Although the
beer list is thin, running only to 30
or so, it is well chosen and well
kept, featuring Dolle Brouwers'
Oerbier and Arabier. The decor is
hand-picked, from the ceiling fans
and statuettes of the saints to the
James Dean clock. Food is limited
but chilli, lasagne and moussaka are
supplemented by house specials like
chicory in cheese sauce, a winter
hotpot and, in summer, an exotic
salad.
Opening hours 16.00 – 03.00
CLOSED MONDAY & TUESDAY

MOUTERIJTJE
25a Kapucijnenstraat
Tel: 056 201414
Café: ✪✪✪ *Beers:* ✪✪✪
Just up from the Brouwzaele is this
converted maltings, with its brick
vaulted roof. The long, deep bar is
on the first floor. Eating is not
compulsory by any means but it is
far more food oriented than its
neighbour. A beer list of 90 includes
Bockor's Kortrijk 800. Brochettes,
zalm (salmon fillet), zeetong (baked
monkfish), stoovlees (stewed beef)
and kikkerbillen (frogs legs) all
feature on the menu, as well as a
selection of smaller snacks.
Friday 11.00 – 03.00
Saturday 16.00 – 03.00
Sunday to Wednesday 11.00 –
01.00
CLOSED THURSDAY

MARIAKERKE
3 km SW of Ostend on the coast
Coastal town, part of the almost
continuous built-up area which lines
the sandy beaches between Ostend
and Nieuwpoort.

BLINCKAERT
177 Zeedijk
Tel: 059 807663
The Olde Sand Dune is a promenade
café on one of the less well known
parts of Ter Streep. Open all year

round. It stocks around 60 beers but
specialises every bit as much in food.
This ranges from ice cream,
pancakes and waffles to steaks and
mussels, and includes a children's
menu. A long deep café with a
conservatory at the back and a small
terrace out front.
Opening hours 11.00 – 24.00
CLOSED TUESDAY and
NOVEMBER

MOEN
12 km SE of Kortrijk on N8
Small town near the Hainaut border.

ST. PIETERSHOF
6 Kraaibos
Tel: 056 456451
Entering Moen from St. Denijs, you
cross a canal bridge. Turn left on
either side of this and continue for 2
km. You will eventually reach
another canal bridge, next to a huge
lock. St. Peter's House is away to the
left, down a track with its own
drawbridge; a proper rural beer
house with environmentally positive
tendencies. On one of the long-
distance footpaths through the area,
it is thus popular with ramblers.
There are over 100 beers on the list,
which tries to discriminate in favour
of Flemish and Hainaut artisan
brewers. It also offers tea and
pancakes, special ice creams and
home-made cheeses. There is a
small-holding with ducks and geese.
Friday (Sep - Jun) 18.00 – late
Other days 15.00 – late
CLOSED MONDAY TO
THURSDAY (Sep - Jun)

NIEUWPOORT AAN ZEE
20 km SW of Ostend on coast
Nieuwpoort (pop. 8,000) is two
towns. The larger, Nieuwpoort Stad,
is a fishing port with a massive
marina, 2 km inland on the Yser
estuary. Nieuwpoort aan Zee, which
is still sometimes known as
Nieuwpoort Bad, is the smaller
coastal resort, draped along the sea
front. The whole area had to be
rebuilt after World War One, during
which a piece of strategic brilliance
led to the opening of the sluice-gates
and the complete flooding of the
area.

VAGANT
139b Albert I Laan
Tel: 058 236631
Café: ✪✪✪✪ *Beer:* ✪✪✪✪

Coming out of Nieuwpoort Stad the continuation of the main road becomes Albert I Laan and goes on to meet the eastern end of the seafront. De Vagant is a pleasant street corner brasserie-restaurant, 100 metres from the promenade. Its specialities are regional beers, of which there are 90 or so, and regional cooking. The table d'hôte lunches, served from 12.00 to 14.00 are excellent value and steer away from steak and chips into more interesting territory. For example, the wild rabbit cooked in Oerbier. The more expensive à la carte menu is available from 12.00 to 24.00 and features traditional Flemish cooking. Although this looks like a restaurant and the background music is usually classical, many people come here simply to have a bottle or two of ale and a civilised chat.

Opening hours 11.00 – 02.00
CLOSED WEDNESDAY and
TWO WEEKS AFTER WHITSUN

OEDELEM
9 km SE of Bruges on N33
Small town, five minutes from the Ostend to Brussels motorway.

KIOSK
4 Markt
Tel: 050 781595
Café: ✪✪✪ *Beer:* ✪✪✪

In the main square opposite the ornate council offices. An archetypal small Flemish tavern in an archetypal small Flemish town. It stocks 60 beers and offers an excellent menu, specialising in smoked Scottish salmon, Zeebrugge prawns and other seafood. The steaks are pretty good too. Outside there is a small terrace, indoors a small bar.

Opening hours 11.00 – late
CLOSED WEDNESDAY and
END JULY/EARLY AUGUST

OSTEND
Major town [IC]
Ostend (Flemish: Oostende) is a highly versatile port (pop. 72,000).

Antwerp and Zeebrugge handle most of Belgium's maritime trade but Ostend deals with much of the rest. It has the terminals for ferries and jetfoils from Dover and is home to the deep sea fishing fleet, a naval base, a commercial dock and a shipyard. On top of this, it manages to retain a major tourist trade due to Ter Streep, the 15 km of dunes and well-kept sandy beaches which stretch westwards from here.

The town survived destruction by the Spanish in 1604, the British assault on the Germans in two world wars and the great tidal wave of 1953. It is a favourite place for weekend trips from Britain. Most visitors remember best the rows of seafood stalls along the Visserskaai, selling all styles and combinations of North Sea fish, plus the excellence of the more formal cuisine in the hundreds of sea front restaurants that run opposite the stalls from the railway station and ferry terminal west to the beginning of Ter Streep. The town's Kursaal leisure complex houses a casino, a restaurant and an exhibition hall as well as hosting some fairly major concerts.

The downside is the increasing number of disagreeable air-heads, not always that young, rolling about the streets in a state of drunken malevolence on weekend or summer nights. The Ostenders have a name for them. They call them "the British". Regrettably, their cynical observation is right. The problem has reached such a level that the civic authorities no longer advertise Ostend in Britain and are trying to close down the small, cheap hotels favoured by the drunks.

Serious British beer lovers should be prepared to behave ultra-politely or be tarred with the same brush. It is a shame, but spend an hour in the town centre late on a Saturday night and you may see how the Brits earned their reputation as the slobs of Europe.

BOTTELTJE
19 Louisastraat
Tel: 059 700928
Fax: 059 502856
Café: ✪✪✪✪ *Beer:* ✪✪✪✪✪

Ostend's two serious beer cafés lie a block apart, 1.5 km from the ferry terminal and railway station. To find the Little Bottle turn right out of the station and walk about 600 metres along the Visserskaai, past the restaurants and seafood stalls until you reach the first bend on the promenade. Turn left down Langestraat, and Louisastraat is the fourth on your left. The café is part of the Hotel Marion. Do not be put off by the presence in Louisastraat of Ronny's Pub, the Ostend Arms, the White Horse Inn and the Restaurant Coventry, nor by the sign on the door saying "Members Only" in English, not Flemish. They are used to welcoming British beer lovers here but cannot abide drunks. The single lounge is decorated with modern Breugelesque murals. The beer range stretches to 220 and is presented at the bar and in guests' rooms on a useful computerised list. Some snacks are available in the café but for more serious eating, move across the corridor to the restaurant (serving from 18.00 to 22.30). This is called the Steakhouse but actually offers a typical range of other high quality Flemish cuisine as well. The hotel now has 24 rooms starting at BFr 1,200 (single) and BFr 1,800 (double), three stars from the Belgian tourist authorities and BBC TV in every bedroom.

Accommodation is best booked in advance, especially in high summer and at weekends. When they play Rodrigo's Guitar Concerto, you know that time is about to be called.
Sunday to Thursday 16.00 – 01.00
Friday 16.00 – 02.00
Saturday 16.00 – 03.00

OSTENS BIERHUUS
48 Kapucijnenstraat
Tel: 059 706701
Café: **OOOO** *Beer:* **OOOO**
If you think the owner of the Ostend Beer House speaks good English it is because he is English, though his café clearly is not. Kapucijnenstraat lies one block behind the Botteltje (above). You will find this friendly café in a row of buildings halfway along it. From the outside it is not

much to look at but indoors is a typically cosy, warm and simple brown café, with carpets on the seats. The range of 180 beers complements nicely the selection at our other café and an evening shared between them is well worthwhile. Jukebox nostalgia experts will appreciate the background music. Most of the customers are Flemish but even the notoriously unadventurous British weekenders seem to leave their customary orders of Pils behind when they alight here. Maybe it is just that an increasing number of British tourists have hear of Tim Smith's reputation. If this is your first time in Belgium and you are overwhelmed by the choice of ales before you, give him an idea of what you would like to try and, unless snowed under, he will usually be happy to pick something appropriate.
Opening hours 15.00 – late
CLOSED TUESDAY

POPERINGE
10 km W of Ieper off N38 [IR]
This typical small Flemish market town near the French border lies at the heart of Belgium's hop-growing area. In September the landscape is dominated by 15-foot hopbines strung up on rows and rows of high tressles. The local tourist office suggests a day-long circular cycle ride through Hoppeland. The National Hop Museum (see Beer Museums) is situated in Gasthuisstraat. Every three years there is a huge hop pageant on the third weekend in Septemvber, called the Hoppestoet. The next one is in 1996.

OUD VLAENDEREN
14 Grote Markt
Tel: 057 335161
Café: **OOOO** *Beer:* **OOO**
At the centre of town, on the large market square. Appropriately, it is decorated outside by a massive garland of hops. The single large bar is spotlessly clean. The service is keen and polite, and they make allowances for the slow English. The floor is tiled, the furnishings are highly polished and there is a

primitive mural on the wall. In Britain, this type of bar feels like drinking in an aircraft hanger; in Belgium it manages to be atmospheric. Food includes soup, rolls, Eurosnax, croques, waffles, pancakes and ice creams. There are often regional dishes such as hennepot and witloof in hesp (chicory and bacon). Among the 47 well-chosen beers is draught Hommelbier (hop beer) from Van Eecke, originally brewed for the hop museum.

Opening hours 10.00 – late
CLOSED MONDAY

VEURNE

25 km SW of Ostend off A18 (E40) [IR]

Veurne (pop. 12,000) is one of the Polder towns, a few miles inland from the North Sea coast and equidistant from the French border. Its main attraction is the ornate architecture round the Grote Markt, from the Spanish period. Many of the buildings needed restoration after the town was severely bombarded during World War One. The annual procession of the Penitents on the final Sunday in July can trace its origins to the 12th century, and is one of Belgium's more bizarre carnivals, the citizens marching through the streets hooded in black cloaks bearing crosses. For the rest of the year, tourists will have to make do with the International Museum of Bread, Rolls, Cakes and Icing on Iepersesteenweg.

FLANDRIA

30 Grote Markt
Tel: 058 311174
Café: ✪✪✪ *Beer:* ✪✪✪✪

If you are coming from Dunkirk or Calais this may well be your first taste of a Belgian café and it offers a useful introduction. One of many bars in the main square it has a single, high-ceilinged, airy saloon bar, a cramped terrace outside in summer, and waiter service. Many of its 120 beers come from West Flanders. The menu of bar snacks features several variations on a local delicacy, a kind of designer brawn in

aspic on an open sandwich. Quite delicious despite the unappetising description. Clean and well-managed, the Flandria gives a good idea of the standards you should expect from a Flemish tavern. Its four immediate neighbours are slowly increasing their own beer lists.

May to September 09.00 – 24.00
October to April 09.00 – 22.00
CLOSED THURSDAY (Oct - Apr)

WATOU

20 km W of Ieper off N 308

Small border community known locally as the brewers' town, though of the three companies currently in production, only Van Eecke can trace its roots back more than 50 years. If arriving from the French ferries, turn off the A25 Lille road at the first turning for Wormhout.

HOMMELHOF

17 Watouplein
Tel: 057 388024

The square in Watou has four cafés and two names (the alternative is Hugo Clausplein). The Hop House is the newest, but its arrival has caused quite a stir. Masterchef Stefaan Couttenye has deliberately created a tavern-cum-restaurant dedicated to cooking with beer. From the outside, the hop garlands, white-painted brickwork and window-box geraniums would not mark out this street corner café as an increasingly famous national institution, but be assured it is. Drinking without eating is allowed but seems a bit pointless. It may be easier when the new extensions are completed and the place is able to seat 300. The menu features a wide variety of specialities with recommendations about which beer should best accompany them. In May you might even find hopshoots. A quieter jar of ale can be had at the attractive **Gasthof De Eendracht** across the square, the unofficial brewery tap of the Van Eecke brewery.

WESTVLETEREN

20 km NW of Ieper off N8

Small village on the much-signposted Hoppeland cycling route. Its St.

Martin's church has an attractive interior. The brewing abbey and our listed café are 2 km down the road.

VREDE
St. Sixtusabdij
Tel: 057 400377

Visit on a quiet weekday and trade is slack, the bar seeming far too large for its remote setting, directly opposite the smallest of the five Belgian brewing monasteries. Indeed, out of season it may be closed by the early evening. The enormous car park looks incongruous at these times, but becomes more understandable on Sunday afternoons when half of Flanders and his dog take a family outing to sample the beers. Food is limited to soup and basic rolls and little else goes on here except drinking and conversation. There is a shop selling all three regular beers and the monastery's orange-waxed, creamy, deliciously flavoured Port Salut style cheese. This part of West Flanders is awash with breweries and if you are travelling by bicycle this is excellent tavern-crawling country, where deserted back roads can suddenly turn up high quality pubs with excellent food and ale. *Opening hours 12.00 onwards CLOSED FRIDAY*

STOP PRESS

IN THE COURSE OF compiling the second edition of The Good Beer Guide to Belgium & the Netherlands we have been recommended a number of bars which, for one reason or another, we have been unable to survey. These may be excellent, dreadful or even shut, we have no way of knowing. But if you visit any, let us know what you find.

EAST FLANDERS
WATERVLIET: ROSTE MUIS
On the border with Dutch Flanders, 25 km NNW of Ghent. Said to be loaded with bric à brac and presided over by a Grand'Dame. No mention of beers.

LIMBURG (BELGIAN)
'S GRAVENVOEREN: CIERLYCKE SWAENE
10k SSE of Maastricht off N627. Large village in a small Flemish-speaking enclave wedged between Liege province and the Dutch border. Marked as Fouron-le-Comte on French language road signs. Beers from Achouffe, De Troch, Strubbe, Palm and Lefèbvre. In the village square. Regional cuisine.

HASSELT: CAFÉ HASSELT
38 Maastrichtsestraat.
It is said that De Smedt brewery created their Dikkenek pale ale, spiced with juniper, for this café. It was supposed to symbolise the genever production of the town of Hasselt. Dikkenek means "Thickneck" and refers to the nickname applied to Limburgers.

NEERPELT: TEUT BROUWERIJ PROEFLOKAAL
97 Stationsstraat.
A large tasting café is planned at the Teut brewery, 30 km S of Eindhoven on N748, next to the railway station of this small fenland town. No signs of progress by November 1993, however.

WEST FLANDERS
RUMBEKE: BROUWERIJ
392 Rumbeeksesteenweg (051 222274).
Closed Thursday, open other days from 16.00 till late. There is said to be another, arty bar at 16 Duizendzinnenstraat, closed on Mondays.

Hop-picking display at Poperinge which has a museum dedicated to the art
(see Beer Tourism) *Photo Iain Lowe*

Dutch Independents

IN THE 1970s the Dutch brewing industry consisted of Heineken plus a few extras. There were 20 or so established independent breweries serving lagers to their local areas but these beers tended to ape the Heineken brands. Literally the only unusual beer producer was the old abbey brewery in Tilburg. Beer was Pils; Pils was Heineken or Amstel; Heineken and Amstel were the same company; the choice was simple, take it or leave it.

People look at the Dutch beer scene and bemoan its lack of diversity and tradition when compared with its neighbours, Belgium, Germany, Britain or the Czech Republic. What they forget is that things have improved enormously from 20 years ago and that the past decade has seen the creation of over 20 new ale breweries.

Improvements began with the re-emergence of bokbier. This black autumnal lager had all but disappeared by 1980. Then a few Dutch beer drinkers and renegade café owners, inspired in part by what CAMRA had achieved in Britain, created enough fuss to persuade a few regional breweries to promote or revive the style.

After bokbier came an interest in a lighter coloured but equally rounded springtime lager, more in the German tradition, called meibok. At the same time came a revival of interest in ale types, such as wheat beer, winter ale and strong golden brews.

Newer brewers began to produce beers of bokbier and meibok character by top fermentation. This led to the production of Pilseners by top fermentation. The precedent for this was the practices of brewers in the German city of Köln (Cologne), where the Kölsch style of straw coloured pale ale has a long pedigree.

In the autumn of 1992 the home brew café called the Amsterdams Brouwhuis had the outrageous idea of producing a top fermented tarwebok, or wheat bokbier. By coincidence, a few weeks later Heineken produced a similar beer in typically Dutch lagered style. This is the only recorded incidence to date of a multinational leading the world in creating a new beer style of interest to beer connoisseurs.

Heineken had also been responsible for confirming the return of wheat beer to the Netherlands, with the production of Wieckse Witte in 1990. The Dutch are even developing their own variant on the style, a sweeter, lighter, more honeyed version than is generally found in Belgium or Germany.

On the brewery side, the bad news is that independent companies continue to be snapped up by larger predators. The multinationals have also limited the inroads which can be made by potential competitors by acquiring control, in practice if not deed, of nearly all the country's major beer distributors.

The two largest of the new breweries, Arcen and Raaf, have already been taken over by multinationals, but 't IJ of Amsterdam and Us Heit of Friesland are doing well in the run-up to their tenth anniversaries. Some of the new boys possess little more than a stewing pot and large bucket in the corner of the brewer's garage and beer quality can vary, but several are already in the major league as far as taste is concerned. They could all do with more encouragement from the specialist beer bars and an accord signed in November 1993 between ABT and a group of small producers may achieve that.

On the quality side, most Dutch Pilseners still contain 10 to 25 per cent of non-malt adjuncts. All-malt brews are definitely staging a comeback and although they do not match most German or Czech brews, are worth trying. Hops are coming back into vogue too. Perhaps the most notable change in our beer ratings for our second edition is the additional star awarded for the recently spruced up Heineken Pils.

With Big H now clearly believing in the future of quality beers in the Netherlands, things are set to improve further.

Label beers are far less of a problem than they are in Belgium and in general the standard of information given to consumers by both breweries and bars is considerably higher than south of the border. The comments about beer descriptions at the beginning of the section on Belgian Independent Breweries (page 66) also apply to our Dutch brewery listings.

ALFA

BIERBROUWERIJ SCHINNEN BV
Thull 15
6365 AC Schinnen
Tel: 04493 2888
Fax: 04493 2835
Established in 1870 at Schinnen, between Maastricht and Aachen, in Dutch Limburg. Known until 1993 as the Meens brewery, after the family who owned and ran it. The significance of the name change is not yet clear but either way the beers have been known for many years under the brand name Alfa. Unusually for the Netherlands these are all-malt brews. This distinction clearly gives them the edge in quality terms over many of their competitors. The Pils is marketed abroad as Fresh Holland Beer but has a distinctly Czech character. Lentebok was new for 1993. Total brewery output is 60,000 hl per annum.
ALFA SUPERDORTMUNDER
7% abv ✪✪✪ Dortmunder

Sweet, strong and clean-tasting. The strongest Dutch Dortmunder.
ALFA BOKBIER*
6.5% abv ✪✪✪ Dark Bok
Middle of the road, softish bok with slight malty fragrance.
ALFA LENTEBOK*
6.5% abv ✪✪✪✪ Pale Bok
Sweetish, clear, amber coloured brew with great staying power.
ALFA EDEL PILS
5% abv ✪✪✪ Pils
Low on hops but full Pils flavour derives from 100% malt in the mash.
    An oud bruin table beer is also produced.

AMSTERDAMS BROUWHUIS

BIERBROUWERIJ
MAXIMILIAANS
Kloveniers Burgwal 6/8
1011 Amsterdam
Tel: 020 624278
Opened in August 1992. Amsterdam's first brew pub, based at the Café Maximiliaan (see Dutch Cafés: North Holland).

Brouwmeester Albert Hofmann spent three years touring the best small breweries of the world before finalising the plans for this remarkable place. Its most unusual feature is that the brew kettles are actually in the bar. The Kölsch and wheat beer are permanent fixtures. One other beer is usually available. Maximator was the Netherlands' first tarwebok. The beers are currently available only on draught, though large stoppered bottles are being introduced.

MAXIMATOR*
6.5% abv ✪✪✪✪ Wheat Bok Ale
Spicy, deep amber wheat beer with a milky haze a delicate afterburn.

TARWE 68
5% abv ✪✪✪✪ Wheat Beer (unfiltered)
Light coloured, appealingly sweet, cloudy draught wheat beer.

BETHANIEN
4.5% abv ✪✪✪ Kölsch
Imperfect, all-malt ale deliberately trying to mimick a Pils.

Other beers include: Caspers Max* (7.5% abv; tripel), Meibockbier* (pale bok ale) and Winterbier* (winter ale).

BAVARIA
BAVARIA BV
Burg. van den Heuvelstraat 35
5737 BN Liesehout
Tel: 04992 8111
Enormous, successful family-owned brewery. Annual production is 3,200,000 hl, making it one of the largest independent breweries in the world. No known Bavarian connections; its Pilseners do not reach the Rheinheitsgebot standard. It brews ordinary lagers for supermarkets such as Tesco. For 1993 its bokbier was replaced by a new tarwebok. It brews Birra Scura (6.5% abv) and Lynx (5% abv; Pils) for export only.

BAVARIA BOKBIER*
6.5% abv ✪✪✪ Dark Bok
Medium dark, mellow and lacking bitterness.

BAVARIA PILS
5% abv ✪✪ Pils

Smooth, sweet, unbitter, all-purpose Pils.

Other regular beers include: 8.6 (8% abv) and Bavaria Tarwebok* (6.5% abv; wheat bok). A light Pils, an oud bruin table beer and an alcohol-free beer are also produced.

BUDEL
BUDELSE BROUWERIJ
Nieuwstraat 9
6021 HP Budel
Tel: 04958 1369
Smallish independent brewery, operating since 1870 at Budel near the Belgian border in North Brabant. Becoming a darling of Dutch beer lovers because of a tendency to try out some interesting ales in addition to the standard lager range. Total production is 20,000 hl a year. Capucijn is top fermented in the vat, then undergoes cold storage similar to lagering.

BUDELS BOCK*
6.5% abv ✪✪✪ Dark Bok
Dark, sweet brew with a lingering light bitterness.

BUDELS CAPUCIJN
6.5% abv ✪✪✪✪ Dubbel
Beautiful, sweet, malty beer, possibly spiced.

BUDELS PAREL
6% abv ✪✪✪ Kölsch
Clean, Pilsener coloured, well-hopped beer with a definite ale character.

BUDELS PILS
5% abv ✪✪✪ Pils
Hoppier than some.

Other regular beers include: Budels Alt (5.5% abv; altbier) and Naardens Stadbier. There is also an oud bruin table beer and a low alcohol beer.

DRIE HORNE
BIERBROUWERIJ DE DRIE HORNE
Berndijksestraat 63
5171 BB Kaatsheuvel
Tel: 04167 75666
Home brewer Sjef Groothuis set up this tiny commercial brewery in Kaatsheuvel, north of Eindhoven, in

1991 to brew bottled sediment beers. He tends to go for artisanal styles of ale at higher strengths than usual Dutch brews. The beers are produced in batches of 140 litres and annual production is 35 hl. On this scale you can expect some inconsistency, though they are well worth seeking out. The business is due for expansion and a proeflokaal is planned for the near future.
TRIPPELAER
8.5% abv ❸❸❸ Tripel
Strong tripel-style bottle-conditioned ale with a home-brewed flavour.
HORN'S WIT
7% abv ❸❸❸❸ Wheat Beer (unfiltered)
High strength witbier, darker and sweeter than most but very pleasant.
HORN'S BOCK*
7% abv ❸❸❸ Dark Bok Ale
Dryish, sediment brown ale, imitating a bokbier.

Other regular beers include: Drie Horne Meibok* (7% abv; pale bok ale), Horn's Wit 5° (5% abv; wheat beer) and Vat'm Rijnburgs Tripel.

DRIE KRUIZEN

DE DRIE KRUIZEN
Postbus 5921
3273 ZG Westmaas
Tel: 01864 3239
When is a brewery not a brewery? Peter Raaijen started brewing in 1991, by borrowing facilities at the now defunct Hopbloem brewery in Middelburg, Us Heit and Zeeuwsche-Vlaamsche (below). The intention was that he would open the Three Crosses brewery at Westmaas, south of Rotterdam in 1993 to produce around 300 hl of beer a year. Before this opened he had announced plans to open a second in Schiedam and there were even rumours about a third. By the time we went to press no brewery was in operation but there were plenty of beers bearing the Drie Kruizen and Schiedamsch names. We have decided to list details of the beers anyway and clarify the situation in our next edition.

PENCIL BIER
7% abv ❸❸❸ Pale Ale
Sweetish, light amber, sediment beer with abrupt hoppiness.
GRIFFOEN
6.5% abv ❸❸ Pale Ale
Hazy pale ale which turns before its "sell by" date. Needs more work.
KOORNBEURS BOKBIER*
6.5% abv ❸❸❸ Dark Bok Ale
Chestnut coloured, filtered bok ale. Bitter but lacking maturity.
KLETS
6% abv ❸❸❸ Pale Ale
Pale amber, lightly sedimented ale. Overtones of demerara and lychees.
OUDE POSTKANTOOR
5.5% abv ❸❸❸ Pale Ale
Lively, orange-brown sediment brew with candy flavours.

Other regular beers include: Koornbeurs Bier (5.5% abv; pale ale) and Drie Kruizen Kerstbier* (winter ale).

DRIE RINGEN

AMERSFOORTSCHE BROUWERIJ
Kleine Spui 18
3811 BE Amersfoort
Tel: 033 620300
Originally founded as the Amersfortsche Bierbrouwerij at Amersfoort in Utrecht province in 1989. Now far better known by its brand name, The Three Rings. Amersfoort was once a great brewing town and around 300 breweries are known to have been operating here at one time or another. Now there is only one. Production has expanded to 1250 hl a year which makes the company one of the largest of the newer breweries. It has a public sampling room (see Dutch Cafés: Utrecht), is a founder member of BAB and possesses a microbiology laboratory which it allows other members to use to help them counteracting yeast infections. The beers are all filtered. For 1993 we believe that the new Tarwebock replaced the old Bockbier.
DE DRIE RINGEN WINTERBIER*
8% abv ❸❸❸❸ Winter Ale

Good blend of fierce hop character on smooth malt backtastes.

DE DRIE RINGEN TRIPEL
7.5% abv ✪✪✪✪ Tripel
Clear, amber brew without sediment but well put together.

DE DRIE RINGEN BOCKBIER*
6.5% abv ✪✪✪ Dark Bok Ale
Darkish, ruddy-amber ale. In the bok style but smoother.

DE DRIE RINGEN MEIBOK*
6.5% abv ✪✪✪✪ Pale Bok Ale
Clear, deep amber brew, sweeter and weaker than the tripel but similar.

DE DRIE RINGEN HOPPENBIER
5% abv ✪✪✪ Pale Ale
Clean, slightly fruity but unmistakably Dutch pale ale.

Other regular beers include: De Drie Ringen Tarwebock* (6.5% abv; wheat bok ale) and Amersfoorts Wit (5% abv; wheat beer).

GANS

BIERBROUWERIJ DE GANS
Ambachtscentrum
Hollandsche Hoeve
Kattendijksedijk
4463 AL Goes
Tel: 01100 12744

A modern microbrewery, founded in 1988 and based in a craft park on the outskirts of Goes, in Zeeland. Named after a long-standing brewery which had been operating in the town until a few years previously. It brews in batches of 120 litres and produces 100 hl a year, principally for visitors to the brewery on Saturday afternoons and for a few local bars. The beers are usually bottle-conditioned and can sometimes be found further afield. For details of brewery trips and the sampling room see Beer Tourism: Brewery visits.

GANZE BOKBIER*
7.5% abv ✪✪✪ Dark Bok Ale
Deep chestnut, fizzy, straight and dry bok ale.

GANZE BIER DUBBEL
7% abv ✪✪✪ Brown Ale
Dry and spritzy sediment brown ale lacking dubbel character.

GANZE BIER BITTER
5.5% abv ✪✪✪✪ Pale Ale
Bitter, firm, lively sediment pale ale.

LA STRADA WIT
5.5% abv ✪✪✪ Wheat Beer
(unfiltered)
Unsweetened, unspiced sediment wheat beer which drops bright easily.

GANZE BIER VARIA
4.5% abv ✪✪✪ Pale Ale
Thin, bitter, sediment beer lacking subtlety.

Other regular beers include: Ganze Kerstbier* (10% abv; winter ale), Ganze Bier Tripel (8.3% abv; pale ale), Karolinger Bier (7% abv; brown ale), Verenigings Tripel* (6% abv; pale ale), Gooie Mie (5% abv) and Ganze Zomerbock*.

GROLSCH

GROLSCHE BIERBROUWERIJ
Eibergseweg 10
7141 CE Groenlo
Tel: 05440 79111
Fax: 05440 61111

The name is a corruption of Groenlo, the Gelderland town in which the original Grolsch Brewery stands. There is a second brewing plant at Enschede in Overijssel. Grolsch is the second largest independent brewer in the Netherlands with annual production of 1,900,000 hl. In 1990 it shocked observers of the European brewing scene by buying Wickuler-Küpper of Cologne at a sharp price. They followed by buying the British firm Ruddles for less transparent reasons. On their home territory they share business interests with Gulpen, such as a share in the distribution company, De Bierelier, also owned by VBBR. No takeover has been broached publicly.

Their famous Pils was always more popular than other Dutch beers because it was unpasteurised and so had more freshness of flavour. The beer has always been served in stoppered bottles, as the story would have it, because beer drinkers in the Protestant north of the Netherlands are both parsimonious and sober characters, so they would only drink half a bottle at a time. When Grolsch tried to phase out these stoppered bottles in the 1950s they faced unexpectedly staunch resistance but used the publicity superbly to manufacture a marketing coup which serves them well to this day.

In the past decade they have introduced new beers at the rate of one every three years, the latest being the Meibok. Grolsch Dark Beer is brewed for export only. The Premium Dry may have flopped, along with all the other imitators of that Japanese style of tasteless lager.

GROLSCH BOKBIER*
6.5% abv OOOO Dark Bok
Very sweet, very dark and very palatable.

GROLSCH MEIBOK*
6.5% abv OOOO Pale Bok
Well rounded, smooth, almost illustrious amber lager.

GROLSCH AMBER
5% abv OOO Pale Ale
Firm and well-brewed if lacking distinctive character.

GROLSCH PILSNER
5% abv OOO Pils
Fresher flavoured and slightly more bitter than most Dutch Pilseners.

Other regular beers include: Grolsch Premium Dry (4.5% abv; Pils). An oud bruin table beer is also produced.

GULPEN

GULPENER BIERBROUWERIJ
Rijksweg 16
6271 AE Gulpen
Tel: 04450 1956
Fax: 04450 3515

Based at Gulpen, between Maastricht and Aachen at the southern tip of Dutch Limburg and brewing since 1825. They share some projects, such as distribution and exporting, with Grolsch (above). They have also brewed beers for Kroon, St. Martinus and others. St. Joris is brewed on commission and may be the ordinary Pils in unpasteurised form.

Perhaps the most interesting of the established Dutch independent breweries and certainly not one afraid to experiment. In 1989 they introduced Mestreechs Aajt, said to resemble a style that was popular around Maastricht in the 1930s. This is made with the help of Interbrew's Belle Vue plant in Brussels and is diluted at some stage. The brewery says it is taken there primarily for fermentation. Most recently they announced plans to produce Gulpener Witte Kerst, thought to be a Christmas wheat beer. Total brewery production is 130,000 hl per year.

GULPENER BOCK*
6.5% abv OOO Dark Bok
Thin, dark and alcoholic but lacking character.

GULPENER DORT
6.5% abv OOO Dortmunder
Light chestnut, sweetish, mellow lager. Produced since 1953.

GULPENER X-PERT
5% abv OOO Pils
Fine all-malt Pils with bite and a distinct bitterness.

GULPENER PILSNER
5% abv OO Pils
Unimpressive.

ST. JORIS
5% abv OOO Pils
Clear and crisp, filtered, unpasteurised Pils lacking panache.

SJOES
4.5% abv OO Unclassifiable
Queer and characterless blend of the Pils and oud bruin.

Other regular beers include: Gulpener Meibock* (6.5% abv; pale bok). An oud bruin table beer and a light lager are also produced.

HOEKSCHE

BROUWERIJ DE HOEKSCHE
Zingweg 102-103
3262 BD Oud Beijerland

The Hook's Brewery started testing recipes in June 1991 and opened its own plant in 1992. Unfortunately it had ceased trading at the time we went to press, though financial backers were being sought to revive it. Brewer Jan Wolfs is involved in the plans to open a brewery in Schiedam and things should be clearer in the near future.

IJ

BROUWERIJ 'T IJ
Funenkade 7
1018 AL Amsterdam
Tel: 020 622 8325

Founded in 1984 on Amsterdam's waterfront. The brewhouse and brewery tap (see Dutch Cafés: North Holland) are in a converted bath-house. The building is topped by an impressive windmill which can be used for milling malt, though it rarely is. The beers are increasingly popular in the capital and deserve greater exposure. Annual production is currently 1,200 hl. Mug Bitter is brewed mainly for De Mug café in Middelburg, Zeeland but can also appear at the brewery proeflokaal. From the marketing viewpoint, Paas IJ is a meibok ale; IJndejaarsbier appears only at Christmas. The Bockbier may now be called Turbock.

STRUIS
10% abv ✪✪✪✪ Strong Ale
Dark, sourish and heavyweight.
COLUMBUS
9% abv ✪✪✪✪✪ Tripel
Innocent but potent, slightly sour, blond ale, stronger than most tripels.
ZATTE
8% abv ✪✪✪✪ Tripel
Strong, sweet, rounded and blond. Better in the bottle.
IJ BOCKBIER*
6.5% abv ✪✪✪✪ Dark Bok Ale
Lively, fruity, dark reddish-brown bok. Improves with age.
NATTE
6% abv ✪✪✪✪ Brown Ale
Dry and bitter, developing a pleasant sourness with ageing.
MUG BITTER
5% abv ✪✪✪✪ Pale Ale
English best bitter brewed with Belgian hops.
PLZEN
5% abv ✪✪✪ Kölsch
Maverick lightly coloured ale, named after the Czech spelling of Pilsen.

Other regular beers include: IJndejaarsbier* (9% abv; winter ale), Paas IJ* (7% abv: Easter ale) and Speciale Vlo.

KONINGSHOEVEN

TRAPPISTENBIERBROUWERIJ DE SCHAAPSKOOI
Eindhovenseweg 3
5056 RP Berkel-Enschot
Tel: 013 358147
Fax: 013 437472

The sixth of the abbey breweries and the only one in the Netherlands. Founded in 1884 at the modern Cistercian abbey of Onze Lieve Vrouw Koningshoeven near Tilburg, it was for many years, before the arrival of Arcen in 1981, the only Dutch brewery producing ales. Far and away the most commercial of the monastic producers despite fairly low production of 22,000 hl a year. The brewhouse is relatively small but has been completely modernised in the past three years.

There are currently either two or four versions each of the dubbel and tripel, depending on who you believe. VBBR (Allied) commission the Koningshoeven brands, which are unfiltered in bottles and filtered on draught. The La Trappe brands are said to be different brews from the Koningshoeven ones and are unfiltered for the Dutch bottled market but filtered when on draught or when exported via John Martin of Antwerp. The old Tilburg brands, which used to be produced for the Grolsch/Gulpen distribution company, Bestebier, disappeared when this merged with the VBBR company Bierelier.

Quadrupel first appeared in 1991 as a one-off but was successful enough to remain in the range. In 1992, they started to produce a lower gravity draught beer called Blond and a special brew called Enkel for a chain of off-licences. And in case you were left with any doubts that this is a commercial brewery first and foremost, they have also brewed wheat beers for VBBR and Kroon when called upon to do so.

LA TRAPPE QUADRUPEL
10% abv ✪✪✪✪ Trappist Strong
Thick, sweet, chestnut brew. Will probably improve to 5✪ with ageing.

KONINGSHOEVEN TRIPEL
(bottled)
8% abv ●●●●● Trappist Tripel
One of the best Dutch beers when
allowed to mature. Full of fruit, nut
and honey flavours.
LA TRAPPE TRIPEL (unfiltered)
8% abv ●●●● Trappist Tripel
Polished, copper-brown ale with a
sanitised beefiness.
LA TRAPPE TRIPEL (filtered)
8% abv ●●●● Trappist Tripel
Like the unfiltered version but less
well rounded.
KONINGSHOEVEN DUBBEL
(bottled)
6.5% abv ●●●● Trappist Dubbel
Complex but smooth when fresh,
delightfully disorganised when aged.
KONINGSHOEVEN DUBBEL
(draught)
6.5% abv ●●● Trappist Dubbel
Simpler and smoother than the
bottled version.
LA TRAPPE DUBBEL (unfiltered)
6.5% abv ●●●● Trappist Dubbel
Increasingly bitter, darker and dryer
but still a beer of character.
LA TRAPPE DUBBEL (filtered)
6.5% abv ●●● Trappist Dubbel
Bitter, dark and dry but a bit simple.
KONINGSHOEVEN BLOND
6% abv ●●● Pale Ale
Draught pale ale, less impressive
than the real trappist brews.

Other regular beers include:
Koningshoeven Tripel (draught) (9%
abv: trappist tripel) and La Trappe
Enkel (5.5% abv; pale ale).

KROON

DE KROON'S BIERBROUWERIJ
Koesstraat 20
5688 AH Oirschot
Tel: 04997 72002
Independent brewery at Oirschot in
North Brabant, tracing its origins
back to 1627. Annual production is
20,000 hl. No relation to the Belgian
brewery of similar name. In the late
1980s they began to extend their
range of interesting bottom
fermented beers and now appear to
be messing about in the ale line. We
know them to be experimenting
with a wheat beer to be called
Kroon Witbier. They also take on
contract brewing for other
breweries.
KROON BOKBIER*
6.5% abv ●●● Dark Bok
Dark and dryish but lacking finish.
KROON MEIBOK*
6.5% abv ●●●● Pale Bok
Sweetish, amber meibok with a fine
aroma.
KROON BRILJANT
6.5% abv ●●● Dortmunder
Clean, light Dortmunder, similar to
Gulpener Dort.
KROON EGELANTIER
5% abv ●●● Münchener
Peculiar, chestnut coloured, bitter
sweet lager. Like Münchener with
molasses.
KROON PILS
5% abv ●● Pils
Darker than average and bitter-
sweet.

Other regular beers include:
Kikbier (5% abv). An oud bruin table
beer and a low alcohol beer are also
produced.

KUIPERTJE

BIERBROUWERIJ 'T KUIPERTJE
Appeldijk 18
4161 BH Heukelum
Tel: 04188 1602
The Little Copper brewery. Founded
in 1988, at Herwijnen in Gelderland,
moving up the road to its current
site in 1991. They specialise in
bottled sediment ales and had a few
problems at the old brewhouse.
They brew with De Koninck yeast in
the spick and span new one in
Heukelen. This also has its own
licensed sampling room (see Dutch
Cafés: Gelderland). After a lot of
experimenting in the early days, the
beer range is stabilising but subject
to change, with a lot of one-off
brews still appearing. Ammerois and
Bom Stad Bier may by now be out of
production. In 1991 they produced
Winterbier but it failed to appear in
1992. There may be an additional
beer called Professor Ich Tripel. The
beers are bottled with a full

sediment but seem to have quite a short shelf life, maybe as little as two months, before developing acid flavours similar to those found in beers from the Belgian brewery, De Teut. Current annual production of 650 hl is expected to rise.

KUIPERTJE BOCKBIER*
6.5% abv ✪✪✪✪ Dark Bok Ale
Delightfully sweet, unbitter bok ale with strong backtaste of peardrops.

SOWIETS
6% abv ✪✪✪ Brown Ale
Tangy, sweet brown beer with heavy sediment.

LINGEWAL VRIENDENBIER
5.5% abv ✪✪✪ Pale Ale
Polished and well-rounded, typically Dutch pale ale.

Other regular beers include: 't Kuipertje's Meibok* (8% abv; pale bok ale), Prater Fritsius (7.5% abv; pale ale), Ammeroois (7% abv), Nicks (7% abv; pale ale), Bom Stad Bier (6.5% abv) and Tuimel Wit (6.5% abv; wheat beer).

LEEUW

BIERBROUWERIJ DE LEEUW
Pater Beatrixsingel 2
6301 VL Valkenberg an den Geul
Tel: 04406 13434
Fax: 04406 13646

The Lion brewery. Largish independent company from Valkenburg an den Geul, near Maastricht in Dutch Limburg. Established in 1886 by two brewers who had been operating in the area since 1870. Traditionally a lager brewery, they dipped a toe into ale brewing by producing a witbier in 1991. They also brew the Europilsner brand, Karlsquell, under contract. Annual production is 135,000 hl.

LEEUW BOCKBIER*
6.5% abv ✪✪✪ Dark Bok
Dry, roasted bokbier.

SUPERLEEUW
6.5% abv ✪✪✪ Dortmunder
Recently up-graded to be a more characteristic Dortmunder.

JUBILEEUW
5% abv ✪✪✪ Pils

Brewed to an all-malt recipe and distinctively Czech but lacking the smoothness of a great Pils.

LEEUW PILSNER
5% abv ✪✪ Pils
Very ordinary, even when served from a flashy bottle! Only just 2✪.

VALKENBURGS WITBIER
4.8% abv ✪✪✪✪ Wheat Beer (unfiltered)
Sampled on draught. Spicy, sweet, gingered and soft.

VENLOOSCH ALT
4.5% abv ✪✪ Altbier
Dark, roasted altbier of little character.

An oud bruin table beer is also produced.

LINDEBOOM

BIERBROUWERIJ DE LINDEBOOM BV
Engelmanstraat
6086 BD Neer
Tel: 04759 2900
Fax: 04759 2750

The Linden Tree brewery. Independent company, established in 1870 at Neer, near the German border in the northern part of Dutch Limburg. Produces only lagers at present. Production stands at 40,000 hl a year.

LINDEBOOM BOCKBIER*
6.5% abv ✪✪✪ Dark Bok
Dark brown beer with a dryish, clinging bitterness.

LINDEBOOM MEIBOCK*
6.5% abv ✪✪✪✪ Pale Bok
Sweetish, but well-attenuated amber coloured meibok.

LINDEBOOM GOUVERNEUR
5% abv ✪✪ Wiener
Characterless but harmless.

LINDEBOOM PILSNER
5% abv ✪✪✪ Pils
Well balanced, pleasant, dryish Pils, bitterness holding to the end.

An oud bruin table beer is also produced.

MAASLAND

MAASLANDBROUWERIJ
Kantsingel 14
5349 AJ Oss
Tel: 04120 38473
Fax: 04120 45218

Microbrewery founded in 1989 at Oss in North Brabant. Already established as the Netherlands' best producer of spiced ales, its production is still limited to 500 hl a year but deserves to be higher. The beers are strongly influenced in flavour and character by the Belgian brewery, Achouffe. Indeed Achouffe are said to have brewed the 1992 Kerst Bier. Whether the breweries are more than friends is not clear.

D'N SCHELE OS TRIPEL

7.5% abv ❶❶❶❶❶ Spiced Ale
Deliciously spicy, orange-amber coloured sediment ale. Highly aromatic with a complex sweetness deriving from malted barley, wheat and rye.

MAASLAND VOLKOREN KERST BIER*

7% abv ❶❶❶❶ Winter Ale
Rich, soft brown sediment ale, slightly spicy and spritzy.

VOLKOREN BOKBIER*

6.5% abv ❶❶❶❶ Brown Ale
Dark, dryish and delightful. Not really a bok, more a cultured brown ale.

MAASLAND MEI BOCKBIER*

6.5% abv ❶❶❶❶❶ Pale Bok Ale
Excellent, dark amber ale, much like a candied tripel with roasted overtones.

HET ECHTE HAAGSCHE MEIBOCK*

6.5% abv ❶❶❶ Pale Bok Ale
Filtered, sweetish pale ale of character with unpleasant bitter backtaste.

WITTE WIEVEN WITBIER

5.5% abv ❶❶❶❶ Wheat Beer
(unfiltered)
Fruity, unfiltered spiced wheat beer, without the typical Dutch softness.

Other regular beers include: Maasland Paasbier* (6.5% abv; Easter ale).

MOERENBURG

BIERBROUWERIJ MOERENBURG
Jasmijnstraat 17
5014 AR Tilburg
Tel: 013 360518

Founded in July 1992 at Tilburg, a microbrewery with a brew run of only 300 litres a go and an output of only 200 hl a year. Brews only sediment bottled beers for cafés and off-licences in Tilburg, Eindhoven and Oisterwijk. It completely overhauled its beer range in the autumn of 1993. Gouwe Ouwe means Goldie Oldie.

GOUWE OUWE

7.5% abv ❶❶❶ Brown Ale
Slightly sour, burnt and acrid, strong brown sediment ale.

MOERENBURG BOKBIER*

7% abv ❶❶❶ Dark Bok Ale
Plain, burnt, dark sediment beer.

KARAKTAR

6.5% abv ❶❶❶ Brown Ale
Thinnish, slightly candied, sediment brown ale.

MOERENBURG MEIBOK*

5.8% abv ❶❶❶ Dark Bok Ale
Dark, filtered brown beer with an aged character.

MOERENBURG WITBIER

5.5% abv ❶❶❶ Wheat Beer
(unfiltered)
Unsweetened, unspiced, sediment wheat beer which drops bright easily.

Other regular beers include: Moerenburg Zomerbier* (5.5% abv; pale ale).

ONDER DE LINDEN

BROUWERIJ ONDER DE LINDEN
Haagsteeg 16
6708 PM Wageningen
Tel: 08370 22845

The Under the Linden brewery. A tiny concern, founded in 1989 at Wageningen in Gelderland. Owner Leo Saaijer tends to brew ales on a single brew run, then stick with the brews which go well. Their longest standing brand, Quintus, is the only current Dutch attempt at a Flemish-style old brown ale. Annual production is around 90 hl, which is small. Additional beers called Herfstbier, Termineel, Veenman Bier and Wampus Wit have appeared.

GELDERS TRIPEL
7.7% abv ✪✪✪ Tripel
Superb fragrant hop. Only sampled when aged, so may be finer.

Other regular beers include: Sinterklaas Bier* (8.2% abv; winter ale), Onder de Linden Bokbier* (6.5% abv; dark bok ale), Quintus (6.5% abv; old brown) and Onder de Linden Meibok* (6% abv; pale bok ale).

QUIST

QUIST BROUWERIJ
Postbus 93
9780 AB Bedum

Long time home brewer Peter Quist started production in September 1993. The first beer is a copper coloured, clear pale ale. The second brew is expected to be a wheat beer, to be called Ijsberg. This is the northernmost brewery in the guide.

ST. CHRISTOFFEL

ST. CHRISTOFFEL
BIERBROUWERIJ
Bredeweg 14
6042 GG Roermond
Tel: 04750 15740
Fax: 04750 16402

Microbrewery, started in 1986 at Roermond, near the German border in northern Dutch Limburg, by Leo Brand, a member of the family which owned the Royal Brand brewery. One of the simplest breweries in the world, dedicated to the production in fairly small quantities of high quality lagers. It started by producing a single, unfiltered Pilsener and sold it in an equally distinctive stoppered bottle. It has since experimented with a Münchener, now out of production, and more recently a stronger Pils. Definitely the best lagers from either Belgium or the Netherlands, the Pilseners are a whisker away from a five star rating. Annual output has now risen to 4,000 hl.

CHRISTOFFEL BLOND
5% abv ✪✪✪✪ Pils
Bottled with a light sediment, darkish and bitter with bags of character.

CHRISTOFFEL BIER
5% abv ✪✪✪✪ Pils
Draught and filtered, bitter and characterful in the best German tradition.

Other regular beers include: Christoffel Robertus (6% abv; Pilsener).

ST. MARTINUS

SINT MARTINUS
BIERBROUWERIJ
Oude Kijk in 't Jatstraat 16
9712 EG Groningen
Tel: 050 189706

The most northerly brewery in the Guide. A microbrewery in every sense. When they started in June 1992 there were only two smaller brewhouses in the world. The current range consists of two regular beers and three seasonal brews which will vary in recipe each year. The Valentijnsbier is for St Valentine's Day. There is also a brew for the local student beer society and there have been other experimental brews. Total annual production is currently 150 hl but a new brewhouse is planned. The company also owns De Bierwinkel off licence (see Beer Shops and Warehouses) and the café Het Paard Van Troje (see Dutch Cafés: Groningen) which are in the same complex of buildings.

CLUYN
8.8% abv ✪✪✪✪ Brown Ale
Dark amber, slightly hazy, sweetish and spicy, though not spiced.

NOORDERBLOND
5.5% abv ✪✪✪ Wheat Beer
(unfiltered)
Very dry with sediment but no protein haze. 30% abv malted wheat.

Other regular beers include: Bommen Berend Meibock* (6.5% abv; pale bok ale), Eindejaarsbier* (winter ale) and Valentijnsbier*.

SCHIEDAMSCH

BROUWERIJ SCHIEDAMSCH
Schiedam

See the comments for the Drie Kruizen and Hoeksche breweries (above). As far as we can piece together, the combined efforts of people from those two projects should create a real brewery called Schiedamsch in Schiedam before the Guide is published. This is a good thing, considering the number of beers already on the market which claim on their labels to come from it! In reality, at the time of going to press we think they are brewed at Zeeuwsche-Vlaamsche (see below) and marketed by the future owners.
SCHIEDAMSCH BOCK*
8% abv ❸❸❸❸ Dark Bok Ale
Dark, sweetish, matured strong bok ale produced for autumn 1993.
SCHIEDAMSCH SINT JAN
5% abv ❸❸❸❸ Pale Ale
Light amber coloured, subtle pale ale with staying power.

US HEIT

FRIESE BIERBROUWERIJ
Lorentzstraat 15
8606 JP Sneek
Tel: 05153 393

Probably Friesland's first brewery for 100 years when it opened in 1985. For a while it operated out of a converted cowshed in Uitwellingerga just down the road but then moved to its current premises to be in the same building as its parent company, Diroy BV, who are drinks wholesalers. All beers are now marketed under the Us Heit brand name that was first introduced in 1990. Current production is 2,500 hl per annum. The two lagers are only matured in the tank for one week, leaving them bland and unimpressive. However, some of the ales are among the best in the Netherlands. Dubbel Wit is only available on draught. Frysk Bier and Kerstbier (introduced in 1991) are only available in 75 cl bottles. Us Heit means "Our Father" in Frysk

and is the name by which Friesland's founder, Count William-Louis of Nassau-Dez is known.
US HEIT FRYSK BIER
6% abv ❺❺❺❺❺ Pale Ale
An accomplished premium pale ale with a delicate sediment. Full aroma of Northern Brewer and Perle hops, beautifully bitter like Orval.
US HEIT BUORREN BIER
6% abv ❹❹❹❹ Pale Ale
Fruity, copper coloured sediment ale with faint herbal undertones.
US HEIT TWELS BOKBIER*
6% abv ❸❸❸ Dark Bok Ale
Dark and sweetish ale-type bok with sediment.
US HEIT TWELS PILSENER SPECIAAL
5% abv ❷❷ Münchener
Dark and sweetish, with Munich malt but drab.
US HEIT TWELS PILSENER
5% abv ❷❷ Pilsener
Lightish lager with unsubtle flavours.
    Other regular beers include: Us Heit Kerstbier* (7.5% abv; winter ale) and Us Heit Dubbel Wit (6% abv; wheat beer). There is also a low alcohol beer.

UTRECHT

UTRECHTSE
STOOMBIERBROUWERIJ
Oude Gracht 99
3511 AE Utrecht
Tel: 030 311864
Fax: 030 367377

Home brew pub in Utrecht (see Dutch Cafés: Utrecht), dating back to 1990. It operates in the cellars of the Stadskasteel, a mediaeval mansion on Utrecht's oldest canal. Brews only wheat beers at present. Jonge Daen is the filtered version of Ouwe Daen. We believe the beer is only available at the Oudaen and on draught. There are brewery tours (see Beer Tourism: Brewery visits).
OUDAEN TARWEBOK
6.8% abv ❸❸❸ Wheat Bok Ale
Copper coloured, filtered ale. Wheat beer sweetness with bok depth, but no bitterness or maturity.

JONGE DAEN

5% abv ❸❸❸ Wheat Beer (filtered)

Sweet, harmless, filtered wheat beer.

OUWE DAEN

5% abv ❸❸❸❸ Wheat Beer
(unfiltered)

The unfiltered version has a more
grainy character and scrapes a
higher rating.

VAETE

BROUWERIJ DE VAETE
N. Kraayertsedijk 2
's Heer-Arendskerke

Not yet brewing at the time of going
to press. A new wave brewery about
to open at Lewedorp on the
outskirts of 's Heer-Arendskerke,
near Goes in Zeeland. The first beer
will be a 5% abv wheat beer and the
second a strongish winter ale.

VERKEERDE WEERELD

BROUWERYE DE VERKEERDE
WEERELD
Ezelsveldlaan 62
Delft

New brewery planned to open in the
tourist town of Delft, South Holland,
shortly after we go to press. It is
being constructed from the old plant
from the Peizer Hopbel brewery in
Drente and we understand that the
old brewing team from there are
involved in the new project. It will
be built in a science and technology
museum.

WEESHUIS

HET WEESHUIS
Herman Heijermanstraat 35
3451 AL Vleuten
Tel: 03407 1221

The smallest production of any
"commercial" brewery in the world,
surely. Annual output is a mere 500
litres a year, brewed at the Onder de
Linden brewery by agreement.
Going since 1991, its future plans
are not yet clear.

Regular beers include: Bijlevelt
Grand Cru Vleutens Tripel (8.5%
abv; tripel).

ZEEUWSCHE VLAAMSCHE

ZEEUWSCHE VLAAMSCHE
BROUWERIJ
Absdaalseweg 2
4561 GG Hulst
Tel: 01140 14339

Unusual new brewery opened in the
town of Hulst, 30 km west of
Antwerp in Dutch Flanders, the
southernmost part of Zeeland
province. Founder and brewer Geert
de Smet hired Chris Wisse from
Domus in Leuven to take over the
brewing at the beginning of 1993.
(Chris's training involved a long spell
as chief barman to Jan de Bruyne at
't Brugs Beertje in Bruges.) Infamous
for producing "colourful" beers,
Paranoia first came out in green,
then pink. The brewhouse seems to
be open to every putative new small
brewery in the Netherlands and it
has test brewed or brewed to
commission a remarkable number of
bottled ales. Here we only list their
own label products. The beers are
improving in quality since the
change of brewer but have a way to
go yet.

PARANOIA GROENE

7% abv ❸❸❸ Pale Ale

Filtered pale ale dyed lime green.
Spicy brew spoiled by chemical
bitterness.

PARANOIA ROOD

7% abv ❸❸ Pale Ale

Like a hazier, pink-dyed version of
the last beer with more chemical
backtaste.

ZEEUWSCHE BRUINE

6% abv ❸❸❸ Old Brown

Sour, hazy brown ale, somewhere
between old brown, lambic and a
dark version of the Witte.

ZEEUWSCHE WITTE

5% abv ❸❸❸ Wheat Beer
(unfiltered)

Cloudy with both protein and
sediment. Goes acid before its sell by
date.

ZON

BROUWERIJ DE ZON
Schaijk

The Sun brewery, founded in 1992,
north east of 's Hertogenbosch in
North Brabant province. As well as
the two existing beers, a dark 6%
abv ale is planned.

Regular beers include: Brabants
Glorie (6.5% abv; tripel) and
Schaijkse Troost.

Albert Hoffmann stirring the pot at the Maximiliaans Brewery in Amsterdam

Dutch Cafés

RECOMMENDED CAFES IN ELEVEN of the twelve Dutch provinces are listed here. We have not located any notable beer cafés in the twelfth and newest province, Flevoland, and so it has been omitted. For further information about the layout of information included here, see the beginning of the Belgian Cafés section.

Drenthe

THE PROVINCE OF DRENTHE is flat, neat, Calvinist and potentially very boring. If the EC ever gives grants for a cultural decoke and rebore, Drenthe will be near the front of the queue.

Its capital, Assen, was still a village at the beginning of the 20th century. Virtually its only claim to fame is the motorcycle track which hosts the Dutch TT Motorcycle Grand Prix on the last Saturday in June. The rest is land which has been reclaimed from nature by draining the fen and cultivating the moor. As you drive through on the way to Groningen you may wonder why they bothered.

For the beer drinker, the good news is the formation of the Alliantie der Gilde Tappers, an organisation formed to promote the beer cafés in Drenthe and nearby Groningen. It is hoped that the beer culture of the province will take several steps forward as a result.

PEIZE

8 km SSW of Groningen on N372
Typically smart and well-ordered northern Dutch village.

PEIZER HOPBEL

3 Hoofdstraat
Tel: 05908 33607
Café: ✪✪✪✪ *Beer:* ✪✪✪✪

Peize's Hopcone used to be famous for being the Netherlands' only home brew house. It produced a beer in the German altbier style and an annual bok ale, under the direction of its co-owners, Gulpen and Grolsch. However, the brewing operation was closed early in 1993, leaving the pub to survive on its reputation for excellent food, an extensive and intelligent beer list and some smart decor. You will find it just off the main road by Peize's prominent windmill. Its huge thatched roof gives a deceptively small appearance to a large building housing a proper restaurant as well as a pleasant, high-ceilinged, wood-panelled, grey-painted, stone-floored café. The menu features excellent seafood and grilled meats. The beer list of over 70 continues to feature beers of the same name as those produced in the defunct brewery. A little birdie tells us they come from the Van Eecke brewery in West Flanders.
Saturday & Sunday 15.00 – 23.00
Other days 11.00 – 23.00
CLOSED TUESDAY

Friesland

FRIESLAND is another country. It has its own language, Frysk, which is said to bear a resemblance to mediaeval English but little else. You can tune in to it on the local radio station. It also has a unique flag; seven red lilies shaped like hearts, on a white background crossed by diagonal, bright cobalt blue stripes. The regional culture reflects quiet, rural traditions rent asunder by the effects of strong Protestantism, and shows in the relative dearth of cafés.

Friesland attracts an increasing number of foreign visitors because of its extensive network of waterways and their associated leisure pursuits. If the tourist industry is to succeed, however, there will need to be changes in the attitude towards drinking. At present, most locals do their drinking at home, so beer houses and attractive cafés are few and far between.

Our first edition listed no entries at all for Friesland. Neither of those below would make our pages in other provinces, but to encourage the process of change we acknowledge their limited success. Even the beers of Friesland's own brewery, Us Heit, are difficult to find locally. It will be interesting to see if the putative new brewery at De Knipe, just north of Heerenveen, manages to bring any more cheer.

LEEUWARDEN
Major town [IR]

The provincial capital of Friesland is an odd place. Friesland's beer lovers could claim to be an oppressed minority and Leeuwarden (pop, 85,000) reflects this. It must be the only city in Europe with no café culture. Indeed, the pervading atmosphere is that anyone found lurking in a café is a low-life, that it is not something a decent person would consider and that real men go to church. Although restaurants are much in evidence, cafés are few and far between and the number selling even a handful of decent ales is tiny. Our advice to visiting beer drinkers is simple. Refuse to go! If for reasons of trade, commerce or posting to the RAF base, you feel obliged to visit, consider becoming tee-total. If desperate, read on. Remember, Mata Hari was born here.

HOFNAR
8 Auckamastraatje
Café: ✪✪ *Beer:* ✪✪✪

The town hall is in Hofplein, a small cobbled square at the geographical centre of the city and the best two cafés we found in Leeuwarden are both situated here. Unfortunately the **Oranje Bierhuis** sells only Heineken but is a classic brown café, worth a peek. The Hofnar is a couple of doors up the tiny street just beyond it and seems to be shaping up to be a beer café. There is no university in town. If there was, the students would flock here. High stools, dark walls, some breweriana, loud music and a smell of burning rope. Your 38-year-old editor was the oldest customer. No food but plenty of soul. Fifteen special beers including four trappists and some German imports. Encourage them.

*Sunday to Wednesday 16.00 –
01.00*
*Thursday to Saturday 16.00 –
02.00*

SNEEK

20 km SSW of Leeuwarden on A7
(E22) [IR]

Sneek (pop. 28,000), known as Snits
in the Frysk language, is saved from
its lack of decent beer cafés by being
perhaps the most attractive town in
the northern Netherlands. Not to be
missed is the dainty brickwork of the
17th century Waterpoort
(Watergate), a hang-on from the old
town fortifications. There is no
university to stimulate beer culture
but it has a teacher training college
and a fair number of tourists in
summer from the waterways. If you
do not like our suggestion, the
attractive café of the **Hotel
Hanenburg** at no. 2, Wijde

Noorderhorne (tel: 05150 12570)
stocks half a dozen special beers and
also has a fine restaurant, an
exceptionally friendly welcome and
smart, good value accommodation.

OUWE VAT

2 Leeuwardeweg
Tel: 05150 17111
Café: ✪✪✪ *Beer:* ✪✪

In any other province, The Old
Barrel would not even get a passing
mention. In Sneek it represents the
only café with 15 beers. A modern
lounge with all-enveloping muzak
and a couple of dartboards. Set back
from the ring road behind the canal
on the corner of the turning to
Leeuwarden. The hopeful sign is the
careful and ornate beer menu with
its worthy write-ups of beers which
would be commonplace elsewhere.
We hope we were unlucky with the
disinterested barman.

CAFÉ RATING:

✪✪✪✪✪ = a classic of its kind

✪✪✪✪ = well worth seeking
out

✪✪✪ = above average

✪✪ = ordinary but pleasant

✪ = lacking something

BEER RATING:

✪✪✪✪✪ = exceptional range
of well-kept beers

✪✪✪✪ = well above average
range and/or quality

✪✪✪ = interesting or above
average list

✪✪ = typical list

✪ = not really a beer café

Gelderland

GELDERLAND HOLDS A PIVOTAL position in modern Netherlands between the flatlands of the Protestant north, the Burgundian traditions of the Catholic south, the urban sprawl of the Randstad in the west and the German border area in the east.

Its three main towns, Apeldoorn, Arnhem and Nijmegen, form the spine, running north to south. In the east is the under-populated Achterhoek region, reclaimed bog which is now a fertile agricultural area, interspersed with woodland. In the north west is the Veluwe, a woody heathland area with a lakeside coastal strip overlooking the new island province of Flevoland.

East of Nijmegen the Waal peels off the Rhine, which divides at Arnhem into the IJssel and the Nederrijn (Lower Rhine). The strategic importance of this led to the south of the province seeing some of the fiercest fighting in the liberation of the Netherlands in 1944, as Allied troops tried to push through to the industrial heartlands of the Ruhr, less than 100 km south east of here.

The best known brewery in Gelderland is Grolsch, at Groenlo. The other four are the newer ale breweries of Raaf, Kuipertje, Onder de Linden and Weeshuis.

ARNHEM
Major town [IC]
The provincial capital (pop. 180,000). On the right bank of the Nederrijn. By April 1945 after the Allies had made a second attempt to take the town after the "bridge too far" offensive, less than 150 houses were habitable. The new Arnhem is an impressive recreation of the old centre.

North of the town is the Openluchtmuseum, a collection of traditional Dutch buildings laid out in a country park. Nearby is the Burgers Zoo and Safari Park. While the latter is a bit sad, the Zoo is worth a visit if only to experience the extraordinary atmosphere of the Burgers Bush, a huge hothouse laid out like a stretch of Indonesian jungle. South of the town is the Hartenstein Airborne Museum at Oosterbeek which illustrates the Battle of Arnhem without labouring the cock-ups.

MOORTGAT
35 Ruiterstraat
Tel: 085 450393
In the centre of town near Korenmarkt. Café-biljart 't Moortgat is a brown café with billiards, stocking around 120 beers. These are mainly ales, of which three quarters are Belgian and most of the rest are Dutch. No food, only nibbles. Christmas Day is the only day it closes. They run special beer evenings and the odd chess tournament.
Monday to Wednesday 12.00 – 01.00
Thursday to Saturday 12.00 – 02.00
Sunday 16.00 – 01.00

DIEREN
15 km NE of Arnhem off N48 [IC]
Small town on the way from Arnhem to Zutphen. In high summer there is a restored steam railway which runs from the main station to Apeldoorn.

WAGERIJ
1 Zutphensestraatweg
Tel: 08330 14105
Two hundred metres from the
station on the corner of Spoorstraat;
a brown café and bistro which is
gently expanding its range of
specialist beers. More reports please.

HARDERWIJK
25 km NW of Apeldoorn off A28
(E232) [IC]
A seaside town which lost its sea.
Once a fortress on an outcrop in the
Zuiderzee, the building of the
Afsluitsdijk and subsequent
reclamation of the island province of
Flevoland has left Harderwijk as a
small lakeside resort that looks out
across the water to a newly
constructed land. Its impressively
enormous, brick-built church (the
Grote Kerk of course) betrays a
greater past.

LUXEMBOURG
42 Smeepoortstraat
Tel: 03410 19019
Café: ●●● *Beer:* ●●●
Once a member of the De Beiaard
chain of beer cafés, the Luxembourg
set its own course in the summer of
1993, as the Hotel-Café-Restaurant
Luxembourg. They have crunched
the beer list down to 40 but this is
still unusually high for the area. It is
a dark, noisy, popular café attracting
a wide range of young and not-so-
young customers. There is a
dartboard and a billiards table. The
restaurant (Wed – Sun: 17.00 to
21.00) was Mexican when we last
checked. The accommodation is
good value (singles from NFl 55,
doubles from NFl 80). If you are
heading across the bridge to
Flevoland and the dyke to North
Holland, we think this is your last
chance of an unusual beer for
50 km.
Sunday to Thursday 16.00 –
01.00
Friday & Saturday 16.00 – 04.00

HEUKELUM
25 km S of Utrecht off A15 (E31)
Small village north east of
Gorinchem, on the banks of the
Linge, which marks the provincial
border with South Holland.

KUIPERTJE BROUWERIJ PROEFLOKAAL
48 Appeldijk
Tel: 04188 1602
Sedate tasting room with heavy
furnishings in a converted coach
house by the brewery. Only the
beers from 't Kuipertje brewery are
available. The only other beverages
available are tea and coffee but
beware: because of brewery
licensing regulations, only 2 kg of
sugar are allowed on the premises at
any one time, so they may run out!

MOLENHOEK
7 km S of Nijmegen on N271
Village on the North Brabant border,
which is home to the Netherlands'
second largest established new wave
brewery.

BROUWERIJMUSEUM RAAF PROEFLOKAAL
232 Rijksweg
Tel: 080 581177
Café: ●●●● *Beer:* ●●
Although postally it is in Heumen,
you will find the Raaf brewery on
the N271 at Molenhoek. Parties can
book a tour of the brewery and for a
small entrance fee anyone can look
around the museum of brewing. The
proeflokaal is free of charge and is
used as a regular meeting place by
locals, especially on Sunday
lunchtimes in summer. Indoors is a
sparse but pleasant tiled café, which
boasts an open fire in winter.
Outdoors, the splendid garden has a
terrace for drinking. The range of
beer is limited to Witte Raaf, Raaf
Tripel and the occasional seasonal
brew. Outside the restricted opening
hours the premises are for private
hire and apparently do a brisk trade
in wedding receptions. Although
food is limited, we can recommend
the Sunday breakfast, served from
from 11.00 to 13.00.
Sunday 11.00 – 18.00
Other days 12.00 – 17.00
CLOSED MONDAY; and
TUESDAY to SATURDAY (Sep -
Jun)

NIJMEGEN
Major town [IC]
Large town (pop. 150,000) near the place where the Nederrijn joins the Maas. It is surrounded by seven "hills". Perhaps the northernmost point of the true south Netherlands culture.

Nijmegen was the bridge in the Battle of Arnhem which was not "too far" but the town still suffered heavy bombardment. As in Arnhem, reconstruction has been extensive, and only completed around the Grote Markt in 1970. The inland port now carries ships of up to 6,000 tonnes on their way from Rotterdam to the Ruhr.

Velorama, the national museum of bicycles at 107 Waalkade and the Afrika Museum in Berg en Dal will reward an inexpensive meander. If you prefer the plainly bizarre, then between Easter and October find the Heiligland Stichting just off the Groesenbeek road, 4 km south east of the city centre. This is a recreation of the major New Testament sites of ancient Palestine, set in 125 acres of drained Dutch fen.

PUMPKE
65 Molenstraat
Tel: 080 229255
From the station, take the boulevard called Burgem van Schaeckmathon Singel to the designer roundabout and then take the second left to find Molenstraat. From the Grote Markt take Broerstraat. Unusually for somewhere in the town centre, there is convenient parking. The splendid old brown café, heavily furnished in wood and decorated with more than its share of old brewery adverts, claims to have been an "academy of beer" for over 50 years. Certainly it was one of the first cafés in the Netherlands to join the beer revolution of the early 1970s. Its current beer list offers 180 choices, including 17 on draught. Food is limited to nibbles. There is some seating outdoors in good weather.
Opening hours 12.00 – 03.00
CLOSED SUNDAY

SAMSON
4 Houtstraat
Tel: 080 233023
At the end of Molenstraat heading away from the station, turn left to find 1944 Plein. Houtstraat runs off this. Samson is a well-run brown café in this street. It gets busy in the evenings and attracts serious billiards players in the afternoons. Sixty beers, of which eight are on draught. Snacks are available at all times and the hot rolls and meatballs are both recommended. There is a terrace outside.
Monday to Friday 10.00 – 02.00
Saturday 11.00 – 02.00
Sunday 14.00 – 02.00

WAGENINGEN
15 km W of Arnhem on N225
Suburban town on the right bank of the Nederrijn. Ten km north east of here is the Hoge Veluwe national park, over 150 Km^2 of woodland and heath, which is home to herds of red deer and packs of wild boar. Within its boundary, near the village of Otterlo, is the Kröller-Muller museum and art gallery with its sculpture park and some 278 works by Van Gogh.

VLAAMSCHE REUS
4 Molenstraat
Tel: 08370 12834
The Flemish Giant is a well-managed, clean, modern-style café in the town centre. It specialises in beers and stocks 110 different varieties, including a good range of trappist brews. They often go for a beer "theme" week with extra varieties bought in. Food is minimal. The owners describe their clientele as mixed, with a heavy smattering of ageing students. Background music is mainly blues and nostalgia pop. They have a beer book library. The town's other café for beer lovers is **Quintus**, the proeflokaal of the Onder de Linden brewery, at 16 Haagsteeg. Unfortunately, we have no details of its opening times or facilities.
Sunday to Wednesday 15.00 – 01.00
Thursday to Saturday 15.00 – 02.00

Groningen

GRONINGEN is the north eastern province of the Netherlands. Like the rest of the Protestant north its traditions are more restrained and less hearty than the cosmopolitan central regions and Burgundian Catholic south.

The province's north coast is still called the Marshlands, though most of that area is now agricultural. Some of the land was reclaimed from the sea but nature has fought back in other areas. The southern and central parts of the province are as flat as a pannekoek.

In our first edition we prophesied a burgeoning of beer culture in Groningen and we have been proved right. The past two years have seen the opening of the province's first new brewery, St. Martinus of Groningen, recently followed by Quist of Bedum. There are now many more cafés with interesting beer lists plus a number of specialist beer shops.

The creation of a new organisation for beer cafés, AGT, also bodes well for the future. The list of its members appears at te end of the listings for Zeeland.

GRONINGEN
Major town [IC]
However you arrive in Groningen, the simplest way to orientate yourself is to start at the railway station, which is alongside the bus station and the only large, free, easily locatable car park in the centre of town.

From the front of the station turn right, past the bus stops for Veendam and Winschoten, until you reach the crossroads. Turning left across the canal, the road becomes Herestraat and if you proceed in a straight line come what may, you will eventually find the Grote Markt, the hub of the city.

In Grote Markt are the tourist information office, the Saturday market and numerous cafés selling an increasing number of ales. Certainly sufficient to keep you busy while you get your bearings. While sober, try the History Museum on Praediniussingel and the Martini (Gothic) and Martinus (neo-Gothic) churches.

GROOTE GRIET
37 Grote Markt
Tel: 050 140939
Café: ❂❂❂ *Beer:* ❂❂❂❂
This long, dimly lit brown café in the city's main square, 100 metres from Tourist Information, divides beer lovers. Some hate it for being noisy and a bit flip with its beer list. Others praise it for being a standard bearer for decent beer in the north. We like it for what it is. Loud, often lively, carrying over 70 beers (including brews from 't IJ and Leeuw) and knowledgeable about the beers (when they want to be). The name could mean "Great Godwit", a species of bird found in the Groningen marshes. In fact, it refers to the same cannon as its namesake in Ghent. The better seating is found at the back of the long bar. They do not serve the terrace area outside on the market place but another beer café, **De Tapperij**, in the basement of the Grand Café Bruxelles a couple of doors down, does. This is a grubby basement brown café stocking

around forty beers. Some other cafés in the Grote Markt show leanings towards interesting beer but none really justifies a full entry yet.
Monday to Thursday 11.00 – 01.00
Friday & Saturday 11.00 – 02.00
Sunday 16.00 – 01.00

PAARD VAN TROJE
5 Kleine Kromme Elleboog
Tel: 050 120050
Café: ❊❊❊ *Beer:* ❊❊❊❊

The Trojan Horse pub, the St. Martinus Brewery and the Bierwinkel off-licence are all part of the same group of small businesses and currently can be found side by side in a small alley off Oude Kijk in 't Jatstraat. To find this, leave the Grote Markt via Zwanestraat (see "Ugly Duck" below) and turn right at the crossroads at the end. The bar is plain and simple but will grow atmospheric with usage. Food is limited to toasted sandwiches. The main reason to come here is the beer list of 60 choices. As well as the two regular beers from the kitchen brewery next door, Cluyn and Nooderblond, you might find one of their seasonal beers. If not, you may find the real trappist version of one or two of the Westvleteren beers - very rare in the northern Netherlands. If you are feeling adventurous, turn right out of the café and then take a left to reach good pub hunting territory. If you are heading home, the Bierwinkel has an excellent selection of beers (see Beer Shops & Warehouses).
Monday to Saturday 16.00 – late
Sunday 19.00 – late

UGLY DUCK
28 Zwanestraat
Tel: 050 123192
Café: ❊❊❊ *Beer:* ❊❊❊

The north western exit from the Grote Markt becomes Zwanestraat (alternatively Swaenestraat). The Ugly Duck is a split-level café with a billiards table at the top of the stairs and high chairs at the bar. The beer list of 35 may not be impressive elsewhere but puts it at the cutting edge in Groningen. The lunchtime snacks are popular but the fuller evening menu (from 17.00 till 21.30) is better and tries to feature a good choice for vegetarians, as well as a range of grills and fish. There is a piano too.
Monday to Saturday 12.00 – late
Sunday 13.00 – late

SCHIERMONNIKOOG
35 km NW of Groningen, off the north coast
Schiermonnikoog is the smallest inhabited island in the Netherlands. It can be reached by a passenger ferry from near the village of Lauwersoog (on N361). In the Middle Ages, this was still part of the mainland but just as the Dutch have reclaimed land from the sea, so nature has reclaimed some of the northern dunes in return. Isolation and geology combine to form beaches on its northern coast which match those found in any tropical paradise. Unfortunately, the climate does not.

OUDE BOOTHUIS
Langestreek
"It Oude Boothuis" is local dialect for The Old Boathouse Inn and indeed the café is just that, a converted lifeboat station. It serves the main settlement of this holiday island but remains open all year round. It is a typical brown café keeping a range of over 40 beers, including the brews from the St. Martinus brewery. Food is practically non-existent. We think it is the northernmost café in the Netherlands. If not, it is certainly the northernmost in the Guide.

VEENDAM
25 km ESE of Groningen off N33
Typically well organised, small northern town served by several industrial waterways and with a pedestrian precinct at its centre. If visiting during the day be sure to find the delightfully peaceful public park with its moated cemetry.

AAIERDOPPIE
9 Kerkstraat
Tel: 05987 18221
Café: ❊❊❊❊ *Beer:* ❊❊❊❊
On the main walkway through the

pedestrian precinct at the heart of the town. A modern, long bar that will become browner as the years pass. Well managed, well maintained and attractive. It stocks an interesting beer list totalling around 80, and including some unusual Belgian finds for the area. There is a small covered terrace out front and a TV at the end of the bar. The café itself serves only small snacks but there are Greek and Mexican restaurants opposite. To find the park, turn left and left again.

Monday to Friday 15.00 – late
Saturday & Sunday 13.00 – late

WINSCHOTEN

35k ESE of Groningen off A7 (E22) [IR]

Pleasant, small market town, 10 km from the border with northern Germany.

CARAMBOLE

2 Blijhamsterstraat
Tel: 05970 24190
Café: ✪✪✪ *Beer:* ✪✪✪✪

The main church in Winschoten sits in the Markt Plein. Blijhamsterstraat runs off this and the Biertapperij Carambole is 50 metres down the street on your right. There are 85 beers, mainly from Belgium, with surprisingly few German imports. The bar snacks menu is broad. The clientele is mixed with an over-representation of young people attracted by the wide variety of table games, including two full-size snooker tables, American pool and a full-size Dutch billiards table (no pockets). Hence the café's name, which means "Cannon", as in hitting two balls with the cue ball. They have a lot of Dutch and German tourists here but the British are still rare. The welcome is warm but expect a few questions about how you came to be in the far north. Your chance to say "I'm only here for the beer".

Opening hours 14.00 – late

Limburg

THE DUTCH PART OF LIMBURG hangs like a tonsil at the bottom right hand corner of the map of the Netherlands. Around the city of Maastricht and industrial area of Sittard, it seems to squeeze itself like toothpaste into a crevice between Belgium and Germany.

Its northern half, organised around the border towns of Roermond and Venlo is part of the agriculturally poor flatlands that continue into Germany. The ceramics industry is a big employer here. The southern part used to be a great mining area but when demand for coal fell, the Dutch government invested heavily to attract businesses like the Volvo (Daf) car plant, to avoid economic decline.

The area between Maastricht and the German border has some beautiful rolling countryside and the nearest thing the Netherlands has to real hills. It remains one of the Netherlands' centres of brewing and still boasts three established independent breweries, Alfa, Gulpen and Leeuw, as well as the Heineken subsidiaries, Brand and Ridder. In 1858 the province was home to 220 commercial breweries.

ARCEN
15 km N of Venlo off N271
Village on the banks of the Maas with a famous revivalist brewery. Kasteeltuinen Arcen is a 17th century castle with landscaped gardens and a few typical tourist trappings.

HARMONIE†
2 Maasstraat
Tel: 04703 1608
The Harmony is believed to stock around 50 beers, including 15 Dutch ones. Of the rest we know little.
Monday to Friday 20.00 – 02.00
Saturday & Sunday 14.00 – 02.00

PROEVERIJ
46 Kruisweg
Tel: 04703 2459
The Sampling Room is Arcener Stoombrouwerij's brewery tap. It serves around 20 beers, including seven on draught. There is no Pils but every beer from the brewery is included plus a range of brews from the Belgian firm, Timmermans. Food is limited to snacks but some of these are quite hearty. Brewery tours can be made by arrangement, preferably from Tuesday to Saturday. The café welcomes families.

Opening hours 11.00 – 19.00
CLOSED MONDAY; and
CLOSED SUNDAY (Sep - Apr)

BEEK
12 km NNE of Maastricht off A2 (E25) [IC]
An industrial and residential suburban town (pop. 17,000) to the north of Maastricht. Convenient for the airport.

GEVELKE
4 Prins Mauritslaan
Tel: 046 371904
Café: ✪✪✪ *Beer:* ✪✪✪✪
From the main line station, Beek-Elsloo, turn left onto the main road and after 600 metres, left again into the town. On your left, after 50 metres is this cosy, modernish, well-managed, suburban high street beer café. The beer list currently runs to around 80. There is a small streetside terrace. Inside, a pool table is prominent. The only food available in the bar is small snacks. However, a proper bistro restaurant operates upstairs (Tue - Sun: 12.00 to 22.00).
Monday 20.00 – 03.00
Tuesday to Saturday 11.00 – 03.00
Sunday 12.00 – 03.00

CADIER EN KEER

5 km ESE of Maastricht on N278
Wayside village on the old road from
Maastricht to Aachen. Reach it by
bus no. 54 from Maastricht station
(half-hourly from 08.00 to 20.00).

AUBERGE CADIER MONTAGNE

17 Rijksweg
Tel: 04407 1253
Café: ✪✪✪ *Beer:* ✪✪✪✪

It has not been an auberge since
1982 and the montagne is the 30
metres worth of gentle hillock
which counts as a mountain around
here but who cares? This large,
friendly roadside café and restaurant
took up an interest in beers in 1985.
Currently it stocks around 75 and
you can drink them in the spacious
high-ceilinged café and bistro, or
outside on the terrace. The kitchen
serves anything from small snacks to
full size meals for all the family (from
opening time to 02.00). There is a
specialist jenever shop 100 metres
up the mountain.
Tuesday to Saturday 16.00 – late
Sunday 10.00 – late
CLOSED MONDAY

GELEEN

16 km NNE of Maastricht off A2
(E25) & A76 (E314) [IC]
Suburban town (pop. 34,000) in the
industrial zone of Sittard, close to
the isthmus between the north and
south of the province. It has two
railway stations on different main
lines, the market square being
equidistant from each.

DOUFPOT

36 Markt
Tel: 046 751023
Café: ✪✪✪✪ *Beer:* ✪✪✪

It is extremely unusual to find two
adjacent cafés in a suburban town,
each worthy of a Guide entry,
especially in such contrasting styles.
This is the smarter one, the decor
being stripped brick, held up with
massively hewn chunks of tree. Like
its neighbour, it has a terrace
overlooking the edge of the market
square. There are candles on the
table and the music is mainstream

jazz. Although the beer list is limited
to under 30 it is intelligently chosen
and seems to try to find one fine
example of most of the major styles.
Brugse Tripel, Arabier and
Rodenbach Alexander were all
available at the time of survey. Food
is limited to snacks.
Monday to Thursday 16.00 –
02.00
Friday to Sunday 14.00 – 03.00

MAXIMILIAAN

35 Markt
Tel: 046 748904
Café: ✪✪✪ *Beer:* ✪✪✪✪

A specialist beer café run by one of
the leading lights of ABT, Max
Massen. He says he has based his
café on the Great British Pub and has
a real GPO telephone kiosk in bright
red to prove it. We know of very few
British pubs, great or otherwise,
which stock over a hundred beers,
play unashamedly gutsy R&B as
background music, string their
customers down the counter of a
long, dark bar and offer them real,
old-fashioned open-top table
football, but there you go. Most of
the beers are Belgian with a dozen
Dutch, including St Christoffel. A
complete contrast to the folks next
door, except for the terrace out
front.
Monday & Tuesday (Jul - Aug)
18.00 – 02.45
Saturday 13.00 – 02.45
Other days 15.00 – 02.45
CLOSED MONDAY & TUESDAY
(Sep - Jun)

MAASTRICHT

Major town [IC]
The capital of Limburg province
(pop. 125,000). An ancient town,
known since Roman times as a place
for crossing the River Maas. It has
been the seat of a bishop since the
4th century and enjoyed a prolonged
period of prosperity from the 13th
to 17th centuries. Despite its
strategic importance, most of its old
buildings have survived many of the
ravages of successive European wars.
It is awash with famous churches. St.
Servatius' is said to be the oldest in
the Netherlands and to be
constructed over the saint's body.

The Church of Onze Lieve Vrouw (Our Beloved Lady) is a rare example of a fortified church, built to withstand serious attack.

The station is on the right bank, in an area called Wijk. Most of the old town is found on the other side of the river. There is a straight road from the front of the station crossing the Maas at St Servaas Bridge, by the Ridder brewery. Buses to most of southern Limburg depart from outside the station.

Despite its fame, Maastricht seems poorly geared up for the numbers of tourists it attracts. Hotels are relatively few and given its pivotal position in the country's best known brewing area, the beer cafés are most notable by their absence. The area around O. L. Vrouwplein seems the most likely for positive developments.

FALSTAFF
6 St. Amorsplein
Tel: 043 217238
Café: ✪✪✪ *Beer:* ✪✪✪✪

From St Servaas Bridge (also known simply as Maastricht Bridge), the main street into the old town heads straight on and then hits a T-junction. Fork left and then first right into Achter Het Vleeshuis to reach St Amorsplein. From the city's main square, Vrijthof, Platielstraat will lead you to the same place. In summer, most of Falstaff's customers drape themselves around and sometimes over the statue of St Amor in the middle of this small enclosed square. At night and at other times of the year, more use is made of the massively beamed gallery upstairs. There are plain, but middle-aged, wooden furnishings throughout. Music seems invariably loud and modern. Staff dress in black T-shirt uniform and are anything but Falstaffian. The 90 beers feature some aged varieties, but probably not intentionally. Food (12.00 to 21.00) includes soups, rolls, salads, single plate meals, pancakes and ices.
Opening hours 10.00 – 02.00

VIERGE†
2 Cortenstraat
Tel: 043 217550

We do not usually include cafés which have been taken over and closed. However, Maastricht is seriously short of decent beer cafés. La Vièrge (pronounced "fee-air-ker" in Dutch) was no ordinary entry and half our informants assure us that it will re-open with some semblance of a decent range once the hotel apartment block above it is completed. You will find it on the corner of Onze Lieve Vrouwe Plein. It used to stock over 300 beers.

MECHELEN
18 km ESE of Maastricht off N278

Not to be confused with Mechelen-on-the-Maas just north of Maastricht, which is in Belgian territory. This Mechelen is a village just south of Gulpen, halfway between Maastricht and Aachen, on one of the pretty backroads to the Belgian border.

PINTJE
25 Hoofdstraat
Tel: 04455 1227
Café: ✪✪✪✪✪ *Beer:* ✪✪✪✪

On the no. 57 bus route from Maastricht station to Gulpen via the (extremely) pretty route through the rolling countryside of southern Limburg. Opposite an eccentric village church built part in brick and part in stone. Co-owner Lei Meisen is a broadcaster on the local radio station and is a strong enthusiast for Limburg culture. With his wife and a partner, they have made strenuous efforts to keep the front bar of this beautiful place in its original 1882 design. When popularity demanded its expansion, the new rooms were created to match, as far as was practicable. There is a clever beer list of 90, mainly Dutch and Belgian. The unexpected delight is the snacks menu, with its strong regional flavour. The strongest flavour of all must be the Limburg cheese, Hervé, eaten as Rommedoe met Stroop, a stinking mutant of Camembert accompanied by an apple treacle and rye bread. This is the sort of pub near which you buy a house. Failing that, a hiking holiday based at one of the many small country hotels in the very English countryside round here, might make a reasonable substitute.

Sunday 11.00 – 02.00
Other days 14.00 – 02.00
CLOSED TUESDAY

OTTERSUM

20 km SE of Nijmegen off N271
Typical small Dutch town in northern Limburg, a few miles from the German border.

OLD INN
13 Siebengewaldseweg
Tel: 08851 11058
Café: ❍❍❍❍ *Beer:* ❍❍❍❍

The Old Inn is not strictly in Ottersum. Siebengewaldseweg is the first road on your right as you are leaving the town in the direction of Germany. Just as you begin to lose faith, the Old Inn should appear on your left. The exterior is more like a modern German hostelry than either a Dutch beer café or olde English inn. There is a large terrace and larger car park. Inside, the darkened atmosphere could be anywhere in Europe. There are alcoves for eating, seats at the bar and tall tables for drinking. The beer list of 150 is strong on Belgian brews and, more surprisingly, good quality British exports including Fuller's Golden Pride and Thomas Hardy's Ale from Eldridge Pope. We did not try the Tsing Tao Porter from mainland China. There is a full menu, with the cooking tending towards Belgian and the portions towards Teutonic. Food is served all day until 01.00. The service is friendly and helpful.

Opening hours 12.00 – 02.00

North Brabant

NORTH BRABANT (Dutch: Noord-Brabant) is the central southern province of the Netherlands and shares a long land border with Antwerp province in Belgium. While it is not strictly part of the Randstad, the areas around the towns of Tilburg, Eindhoven, Breda and 's Hertogenbosch are very much akin to the modern urban areas of the western Netherlands.

The northern border is marked by the River Maas, and the southern by Belgium. To the west are the Zeeland marshes, while to the east is the northern part of Limburg. The province is criss-crossed by canals and other waterways.

As part of the grand plan for agriculture the government has assisted the creation of good quality farmland and, where farming remains difficult, the planting of forest. The old style landscape has become so scarce that it is now being preserved in nature parks. Travelling in the countryside, you will find small holdings where goats and geese, cattle and corn, beehives and beetroot are all shoved into an area the size of a typical British field.

Along with southern Limburg, North Brabant is the Netherlands' traditional brewing area, nowadays offering a great diversity. As well as the abbey of Koningshoeven, Heineken, Interbrew and Allied have major plants here. There are also three established independent companies, Budel, Kroon and Bavaria. New, smaller ale breweries seem to crop up almost monthly and include the excellent Maasland.

BREDA
Major town [IC]
The province's third largest town (pop. 120,000); a blueprint of the old design of Dutch town, its city centre is ringed by concentric canals. At the heart is the Grote Markt, ringed by the city's architectural centrepieces, the Grote Kerk and Stadhuis. Note also the former castle of the Dukes of Orange and the statue of William of Orange (Britain's King William III). The Beguinage, a traditional home to Dutch nuns who have not taken vows, is still in use. Be warned that there are very few budget hotels.

BEYERD
26 Boschstraat
Tel: 076 214265
Café: ❍❍❍ *Beer:* ❍❍❍❍❍
The Carillon has been a café for over 150 years and for the past 26 of

these it has been run by Piet de Jongh, current chairman of the ABT group of privately owned cafés and one of the leading players in the Dutch beer world. The best way to get here is either from Dulle Griet (below) or else by noting the town plan at the station and walking; it is less than ten minutes. There is a tiny terrace on the street and a large bar inside, attracting reverent customers of all ages. At the back is a separate restaurant with serious cooking, some of it beer related, which is gaining a good reputation in its own right. The beer list usually runs to around 150 and often includes special promotions of Belgian or Dutch brews. Even when the three members of the family are busy, the other bar staff are refreshingly knowledgeable about the beers and can guide the weary traveller.
Saturday 14.00 – 02.00

Sunday 10.00 – 02.00
Other days 12.00 – 02.00
CLOSED WEDNESDAY

DULLE GRIET
6 Regierstraat
Tel: 076 212776
Café: ✪✪✪✪ *Beer:* ✪✪✪✪

Just off the Grote Markt is Breda's other fine beer café, a specialist in better ales only since 1990. The tables in this long brown café often sport candles and if you are lucky, one of the owners will serenade you on the piano with a guarantee of 95 correct notes in every hundred. The beer list usually tops a hundred with an above average range of brews from small Dutch breweries like Maasland. A small but varied dinner menu operates from 17.00 to 21.00 and a wide range of snacks is available at other times. To move on to the Beyerd, turn left out of the door and carry straight on for 300 metres. **Beyerd** is such an institution that the town council signpost it!
Monday to Wednesday 16.00 – 01.00
Thursday to Sunday 16.00 – 02.00

EINDHOVEN
Major town [IC]

North Brabant's second largest town (pop. 190,000) was created almost entirely by the Philips electronics group, whose headquarters is here. They have helped create a technical university, a school of industrial design, some excellent scientific libraries and a space age science museum called Evoluon.

Most travellers come here on business or to watch the local football team. Regrettably it is not exactly the beer capital of the southern Netherlands. For light relief try the Animali Zoo just south of the town. For simple tourism, be sure to clock the modern carillon on Jacob Oppenheimstraat, finished in 1966 and the largest in the Netherlands.

OUDE ST. JORIS
25 Pastoor Dijkmansstraat
Tel: 040 114636
Café: ✪✪ *Beer:* ✪✪✪

Shortly before going to press we heard about another beer café in Eindhoven (see Stop Press). Until now the Old Saint George has been the best bet, despite being inconveniently placed 1.5 km out of the centre, off the main road to Geldrop, turning right just before the road down to St. Joris' church. What the Dutch call a dark brown café and our big sister publication for Britain calls "a traditional back-street local". Friendly, if a little exclusive, beery, if decidedly coy about how many beers are in stock and not the sort of place to impress your business contact. Darts, billiards and students in the evenings.
Opening hours 10.00 – 02.00

'S HERTOGENBOSCH
Major town [IC]

Known universally as Den Bosch (pronounced "dane boss"), the provincial capital (pop. 90,000) is the smallest and most traditional of the four large towns in the province. Its sprawling market square has a statue to the town's most famous son, the artist Hieronymus Bosch. The most impressive building is St. John's Cathedral, dating mainly from the 15th and 16th centuries with some older bits. Well worth a saunter inside.

DUVELKE
55 Verwerstraat
Tel: 073 140308
Café: ✪✪✪✪ *Beer:* ✪✪✪✪

The Markt in Den Bosch is a strange-shaped affair. The statue of Hieronymus Bosch is hidden away in a corner and opposite this is Ridderstraat. Take this street and at its end turn left and immediately right to find Verwerstraat. The Little Devil is 100 metres further on, to the right. A candle-lit, friendly café with a peaceful atmosphere and helpful bar staff. The beer list is around 120 and, since the closing of Anders beer café, is a long way ahead of anything else in town. Food is limited to simple snacks.
Opening hours 15.00 – 01.00
CLOSED TUESDAY

TERMINUS
19 Stationsplein
Café: ✪✪✪ *Beer:* ✪✪✪

This small hotel in the square at the front of Den Bosch's railway station has been known to Guide inspectors for some years because of its budget accommodation and the robust cooking in its restaurant. It is also perhaps the only beer café in the world to have an Orthodox Jewish billiards team. In the past the beer list was small but spiked with highly unusual finds like a Bamberg Rauchbier, a smoked lager from Bavaria. We now hear that the list is slowly expanding and that a full entry is justified. More reports please.

OISTERWIJK
8 km ENE of Tilburg off N65 [IC]
Typical small southern Dutch town with a parish church designed by Cuypers, the architect responsible for Amsterdam's Centraal Station and waterfront. There is a 1500-acre fenland nature reserve to the south.

BELLE EPOQUE
69-71 Lind
Tel: 04242 84850
Café: ✪✪✪ *Beer:* ✪✪✪✪

The road called Lind is Oisterwijk's pleasantly quiet high street. La Belle Epoque has a pleasant, sheltered terrace of cane-back chairs out front, overlooking the boulevard. Inside is a single large lounge with seats around the bar. Its main purpose is to promote the consumption of good ales. They run their own beer club and hold a beer festival on the first Sunday in July. Daytime opening hours are a bit vague.
Opening hours 19.00 – late
CLOSED TUESDAY & WEDNESDAY (winter)

BOSHUIS VENKRAAI
162 Bosweg
Tel: 04242 82396
Café: ✪✪✪✪✪ *Beer:* ✪✪✪✪

The Fenlock Woodhouse has perhaps the best setting of any café in the Guide. At the junction of several footpaths and bridlepaths, it lies at the end of Oisterwijk's "millionaire's row", a kilometre or so into the woods. From the station, head up Stationstraat and carry on for a kilometre in a straight line, until you can go no further. This should be the T-junction with Merodalaan, where you turn right and then first left into Wierdsmalaan. This becomes Bosweg after 500 metres. This splendid single room café, with a lovely atmosphere, is a country pub Dutch-style. Outside you can tie up your horse or let the children roam across the imaginative playground in the woody paddock that is the garden. Inside, just be mellow and enjoy the hundred or so beers. Small snacks are available.
November to Easter 09.00 – 19.00
Thursday & Friday (summer) 12.00 – sundown
Other days 09.00 – sundown
CLOSED THURSDAY & FRIDAY (Nov - Easter)

OOSTERHOUT
7 km NE of Breda off A27 (E311)
Tidy suburban town, a bus ride from Breda but off the train routes.

BEURS
4 Klappeijstraat
Tel: 01620 53477
Café: ✪✪✪✪ *Beer:* ✪✪✪✪

Just off the Markt, in the centre of Oosterhout, the Exchange came within a whisker of a five star rating of both café and beer list. For a town centre café in a small place off the beaten track, that is quite an achievement. The intelligent design of this large, light brown café creates a relaxing and up-market atmosphere, though it still clearly functions as a proper local pub. There is a real wood fire and plenty of candle light but still an airy, spacious feel. They manage to fit in a billiards table without detracting from the unusual and attractive furnishings. The beer list of 90 or so is also intelligent and unusual. From the Netherlands' smaller brewers come Mug Bitter, Witte Wieven and Schele Os. From their Belgian equivalents come Bink, several beers from Achouffe and Kerelsbier. There is even a decent wine list. Food is limited to small snacks. They

accumulate beer magazines and books. Well worth finding.
Monday to Friday 10.00 – late
Saturday 12.00 – late
Sunday 11.30 – late

TILBURG
Major town [IC]
North Brabant's largest town (pop. 210,000). A modern affair, traditionally a wool town but now supported by a wide variety of industries brought by the good road, rail and canal links. It boasts two interesting museums, one dedicated to international textiles, the other to ethnic cultures, but these attractions pale into insignificance alongside the De Efteling themepark, just up the road in Kaatsheuvel.

If you are travelling with children or else have an urge to liberate the child within for a day, De Efteling is an essential port of call, provided you have no conscience about spending 100 Guilders a head. Apart from the "magic" woods, "haunted" castle, overhead bikeway, Trolls' cave etc:, the major attraction is the wide selection of ways in which to enjoy a heart attack. The waterchutes and sky-tower are are at the mild end of the scale. They ban you from the loop-the-loop rollercoaster if they discover cardiac problems on physical examination.

KANDINSKY
58 Telegraafstraat
Tel: 013 444924
Café: ✪✪✪✪ *Beer:* ✪✪✪✪
Kandinsky was a Polish artist who lived in France in the 1920s, some of whose works are in the collection at the Boymans Museum in Rotterdam. You have to name a café after something. To reach it from Tilburg station, turn left and cross the dual carriageway. The first road on the right is Willem II Straat and after 100 metres on the left is Telegraafstraat. Tilburg's newer specialist beer café consists of a single long room with a semi-circular bar and light brown saloon area. It started up in 1993 with around 85 beers, including the complete range from the town's Moerenburg brewery. The rest of the list includes a few other

extraordinary items and there are similarities with De Beurs at Oosterhout (see above). Small Flemish breweries like De Bie and Steedje feature. It is clear that the owners may well collect unusual beers for fun, so ask about anything not on the list. It may rise to a five star list if the first few months are anything to go by. Food is limited to simple snacks. There is occasional live music.
Opening hours 14.00 – late

ZOMERLUST
15 Oisterwijksebaan
Tel: 013 425292
Café: ✪✪✪✪✪ *Beer:* ✪✪✪✪✪
There is no literal translation of Zomerlust, but Spring Fever comes close. Although this excellent café is only 2 km out of the centre of town, on the old road to Oisterwijk, you could be forgiven for believing you were in a rural tavern. The best way to get there is by taxi, hoping that you do not have to stop for the canal bridge, a few hundred metres short of the pub. Until recently it was swung round by hand by a long-suffering bridgeman. However you get there, the journey is worth the effort. The beer list of about 90 is usually in excellent condition and features some well-chosen and very unusual beers, not all of them of mind-warping strength. There are usually some traditional gueuzes, an unusual find for the Netherlands, plus a few real oddments which have appealed to owner Tejo Kromhout. Attractively laid out, with a mixture of furnishings, it adopts an art deco or belle époque style inside. True to Dutch café tradition from that era, there are carpets on the tables. Outdoors is a useful summer terrace overlooking the fields. Food is normally limited but on Fridays they offer "beer gastronomy" and an enterprising fuller menu. The final Friday of the month is famous in this regard and you will have to book. They also do breakfasts on Sunday and Public Holidays from 11.00 to 13.30. One of the best cafés in the Netherlands.
Wednesday & Thursday 19.00 – 02.00

Friday & Saturday 15.00 – 02.00
Sunday & public holidays 11.00 –
02.00
CLOSED MONDAY & TUESDAY

TRY ALSO: in the city centre, a
street called Heuvel (not
Heuvelstraat) has several cafés
which do not quite reach a full
entry. At no. 10, **Polly Maggoo** has
a good value upstairs restaurant; at
no. 14, **Tribunaal** has over 30 beers;
at no. 16, **Buitenbeentje** usually
tops 40; there is also an interesting
off-licence at no. 42.

VALKENSWAARD
8 km S of Eindhoven on N69
The inadequate border road from
Eindhoven to Hasselt bottlenecks in
Valkenswaard, a small Kempish
town. Despite its size, it has three art
galleries and a couple of museums.

BOLLEKE
38 Leenderweg
Tel: 04902 16768
Café: ✪✪✪ *Beer:* ✪✪✪✪
Where the traffic jam reaches its
most absurd you are at the centre of
town, which is where Leenderweg
branches off. The Goblet is on the
right after 300 metres. A light brown
café with a single, large room
offering billiards, darts and
compulsory music, its fame comes
from its list of 150 beers. Limited
food stretches to single plate meals.

There are some seats outside. It
would get more trade from travelling
beer lovers if the transport links
were better but in this part of the
southern Netherlands links with
Belgium have been such that there is
not even a train connection between
the two countries.
Monday & Tuesday 19.00 – 01.00
Wednesday 14.00 – 01.00
Thursday 13.00 – 01.00
Friday & Saturday 12.00 – 02.00
Sunday 12.00 – 01.00

VELDHOVEN
5 km SW of Eindhoven off A67
(E34) & N269
Effectively a suburb of Eindhoven,
heading out towards the main
motorway from Antwerp to the
German border. There is a go-kart
track on Landsardweg.

BLUES
1 Heerseweg
Tel: 040 545406
Suburban café specialising in beer
and blues music. It has 40 different
versions of the former and loads of
the latter. Attracts a lot of live
musicians and this may determine its
opening times, which are otherwise
just reported as "from the evening
until much later". Over 100 people
can sit outdoors.
Opening hours 20.00 – late
CLOSED MONDAY

North Holland
including Amsterdam

NORTH HOLLAND (Dutch: Noord-Holland) is virtually three different places. At its heart is the unique conurbation of Amsterdam, one of the great cities of the world. Encircling this on all sides and overflowing into the equally heavily populated provinces of South Holland and Utrecht are the suburban areas of the Randstad, where over half the Dutch population lives. Finally, there is the surprisingly deserted north of the province. Alkmaar, Hoorn and all points north, including Texel, the largest of the Frisian Islands.

Much of North Holland is surrounded by water. To the west is the North Sea coast, breached only by the canals which serve the port of Amsterdam. To the east are the IJsselmeer and smaller Markermeer, massive fresh water lakes formed when the old Zuiderzee was cut off from the North Sea in 1932 by the Afluitsdijk. This 30 km sea barrier which nowadays carries the motorway to Friesland is one of the wonders of the modern world. To gauge the achievement, imagine building a motorway across the English Channel.

The revival in Dutch beer culture owes a lot to the beer drinkers of Amsterdam and its surroundings. Their failure to be impressed with the uniformity which the Heineken-Amstel merger of 1967 had imposed led inevitably to the more import-orientated beer market of the 1980s and 90s and the current burgeoning of small ale producers. Regrettably only two, 't IJ brewery and the Amsterdams Brouwhuis, both of Amsterdam, function in the province itself.

ALKMAAR
32 km N of Haarlem off A9 [IC]
Picturesque old town (pop. 70,000), built below sea level and enclosed by canals. Home to the Museum of Cheese and the national Museum of Beer. The famous Kaasmarkt is held on Friday mornings between April and October, when cheese merchants in traditional costume make a right to-do of weighing, testing, carrying and loading several lorry loads of cheeses, while a thousand Nikon shutters click and wind.

BOOM
1 Houttil
Tel: 072 115547
Café: ✪✪✪✪ *Beer:* ✪✪✪
At the heart of the town centre, in the basement of the Biermuseum de Boom (see Beer Tourism), at canalside level, is this attractive single-room café, complete with its painted piano. There is a floating terrace moored alongside. When it first opened, it aimed to stock every beer produced in the Netherlands, but as the number of breweries and beers expanded so the number on sale has, if anything, reduced. There are rarely as many as 80 in stock. Surprisingly, they have no beer list and the staff encountered on recent visits know little or nothing about the brews or the breweries. The customer who wants to look beyond the range of draught beers is handed, rather limply, an old copy of Dave Vlam's Nederlands Bierboek and told to pick a beer. As two-thirds of those mentioned are unavailable, this can be a frustrating experience. The museum entrance is at the back and the museum buildings are upstairs. Snacks are limited.
Sunday (Apr - Oct) 13.00 – 20.00

Other days 10.00 – 20.00
CLOSED MONDAY; and
SUNDAY (Nov - Mar)

AMSTELVEEN
8 km S of Amsterdam on A9
Suburban town swallowed by
greater Amsterdam.

ABINA
193 Amsterdamseweg
Tel: 020 412261
Café: ✪✪✪ *Beer:* ✪✪✪✪
In the older, post-war part of town.
Inconvenient for the tram service to
Amsterdam Centraal Station but the
no. 63 bus to Marnixstraat, near
Leidseplein, leaves from the
opposite side of the road and takes
30 minutes to reach the city centre.
This is a small town hotel, street
corner suburban restaurant and
young people's brown café. Some of
the enamel beer adverts on the walls
are real collectors items. The early
opening time is extraordinary, as is
the sight of night workers drinking
trappist beers while you eat
breakfast. They claim to stock 120
beers but the more unusual ones
may not be available. Great pancakes
and a fuller menu if required. There
are billiards and snooker tables. The
bedrooms could be cleaner and the
hotel decor is not up to usual
continental standards. Twelve rooms
from NFl 75 (single) and NFl 95 NFl
(double).
Monday to Friday 06.30 – 02.00
Saturday & Sunday 08.00 – 03.00

AMSTERDAM
Capital city [IC]
Amsterdam is unique. A city of
bicycles and trams, of sex shops and
car thefts, of fresh flowers and raw
herring, of dog poop and dope, of
free live music in the streets and
women for sale in shop windows. A
man on the fourth floor of a gabled
house in a canalside terrace uses a
winch to hoist his furniture from the
cobbled street. A needle-scarred
Englishman sells you a story of lost
passports and humility for 25
Guilders. The coffee is always the
best. The trams run all night. You
never let go of your wallet.
    Amsterdam is relaxed and

frenetic, classy and dangerous,
abrupt and charming. People spend
a part of their lives here. Never to
move would be like sticking rigidly
to a diet of steak and fresh oranges.
After a while they move on; they get
fed up with the burglaries.
We tourists come here mainly to
stare. In the morning we stare at the
Van Gogh Museum and the nearby
Rijksmuseum. In the afternoon we
stare from a glass topped boat at the
townhouses and swing bridges on
the canals and the massive office
blocks on the waterfront. In the
evening we stare at the Paraguayan
flute band playing the same haunting
native rifts that they did when you
saw them outside the Coliseum and
the Pompidou Centre. At night we
stare at the crowds milling past the
rows of red windows and brightly lit
"video" stores around the Oude
Kerk, as the professionals stare back.
    You leave your car in another
town and come by train to Centraal
Station. Otherwise somebody will
steal your music and leave a pool of
shattered glass on the back seat as an
unwelcome souvenir.
    Amsterdam cafés are, like the city
they serve, very much a matter of
how you find them. In a place which
manages to combine perpetual rapid
change with timeless solidity it is
inevitable that new heroes emerge
and fade while a few old friends
keep on rolling. There are many
dreadful cafés, especially around the
tourist haunts, but also some which
will impress even the fiercest critic.
    None of our entries is a "smoking
café". Dope and fine ale are
generally a bad mix. The same can
be said about beer of any sort and
jenever, which is why we have
removed our upgraded list of spirits
houses to a special feature (page
238).
    We strongly advise you to invest
in the cheapish but well-designed
city map (Falkplan) available from
the VVV tourist office next to
Centraal Station. Without it, finding
your way about can be difficult. All
but a couple of the entries are in or
near the city centre, so be prepared
to walk a lot.

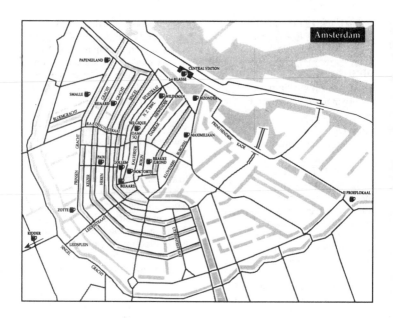

1er KLASSE
Platform 2
Amsterdam Centraal Station
Tel: 020 625 0131
Café: ✪✪✪✪ *Beer:* ✪✪

If you have not started whistling the theme to "Murder on the Orient Express" within 30 seconds of entering this wonderful station café, then you are no romantic. Amsterdam Centraal was designed by the 19th century Dutch architect P.J.H. Cuypers and 1er Klasse Café Restaurant was originally its first class waiting room. It had fallen into disrepair until, in 1985, some perverse genius decided to renovate it: the high ceiling has painted girders as beams; Parquet floor, umbrella stands, painted mahogany-panelled walls; hanging lights from the Belle Epoque; rubber plants and flower arrangements; a distant bar beyond the starched white table-clothed dining area. It could do with aspidistras. Very few Amsterdammers even know of its existence. The beer range of 20 is small but includes some of the commoner classics. Food is served from 12.00 to 14.00 and from 17.00 to 22.00. The evening menu includes soup, bouillon with coriander, profiteroles, fried squid, gravlax, carpaccio, tagliatelle, country salad and various tartes. There are special tokens to use for the toilet.
Monday to Saturday 09.30 – 23.00
Sunday 10.30 – 23.00

BEIAARD
90 Herengracht
Tel: 020 625 0422
Café: ✪✪✪ *Beer:* ✪✪✪✪

You will find the first of our two cafés called The Carillon, on the east side of the town, towards the northern end of the canal, between Herenstraat and Leliegracht. It sits in a terrace of high gabled houses on a typical Amsterdam canalside row. Inside is a simple long bar, a range of 80 beers, a relaxing atmosphere and the chance of escaping the sillier side of this cosmopolitan capital. Below it is a snooker hall and aerobics gym. There are only small snacks but these include osseworst, made from macerating very lightly cooked beef. If you want something more substantial, the Belgian restaurant next door at no. 88 (tel: 020 624 9635) serves excellent and authentic Flemish cuisine and 40 beers to accompany it. You must eat, however, it is not a café.
Sunday to Thursday 16.00 – 01.00
Friday & Saturday 16.00 – 02.00

BEIAARD
30 Spui
Tel: 020 622 5110
Café: ✪✪✪✪ *Beer:* ✪✪✪

At the southern end of Spuistraat is a pleasant, small square called simply Spui, which houses an occasional street market in paintings and curios. Overlooking it is Amsterdam's other Beiaard beer café, which opened in March 1992. It is the sister café to the Beiaards in Enschede and Hengelo but only a distant cousin of the café in Herengracht. The layout is split-level, with the upper floor next to the bar overlooking an airy, covered terrace with a fine view of the comings and goings of the square. There are around 70 beers and simple snacks to accompany them. The atmosphere is modern street café and the music can be intrusive. It is becoming beerier and three stars may be mean. For an attractive old café in the traditional Amsterdam style, try the two halves of **De Hoppe** at no. 18 Spui, 30 metres away. The public bar on the right is typical brown café while the saloon on the left has carpeted tables and waistcoated barmen.
Monday to Thursday 11.00 – 01.00
Friday to Sunday 11.00 – 02.00

BELGIQUE
2 Gravenstraat
Tel: 020 625 1974
Café: ✪✪✪✪ *Beer:* ✪✪✪✪

Just off Dam Square behind the Nieuwe Kerk, this pleasant small, ancient-and-modern café stands in one of the quieter parts of the central tourist area. Set up by a former employee of In de Wildeman (below). Stocks around eighty beers,

with a special emphasis on Belgian brews. There is an impressive range of trappist beers, including all three of the real Westvleteren brews. You will usually find La Chouffe on draught and the excellent draught version of the Dutch pils, Christoffel Bier from the St. Christoffel brewery in Dutch Limburg. Food is limited to sandwiches, trappist cheeses with toast or French bread, or pizzas. Background music tends to be classical during the day and light jazz at night. One of the few cafés in Amsterdam to stock good Belgian genever, the small range including those from St. Pol and Filliers.
Monday 11.00 – 20.30
Wednesday to Sunday 11.00 – 01.00
CLOSED TUESDAY

BIZONDER
66 Prins Hendrik Kade
Tel: 020 556 4564
Café: ✪✪✪✪ *Beer:* ✪✪✪

As you walk out of Centraal Station and look over to your left beyond the tramstops, a gawdy yellow sign atop a terrace of faraway buildings announces the Barbizon Palace. This is stuck to the roof of the Golden Tulip Hotel, whose public bar, next door to the left, is called the Bar Bizonder. Beer cafés are not common in five-star hotels in Holland but then this is not your average beer café. The range of 60 beers is mainly Belgian and so well chosen that it nearly warrants four stars. They have a fuller version of the beer list, clearly compiled by an enthusiast and containing history lessons as well as beer descriptions. The bar staff are splendidly turned out in dicky bows and waistcoats and the ambience is relaxed but polite. You are expected to behave in a civilised manner. Handfuls of peanuts in their shells come with your beer. The principle is that you peel them, throw the shells on the floor, then trample these into the wooden floor to help season it. The mess created is an essential part of the atmosphere. Expensive but high quality snacks are available, plus one option of a full meal. During the Happy Hour, from 17.30 till 18.30

they offer hot snacks with your beer. If you are thinking of staying, the 270 rooms start from NFl 440 (single) or NFl 520 (double). Round the corner in Zeedijk is a plethora of civilised small cafés such as **'t Aepjen** (no. 3), **Verhoeff** (no. 12) and **De Roode Baron** (no. 17).
Opening hours 13.00 – 01.00

BRAKKE GROND
43 Nes
Tel: 020 626 0044
Café: ✪✪✪ *Beers:* ✪✪✪

Parallel with Rokin, moving south from Dam Square is the narrow street called Nes. After 100 metres you come across this theatre-café-restaurant in the Flemish cultural centre, which also houses regular exhibitions of paintings and a small theatre. The modern, tile-floored, open-plan café currently stocks around 30 beers but the list is building. It is particularly well stocked with high quality stronger ales. Upstairs is a proper restaurant featuring good value Flemish cuisine (Tuesday to Friday: 17.30 to 22.00). There is a small lunchtime menu and snacks all day in the café. They use the square outside as a terrace in summer. It may close earlier if trade expires, especially on Sunday evenings.
Sunday to Thursday 11.30 – 01.00
Friday & Saturday 11.30 – 02.00

DOKTORTJE
4 Rozenboomsteeg
Café: ✪✪✪✪✪ *Beer:* ✪

We fell across this little gem completely by accident. Heading south from Dam Square down the pedestrianised Kalverstraat, Rozenboomsteeg is the last alley on the right before you hit the junction with Spui. The Little Doctor is the ultimate brown café; the principle taken to extremes. Its all wooden bar is tiny, able to seat perhaps a dozen people, mainly at the counter. The tight spiral staircase leads to a nautical size toilet. It is packed with ephemera but without any theme, as though this is a collection of items left by forgetful customers over the centuries. Most remarkable of all, though the serving and seating areas are as well kept as anywhere, the rest of the pub has simply not been cleaned, apparently for 40 years or more. The candelabra drip cobwebs. The saxaphone has gone rusty. The curtains have holes made by a dynasty of moths long since fossilised. The effect is magnified by the use of 10 watt bulbs and candles as the only forms of light. But there is Champagne starting at NFl 30 a bottle and a CD player stacked with light classics and jazz. The couple who run it blend effortlessly with the institution and you are left with the uncomfortable thought that life sometimes mimicks theatre. Bierwurst hangs drying at the back of the bar. The opening times we quote are official but not that reliable.

Opening hours 16.00 – 20.00

GOLLEM
4 Raamsteeg
Tel: 020 626 6645
Café: ❍❍❍ *Beer:* ❍❍❍❍

Beer lovers from so many nations made pilgrimages here in the late 1970s and early 1980s, before the old team went their separate ways, that its present owners cannot win. Find it in an alley linking Spuistraat to Singel, two bridges south of Raadhuisstraat. The old brown café's beer list is more commercial than in its heyday, but just as international. They offer currently around 200 choices, which is still the widest selection in Amsterdam. The staff seem to know less about their beers than was the case and sometimes they can appear rude in this regard. But even if the café is run more like a business nowadays, at least it has not disappeared without trace like some of the other old institutions. French bread with trappist cheese or ham and cheese sandwiches is the extent of the food. Background music tends to be jazz, blues or hits of the 1950s.

Sunday to Thursday 16.00 – 01.00
Friday & Saturday 16.00 – 02.00

IJ PROEFLOKAAL
7 Funenkade
Tel: 020 622 8325
Café: ❍❍❍❍ *Beer:* ❍❍❍

Amsterdam's own independent brewery, 't IJ, is situated near the Eastern Dock at the point where the Singel Gracht all but meets the waterfront. The simplest way to find it is to take the no. 22 bus from Centraal Station or anywhere east along Prins Hendrik Kade and ask for Zeeburgerstraat. The converted bath house sports an impressive windmill. The café at the side of the brewery keeps limited opening hours but is well worth a visit. As well as keeping all five of the brewery's beers on draught, it boasts an extraordinary collection of empty beer bottles from almost every brewing nation in the world. Perhaps 2,000 are on show with little or no duplication. The café welcomes children but not dogs and provides board games for amusement. Food is limited to cheese and salami. At closing time many customers move on to East of Eden in Wagenaarstraat, on the corner of Linneausstraat opposite the Tropical Museum, which also keeps most of IJ's beers.

Opening hours 15.00 – 20.00
CLOSED MONDAY & TUESDAY

MAXIMILIAAN
6 Kloveniers Burgwal
Tel: 020 624 2778
Café: ❍❍❍❍ *Beer:* ❍❍❍

Just off the Nieuwe Markt, one block east of the Red Light District. A unique and daring project combining a home brewery, a modern café and a serious restaurant all in one building. The bar is cleverly lit with natural light and designed to be a stripped wood and designer colour scheme open-plan affair which will age beautifully – time will tell. Maximiliaan's gimmick is that its home-made beers are actually brewed in the café. Some customers have thought that brouwmeester Albert Hofmann, brother of manager Caspar, dresses up in rubber gear for the same reasons as some of the characters in the nearby magazine shops. In fact he is supervising the mash in the gleaming coppers at the far end of the room. The fermenting tanks and racking suite can be seen in the rooms beyond. The beers are detailed under Dutch Independent Breweries and three are usually available at any one time. The restaurant offers serious cooking and opens every evening. It also caters for parties visiting the brewery. There is a small range of tasty bar snacks and a plat du jour in the bar. On the opposite side of the canal at no. 59 is the **Engelbewaarder**, a literary café with frequent live jazz, which was the very first beer café in Amsterdam, but which has now reduced its range, though there are still high spots. Round the corner at 2 Nieuwe Hoogstraat is the **Hoogte**, with 40 beers and a cosmopolitan young clientèle.

Opening hours 12.00 – late

PAIX
22 Wolvenstraat
Tel: 020 624 2026
Café: ✪✪✪✪ *Beer:* ✪✪

To find Wolvenstraat, head west of Dam Square behind the Royal Palace on to Raadhuisstraat and turn left on the far side of Herengracht. Wolvenstraat is at the second bridge on the right. One of the problems with Amsterdam is that the beer cafés do not serve great food and the restaurants seem to ignore beer. The Café de la Paix is nowadays primarily an eating house but was once a specialist beer café and it is as though its customers will not let it leave that tradition behind entirely. The menu is wide-ranging and alters sufficiently often to make nominating individual dishes a waste of time. The portions are more than adequate, the cooking varies from good to excellent, the service is friendly for Amsterdam and the atmosphere cosy and agreeable. There are carpets on the table and a Bohemian atmosphere enhanced by incongruous 19th and 20th century curios of various sorts. On a brief trip to Amsterdam, this is the place for the splurge meal. Beers such as Westmalle Dubbel and Tripel, Duvel and other Belgian favourites are

available. The wine list is above average.

Opening hours 16.00 – late

PAPENEILAND
2 Prinsengracht
Tel: 020 624 1989
Café: ✪✪✪✪ *Beer:* ✪✪

The Café 't Papeneiland is agreed to be the oldest café in Amsterdam, a fact which it is now exploiting more than it used to, though in a civilised manner. To find it, take Brouwersgracht, due east of, and slightly inland from, Centraal Station. This is the area called Jordaan. Papeneiland is at the corner with Prinsengracht, the fourth of the canals which encircle the town centre. The café is small but interesting with the charm of an olde-worlde pub. The small beer list includes a couple of brews from 't IJ and an expanding number of others. Bar snacks are simple but adequate for a small lunch. There is a genuine welcome, even at busy times. On the opposite side of Prinsengracht is another café, **'t Smackzeyl**, which has a long-standing reputation, justified or otherwise, for the best Guinness in Amsterdam. Fifty metres in the opposite direction is **Thijsen**, an up-market modern café with an above average beer list.

Opening hours 11.00 – 01.00

RIDDER
85 Jan Pieter Heijestraat
Tel: 020 683 4348
Café: ✪✪✪ *Beer:* ✪✪✪✪✪

First there was a beer café here, then it disappeared and became a shop. Now it is a beer café again. If you are staying at one of the hotels near the Van Gogh Museum then it is only a short walk across the Vondelpark to the end of Jan Pieter Heijestraat (or Heyestraat). Otherwise, take tram no. 1 from Centraal Station or Leidseplein. Thoroughly recommended by those who live in Amsterdam as an excellent and reliable place for both beer and substantial bar food. The beer list is billed as 200. The kitchen is open from 18.00 until the wee small hours, which is unusually late for Amsterdam. They also feature live

music, which can be folk, jazz or country, on a fairly regular basis.
Opening hours 17.00 – late

SMALLE
12 Egelantiersgracht
Tel: 020 623 9617
Café: ✪✪✪✪ *Beer:* ✪✪

Heading south from Papeneiland (above), Egelantiersgracht leaves Prinsengracht just before the second canal bridge. Almost immediately on the right is an archetype of the "period" style of Amsterdam café, the sort where you wear your new leather jacket. The beer range is only 20, but includes Zatte from the capital's 't IJ brewery. There is a broad range of spirits including several rare jenevers. There is a wide range of teas and coffees too. Food includes filling and imaginative bar snacks such as salmon and wild spinach pie or a variety of fruit flans with a volcano of whipped cream. The split-level bar is well managed and tidy but attractively traditional at the same time. There is an old wall clock from James Ritchie and Son of Edinburgh, some ornate outside windows and of course plenty of candle light. Three streets north, at 120 Westerstraat, is one of the better down-market equivalents, **'t Monumentje**. There you will need your battered old leather jacket.
Sunday to Thursday 10.00 – 01.00
Friday & Saturday 10.00 – 02.00

WILDEMAN
5 Kolksteeg (a.k.a. Nieuwe Zijdskolk)
Tel: 020 638 2348
Café: ✪✪✪✪✪ *Beer:* ✪✪✪✪✪

Henk Eggens is a major figure in the Dutch beer revival. For a start he stands six foot eight, not including the moustache. He first became well known as the manager at the Gollem Bar (above) more years ago than anyone cares to remember. He now presides over his own place, The Wild Man Inn, one of the finest cafés in the Netherlands. The road called Damrak runs from the front of Centraal Station to Dam Square. From the station end there are numerous alleys off to the right which link up to a pedestrianised street called Nieuwedijk. The third of these, Oude Brugsteeg, emerges onto Nieuwedijk more or less opposite Kolksteeg. In de Wildeman is halfway along on the left. If you are in town for more than half an hour, make the effort to find it. The bar is like a smart version of Coronation Street's Rovers Return, circa 1957, with the addition of an impressive bank of spirits casks, 160 beers (including 30 from Dutch breweries) and a great deal of attention to detail. All aspects of the decor are strongly traditional but carefully understated. In a country steeped in the nicotine stains of black cigars, the non-smoking bar to the right of the entrance comes as a great relief. Snacks are limited but an adequate light lunch or supper is possible. In summer there are a few tables outside.
Monday to Thursday 12.00 – 01.00
Friday & Saturday 12.00 – 02.00
CLOSED SUNDAY

ZOTTE
29 Raamstraat
Tel: 020 626 8694
Café: ✪✪✪ *Beer:* ✪✪✪✪

The area around Leidseplein, the meeting place for Amsterdam's younger tourists, may have some nice art deco places, but it is notoriously awful for beer cafés. The Jester is two blocks west of the square and off the beaten tourist track. Despite this it has one of the best selections of Belgian beers in town and has smartened up its image a lot since our first edition. You will still find some interesting characters there but it is not the noisy, smoke-filled basic drinkers' bar it once was. Bar snacks remain basic but are sufficient to help you through the list of over 80 beers.
Monday to Friday 11.00 – 01.00
Saturday & Sunday 16.00 – 01.00

DEN BURG
On Texel Island N of North Holland mainland.
The hourly trip by car ferry from Den Helder only takes 20 minutes

but is made more expensive by the cost of transport on Texel Island. A "boottaxi" ticket includes a journey to and from anywhere on the island and works out the same price as the slower, less convenient buses. Den Burg is the main centre of population on this peaceful, windswept holiday island, which boasts more sheep than people for most of the year. Watersports and gross tourism are deliberately minimal. Gîtes, bird reserves and scientific exploration of the undersea world are more Texel's style.

GROOTEN SLOCK
36 Parkstraat
Tel: 02220 13161
Café: ✪✪✪✪ *Beer:* ✪✪✪
Parkstraat is the main shopping street off the square by the church. One hundred metres down on the right is this pleasant brown café with its J-shaped bar and small outside terrace. Despite the seasonal nature of the island's drinking population, it remains open every day of year including Christmas Day, which underlines its role as a proper social centre, not just a tourist haunt. Prices are reasonable, especially for Texel and a creditable list of 45 beers is available which includes Chimay Bleue and others. Food is limited to toasted sandwiches.
Opening hours 12.00 – 02.00

HAARLEM
Major town [IC]
The second largest city (pop. 150,000) and provincial capital of North Holland. It is not as prosperous as it once was and not as beautiful as the tourist brochures would have you believe. Nonetheless, Haarlem is attractive enough for a half day trip. The area around the Grote Markt is the cultural centre. Be sure to try the Frans Hals Museum in Groot Heiligland, 600 metres south of the Grote Kerk, one of the best traditional art galleries in the Netherlands featuring all the painters who made Haarlem famous in the 17th century and a collection of those who may in the 21st century.

St. Bavo's Church and the Stadhuis are worth a look too. The church's organ is 150 years older than the church building. Hear it for free at 15.00 every Saturday from April to September.

BRUXELLES
16 Lange Wijngaardstraat
Tel: 023 314509
Café: ✪✪✪ *Beer:* ✪✪✪✪
Midway along the north side of the Grote Markt you will find Smedestraat. Its other end forks off Kruisstraat on the way to the station. Half way along Smedestraat is the residential backwater called Lange Wijngaardstraat, its cobbled quietness ripped asunder by the CD machine of this Belgian-style beer café. The musical range is broad but does impose unnecessarily. There are no prizes for decor either, though the small collection of modern paintings and drawings which sometimes adorn otherwise drab walls can be interesting. The beer list is now down to 150 and tending to fall. The food has been excellent, but we have no recent reports and at our last visit we were ushered away from the open doors, ten minutes before opening time with such disinterested rudeness that we do not care, frankly. Food is said to be available from 18.00 to 22.00.
Sunday to Wednesday 16.00 – 01.00
Thursday to Saturday 16.00 – 02.00

MELKWOUD
63 Zijlstraat
Tel: 023 313535
Café: ✪✪✪ *Beer:* ✪✪✪
Zijlstraat is a cornucopia of small shops, interspersed with pubs and restaurants. It leads directly off the Grote Markt; 100 metres on the right is the Milk Wood, a typical brown café with an increasing interest in special beers. The long bar and darkened saloon have some ancient attributes. The beer list currently reaches 40 but includes some unusual finds for this area, such as Crombé's Kriekenbier and Oud Zottegems. Food is minimal. You can

play darts and billiards at the far end. The music can be oppressively loud and the beer can be too cold, but this is early days.

Sunday to Thursday 14.00 – 02.00
Friday & Saturday 14.00 – 04.00

UIVER

13 Riviervischmarkt
Tel: 023 310391
Café: OOOOO *Beer:* OO

In the shadow of the Grote Kerk, next to the Grote Markt lurks this extraordinary old café, created to a classical multi-roomed design. At the front is a supping area with a small bar, sat opposite an impressive bank of spirits casks. In the other rooms there are bare floors and aeronautical bric à brac. There is a piano too. At the back is a wood-panelled drawing room in the style of an Edwardian parlour, called the Parmentier room. An excellent place to while away an hour or two. The beer range is pedestrian but there are a few of the better known classics. Food is limited to cheese, leverwurst and the Amsterdam specialty, ossewurst.

Monday to Thursday 11.00 – 01.00
Friday & Saturday 11.00 – 02.00
Sunday 17.00 – 01.00

HOORN

30 km N of Amsterdam off A7 (E22) [IR]

Lovely old town which used to be a sea port but now looks out over the Markermeer. The old town is just to the north of the waterfront and can be reached easily on foot from the station.

BEIAARD

35 Kerkplein
Tel: 02290 16627
Café: OOO *Beer:* OOOO

Situated on the square which houses the disused Grote Kerk. This is the café which developed the house style for the De Beiaard group of beer cafés. The formula was to provide 70 or so beers in a "Burgundian", or civilised and relaxed atmosphere. Recently it has left the chain and we have not found

out why. Peace and quiet were never a feature of its weekend nights, which are popular. A modernish place with plenty of seats around the counter and an overflow bar upstairs. Usually they offer only small snacks but between 17.00 and 20.00 they offer heavier Flemish cooking. On the last weekend in October they run a festival of bokbiers, using a marquee by the church. At other times they are allowed to use the large seating area on the other side of the road.

Saturday 14.00 – 02.00
Sunday 15.00 – 02.00
Other days 16.00 – 02.00
CLOSED MONDAY (Nov - Easter)

NAARDEN

20 km SW of Amsterdam off A1 (E231)

An extraordinary little town on the Gooimeer, opposite the coast of Flevoland. At the heart of the modern town is Naarden-Vesting, a star-shaped, moated, fortress town within a town. This area is now made over to quiet cobbled streets and parkland. Most of its older buildings date from the 16th century.

DEMMERS

52 Marktstraat
Tel: 02159 45478
Café: OOOO *Beer:* OOO

A street corner beer café with seating on the pavement, a pleasantly designed and furnished, split-level brown café in the heart of Naarden-Vesting, half a mile walk from the station. Probably about 150 years old. They say they stock around seventy different beers with a tendency to go for better known Belgian brews. There is a snack menu including "Antwerp Rolls" of sufficient size to make a filling lunch.

Tuesday to Thursday 17.00 – 01.00
Friday 15.00 – 02.00
Saturday 12.00 – 02.00
Sunday 15.00 – 01.00
CLOSED MONDAY

UITGEEST

18 km N of Haarlem off A208 [IC]
Small town at the northern end of the Amsterdam commuter belt.

THIJS

7 Lange Buurt
Tel: 02513 12617
Café: ✪✪ *Beer:* ✪✪✪✪✪

Only in the Netherlands! This street-corner café in a small estate off the centre of a pretty boring commuter town manages to sell three hundred brews, more than almost any other Dutch café in the Guide. The reason is that it is the on-licence premises for a drinks supermarket called Drankenmarkt Vreeburg (see Beer Shops & Warehouses). Considering its limited opening times, it is remarkably large. There are dartboards and occasional live music.

Friday & Sunday 15.00 – 02.00
Saturday 17.00 – 02.00
CLOSED MONDAY to
THURSDAY

ZAANDIJK

12 km NE of Amsterdam on N203 [IC]
Suburban town in the northern commuter strip on the main line to Alkmaar. It boasts a major watersports park called the Zaanse Schans, lined by windmills, on the opposite side of a road bridge from an industrial waterfront.

KONINCKSPLEIN

13 Lagedijk
Tel: 075 215367
Café: ✪✪✪✪ *Beer:* ✪✪✪✪

Opposite the railway station, Koog Zaandijk, on the other side of the N203 main road is a chocolate factory. Behind this is a windmill. On the opposite side of the road is an expensive small hotel and, unconnected with it, this pukkah little café and off-licence. The cultured decor, relaxed music-free atmosphere and smart small terrace allow civilised enjoyment of a list of 70 beers. There are also small bar snacks. The off licence is listed under Beer Shops & Warehouses. Fifty metres away, beyond the bridge is the watersports complex.

Tuesday to Thursday 16.00 – 24.00
Friday & Saturday 15.00 – 24.00
CLOSED SUNDAY & MONDAY

ZANDVOORT

6 km W of Haarlem on the coast [IR]
Zandvoort is a seaside resort and international conference venue, close to the urban centres of the Randstad. There are plenty of good value, pleasant hotels, especially along Hogestraat. It is linked by regular train to Haarlem (10 minutes) and Amsterdam (30 minutes). If you are driving around the Netherlands, it can make sense to stay here and rail it into these two car-phobic cities.

BIERWINCKEL

1a Raadhuisplein
Tel: 02507 12197
Café: ✪✪✪ *Beer:* ✪✪✪

On the first floor above a general provisions supermarket. The open-air terrace and panoramic windows overlook one of the main shopping streets. There are numerous games, such as pool, darts and billiards at one end and a pleasant open lounge area for eating and drinking. The beerlist includes around 60 brews most of the time, with slight increases in the bokbier season. Food is of the burgers, satay and schnitzel variety.

Opening hours 12.00 – 01.00

Overijssel

OVERIJSSEL is the province which spreads across the northern part of the central Netherlands from the German border to the IJsselmeer. The bulk of the area consists of flat sandy plains cut through by the major north-south and east-west trunk roads and the major ship canals which link the eastern Netherlands and northern Germany to the sea. The shore of the IJsselmeer and the waterways that run from it are popular areas for boating and watersports.

Overijssel's principal towns are either modern and industrial, like Enschede and Deventer, or else date from the 14th century and the era of the Hanseatic League, like the provincial capital Zwolle and nearby Kampen.

The north western part of the province, the so-called "North East Polder", is reclaimed from the Zuiderzee.

ALMELO
22km NW of Enschede on N35 & N36 [IC]

Largish town at the north western end of the industrial strip of southern Overijssel province, made up of Almelo, Hengelo and Enschede. At the point where the central Netherlands gives way to the north.

HOOKHOES
126 Grotestraat

Very much a beer house, in a town which lost its only brewery in 1990. You are in the hinterlands of the Calvinist north here and the Hookhoes is a beacon of enterprise, having been promoting traditional brews for over a decade. The list has consistently topped 100 beers. It opens at noon in summer.
Monday to Thursday 15.00 – 02.00
Friday & Saturday 15.00 – 03.00
CLOSED SUNDAY

DEVENTER
35 km NNE of Arnhem off A1 (E30) [IC]

Lively modern town (pop. 65,000) with a few old buildings at its centre, especially around its massive main square, Brink. The old church of St. Lebuinus on the Grote Kerkhof is also worth a visit. Further afield, just

north of Apeldoorn is Het Loo, the Dutch Blenheim; a huge, manicured palace set in formal grounds, it was the seat of the House of Orange.

HEKSENKETEL
62 Brink
Tel: 05700 13412

The square called Brink is Deventer's equivalent to a Grote Markt. The Witch's Cauldron is found near the old Gothic weigh-house (De Waag). Inside is a strangely attractive, cluttered old brown café. Outside are seats and tables from which to watch the business of daily life pass by and absorb the finer points of the 16th century buildings which are its back-drop. The café offers around 120 different beers and a range of simple snacks, plus a dish of the day. The background music is nostalgia for baby boomers.
Sunday & Monday 17.00 – 02.00
Tuesday & Wednesday 11.00 – 02.00
Thursday to Saturday 11.00 – 03.00

ENSCHEDE
Major town [IC]

Close to the German border, Enschede is the business and cultural centre of the part of the eastern Netherlands called the Twente. Much of the old town burned down in 1862 and has been replaced by a number of impressive 20th century buildings, the oddest of which must be the copper-domed Synagogue. There are three major museums dedicated to textiles, natural history and general collections (the Rijksmuseum). If you are seconded to the University of Twente for any reason, or have an international student card, then also try **Vestingbar** (tel: 053 892397), the local students' union bar on the university campus.

BEIAARD
22 Oude Markt
Tel: 053 306267
The Oude Markt pre-dates the 19th and 20th century rebuilding of the old town. Enschede's two most interesting cafés for the beer drinker are arranged around what was once the village square. At De Beiaard, part of the chain of the same name, they have a club for beer lovers which organises evening tastings and brewery trips. On the café's menu are the usual 70 or so beers with ten on draught. The background music is nostalgia for ageing evacuees.
Monday to Thursday 19.00 – 02.00
Friday 15.00 – 02.00
Saturday 14.00 – 04.00
Sunday 16.00 – 02.00

GEUS
2 Oude Markt
Tel: 053 310564
In the same square is De Geus (roughly translatable to "The Vagabond", though it is named after its owner's surname), a beer café which bills itself as a "light brown café". The beer range here reaches around 150 choices. About 120 of these are Belgian, the others being mainly Dutch with occasional other imports. This is a lively café, popular with all ages. There is a large terrace outside. Once a month, on the last Friday, they have a live band. Food is limited to simple snacks. They are open every day except Christmas Day.
Monday to Friday 10.00 – 02.00
Saturday 11.00 – 02.00
Sunday 14.00 – 02.00

GIETHOORN
23 km N of Zwolle on N334
Village in the far north west of the province, in what used to be the marshlands of the North East Polder. Now popular as an up-market holiday area for yachties and cyclists, near to Boven Wijde and Beukeler Wijde lakes. Lots of marinas and tasteful second homes.

KUIN'S CABARCA
1 Binnenpad
Tel: 05216 2229
Café: ✪✪✪✪ *Beer:* ✪✪✪
Those who know middle class Cornwall or, for American readers, Cape Cod, will be familiar with the sort of thing that Mr. Kuin has created. A superficially simple, converted shack where you expect to see sun-bronzed surfers swapping share prices with middle-aged, cigar-smoking men in loud shirts. The Dutch do not behave like that, but you get the picture. The clientele is pretty mixed, really. The beer list is only around 30 but is intelligently selected. Food is not in evidence. Friendly chat from behind the bar. Not the Guide's usual sort of place, but it works.
Opening hours 10.00 – 02.00
CLOSED MONDAY to FRIDAY (winter)

HENGELO
9 km NW of Enschede off A1 (E30) & A35 [IC]
Enschede's smaller, less bustling neighbour.

BEIAARD
25 Langestraat
Tel: 074 915727
Another café of the De Beiaard group, with the same formula of 70 beers. This is more of a country pub, despite its city-centre location. There is a conservatory and a large beer garden. They have quite a lot of beer-oriented promotions including an October bokbier promotion and beer tasting evenings.
Opening hours 12.00 – 02.00

PLEINTJE
25 Burger Janssenplein
Tel: 074 912425

In the centre of town, next to the
Town Hall (Stadhuis), 600 metres
from the station. Largish café with a
larger terrace outside. Makes
reasonable attempts at an olde-
worlde atmosphere and is proud of
its mixed clientele. Offers 80 beers.
There is a billiards table. Features
live music on the first Thursday of
the month and blues from the
commercial end of the spectrum at
other times. Snacks are limited.
*Monday to Wednesday 11.00 –
02.00*
Thursday & Friday 11.00 – 03.00
Saturday 12.00 – 03.00
Sunday 14.00 – 02.00

ZWOLLE
Major town [IC]
The provincial capital (pop. 90,000).
Not as big as Enschede but much
prettier, the old town being built on
a star-shaped island surrounded by a
canal called the Stadsgracht. It is the
cultural and business centre for a
large rural area and has some
unexpected treasures. Try the 15th
century Dutch Reformed Grote Kerk
of St. Michael with its 4,000-pipe
organ and grotesque carvings. The
nearby Catholic Church of Our Lady
boasts a taller tower, the Peperbus
(Pepper Pot), from which there is an
impressive view of the town and its
surroundings.

CASTELIJN
33 Kamperstraat
Tel: 038 218099
To find this cosy old brown café,
head for the Peperbus (above). It
stands near the foot of the tower. An
easy-going, well-used sort of
atmosphere pervades, helped along
by a beer list of around 40 brews –
impressively large for this part of the
Netherlands – and simple bar food.
The background music is fifties and
sixties, with a leaning towards the
blues. Our informant assures us that
they mount occasional fancy dress
cocktail parties. Why they should do
so remains a mystery.
*Monday to Thursday 16.00 –
02.00*
Friday 12.00 – 02.00
Saturday 14.00 – 03.00
Sunday 18.00 – 01.00

South Holland
including Rotterdam

SOUTH HOLLAND (Dutch: Zuid-Holland) is the most populous of the Dutch provinces and connects the Netherlands by sea to the wider world. The south is dominated by the deltas of the Rhine and the Maas, helping to create Rotterdam and its Europoort. Most of the rest is part of Randstad Holland, one of the densest centres of population in Europe.

The Europoort is the largest sea terminal in the world. At its north western tip is the Hook of Holland (Dutch: Hoek van Holland), the ferry terminal for Harwich. On the opposite side of the estuary is the terminal for Hull. In all, there are over 2,000 separate harbours. 12,000 ships, 500 million tonnes of goods and nearly two million ferry passengers pass through its docks each year. The surrounding area is filled with container warehouses, oil terminals, fish processing plants and naval supply depots in one form or another. To drive round the port on the recommended tourist route takes 150 km!

To the north is the state capital of 's Gravenhage, known better to the Dutch as Den Haag and to the English-speaking world as The Hague. It was recently amalgamated with the port of Scheveningen. More popular with tourists are the attractive town of Delft and the historically important city of Leiden.

The north west coast has a dozen seaside resorts which also act as commuter towns to the urban conurbations. Where there are rural areas, these are frequently turned over to the intensive cultivation of bulbs, especially in the north. South Holland also claims to have more windmills than any other part of the Netherlands.

BRIELLE
20 km W of Rotterdam on N218
Small town dating from the 14th century, beyond the Brielsemeer waterway to the south of Rotterdam Europoort. A market is held every Monday in the old town centre.

KONT VAN HET PAARD
1 Kaatsbaan
Tel: 01810 16161
About 4 km from the North Sea Ferries' terminal. It is only 6 km as the crow flies from the Hook of Holland but due to the estuary of the Oude Maas, more like 20 km by road. In the centre of town, stands this large café which has specialised in beer in the past few years. 120 brews are available, along with a fair range of food.
Sunday to Friday 16.30 – 01.00

Saturday 16.30 – 02.00

DELFT
6 km SSW of Den Haag off A13 (E19) [IC]
Delft (pop. 90,000) is the Netherlands' Bruges, a picturesque old town encircled by canals. Unfortunately, expanding to its current size has left it effectively as a suburb of The Hague. Yet it has retained a traditional townscape and is a pleasant place to potter round. Appropriate really, as Delft's best claim to fame is its porcelain. Some ceramics factories are open for view and specialist shops can be found without difficulty.

There are a number of interesting museums and churches in the town. The Van Meerten Museum is probably the best of these, with its collection of various arts and crafts including some rare old pottery.

LOCUS PUBLICUS
67 Brabantse Turfmarkt
Tel: 015 134632
Café: ✪✪✪ *Beer:* ✪✪✪✪✪
Founded 16 years ago, Locus Publicus is one of the Netherlands' best respected specialist beer cafés, just off the town centre. From the main Markt, take Jacob Gerritstraat to find Brabantse Turfmarkt, the home of the Saturday market. The pub is on the right. It consists of a long, thin, wood-panelled brown café and a small terrace on the street. They stock around 200 different beers, 30 of which come in 75 cl bottles. At the last count, the range of teas had reached 29. Background muzak hampers conversation. Food is limited to soup and sandwiches. If you want a more substantial and memorable meal try **Chez Vincent**, a few doors up, an excellent restaurant specialising in haute cuisine, Dutch style and not averse to storing the odd interesting brew.
Monday to Thursday 11.00 – 01.00
Friday & Saturday 11.00 – 02.00
Sunday 12.00 – 01.00

DEN HAAG
Major town [IC]
Den Haag (The Hague) is home to the Netherlands' parliament and much of its civil service but even so, it is not considered by the Dutch to be the nation's real capital. That honour goes to Amsterdam, an altogether more sophisticated and confident city. And cleaner too.

Since its fusion with the seaport of Scheveningen, Den Haag has become the third largest conurbation in the Netherlands (pop. 450,000). Most visitors come here on business, but if you find yourself in town, consider viewing the Royal Picture Collection at the Mauritshuis in Korte Vijverberg, the world's best collection of 17th century Dutch masters. The less elegant Museum of Toffees is at 20 Oude Molstraat. To amuse younger children, try the famous scale-model

city of miniaturised buildings called Madurodam, on Haringkade. There are good facilities on the coast, too.

LABIERINT
9 Nieuwe Schoolstraat
Tel: 070 346 0411
Café: ✪✪✪✪ *Beer:* ✪✪✪✪
On the way from Centraal Station to the city centre, the first major road parallels a canal. Turning right along the bank on its city side, the road becomes Prinsessegracht and then Koninginnegracht. After 800 metres on the left is Dr. Kuijperstraat, which becomes Mauritskade. A further 800 metres brings you to Nieuwe Schoolstraat on your left. A long walk perhaps but be grateful you are not trying to park. All worth it for a long brown café serving over 100 beers and a full menu of Flemish cuisine. Do not be put off by the suburban estate setting. Our directions are accurate – there really is a café down there.
Opening hours 16.00 – 01.00

PAAS
16a Dunne Bierkade
Tel: 070 360 0019
Café: ✪✪✪✪✪ *Beer:* ✪✪✪✪
Dunne Bierkade is not on most maps. The quickest way to find it from the town centre is to take Lutherse Burgwal from the Grote Markt. This becomes Paviljoensgracht and 800 metres further on to your left is one of the few attractive, cobbled, canalside streets left in town. If you are starting from one of the two main railway stations, locate Bierkade on the display map and head for the end which merges into Zuidwal. Despite its limited opening hours and obscure position, Den Paas is well worth finding. An attractive, candle-lit, atmospheric old café with plenty of wood and exposed brickwork. There are 150 beers on offer. Background music tends to be jazz. Usually the food is limited to bar snacks but on occasions they can branch out into larger meals with elements of French cuisine.
Sunday to Thursday 20.00 – 01.00
Friday & Saturday 15.30 – 01.30

DORDRECHT

14 km SW of Rotterdam between A15 (E31) & A16 (E19) [IC]

Known locally as Dordt, the City of Dordrecht (pop. 190,000) has lived twice. Once in its ancient incarnation before the great flood of 1421 and again since its revival a century ago. Despite its inland position it has always been a trading port and nowadays turns over five million tonnes of goods each year.

TIJD

170 Voorstraat
Tel: 078 133997
Café: ✪✪✪✪ *Beer:* ✪✪✪✪

The city is tourist friendly. All points lead to the railway station and from here it is a ten minute walk to the Times. Bus nos. 8 and 9 stop nearby on Wijnstraat. This is a delightfully relaxed, rather cool and artistic light brown café on the ground floor of a building which dates from 1603. Background music is mainly jazz, the clientele is mixed and the decor features modern art, potted plants, budgerigars and green benches. The boss is Corinne Smeyer van Aart, the only woman to own and manage a long-standing beer café in the Netherlands and a pioneer in this respect. The beer list hovers around 100 and may feature unusual brews from new small Dutch breweries like 't Kuipertje or Gans. Small snacks are always available. There is a full menu served between 20.00 and 22.00 at night. There is no admission after 01.00, even at weekends.

Tuesday 17.00 – 01.00
Friday & Saturday 14.00 – 02.00
Sunday 15.00 – 24.00
Other days 15.00 – 01.00

GORINCHEM

35 km SSW of Utrecht off A27 (E311) & A15 (E31) [IR]

Attractive market town dating from 1224, with excellent road and river links.

KEIZER

114 Keizerstraat
Tel: 01830 34661

Town-centre brown café, stocking 160 beers. Limited snacks. Seats at the bar. Quieter alcoves. Pool table. One of the very few long-standing members of the ABT group of cafés not to have been visited by an accredited Guide inspector. Most the others are excellent so we assume The Emperor is too.

Sunday to Thursday 19.00 – 02.00
Friday to Saturday 15.00 – 04.00

LEIDEN

12 km NW of Den Haag between A44 & A4 (E19) [IC]

Historic and picturesque university town (pop. 105,000) on the Old Rhine, surrounded by canals. Much of the old town has been pedestrianised. Amsterdam and Hook of Holland are just a train ride away making it a possible weekend venue for those not wishing to stay in the capital.

Amongst many dubious claims to fame, Leiden can be held to blame for gin and American Christianity. The former is said to have been distilled for the first time by scientists (or bootleggers) in the town in 1483. The latter connection is due to the Pilgrim Fathers who, contrary to Plymouth's version of history, departed for the New World from Leiden in 1620, eleven years after they had been unceremoniously booted out of England. See the full story in the Leidse Pilgrim Collectie at 45 Vliet.

The university's Botanical Gardens and Observatory are notable sights and happen to be halfway from the station to the area which boasts the best cafés.

BONTE KOE

11 Hooglandschekerk Koorsteeg
Tel: 071 141094
Café: ✪✪✪✪✪ *Beer:* ✪✪

For our first edition, the owner wrote to say that with regret his café was closing. In his shoes, we would want to keep the tourists away, too, but the Guide is no amateur concoction and we know that the Speckled Cow is still going strong. It is a splendidly convivial place found in a side street between Hooigracht, a main road which spans both the New and Old Rhine, and St. Pancras'

Church. Its ludicrous but attractive tiled wall decorations of Friesians at leisure are evidence that the building was originally designed, though never used, as a butcher's shop. The piano is rarely used but the ceramic stove and fire are lit in winter. There are only around 20 beers but these are chosen cleverly. There is no food. We include it for its atmosphere, created mainly by an intensely loyal group of regulars, unaffected by the waves of students and campus followers from the Eurochic end of the market. There is a terrace defined in the alley outside in summer. Probably the best café in town.
Monday to Friday 16.00 – late
Saturday & Sunday 12.00 – late

VATTEGAT
16 Garenmarkt
Tel: 071 143066
Café: ✪✪✪ *Beer:* ✪✪✪
Behind the Museum of Natural History in Raamsteeg lies the Van der Werf Park. Garenmarkt is the road which runs alongside the eastern aspect of both. The Fat Cat offers the best beer list in town among the proper cafés. This stretches to around 60. There are also bar snacks and a small barbecue behind the bar. The atmosphere is darkened Mallorca beach café and now bills itself as "a bodega and beer café". The bimbettes and azure waters are missing but the Phil Collins CDs and other essential features are there in force. It can be quite lively on Friday and Saturday nights.
Monday to Thursday 16.00 – 01.00
Friday 16.00 – 02.00
Saturday 16.00 – 03.00
CLOSED SUNDAY

TRY ALSO: **De Burcht** at 14 Burgsteeg, near the Burcht castle ruins is recommended for its stylishness and the **Barrera** at 56 Rapenburg for its brown café atmosphere. Neither boasts more than 30 beers.

MAASSLUIS
12 km W of Rotterdam off A20 (E25) [IR]

Attractive old port, ten minutes by train from Hook of Holland on the main line to Rotterdam, now absorbed into the Europoort complex but maintaining its old functions. The split-level town layout is odd enough without the impression that the smaller fishing boats manage to moor on the high street. Wandering around, you may chance upon the Museum of Salvage Boats, a gallery devoted to fishing pictures and S.S. Furie, the last Dutch steam-powered tug.

OPORTO
7 Noorddijk
Tel: 01899 20247
Café: ✪✪✪✪ *Beer:* ✪✪✪✪
Near the centre of town, close to the Grote Kerk, this attractive, long, narrow beer café has seats outside in the summer. Popular with students at weekends but generally attracting a mixed clientele. There are a number of house beers such as Sluyzers Pils and Maessluys Nat from a variety of breweries including the Friesland concern, Us Heit, and the West Flanders firm of Van Eecke. Food is usually minimal but they have a special mussels evening on the first Wednesday of the month. Although they limit the number of beers available in the café to around 70, the range is constantly changing. This is helped by the fact that they run a weekend beer shop from the cellar (see Beer Shops and Warehouses).
Tuesday to Thursday 20.00 – 01.00
Friday & Saturday (Oct - Apr) 21.00 – 02.00
Other days 15.00 – late
CLOSED MONDAY; and SUNDAY (Oct - Apr)

ROTTERDAM
Major town [IC]
The population of Rotterdam is quoted as 1,050,000, making it the largest city in the Netherlands and rivalling Brussels as the largest in the Low Countries. It all depends where you think Rotterdam ends and the rest of the world begins. In reality the non-stop urban sprawl spreads almost from Hoek van Holland to

Dordrecht. The city is in and of its port, quintessentially Dutch, a place for merchants and their courtiers.

Rotterdammers have the reputation of being business-like but philosophical. Go for the deal but do not worry if it fails; tomorrow is more important than today. However, they are not without an outrageous sense of fun, as can be seen in the extraordinary architecture around Blaak station where many of our listed cafés are found.

Getting around is a matter of mastering the metro. The main line leaves from the front of Centraal Station and runs underneath the city's main boulevard, Coolsingel, before crossing under the River Maas towards the southern suburbs. Blaak and Oostplein, on the other main line bring the beer tourist to most of their places of interest.

The best known museum in town is the Boymans-Van Beuningen Gallery in Mathenesserstraat, with a broad-based collection of paintings and objets d'art. There are works from most of the old Dutch and Flemish masters but also a significant number of more modern paintings including Picassos, Monets and Gaugins, plus an Italian collection.

To the south west of the Boymans is an area of parkland leading down to the River Maas. Near the waterfront is the 185-metre high Euromast, housing a mock-up of a ship's bridge, two restaurants and a Space Tower. Back towards the city centre is the Prins Hendrik Maritime Museum on Burgermeester Jacobsplein, detailing the history of seafaring over 300 years.

CAMBRINUS
4 Blaak
Tel: 010 414 6702
Café: ✪✪✪✪ *Beer:* ✪✪✪✪✪
Rotterdam's three best cafés for beer tourists plus one of the also-rans are all found within an easy walk of Blaak railway and metro station. Blaak is what happened when H. G. Wells and Pablo Picasso were let loose with a virtual reality architect's kit. At ground floor level in the block between it and the waterfront is

Cambrinus, a modern, open-plan, tile-floored, stand and swig, sit and theorise café. The tone and atmosphere are modulated by music, varying from moderately serious classical via noise to avant garde jazz. At the back is a dining area. Beyond that, a terrace overlooks the old harbour. It lists around 300 beers but be prepared to be disappointed by stock or time problems, especially obvious when it is busy; and it can get very busy, as in eight bar staff fully occupied non-stop-type busy. The food is also surprisingly impressive, especially when they make serious attempts to offer proper Flemish cooking or cuisine à la bière. There are simpler snacks too.
Monday to Thursday 12.00 – 01.00
Friday 12.00 – 03.00
Saturday 14.00 – 03.00
Sunday 14.00 – 01.00

DOELENCAFE
52 Schouwburgplein
Tel: 010 414 8688
Café: ✪✪✪ *Beer:* ✪✪✪
The Doelencafé is the only café we list that is off the waterfront area. In fact it lies within easy reach of Centraal Station. To find it, head out of the main exit across the tramlines, into Kruisplein in the direction of the Holiday Inn. Just before you reach it, turn left and the Doelencafé is on your left. There is a huge terrace on the street and an equally huge bar area inside. It makes up part of the ground floor of the Doelen concert hall. They have between 40 and 50 beers on the list and some bar staff are more knowledgeable than others. The house speciality is jazz. They sponsor the Rotterdam Jazz Festival in October and November and for the rest of the year, put on live jazz every Sunday between 15.30 and 18.00. Their cooking (from 11.00 each day), which is said to be French, has a good reputation and includes dishes of all sizes, and reasonable vegetarian options.
Opening hours 10.00 – 01.00

LOCUS PUBLICUS
364 Oostzeedijk
Tel: 010 433 1761
Café: ✪✪✪✪ *Beer:* ✪✪✪✪

You change metro at Churchillplein to reach Blaak. If you carry on one more station you reach Oostplein. Follow signs to the Oostzeedijk exit and with luck you will stumble across Locus Publicus within 50 metres of the stairway. The claim is 300 beers but we think this is an overestimate. The list does include some unusual brews, though. Look carefully around the many blackboards around the walls. The café itself is simple but special. There is an open log fire in winter, loads of wood panelling, marble and mosaic, Art Deco lighting, pictures of rustic Nederland and blah blah blah, all absorbed into a brown café atmosphere. None of it matches particularly well but so what? The background music tends to be classical or old-style jazz. Catch it at a quiet time and you will appreciate it best. It gets popular with keen young people at night.

Monday to Saturday 17.00 – 01.00
Sunday 21.00 – 01.00

PENCIL
172 Rijstuin
Tel: 010 213 1170
Café: ✪ *Beer:* ✪✪✪

If you like the yellow and turquoise stained glass panels and steel imagery of Blaak station, you will love the stunted pencil called Blaak Tower, and the nearby tiled yellow and black cubes pointing diagonally heavenwards. This is what Frank Lloyd Wright could have done on mescaline. At the base of the tower is a young persons' games café with loads of billiards and pool tables, open-top table football, table ice hockey and, a little incongruously, 80 beers including its own brand. It has all the culture of a bar in a bowling alley.

WEIJMAR
637 Haringvliet
Tel: 010 414 8835
Café: ✪✪✪✪ *Beer:* ✪✪✪

From the back door of Cambrinus (above), head left along the harbour's edge until you reach Haringvliet. Alternatively, from Locus Publicus cut across Oostplein to Oostmolenwerf, then turn right to hit its other end. The high street number is due to the multiple, individually numbered blocks of flats on the quay. The best of the cafés listed for Rotterdam, if you like smart, candle-lit, up-market, food-oriented cafés. Nearly a five star rating. Serious food, especially in the evenings, is best consumed in the glass fronted restaurant area overlooking Haringvliet harbour. Although the beer list only reaches 50, they do a good range of bokbiers, meiboks and Christmas ales in season and as mein host remarked cryptically, they have the whole list in stock. There is also an above average wine list. There are newspapers and magazines to browse through. Very civilised. Formerly the Spaanse Poort, it reverted to its old name in 1991. It has no connection with the Indonesian restaurant in the same building.

Monday to Saturday 11.00 – 03.00
Sunday 14.00 – 03.00

SASSENHEIM
10 km N of Leiden off A 44
Small commuter town, north of Leiden. There is a market on Thursdays.

TWEE WEZEN
2 Oude Haven
Tel: 02522 16560
Café: ✪✪✪ *Beer:* ✪✪✪✪

In the centre of the town, on the corner of a small square which served as the main canal moorings 70 years ago. Chairs and tables spew out onto the square at weekends. Indoors there is a simple bar and upstairs a games room with machines and table football. The beer list stays around 80, with a quarter of these Dutch. There is house beer, a tripel from Raaf called Wezenloos, which may simply be the usual tripel with more sediment. Food is limited to rolls. Damn fine coffee.

Monday to Thursday 12.00 –
01.00
Friday & Saturday 12.00 – 02.00
Sunday 13.00 – 01.00

SCHIEDAM

Western suburb of Rotterdam [IR]

A suburb of Rotterdam like Salford is
of Manchester or Leith is of
Edinburgh. Its station is sub-titled
Rotterdam West. Effectively part of
the city. It is home to one of the few
functioning distilleries left in the
Netherlands, Branderij de Tweelingh
at 93 Noordvest. There is also a small
museum of distilling (closed
Monday) at 112 Hoogstraat.

WEESHUIS

76 Hoogstraat
Tel: 010 426 1657
Café: ✪✪✪✪ *Beer:* ✪✪✪✪

The beer and café ratings here may
be underestimates as the assessment
was made in the harrowing
conditions which prevail at ten
o'clock on a Thursday night, which is
to say that it gets a tad full. A famous
small, long, brown café allegedly
stocking 200 beers. The background
music tends to be jazz and there are
musical instruments on the wall.
From the station either take bus no.
52 or else walk straight ahead to the
spired church of St. Liduina OLV

Rozencrants, then head left and ask.
Hoogstraat is pedestrianised. In
summer they put chairs and tables in
the courtyard at the front. There are
accounts of good cooking. They now
promote a likeur called Weeskind,
which implies some connection
with the distillery, Erven Post. They
are also believed to be financially
involved with the attempts to create
a brewery in Schiedam. The station
is on the route from Rotterdam
Centraal to Hoek van Holland.
Opening hours 12.00 – late

SPIJKENISSE

12 km WSW of Rotterdam on
N218

Small town, halfway along the south
side of the Europoort. An old
community, its 15th century late
Gothic church has a 47-bell carillon
dating from 1988. The futuristic
building on the waterfront is a water
purification plant.

GEBEUREN

13 Voorstraat
Tel: 01880 24220
In the centre of town. All-round café,
trying to be Belgian, offering over
150 beers, plus bar snacks and fuller
meals.
Monday & Tuesday 16.00 – 01.00
Friday & Saturday 14.00 – 02.00
Other days 14.00 – 01.00

Utrecht

UTRECHT PROVINCE is at the north east of the crescent-shaped urban area of the Randstad and forms part of the southern shore of the Markermeer and adjacent Eemmeer, opposite Flevoland.

The bulk of its population lives in the city of Utrecht and its environs or else in the area which spreads north east towards Zeist, Soest and Amersfoort. The more rural south is criss-crossed by major natural and man-made waterways including the branches of the Lower Rhine and the Amsterdam-Rhine Canal.

The province's two breweries are both newish, Drie Ringen of Amersfoort and the Utrecht brewery at the Oudaen in Utrecht.

AMERSFOORT

20 km ENE of Utrecht off A28 (E232) [IC]

The province's second town (pop. 90,000) is awash with historic buildings and surrounded to the south and west by forest. It is ringed by canals and its main square is dominated by the Gothic Church of St. George. Town trumpeters perform every Saturday morning in summer. A nine ton irregular lump of stone reminds the population of the day they were conned by a 17th century prankster into dragging it 6 km from Lensderheide, so that he could win a bet that he could make them do it. The collective nickname for Amersfoorters is "stone heads" as a result.

DRIE RINGEN

18 Kleine Spui
Tel: 033 620300

Small café inside De Drie Ringen brewery. It serves only drie Ringen beers. If the brewing process is operating at the time you can get a great view. Food is limited to small snacks.
Sunday (Apr - Sep) 13.00 – 17.00
Other days 12.00 – 18.00
CLOSED SUNDAY & MONDAY (Oct - Mar)

MARIPOSA

10 Valkestraat
Tel: 033 611176
Café: ❍❍❍ *Beer:* ❍❍❍❍

Leave Markt, the pedestrianised main square, to the right of St. George's church. Turn first right and Valkestraat is 50 metres on your left. The gorgeous looking **In den Grooten Slock**, which you pass, has an unfortunate tendency to play "Why why why Delilah" loudly to its fruit machine lolling younger customers. Mariposa is a deep, dark, long café with a slightly raised seating area. It is popular with younger drinkers at weekends but cosmopolitan the rest of the time. It stocks well over a hundred beers and the bar staff know what is what. They experiment with unusual new beers and will stock "anything we can lay our hands on" once. Pine top bar, wooden floors, tabled alcoves. Noisy at night. There are dartboards. Food is minimalist. There is a sedate upstairs room for beer tastings which is sometimes open.
Monday to Thursday 16.30 – 02.00
Friday & Saturday 14.00 – 04.00
Sunday 14.00 – 02.00

ROOIE CENT

34 Hooglandseweg
Tel: 033 756035
Café: ❍❍❍ *Beer:* ❍❍❍❍

Out in the sticks, a five-minute walk from the centre of town using a local map. The name means roughly the Scraped Ha'penny. A pleasant, if basic single room brown café with bare floorboards, painted wooden walls and a pavement terrace. Friendly bar staff will guide you through the list of over a hundred beers with strength in trappist ales and other Belgian brews. During the day they mix and match bar snacks with some of these. In the evenings a younger crowd can dominate, especially at weekends. There is occasional live music.

Sunday to Thursday 20.00 – 02.00

Friday & Saturday 20.00 – 03.00

UTRECHT
Major town [IC]

The City of Utrecht (pop. 250,000) is the fourth largest in the Netherlands. It is built at the place where the lower waters of the Rhine traditionally divided into the Old Rhine and the Vecht. It has been an important crossing place of the great river since Roman times and an influential religious town since Christianity first reached this part of the world in the 7th century.

The influence of church on state in the Duchies, Kingdoms and Empires which pre-dated the modern Netherlands was traditionally focussed on Utrecht. Its most famous son was probably Adriaan Boeyens who became first the tutor to the young Emperor Charlemagne and then went on to be Pope Adrian VI. It was in Utrecht in 1568 that the seven Protestant provinces announced their declaration of independence from the southern Catholic states, starting the Eighty Years War.

Modern Utrecht is the city of a thousand shops. High streets in the rest of the western world are becoming showcases for the local branches of internationally known chain stores, but Utrecht seems to revel in the obscure, like a mix of York, Oxford and Camden Lock. We found one which sold only nuts, tea and honey.

Its magnificent religious centres such as the Protestant Cathedral of St. Michael are drowned by an appealingly disorganised town centre with loads of unmatched buildings and randomly interspersed canals. The famous university is a presence in the town but night life is not dominated by students.

Vredenburg is signposted through the Hoog Catharijne shopping complex which tops Utrecht Centraal Station. Follow these signs to find the VVV tourist information office and the way into town. You will need VVV if you want either accommodation or a map. If you have half an hour to kill, try the Phonograph Museum, nearby at 43 Gildenkwartier.

BELGIE
196 Oude Gracht
Tel: 030 312666
Café: ✪✪ *Beer:* ✪✪✪✪✪

To find Oude Gracht from Centraal Station, see Oudaen (below). However, finding no. 196 is a tricky business as the street changes name to Stadhuisbrug then Vischmarkt then Lichtegaard then Donkeregaard before becoming Oude Gracht again. You know you are on the right track if you pass Piet Snot's comic shop (old and new) which readers of our first edition will be pleased to hear outlived the fine art showroom next door. The Kafé België announced that it was radically upgraded in 1993. As far as we can tell, this involved shifting the bar to the opposite side of the room, putting a blown-up old photo of the late King Baudoin at the far end of the room and installing a row of 20 beer founts. Otherwise it remains its lovable, grotty, incongruous self. No stars for elegance but still sporting one of the best beer lists in the Netherlands, at nearly 180 choices. Furthermore, the list is clearly displayed, in stock and often good value. Student food such as burgers, vegetarian tart and beignets, bean stew or a plate of pasta is available from 17.30 to 19.45. (Q: Why no later? A: The cook gets hungry so he knocks off, sir.) Smaller snacks at other times.

Sunday to Thursday 11.00 – 03.00

Friday & Saturday 11.00 – 05.00

JAN PRIMUS
27 Jan van Scorelstraat
Tel: 030 514572
Café: ✪✪✪✪✪ *Beer:* ✪✪✪✪

Jan Primus, alias Duke John I of Brabant, would approve of the café which took his name. Hidden in the suburban wastelands of eastern Utrecht, in the area known as Wilhelmina Park, the simplest way to get here is by taking bus Lijn 4 from outside the Centraal Station and asking for Prins Hendriklaan. On foot the route is possible with the aid of the tourist map (from the VVV office at the back of Centraal Station) but takes about 20 minutes. Either way the effort is rewarded by the chance to enjoy the best light brown street-corner café in the Netherlands. Few places quote as one of their attractions, "the customers" but here it is true. Strangers are actively courted for civilised and animated conversation. The all-comers atmosphere is free from muzak and games machines. The bar design is simple but clever. The beer list hovers around 130 and often contains a few surprises. Food is gently expanding to include some Eurosnax and is enough to sustain a longer visit. They are genuinely pleased that you took the trouble to find their café. [Editor's note: things happen when I visit Jan Primus. On the check-up tour for this edition I managed to hail the only tee-total taxi driver in Utrecht. After assuring me that if he were a drinking man Jan Primus would be his favourite café, he really did say "I had that beer bloke Michael Jackson in the cab, once. You know him?".]
Sunday to Thursday 15.00 – 01.00
Friday & Saturday 15.00 – 02.00

OUDAEN
99 Oude Gracht
Tel: 0030 311864
Café: ✪✪✪✪ *Beer:* ✪✪✪
Heading into the city centre from the VVV tourist office will bring you, after 200 metres, to a canal. Turn right and Oudaen is on your right after 30 metres, in the Stadskasteel Oudaen, a 14th century building which operated for centuries as an old people's home. People come here for the home-brewed wheat beers (see Dutch Independent Breweries) but these are not the only

attraction. The café is on the grand Bohemian scale, with a 25-foot ceiling supported by tree-sized beams, massive candelabrae and plenty of candlelight. Jar and jaw standing by the long bar or retreat up the steps to the quieter, raised tabled area at the back. Eating is big here. There is a restaurant called Tussen Hemel en Aarde (Twixt Heaven and Earth) in the evenings. The café too offers a full menu from 11.00 to 17.00 and from 17.30 to 21.00. Lunch includes tagliatelle, satay, quiche and sukiyaki. Dinner expands to include, for example, grilled prawns, lamb cutlets with honey and thyme, and tournedos in red wine, cooked to the standard of an above average British pub. Food prices are average for this grade of café but be warned that the beer is expensive. Simpler snacks are available all day. The gemengd bittergarnitur is a massive plate of nibbles on sticks. We love the bar staff's braces and dicky bows, rolled-up white sleeves and black trousers. The brewery is in the cellars and can be visited sometimes, for a small fee.
Opening hours 10.00 – 02.00

ZES VAATJES
32 Monseigneur van de Weteringstraat
Tel: 030 318990
Café: ✪✪✪✪✪ *Beer:* ✪✪✪
Britain still has a few examples of parlour bars – the landlord's own room into which friends may come to drink. But these make up only one part of the pub. At the Six Little Barrels one gets the impression that entry to any of the pub is by invitation only. This is essentially a sampling café for the up-market off-licence next door, and perhaps the owner's hobby, too. Its opening hours owe nothing to market forces but if your time in Utrecht is convenient to mine host, make a special attempt to find and enjoy this delightfully well-kept and traditional proeflokaal. We list the official hours but droit de seigneur also applies. The range of beers is above average, usually. Bus no. 3 takes you up Nachtegaalstraat and there is a stop opposite the end of Mgr. van de

Weteringstraat.
Thursday 14.00 – 20.00
Saturday 10.00 – 17.00
Other days 14.00 – 18.00
CLOSED WEDNESDAY &
SUNDAY

ZEIST

10 km E of Utrecht off A28 (E232)
[IC]
Market town (pop. 60,000) halfway
between Utrecht and Amersfoort,
surrounded by woodland. The 17th
century mansion, Slot Zeist, is open
every weekend and daily in summer.

SCHAVUIT

21 Steynlaan
Tel: 03404 17714
The Rascal is an up-market, town-
centre brown café which regularly
features live music. The beer list is
limited to 35 choices but they offer
occasional beer tasting evenings.
Open every day except New Year's
Eve.
Monday to Thursday 20.00 –
02.00
Friday & Saturday 14.00 – 03.00
Sunday 14.00 – 02.00

Zeeland

ZEELAND, still sometimes known in English as Zealand, is the south western province of the Netherlands. It is made up from the islands of North and South Beveland, Walcheren and Schouwen-Duiveland, now linked by dykes and reclaimed land, making the area a delta of the Rivers Schelde and Maas. Work continues, to alter the flow of the great rivers, so as to make them better waterways and less erosive of the fertile land.

In many parts of the province, residents refer to their bit as "the island". The exception is the southernmost part, Zeeuwsch Vlaanderen, which translates as Coastal Flanders but is more often called Dutch Flanders. This is geographically contiguous with Belgian Flanders and is linked to the rest of the Netherlands only by the two car ferries at Breskens and Perkpolder.

Zeeland's two new wave breweries, Gans of Goes and Zeeuwsche-Vlaamsche of Hulst in Dutch Flanders, are scheduled to be joined by a third in 1994. This is ironic, given the disappearance of many of the beer cafés in the province.

GOES

15 km ENE of Vlissingen off A58 (E312) [IC]

The old town of Goes is in South Beveland. As the decades go by and the routes taken by the great rivers to reach the sea become better organised by major engineering projects, this part of Zeeland becomes more convincingly a part of the mainland. The town has the small but interesting Beveland Museum, by St. Katerin's church and a theme park of ancient crafts, which houses the Gans brewery (see Beer Tourism: Brewery visits).

STRADA

48 St. Jacobstraat

Café: ✪✪ Beer: ✪✪✪

In the pedestrianised centre of the town, not far from the Markt; a young person's café complete with funfair dodgems, half a pink Cadillac, a GPO telephone kiosk and all the styles of nineties bop. Almost incongruously it also commissions a genuinely unique house beer, La Strada Wit (5.5% abv) from the town's Gans brewery. Among its 30 other beers is its Ganze Tripel.

Minimal snacks only.
Monday 10.00 – 18.00
Saturday 12.00 – 02.00
Other days 10.00 – 02.00

MIDDELBURG

4 km N of Vlissingen off A58 (E312) [IC]

The ancient town of Middelburg has a lovely centre, dominated by an impressive Gothic town hall and restored 13th century abbey. It is an easy bus or train ride from the ferry terminal at Vlissingen.

MUG

54 Vlasmarkt

Tel: 01180 14851

Café: ✪✪✪✪✪ Beer: ✪✪✪✪

Walcheren "Island" used to have several beer cafés, particularly in Vlissingen. Now we could only find one worthy of mention – but how worthy! You will find Vlasmarkt branching off the main Markt, which is the heart of Middelburg, opposite the VVV Tourist Information office. It is an unusually cosmopolitan street, boasting an Arabic grocer, antiques shops, a film theatre, a pets emporium and The Midge, a café-restaurant in the classic mode. There is wood everywhere. The furniture is rickety-rackety and the decor is carefully selected. The lighting is mainly candles, the atmosphere is fin de siècle bistro and timeless Bohemian tavern. The music ranges from Beethoven to bee-bop. The beer list stretches to 80, though only 60 are advertised. 't IJ brewery's Mug Bitter was originally commissioned for this café. You will also find most of the other IJ beers and real Westvleteren 8° and 12°. The wine list is expensive but high quality. There are wooden casks of sherry, port, Madeira and notenwijn, a Sicilian wine fortified with a bitter almond likeur. The menu is unusually full and generally high quality, especially the grills. There is a main bar, a restaurant and a meeting room which doubles as the overflow for the eatery. The full restaurant menu runs from 17.30 to 23.00. At other times there are snacks. Hams and bierwurst can be seen drying over the bar. There is live jazz on the last Tuesday of the month. Owner Barend Midavaine dines here, as he has done with great relish for the past 20 years. Long may he continue to do so. His establishment is excellent.

Opening hours 16.00 – late
CLOSED SUNDAY & MONDAY

TERNEUZEN

25 km SE of Vlissingen on opposite bank of the Schelde Estuary

The largest town in Dutch Flanders. On the south bank of the western branch of the Schelde estuary, at a point where the river mouth is 4 km across. The people here are fiercely Dutch but regarded by many of their countrymen as honorary Belgians. The town centre is effectively an island formed by a canal which parallels the estuary. The pedestrianised town plan is unmistakably Dutch.

VRIENDSCHAP

1 Noordstraat
Tel: 01150 12593
Café: ✪✪✪✪ *Beer:* ✪✪✪

Dutch Flanders was a beer desert at the time of our first edition. Since then it has acquired a brewery (see Dutch Independent Breweries: Zeeuwsche-Vlaamsche) and the Friendship, a specialist beer café with a unique atmosphere. You will find it on the numerous street maps at the land end of the main shopping street. The biggest draw here is the decor. A high-ceilinged, large, single room café is made most attractive by the use of carpets on the tables, stuffed birds and fishing memorabilia on the walls and the use of all manner of seating to create several drinking areas of different character in one place. The bar front is carved and there are plenty of potted plants. The walls are wooden and floorboards bare. The other draw is the seventy-five beers on the list, which include a few from the Dolle Brouwers. From 12.00 to 14.00 they serve omelettes, uitsmijter and beef steak. At other times there are pancakes and ice cream. Background music includes traditional melodies played with accordions and bass drums. They have a billiards table.

Opening hours 11.00 – late
CLOSED SUNDAY

STOP PRESS

IN THE COURSE OF compiling the second edition of The Good Beer Guide to Belgium & the Netherlands we have been recommended a number of bars which, for one reason or another, we have been unable to survey. These may be excellent, dreadful or even shut, we have no way of knowing. But if you visit any, let us know what you find.

FRIESLAND

BLIJA: VELDZICHT
Small town 20 km north of Leeuwarden on the N357. Said to be an authentic brown café with a selection of better known Belgian ales.

GRONINGEN

Shortly before going to press we were supplied with the names of the bars which have joined AGT, the new beer café organisation for the northern Netherlands. Those not already listed in the Guide are:

BEDUM: FLAIR
36 Grotestraat.
Six kilometres north of Groningen.

DE WILP: SPORTLUST
9 Plantsoen.
Twenty kilometres south west of Groningen.

GRONINGEN: TOETER
6 Turfsingel.
In the provincial capital itself.

LEEK: OUDE BANK
6 Tolberterstraat.
Twelve kilometres south west of Groningen.

STADSKANAAL: CHAPLINS BAR
56 Handelsstraat.
Forty kilometres south east of Groningen.

VEENDAM: TOETER
5 Beneden
Westerdiep. In the same town as the Aaierdoppie.

WINSCHOTEN: BLOEM
1b Marktplein.
In the same town as the Carambole.

NORTH BRABANT

EINDHOVEN: VONDERKE
On Napoleonplein and said to sell special beers.

ETTEN-LEUR: NE'ERLANDS KOFFYHUIS
Suburban town 8 km WSW of Breda. Venue for sampling sessions by PINT. No other information available.

NORTH HOLLAND

AMSTERDAM: BAARSJES
578 Overtoom (tel: 020 612 9983).
In the south western suburbs, on the way to Schipol Airport. Beer café and steakhouse with a pleasant modern atmosphere.

AMSTERDAM SPIRITS HOUSES

Amsterdam boasts many weird and wonderful styles of café. Several particularly characterful places specialise in stocking an array of jenevers, likeurs or other spirits.

Be warned that mixing beer and spirits is not really approved of in Amsterdam and care must be taken if you intend to visit some of our beer cafés before or after a visit here.

The **Admiraal** at 319 Herengracht (tel: 020 625 4334) is just around the corner from the Café de la Paix (see listings) and is named after Ruyters, who is buried in the church on Dam Square. This beautiful café-restaurant is the proeflokaal for the jenevers, likeurs and brandewijns produced by the Distilleerderij Van Wees (AVW). They sell jenevers up to twenty years old from stone jars and the likeurs of fruits steeped in alcohol from large glass bottles. Little of the furniture matches and there are plenty of nooks and crannies. The bar meals are neither cheap nor ordinary, from light snacks to full and heavy Dutch cooking. (Mon – Fri 12.00 – 24.00, Sat 17.00 – 24.00).

The **Drie Fleschjes** at 18 Gravenstraat (tel: 020 624 8443) is in the same street as Café Belgique (see listings). It serves around forty likeurs and other spirits, mainly from Bols and Bootz. There are bare floorboards, lightly sanded and a stacked bank of oak casks with padlocked taps. The contents of these are privately owned by companies and used for hospitality. (Mon – Sat 12.00 – 20.30).

The **Olofspoort** at 13 Nieuwe Brugsteeg (tel: 020 624 3918) is fifty metres from Bizonders Bar (see listings), turning left. It is undoubtedly the most elegant of the spirits houses we list and has the best array of drinks. As well as grain jenevers up to seventeen years old you will find old moutwijn jenever, old corenwijn jenever, Amsterdamse kruidenbitter Olofspoort (a spiced bitter tonic) and fifty likeurs of the Oud Amsterdam brand. There is plenty of jenevriana in this immaculately kept two-roomed proejflokaal. No food. (Tue – Thu 15.00 – 01.00, Fri & Sat 15.00 – 02.00).

The **Oosterling** at 139 Utrechtsestraat (tel: 020 623 4140) is off the beaten track. Take tram no. 4 from Centraal Station to Frederiksplein and backtrack 100 metres. Dutch bars rarely have off-licences but here is an exception. The impressive range of spirits includes good examples from innumerable international styles plus a good range of Dutch ones, including several which are "own brand" for the café. These include a jenever and a spiced, bitter "tonic". The atmosphere is Victorian liquor saloon. (Daily 12.00 – 01.00).

The **Wijnand Fockink** at 31 Pijlsteeg (tel: 020 639 2695) is situated on a back alley between Dam Square and the Red Light District. It is the simplest of Amsterdam's spirits houses, with just a small bare-floored, plain room and few seats. It re-opened in 1993 after three years. By early 1994 it should have its own distillery just own the street, to make traditional jenevers and eaux de vie. Meanwhile it stocks sixty different likeurs from AVW plus a variety of other distillers' jenevers. (Daily 16.00 – 20.00).

Multinationals
Brewery groups

SITTING IN A BELGIAN or Dutch café looking at a list of 300 different beers, it is hard to imagine that four companies control 85 per cent of beer production in the two countries.

If Heineken, Interbrew, BSN and Allied-Carlsberg wanted to cut up rough, they could effectively close down the Dutch and Belgian artisan brewing traditions tomorrow. The reason that they do not do so has little to do with sentimentality or consumer campaigning. It is a reflection of the fact that each of them currently sees a future for specialist beers in Europe and sees small producers as the best judges of this market.

For our second edition, we have listed the breweries of these four conglomerates under each parent company. You are also referred to the comments at the beginning of the section on Belgian Independent Breweries concerning listings.

ALLIED-CARLSBERG
The full extent of the relationship between Allied Breweries (UK) and Carlsberg of Copenhagen is not really in the public domain. They have many co-operative ventures but there has not been any formal merger or takeover. If they were to be fully merged they would become the second largest brewing group in Europe.

The part of the Allied-Carlsberg empire which lies in the Low Countries is Verenigde Bierbrouwerijen Breda-Rotterdam (VBBR). In the not too distant past its beers were better known as Skol, Allied Breweries' bold, but thankfully unsuccessful attempt to create an international brand of Eurofizz, consistently awful wherever you tried it.

The leading brand name for VBBR nowadays is Oranjeboom, taken from the name of the now defunct Rotterdam brewery. Lager production is now centred on the Breda plant, originally the Drie Hofijzers brewery.

Since our first edition, the company has expanded and refined its interest in brewing ale in the Netherlands. In 1991 they acquired effective control of the Arcen brewery which, ironically, had been founded in 1981 as the result of an employee buy-out of the Vriendenkring brewery when it was closed by its then owners, Allied Breweries (UK). In 1992 they added Raaf to their collection.

The link between VBBR and the Koningshoeven abbey brewery is more subtle. They own the "Koningshoeven" brand name and distribution rights. However, sources close to God assure us that they have not bought the abbey, its brewery or the religious order. At least, not yet.

ARCEN
ARCENSE STOOMBROUWERIJ
Kruisweg 44
5944 EN Arcen
Tel: 04703 2427
Fax: 04703 1297
The Arcener Bierbrouwerij BV was formed in 1981 by a management buy-out. This was the first of the new wave of artisanal breweries to set up in the Netherlands. It pioneered the introduction (or re-introduction) of a number of ale styles to the country and was the first company to produce bokbiers by top fermentation.

Their early success came as the result of a deal with Hertog Jan, a large distributor which commissioned own brand ales from them. Somehow this led to them rejoining the Allied stable in 1991. Recent developments include the withdrawal of a large number of beers and the introduction of a Pilsener, brewed for a supermarket chain. These reverses are not welcomed by Dutch beer lovers.

The company also brews Lurkbier for the mischievous trolls of De Efteling theme park in Kaatsheuvel, a filtered version of the Dubbel. Arcener Stout and Oud Limburgs still appear at the brewery tap but are off sale elsewhere, so we have not listed them. They sometimes brew Witte Raaf when that brewery is over capacity. Current production is 20,000 hl a year.

HERTOG JAN GRANDE PRESTIGE
10% abv ✪✪✪✪ Strong Stout
Dark, fruity and powerful but lacking the panache of a 5✪ brew.

ARCENER WINTERBIER*
9% abv ✪✪✪ Winter Ale
Strong, filtered, straw coloured ale, sold mainly from November to January.

HERTOG JAN TRIPEL
8.5% abv ✪✪✪✪ Tripel
Clear, dark amber ale in the tripel style but lacking the abbey complexities.

HERTOG JAN DUBBEL
7% abv ✪✪✪ Dubbel
Dark, firm and bitter but a bit too "clean". Starts well but fades away.

ARCENER ZOMERBOK*
7% abv ✪✪✪ Pale Bok Ale
Variable from year to year. Also sold as Hertog Jan Meibok.

ARCENER OERBOCK
6.5% abv ✪✪✪✪ Dark Bok Ale
Smooth, subtle, sienna coloured, all-year-round, top fermented bokbier.

HERTOG JAN BOCKBIER*
6.5% abv ✪✪✪ Dark Bok Ale
Dark, dryish, roasted bok; a separate brew from Oerbock.

ALTFORSTER ALT
5% abv ✪✪ Altbier
Medium brown, simple but clean.
Other regular beers include:
Arcener Pils (5% abv; Pils).

ORANJEBOOM

VERENIGDE BIERBROUWERIJ BREDA-ROTTERDAM
Ceresstraat 13
4811 CA Breda
Tel: 076 252472

In the three centuries between 1671 and 1967, the Orange Tree brewery in Rotterdam had grown by takeover and merger to be one of the largest in the Netherlands. Allied grabbed it in 1967 as part of their efforts to create Skol and eventually closed it in 1990. In 1968 Allied had added the scalp of the 450-year-old Drie Hoefijzers (Three Horseshoes) brewery in Breda, 40 miles to the south east. Ironically, many of the beers produced at the Drie Hoefijzers plant are called Oranjeboom. Its first ale appeared in 1992 and more have followed, though Elfde Gebod is rumoured to be brewed at Arcen.

The plant also brews Titan Super Strength, Skol 1080 Strong Lager (8.5% abv; strong lager), Fernandes Extra Stout and, would you believe, Double Diamond for export only. Output is 2,100,000 hl per year.

HET ELFDE GEBOD
7.5% abv ✪✪✪ Pale Ale
Heavily hopped, sweetish and horribly innocent.

ORANJEBOOM HERFSTBOCK*
6.5% abv ✪✪✪ Dark Bok
Sweet, dark and porter-like.

ORANJEBOOM LENTEBOCK*
6.5% abv ✪✪✪✪ Pale Bok
Clear, sweet, mellow amber brew, with a pronounced hop and background candy.

TRIO EXTRA STOUT
6.5% abv ✪✪ Stout Lager
Drab, medium dark, bottom fermented stout, originally popular in Surinam.

ORANJEBOOM ROYAL
6% abv ✪✪ Pils
Dull premium Pils, rather like a British attempt at the same style.

KLASSIEK 1628
5.5% abv ❂❂❂ Pils
Dryish pils-style beer, recently re-jigged and strengthened.

ORANJEBOOM PILSENER BIER
5% abv ❂❂ Pils
Ordinary mass-production Pils.

Other regular beers include: John Bull Bitter and Royal Dutch Posthorn. There is also an oud bruin table beer, a light Pils and three low alcohol beers.

RAAF

BIERBROUWERIJ RAAF
Rijksweg 232
6582 AB Heumen
Tel: 080 581177

The Raven brewery was founded in 1983 in Gelderland and in a short independent existence produced a vast range of beers in a wide variety of styles. It used organic malt and hops and some of its beers were among the best in the Netherlands.

In 1992 it was taken over by Allied Carlsberg and within months there was a radical reduction in its range.

Their current policy is not to produce a bokbier, on the grounds that everybody else does. The Paasbier was not spotted in 1993. Overall annual production is 6,000 hl. Half is now draught beer and the brewery is frequently over capacity. On the plus side, the quality is certainly more consistent nowadays and there has been no decline in the recipes. It is not clear why Allied Carlsberg should want to grab both Raaf and Arcen as well as holding a contract with the Abbey of Koningshoeven.

There is a traditional beer café and brewing museum at the brewery, open to the public. Tours of the museum include a look round the brewery. For further details see Dutch Cafés: Gelderland and Beer Tourism.

RAAF TRIPEL
8.5% abv ❂❂❂❂ Tripel
Sourish amber ale, refreshing despite its gravity. Nearly a five ❂ brew.

WITTE RAAF
5% abv ❂❂❂❂ Wheat Beer (unfiltered)
Fruity, but slightly sour wheat beer with undertones of Hock or Moselle.

Other regular beers include: Raaf Kerstbier* (10% abv; winter ale), Raaf Paasbier* (7% abv; Easter ale) and Raaf Verjaardagsbier* (7.5% abv).

B. S. N.

The French are seen as wine drinkers. Tell people that the third largest brewery group in Europe is based in Strasbourg and they scratch their heads. The brand name Kronenbourg is perhaps better known. BSN was actually a bottle manufacturing company before it bought out a large number of the makers of the stuff which filled the gap in the glass.

Currently the BSN subsidiaries control around one fifth of the Belgian beer market. Kronenbourg had co-owned Alken for some while before linking up with the Maes brewery, that was briefly owned by Watneys in the 1970s. The amalgamated company is called Alken-Maes in Belgium, though to some extent this is to avoid the embarassment of acknowledging that the French have a major stake in the Belgians' favourite industry.

The Maes family did not sell its large stake in the company until November 1993 but even before that, there was no doubt that its business affairs were largely controlled by BSN head office. Even without Alken-Maes, BSN is ranked as the world's eighth largest beer manufacturer. It is clearly one of the players intending to control European brewing.

Alken made their reputation on the quality of their Cristal lagers. Unfortunately, in common with many of their rivals, they seem to pay less attention to distinctiveness nowadays and Cristal Alken has dropped a star since our first edition.

In the ale line, Union brewery seems to be employed in producing more potentially excellent beers which are made more bland and less interesting by filtration and pasteurisation. The Grimbergen range and the Cuvée de l'Ermitage brands seem to have flavour components, from the recipe or the yeast, which would go well in a refermented beer, but alas they do not get the chance.

Surprisingly, the group does not produce a single wheat beer. It may be that to do so would require a change of policy regarding sedimentation or could equally be a forewarning that an acquisition may be looming. Moortgat, Palm, Riva and Haacht spring to mind.

In the field of lambic beers, the picture is confusing. The Mort Subite brands produced at the De Keersmaeker plant are relentlessly commercial; weak, unimpressive beers with a catchy name. In the past five years, the group has shut down its other lambic breweries, the confusingly unrelated De Keersmaecker plant closing in 1990 and the Eylenbosch plant being downgraded to fermentation and storage only in 1991. However, the Eylenbosch brands have reappeared recently as the sourer, stronger, filtered partners of the Mort Subite brands at the same time as a rumour is passing through the cafés that De Keersmaeker's traditional gueuze will no longer be produced. If so, this is in sharp contrast to the developments at Interbrew, Van Honsebrouck and De Troch.

ALKEN

BROUWERIJ ALKEN-MAES
Stationsstraat 2
3570 Alken
Tel: 011 312711

The original Alken plant, dating from 1881, where Alken Cristal beers were perfected. One of two massive beer production units within the Belgian company, annual production is 950,000 hl. A small amount of ale brewing probably continues. We are not certain which plants brew which beers so for the sake of simplicity and at the expense of accuracy, we have listed all the group's ales, other than the lambic-based ones, as coming from the Union brewery. The Tourtel range of beers are alcohol-free.

CRISTAL ALKEN
4.8% abv ✪✪✪ Pils
Pale, flowery, well-hopped Pils, filtered but not pasteurised.

Other regular beers include: Kronenbourg (4.8% abv; Pils). There are also four table beers, a low-alcohol beer and three alcohol-free beers.

DE KEERSMAEKER

BROUWERIJ DE KEERSMAEKER
Brusselstraat 1
1730 Kobbegem
Tel: 02 452 4747

Established Senne Valley lambic brewer and gueuze blender at Kobbegem, north west of Brussels, tracing its origins to 1721. Its most commercial beers bear the brand name Mort Subite, taken from the Brussels café of the same name (see Belgian Cafés: Brabant). Even before they were taken over by Alken-Maes in 1989, the beer production had swung strongly towards filtered, unnaturally sweet, commercial, lambic-based drinks, though traditional gueuze is still available. The validity of rumours saying production has ceased is not known. Cafés say yes, OBP says no and the brewery has made no comment. If OBP is wrong, they will be upset, as a microbiological analysis of gueuze beers carried out in the summer of 1993 showed the De Keersmaeker brew to be very traditional. Annual production is 30,000 hl, giving them eight per cent of the market in lambic-based beers.

DE KEERSMAEKER GUEUZE
5% abv ✪✪✪✪ Gueuze (unfiltered)
Sweeter, darker and weaker than the best traditional gueuzes.

MORT SUBITE KRIEK
4.5% abv ✪✪ Cherry Gueuze (filtered)
Filtered and clear, semi-sweet with vaguely acid backtastes.

MORT SUBITE CASSIS
4% abv ✪✪ Fruit Lambic
Anaemic lambic with blackberry
liquid.
MORT SUBITE GUEUZE
4% abv ✪✪ Gueuze (filtered)
Filtered, clear, sweet and innocuous.
MORT SUBITE PECHE
4% abv ✪✪ Fruit Lambic
Clear, semi-sweet peach drink with a
hint of beer in the background.

Other regular beers include: De
Keersmaeker Kriekenlambic (4%
abv; cherry lambic), De Keersmaeker
Lambic (4% abv; lambic) and Mort
Subite Framboise (4% abv raspberry
lambic).

EYLENBOSCH

BROUWERIJ EYLENBOSCH
Ninoofsesteenweg 5
1703 Schepdaal
Tel: 02 569 1478
Just as with Schepdaal's other lambic
brewery, Interbrew's De Neve plant,
brewing ceased in 1991 but hot wort
is still transported from Kobbegem
to be spontaneously fermented here
and then matured. Lambics up to
three years old are used in the
production of the gueuze and kriek
but as far as the Guide is aware, all
the beers are filtered at present.
They do not taste to be pasteurised
but with lambic-based beers,
tastebuds can be notoriously
inaccurate in this regard.
EYLENBOSCH KRIEK LAMBIC
CUVEE SPECIALE
5% abv ✪✪✪ Cherry Gueuze
(filtered)
Refreshing, fruity, garnet-coloured,
slightly sour beer, close to a fourth
star.

Other regular beers include:
Eylenbosch Gueuze Lambic Cuvée
Spéciale (5% abv; gueuze).

MAES

BROUWERIJ ALKEN-MAES
Waarloosveld 10
2550 Waarloos
Tel: 015 312931
The original Maes brewery at
Waarloos, south of Antwerp,
brewing since 1880. Owned by
Grand Metropolitan (Watneys!) for a

time in the 1970s and early 1980s.
This is the group's largest plant with
a production of 1,300,000 hl per
year. In addition to those listed,
there is a product range broadly
similar to the Alken plant. We do not
know whether they are simply
variations on the same lager recipe.
MAES PILS
5.1% abv ✪✪ Pils
Ordinary mass-market Pils.
GOLDING CAMPINA
4.8% abv ✪✪✪ Pils
Sweetish, bitter and slightly unusual.

Other regular beers include:
Anglo Pils (5% abv; Pils).

UNION

BRASSERIE UNION
Rue Derbeque 7
6040 Jumet
Tel: 071 350133
The major ale brewery of the Alken-
Maes chain, at Jumet, near Charleroi
in Hainaut province. Produces a
number of Grimbergen and Cuvée
de l'Ermitage beers, roughly in the
abbey style, which are pretty
passable despite the absence of
sediment. The annual output from
Union is 175,000 hl. They took over
brewing the Ciney range from
Interbrew in 1991 and do so to
contract specifications rather than
their own recipe.

The Watneys range is a hang-on
from the days when Grand
Metropolitan owned the then parent
company in the 1970s. Watneys Red
was the symbol of everything hated
by British beer lovers 20 years ago.
The remaining Belgian version is
recognisably related to the original.
The other Watney brews never had a
British equivalent.
GRIMBERGEN OPTIMO BRUNO
10% abv ✪✪✪✪ Strong Ale
Clear, potent, amber ale in the style
of a strong tripel. Who remembers
the taste of "Spangles"?
CINEY SPECIALE 10
9% abv ✪✪✪✪ Abbey Strong
Deep and dark filtered ale with
enough flavour mixes to scrape four
stars.
JUDAS
8.5% abv ✪✪✪ Strong Golden

Drier and less aromatic than Duvel, with no defining character.

GRIMBERGEN TRIPEL
8.1% abv ✪✪✪✪ Abbey Tripel (dark)
Dark, sweet and strongish. Backtastes of bananas, blackcurrant and aniseed.

CUVÉE DE L'ERMITAGE
7.2% abv ✪✪✪ Brown Ale
Umber coloured, strong and bitter-sweet, tending to cloy.

CINEY BLONDE 7
7% abv ✪✪ Pale Ale
Ridiculously sweet, dead blond ale.

CINEY BRUNE 7
7% abv ✪✪ Brown Ale
Slightly drier dead brown ale.

WATNEYS SCOTCH
6.7% abv ✪✪✪ Scotch Ale
Very dark, very sweet and very caramelised.

GRIMBERGEN DUBBEL
6.2% abv ✪✪ Abbey Dubbel

Dark, sweet and bitter, lacking class since it became brewery conditioned.

WATNEYS RED BARREL
5.3% abv ✪✪ Pale Ale
Stronger than Olde Gnatpee used to be. Still tastes of scalded sugar.

ZULTE
4.7% abv ✪✪ Old Brown
Sweet brown ale with lactate. Alken closed the Zulte brewery in 1990.

RUBENS GOLD
4.3% abv ✪ Pale Ale
Dreary, weak pale ale.

RUBENS ROOD
4% abv ✪✪ Pale Ale
Sweet, slightly hazy, almost wheaty light ale.

Other regular beers include: Cuvée de l'Ermitage Christmas* (7.5% abv; winter ale) and Grimbergen Blond (6.5% abv; pale ale).

HEINEKEN

Heineken is the world's second largest brewer. Only the American Budweiser group, Anheuser-Busch, brews more beer. They knocked the other US giants, Miller, into third place in 1990. Heineken is also the world's biggest exporter of beer and brews as much as BSN and Interbrew put together. Remarkably, there is still a considerable stake and management interest held by the Heineken clan, though it is no longer, as some believe, a privately owned concern.

The first Mr. Heineken entered the industry in 1864 by purchasing an Amsterdam brewery. Four years later he replaced it and over the following century the company bought widely and wisely in the Netherlands and abroad. They currently own, dominate, or have significant interests in, nearly 100 breweries worldwide and, like their major European rivals, are back on the acquisitions trail close to home. In the Netherlands alone the group produces over 13,000,000 hl of beer each year.

Heineken's domination of the limited Dutch market was finally cemented in 1968 when they merged with their main competitors, Amstel. Their overseas connections are almost as old as the company itself, dating back to the beginnings of the Dutch colonial trade in the 1870s. In addition to their significant interests in foreign companies they have licensed other breweries to use the names Heineken and Amstel in most major beer drinking nations of the world. British Heineken originally came from Whitbread and contained significantly more water than its Dutch counterpart. The Dutch version is now more common.

Heineken has an appalling track record of taking over rival companies, closing their breweries and banishing their beers. They have also taken control of a significant part of the beer distribution business in the Netherlands and have effectively tied up large numbers of cafés and bars by the use of loans and trading agreements.

In recent years, there have been a number of indicators that attitudes have been changing and that they recognise the re-emergence of a quality market in beer. Their distribution company is largely responsible for increasing the beer range in the average Dutch bar from three to twelve. They have not yet closed any of their recently acquired regional breweries. Finally, they are beginning to branch out into new beer styles.

As well as the beers already on the market, they plan to introduce at least two more beers in 1994. Kylian will be a 6.5% abv copper coloured ale, and "1994" a special brew for the New Year.

Official company information is that they hold no major shareholdings in any Belgian brewery. This is hard to believe and their names have been linked by gossips in the industry to companies like De Koninck, Palm, Moortgat and Rodenbach, though without any firm evidence.

Whatever reservations consumers may have, there is no doubting that Big H is not just the biggest player in the European beer market, it is also the most accomplished. So expect to hear less of them.

BRAND

BIERBROUWERIJ BRAND
Brouwerijstraat 2
6321 AG Wijlre
Tel: 04450 8282
Fax: 04450 1354

There is known to have been a brewery at Wiljre, near Maastricht since 1340 and it was owned by the Brand family from 1871 until Heineken seized it in 1990. Queen Beatrix honoured its products by Royal Proclamation in 1971 and for a time both the brewery and its beers adopted the title Koninklijke (Royal) Brand. The Pilsener is sold in Britain and the US as Royal Brand Beer. Cynics in the Dutch beer world feared that the takeover would limit Brand's future to about 650 days but so far have been proved wrong. Annual production is 500,000 hl.

BRAND SYLVESTER*
8% abv ✪✪✪ Winter Ale
Copper-brown, sedimented winter ale which fails to drink to its strength.

BRAND DUBBELBOCK
7.5% abv ✪✪✪ Dubbelbock
Strongish, dryish, bitterish lager, vaguely in the German dubbelbock style.

BRAND IMPERATOR
6.5% abv ✪✪✪✪ Bock
Amber lager, close to the German bock style. Available all year.

BRAND URTYP PILSENER
5% abv ✪✪✪ Pils
Soft, smooth, 100% malt Pils.
Sometimes sold as "Brand UP".

BRAND PILSENER
5% abv ✪✪✪ Pils
Clean, crisp Pils with a hoppier character than most.
There is also an oud bruin table beer.

HEINEKEN

HEINEKEN NEDERLAND NV
Postbus 28
1000 AA Amsterdam
Tel: 020 523 9239
Fax: 020 626 3503

Despite the address, Heineken's two major beer factories are now at 's Hertogenbosch and Zoeterwoude, both in central Netherlands. Heineken and Amstel products continue to use different yeasts and it is logical that they are brewed at separate plants but we have not been able to confirm this. It is interesting that Heineken Pils, the company's bog standard product is being brewed to a more bitter recipe than it was two years ago. It was assumed that the Heineken plants would be used for mass production only, until the appearance of Tarwebock 1992, the first bottom fermented wheat bok in the world. The future may be more interesting than the past. Annual production at the two plants is 12,500,000 hl. There is also a beer called Heineken Special Dark (4.9% abv; dark lager) which is brewed for export only. Heineken Bokbier was replaced by Tarwebock for 1993.

AMSTEL BOCKBIER*
7% abv ✪✪✪✪ Dark Bok
Surprisingly assertive dark, bitter-

sweet bok of above average
strength.
AMSTEL GOLD
7% abv OO Pils
Stronger than average Pils.
HEINEKEN BOKBIER*
7% abv OOO Dark Bok
Sweetish, strongish but otherwise
middle-of-the-road filtered bok.
HEINEKEN TARWEBOCK*
6.5% abv OOO Wheat Bok
The 1992 (OOOO) was a nicely
balanced chestnut brew; 1993 saw a
black, sweet concoction.
HOOIBERG BOKBIER*
6.5% abv OOO Dark Bok
Filtered but unpasteurised bokbier.
SLEUTEL BOKBIER*
6.5% abv OOO Dark Bok
Pasteurised version of Hooiberg
VAN VOLLENHOVENS STOUT
6.5% abv OOO Stout Lager
Bottom fermented stout named after
a long-closed brewery.
AMSTEL 1870
5% abv OOO Pils
Superior bottled Pils, brewed with
100% malt. Almost 4O.
AMSTEL PILSENER BIER
5% abv OO Pils
The ordinary brew.
HEINEKEN PILSENER BIER
5% abv OOO Pils
The Dutch for "beer". Improving.
    Two oud bruin table beers and a
light lager are also produced.

RIDDER

BROUWERIJ DE RIDDER BV
Oeverwal 3-9
6221 EN Maastricht
Tel: 043 216057
Fax: 043 254049

Typical regional brewery on the
banks of the Maas in Maastricht,
privately owned from its inception
in 1857 until the Heineken takeover
of 1982. During 1990 it began
producing an ale for the first time in
living memory. It is also used to
produce test brews for the parent
company. Annual production is
35,000 hl.
RIDDER BOCKBIER*
7% abv OOOO Dark Bok
Dry, bitter, umber coloured with
stout-like qualities.
RIDDER MALTEZER
6.5% abv OOOO Dortmunder
Surprisingly robust, fruity, amber
coloured lager.
RIDDER PILSENER
5% abv OO Pils
Another standard Pils.
WIECKSE WITTE
5% abv OOOO Wheat Beer
(unfiltered)
The archetypal Dutch wheat beer.
Sweet, mellow, hazy and toffee
flavoured.
    There is also an oud bruin table
beer.

INTERBREW

Europe's second largest brewery group, based in Leuven, East of Brussels. It
was formed by the merger of Artois with Piedboeuf in 1988. It is more family
dominated than Heineken, to the extent that its shares are not listed on the
open market. Interbrew holds 63 per cent of the Belgian beer market and with
its takeover of Van Den Stock (Belle Vue) in 1991, took 65 per cent of the
market in lambic beers.

    In 1987 Artois had injected considerable cash into the De Kluis wheat beer
brewery in Hoegaarden. Interbrew completed the takeover in 1989. It also
owns breweries in France, the Netherlands and Italy and intends to remain a
major player when Europe is reduced to just five or six megacompanies.

    Interbrew may well go on to acquire more Belgian and Dutch breweries
and certainly has injected "technical assistance" to important ones like
Rodenbach. It has low-key trading agreements with Carlsberg in Denmark and
Whitbread in Britain but is too small to take over the former and sees no great
advantage to making a bid for the latter.

    Leuven no. 2, one of the most massive beer factories ever constructed, is
now in production. The orginal Leuven plant has been redesigned to include

an ale plant capable of producing smaller runs of beer for the specialist markets. The only lager plant expected to survive in the medium term is Jupiler, though no clear statement has yet been made about Dommelsch in the Netherlands.

Of the ale breweries, the fate of Lamot is sealed and St. Guibert will probably go too. De Kluis looks to be safe. It has a lot of new plant, its production is expanding and unlike St. Guibert, it has the knack of producing first rate beers. The fate of the three lambic breweries will depend on the changes in the lambic market. It is highly unlikely that either Belle Vue brewery will go, but unless the early signs of a rekindling of interest in artisanal gueuze continue, it seems unlikely that the De Neve fermentation and storage plant will last beyond 1996.

Interbrew's range of bottom-fermented beers has been decimated and unless there is a revival of the quality issue in the Belgian lager market generally, it is safe to assume that they will concentrate on building up the Jupiler, Artois and Loburg brand names, while brewing some major foreign brands under licence.

On the ale side, the mediocre Leffe beers sell well and the De Kluis beers are expanding remarkably. The other ales, some of which are brewed in co-operation with Bass and Whitbread, could do with a bit of thought and a facelift. The lessons which are eventually learned from the experiments in the field of serious lambic beers can be applied elsewhere.

The group's total production in Belgium and the Netherlands is around 10,400,000 hl per year.

ARTOIS

BROUWERIJ ARTOIS
Vaartstraat 94
3000 Leuven
Tel: 016 247111

Leuven no. 1 is a monumental factory near the centre of Leuven (Louvain). Its riverside frontage comes out of Gotham, via Stalin. Leuven no. 2 employs so much concrete that it looks to be safe against nuclear attack. Between them, by 1996, these breweries will produce about 9,000,000 hl of beer annually. The problem of brewing with different yeasts should have been overcome by effectively sealing off a part of the original plant and creating what the company calls a capacity for "short" brew runs, which we understand may amount in British terms to up to 1,000 barrels a time! There are no plans to produce ales which referment in the bottle and so Leffe Tripel and the De Kluis beers seem set to stay in Hoegaarden.

CAMPBELL'S CHRISTMAS*
7.5% abv ✪✪✪✪ Winter Ale
Firm, filtered, aged, dark and dangerously drinkable.

CAMPBELLS SCOTCH
6.8% abv ✪✪ Scotch Ale
Dark and sweet but nothing special.
LOBURG
5.7% abv ✪✪ Pils
85% malt. Stronger than most Belgian Pils but no more impressive for that.
WHITBREAD PALE ALE
5.6% abv ✪✪✪ Pale Ale
Distinctly English, dry, bitter pale ale, far superior to the British version.
STELLA ARTOIS
5% abv ✪✪ Pils
Generally accepted as being inferior to the British version!
WHITBREAD EXTRA STOUT
4.5% abv ✪✪✪ Dry Stout
Dark and bitter-sweet. Not at all bad. A potential Whitbread import?
  Other regular beers include:
Bergenbier (5.7% abv; Pils) and Bergenbraü (4.3% abv; Pils)

BELLE VUE (MOLENBEEK)

BRASSERIE BELLE VUE
Rue Delaunoystraat 58
1080 Sint Jans Molenbeek
Tel: 02 522 1935
There are two Belle Vue breweries.

At Molenbeek, 2 km from the centre of Brussels is the traditional one. Originally the Decoster brewery of the Van Den Stock family, it was founded in 1913. After World War Two, several smallish lambic brewers began to work together to form an agglomeration of companies called Belle Vue, part of the aim of which was to save lambic brewing by making its products more commercially acceptable to mainstream drinkers who were becoming used to sweet ales. When Interbrew took over in 1990, all the Belle Vue products were in this style. The only traditional products remaining were one or two of the De Neve beers, brewed at the Brabrux plant in Schepdaal, and even these were becoming commercialised.

At Molenbeek there are 10,000 oak casks and a further 1,000 chestnut ones, all filled with lambic, cherry lambic or raspberry lambic. The largest, the foudres, hold 80 hl (1,750 gallons). The lambic brewed here is produced by fully traditional methods, there is no dilution and old lambics used in blending gueuze are stored for up to five or six years. The raspberry lambic is made by adding 80 litres of raspberry juice to 570 litres of eight-month-old lambic. The cherry lambic utilises largely whole fruit, mainly Gorsem cherries, with some Schaerbeek and Du Nord varieties.

Regardless of the traditional methods, until recently the Belle Vue brands were, without exception, bland and simple. The reason for this was the heavy emphasis on the use of young lambic, much of it produced at Zuun (below) and of "old" lambics which were not old enough to have matured the typical flavours created by the slow activity of Brettanomyces organisms.

However, 1993 saw an extraordinary development, when Belle Vue launched an excellent and completely traditional gueuze called Sélection Lambic. This will improve with ageing for at least five and perhaps up to 20 years in the bottle.

There are also mutterings about an unfiltered cherry gueuze and making available the cherry lambic on draught.

Unbeknown to many beer lovers, the Molenbeek brewery has for many years run a system by which café owners, mainly from Pajottenland, have been able to bring wooden casks to the brewery and have them filled with lambic, young or old or even blended. In the Brussels area they also supply a filtered draught lambic, sweetened with brown sugar, called lambic doux. In both cases this is likely to billed by the café as a house beer.

Cherry lambic is produced by adding cherries to four-month-old lambic. When this is eight months old, some is blended with young lambic to make Primeur, the Beaujolais Nouveau of the lambic-marketing world. Belle Vue Kriek relies on older (12- to 18-month-old) cherry lambic being added to young lambic and balanced with a little cherry juice.

250,000 hl of beer is produced at the two breweries. Gueuze and cherry gueuze account for 45 per cent each. The exports to France are called Bécasse and to the Netherlands, until recently, Caves Bruegel.

BELLE VUE FRAMBOZEN
5.2% abv ✪✪ Raspberry Lambic (filtered)
Naturally perfumed, ruddy sweet, beery substance.

BELLE VUE GUEUZE
5.2% abv ✪✪ Gueuze (filtered)
Clear, sweet and wheaty. Not unpleasant but far removed from traditional gueuze.

BELLE VUE KRIEK
5.2% abv ✪✪ Cherry Gueuze (filtered)
Dark, clear, sweetish, cherried and undemanding pasteurised fruit beer.

BELLE VUE SELECTION LAMBIC
5.2% abv ✪✪✪✪✪ Gueuze (unfiltered)
Straight in at the top. A superbly challenging, properly sedimented, cleverly blended, sour traditional

gueuze that stops short of frank acidity.

KRIEK PRIMEUR
5.2% abv ❂❂❂ Cherry Gueuze (filtered)
Drier, slightly fruitier version of the pasteurised Belle Vue.

BELLE VUE (ZUUN)

BRASSERIE BELLE VUE
Steenweg naar Bergen
1600 St. Pieters Leeuw

Belle Vue's Zuun plant has the reputation of being the source of all evil in the world of lambic. This is not entirely fair, though it is certainly no Molenbeek. Unlike at Molenbeek, we have not seen the tank in which spontaneous fermentation is seeded by micro-organisms falling from the night sky as the wort cools. However, we are assured that it exists and if it did not, this would make the operation illegal. Equally there is no down-grading of the recipe at Zuun to our knowledge.

What is different here is that fermentation occurs in steel cylinders, not oak casks. The fermentation of lambic is described elsewhere (see Beer Styles). The third and fourth stages of fermentation are not really possible in metal containers as they rely to some extent on the spores found in the wood of the casks. However, the alcohol-forming second stage does not require these conditions. Therefore the production of young lambic, which is the biggest need for a commercial producer, is most economically produced this way.

The only faintly dubious practice is the way in which the enterobacteria of the first stage of production are killed off. While in oak casks this is brought about by sulphurising the cask before filling; in steel tanks the degree of acidity is lowered by using a by-product of the third stage of fermentation.

All the beers produced here are sent to Molenbeek for filtering, blending, packaging and distribution. The one beer we list

here is a blend of young lambic with a brown ale called Mengbier, also produced at Zuun but not available in its own right on the market.

JACK-OP
5% abv ❂❂❂ Unclassifiable
Strange, darkish, sweetish, pasteurised ale of unusual character.

BRASSICO

BRASSERIE BRASSICO
Route de Wallonie 4
7410 Ghlin

Despite being one of the founders of the Interbrew group, Brassico allowed their main brewery at Ghlin, near Mons, to be downgraded to just another Jupiler production plant. Created in 1960 to replace two Brussels breweries and two from Mons, it was due to close at the end of 1993.

DE KLUIS

BROUWERIJ DE KLUIS
Stoopkensstraat 46
3320 Hoegaarden
Tel: 016 767676
Fax: 016 767691

Founded in 1966 at Hoegaarden in eastern Brabant on the site of the old Tomsin brewery by Pierre Celis, the beer enthusiast and milkman who effectively re-invented the Belgian style of wheat beer. By 1978, the brewery's products had become so successful that an old soft drinks factory was purchased. A series of delicious and highly successful stronger beers was introduced but disaster struck in 1985 when a fire destroyed the brewery. The amount of new investment required led to funding having to be sought from Interbrew, who had effectively taken over by 1989. Unbelievably, production is now 650,000 hl per year of the wheat beer alone and nearer 800,000 hl in total. In 1992, production of the only sediment beer in the Leffe range was transferred here. Original fears that the brews and their brewery would be completely wrecked have proven to be exaggerated, so far.

VERBODEN VRUCHT
9% abv ❂❂❂❂ Brown Ale

Dark, mellow and distinctive, with complex mixed herbal flavours. Known as Fruit Defendu in French.

HOEGAARDEN GRAND CRU
8.7% abv ✪✪✪○ Strong Golden
Light in colour, heavy in character. Becoming a "simpler" beer.

JULIUS
8.7% abv ✪✪✪○ Spiced Ale
Once a classic beer but now tasting more like Grand Cru with added perfume.

LEFFE TRIPEL
8% abv ✪✪✪○ Abbey Tripel
Westmalle Tripel without the final panache. Typical sediment abbey tripel.

HOEGAARDEN
5% abv ✪✪✪○ Wheat Beer (unfiltered)
Sweet and spicy, light and cloudy. More honeyed after a few weeks' ageing.

DE NEVE

DE NEVE
Isabellastraat 52
1703 Schepdaal
Tel: 02 569 0902

Strictly speaking the De Neve plant in Schepdaal is not a brewery, as it no longer brews. However, for the next few years at least, it will continue to ferment and blend lambic ales brewed elsewhere.

Hot wort is transported from one of the Belle Vue breweries to Schepdaal for pumping into the fermentation tray at De Neve. Here the same cooling and spontaneous fermentation process occurs as at other lambic breweries. After 24 hours the beer is then racked into some of the 6,000 oak casks still in use in the storage rooms.

The same fermentation process will occur as at the Belle Vue (Molenbeek) plant but as the microflora in the atmosphere here are different from those 10 km down the road, the lambics produced will have a different character.

De Neve Gueuze comes filtered/pasteurised and also partially filtered/unpasteurised. Unfortunately they have the same name, though

the black label of the more traditional version says "refermented" on it, while the yellow and orange label of the dead version does not. Sales are currently about the same for each. The refermented version improves with ageing.

De Neve Kriek is made from two-year-old cherry lambic, blended with old and young lambics and a little cherry juice. It is then pasteurised. De Neve Framboise is the same product as Belle Vue Framboise.

The plant is pencilled in for closure in 1996 but if the lambic market turns head-over-heel, as it may, anything could happen.

DE NEVE GUEUZE LAMBIC
5.2% abv ✪✪✪○ Gueuze
Sharp, bitter and commendably dry gueuze with a light sediment, which matures to a 5✪ rating after two years in the cellar.

DE NEVE GUEUZE LAMBIC (filtered)
5.2% abv ✪✪○ Gueuze
Drier and more accomplished than some commercial gueuzes but not great.

DE NEVE KRIEK (draught)
5.2% abv ✪✪○ Cherry Lambic (filtered)
Horribly perfumed, solid, darkish, sweetish cherry beer of no great character.

Other regular beers include: De Neve Kriek (bottled) (5.2% abv; cherry gueuze).

DOMMELSCH

DOMMELSCHE BIERBROUWERIJ
Brouwerijplein 84
5551 AE Dommelen
Tel: 04902 87911
Fax: 04902 44385

Founded in 1744 at Dommelen, just over the Dutch border in North Brabant. Taken over by Artois in 1968, its production has reached 650,000 hl a year. It is the only surviving Dutch brewery in the Interbrew conglomerate, since the closure of the 220-year-old brewery at Hengelo in 1988 with the loss of all its beers. Brews some of the lagers for the Dutch distributor

Hertog Jan, whose ales are brewed by the Allied-Carlsberg brewery at Arcen. At least some of the Pils is now brewed in Leuven, as is their alcohol-free lager, Dommelsch NA. This must imply a limited life expectancy after Leuven no. 2 opens.

DOMMELSCH BOKBIER*
6.5% abv ✪✪ Dark Bok
Supposed to be very bitter and sweetish. Sampled on draught it is a kitten!

DOMMELSCH DOMINATOR
6% abv ✪✪✪ Dortmunder
Fruity, strongish pale lager also sold as Hertog Jan Speciaal.

DOMMELSCH PILSENER
5% abv ✪✪ Pils
Bland and undistinguished. Also sold as Hertog Jan Pilsener.

An oud bruin table beer is also produced.

JUPILER

BRASSERIE JUPILER
Rue de Visé 243
4020 Jupille-sur-Meuse
Tel: 041 627800

This is the brewery, founded in 1853 at Jupille-sur-Meuse, near Liège, that created Jupiler Pils, Belgium's top-selling beer brand. It is Interbrew's second largest plant, producing 2,200,000 hl per annum. It is one of the few not earmarked for closure after Leuven No. 2 is on full production, which the sentimentalists say is because the beer is associated with the brewery and the cynics say is because the plant is the last one left in Wallonia. Other plants imitate the beer.

JUPILER
5.2% abv ✪✪ Pils
Belgium's top-selling beer. How could this be possible?
There are also three table beers.

LAMOT

BROUWERIJ LAMOT
Van Beethovenstraat 10
2800 Mechelen
Tel: 015 412826

Large plant between Antwerp and Brussels, brewing 1,000,000 hl per year. Once owned by the British brewery group, Bass, who tried to tempt 1970s British lager drinkers with Lamot Pils. Some of the brewery's output of ales has already been transferred to Leuven and the rest will follow with the lagers before 1996.

McEWANS CHRISTMAS ALE*
7.2% abv ✪✪✪✪ Winter Ale
Strongish, brownish and Christmasish.

McEWANS SCOTCH
7.2% abv ✪✪✪ Scotch Ale
Dark, bitter-sweet ale, easily bettering McEwans' Scottish-brewed ales.

BASS PALE ALE
5.2% abv ✪✪ Pale Ale
Feeble beer, unworthy of Bass abroad.

BASS STOUT
5.2% abv ✪✪✪ Sweet Stout
Dark, thick, bitter and syrupy.

LAMOT PILSOR
5.2% abv ✪✪ Pils
Neutral Pils.

GINDER ALE
5.1% abv ✪✪✪ Pale Ale
Stylish but uninspiring pale ale.

HORSE ALE
4.8% abv ✪✪✪ Pale Ale
Distinctly Belgian pale ale.

Other regular beers include: CTS Scotch (7.5% abv; Scotch ale), Setzbraü (6% abv; Pils), Kassel (5% abv; Pils) and Krüger Export (4.8% abv; Pils).

ST. GUIBERT

BRASSERIE SAINT GUIBERT
Rue de Riquau 1
1435 Mont Saint Guibert
Tel: 010 655771

Artois' original attempt to run an artisan ale brewery, at Mont St. Guibert, south of Brussels. The company which has taken over had the contract to brew beers for the Abbaye Notre Dame de Leffe. The range has continued and sells well but is hardly the connoisseur's favourite. The brewery is earmarked for closure in 1995, when the rest of the range plus Vieux Temps will follow Leffe Tripel to Leuven. Current production is 350,000 hl a year. A beer called Leffe Birra Rossa

(6.2% abv; pale ale) is brewed for the Italian market.

LEFFE RADIEUSE
8.2% abv ✪✪✪ Brown Ale
Sweet, dark brown, bitter and warming but too simple for its strength.

LEFFE VIEILLE CUVEE 8°
8.2% abv ✪✪✪✪ Abbey Dubbel
The best of the St. Guibert brews, a mature brown ale with faint sourness.

LEFFE BLONDE
6.3% abv ✪✪ Pale Ale
Rather ordinary pale ale which fails to drink to its strength.

LEFFE BRUNE
6.3% abv ✪✪✪ Brown Ale
Not bad for a strongish brown ale but not an abbey beer.

VIEUX TEMPS
5% abv ✪ Pale Ale
One of the few really bland Belgian ales.

IMPORTED BEERS

THE DUTCH BEER MARKET features a large number of imported beers, though curiously the Germans are not as heavily represented as one might expect. The Belgians are not great beer importers but do have a tradition of enjoying English pale ale, stout and dark, strongish Scottish ales.

In 1908 an ex-pat Englishman, John Martin of Newmarket, Suffolk, set up an importing company in Antwerp which, even though it has expanded to trade mainly in Belgian and Dutch beers, continues to import some brews from the British Isles which are not generally available in their native countries.

The only beers we list here are the brews created especially for the Belgian and Dutch markets.

GUINNESS

The Dublin brewery produces mainly low strength stout for its native Irish and British markets but also brews for export at higher gravities. Recently the American export version has been appearing with greater frequency in the Netherlands, but the uniquely powerful, strong Guinness stout is still available, as it has been since 1912.

GUINNESS EXPORT
8.3% abv ✪✪✪✪ Strong Stout
Dark, dry, bitter and treacly. Like Irish Guinness with half the water removed.

SCOTTISH & NEWCASTLE

You will not find many brews of exceptional gravity from S & N in Britain, though Scotland's ale tradition is certainly littered with such creations. The Traquair House brewery of Innerleithen continues to produce fine dark beers to the exclusion of all else. Scotch ale in

Belgium is held in high regard and certainly as a superior drink to that warm, flat, weak stuff which comes out of handpumps. The mythical "Gordon's" does not come from the real Highlands, of course, but even Edinburgh's Mount is pretty Himalayan compared to much of Belgium and the Netherlands.

GORDON'S FINEST GOLD BLOND
10% abv ✪✪ Strong Ale
Unimpressive, straw coloured fire water tasting of sweetcorn and rotted rubber.

GORDON'S XMAS ALE
8.8% abv ✪✪✪✪ Christmas Ale
Burnt umber in colour, rich, bitter and sweet; almost oppressive.

GORDON'S HIGHLAND SCOTCH ALE
8.6% abv ✪✪✪ Scotch Ale
Sweet, powerful, chestnut coloured brew served in a distinctive thistle glass.

DOUGLAS SCOTCH
8.3% abv ✪✪✪✪ Scotch Ale
Sweet, strong, smooth and black.

Beer shops
and warehouses

ONE GOOD THING about the single European market is that you can now import to Britain from any EC country as much beer as you can show is for personal consumption. Beer bought in Duty Free shops, for example on the ferries, is still limited to the pre-1993 limit of fifty litres per head. However, if you buy from shops or warehouses in another EC country, the nominal limit is one hundred and ten litres a head. If you can convince the customs' officials that you have a legitimate reason to buy more, they can allow this through. It is not legal to re-sell beer imported in this way.

The mark-up for beer in Belgian and Dutch bars is around 100%, so beer shops offer particularly good value, as well as an opportunity to continue your enjoyment and educate your friends back home.

The limit sounds great but unless you have a large truck is impractical. It weighs the same as two average-size beer drinkers. In crates, you will be lucky to fit more than fifty litres in the boot of an average family saloon. Consider taking fold-away cardboard cases but be aware that this may put you over the legal weight limit for carrying goods in you car or van.

Once your beer has arrived back home, examine the bottles closely for recommendations about storage temperature. When in doubt, store at between 6° and 8° Centigrade. As a general rule, lagers are best served at that temperature too. Ales generally taste best at between 11° and 13° Centigrade.

Belgium and the Netherlands have hundreds of shops, warehouses and wholesalers specialising in beer, some of which sell many hundreds of different varieties, including those found only rarely in cafés. They range from specialist off-licences to drive-in hypermarkets. The only hassle with most is that they often will not take credit or charge cards and some will not even take Eurocheques.

The Guide gives preference to stores which are convenient for tourist areas or for the channel ports. All those listed retail directly to the general public and most allow purchases of as little as one bottle, though there may be discounts for larger orders. If you find other convenient shops and warehouses, let us know.

ANTWERP

ANTWERP

BELGIUM BEERS
2 Reyndersstraat
Tel: 03 226 6853
On one of the best pub crawls in Europe is this excellent off-licence, with its range of around 280 different beers, mostly Belgian. The selection is impressive and includes many Flemish beers which are usually difficult to find, such as Bink and Zatte Bie. They also sell glasses.
Daily 11.00 – 19.00

BAARLE-HERTOG

BROUWERSHUIS
42 Molenstraat
Tel: 014 699403
Fax: 014 699397

In an enclave of Belgium surrounded by the Netherlands. Its proeflokaal is listed under Belgian Cafés: Antwerp. A beer shop with tasting facilities and an extraordinary gueuze cellar downstairs, stocking an excellent range of traditional gueuzes, old and new; 700 beers in all, mainly Belgian but several dozen Dutch brews. Eurocheques but no credit cards.
Friday 09.00 – 20.00
Other days 10.00 – 18.00
CLOSED MONDAY

ESSEN

This small town is at the Dutch border on the N133 to Roosendaal. It supports three major beer warehouses. **Baetens** (stocking 350 beers) is at 303 Horendonksteenweg, **Caigny** (400 beers) is at 79 Spijker and **Van Oevelen** (350 beers) is at 47a Moerkantsebaan. You will find one or other open Monday to Saturday between 09.00 and 18.00 and Sunday from 09.30 to 16.00.

BRABANT

BRUSSELS

BIERES ARTISANALES
174 Chausée de Wavre (Waversesteenweg)
Tel & Fax: 02 512 1788
Two kilometres from the city centre in the inner suburb of Ixelles (Elsene). The best off licence in the capital, selling nearly 400 beers and specialising in Belgian artisanal ales. Glasses too. They have numerous suggestions for gift-wrapped presents.
Tuesday to Saturday 11.00 – 19.00
CLOSED SUNDAY & MONDAY

LEUVEN

TERCLAVERS
203a Mechelsestraat
Tel: 016 202000
Fax: 016 205638
North of the Grote Markt but within the older part of town. Stocks around 300 beers. They will allow some tasting. Gift-wrapped presents.
Monday to Friday 09.30 – 18.30
Saturday 09.30 – 18.00
CLOSED SUNDAY

EAST FLANDERS

GHENT

HOPDUVEL
625 Coupure Links
Tel: 091 252068
Fax: 091 241406
On a canal bank a couple of blocks from the bar of the same name (see Belgian Bars: East Flanders). Stocks 400 beers, mainly Belgian and boasts a gueuze cave with a reasonable stock of traditional lambic-based beers. Very user-friendly. Stocks numerous special bottles and beer books. Eurocheques but no credit cards.
Daily 10.00 – 12.30
13.30 – 19.00
CLOSED SUNDAY & MONDAY

MELLE

BIERHALLE
36a Hovenierstraat
Tel: 091 308844
Fax: 091 319838
On the outskirts of Ghent and convenient for the E40. Stocks 350 beers.
Tuesday to Saturday 09.00 – 12.30
Monday to Friday 14.00 – 19.00
Saturday 14.00 – 18.00
CLOSED SUNDAY

ZOTTEGEM

DE PIKARDIJN
44 Nieuwstraat
Tel: 091 607504
The excellent beershop owned by the people who run one of Belgium's best country pubs, the Pikardijn at St. Lievens Houtem (see Belgian Cafés: East Flanders). Around 350 beers are available.
Thursday & Friday 13.30 – 18.00
Saturday 10.00 – 18.00
CLOSED SUNDAY TO WEDNESDAY

LIEGE

LIEGE

BIERERIE
45 Rue Hemricourt
Tel: 041 542040

Stocks 800 beers, mostly Belgian.
Tuesday to Friday 11.00 – 18.30
Saturday 10.30 – 17.00
CLOSED SUNDAY & MONDAY

LIMBURG (BELGIAN)

For historic reasons, neighbouring countries may have widely different rules about taxing or licensing the sale of particular commodities. The result is that where two countries share a border, you can bet that some entrepreneur in the country with the lower prices or greater availability will have a opened a warehouse full of whatever it is, within an easy drive of the customs post. In Belgium this is beer, leading to a string of specialist beer warehouses laced along the Dutch border. These are aimed at Dutch beer drinkers, so are a bit off the beaten track for most tourists.

The ones we know of are found, working anti-clockwise from Maastricht to Eindhoven, at: Riemst (**Janssens**, on N79), Lanaken (**Willems**, off N77), Neertoeren (**Nies Cox**, on N773), Maaseik (**Corstjens**, off N773/N762), Molenbeersel (**Nies Cox**, off N762), Hamont-Achel (**Bieren en Pintelieren**, off N71) and Lommel (**Pauwels**, off N746).

Opening times vary but few are open on Sunday, about half open on Monday and on other days 09.00 to 18.00 with a break for lunch on weekdays is typical.

LUXEMBOURG

BOUILLON

CAVE A BIERE
26 Rue de la Maladrerie
Tel: 061 467719
250 beers are on sale in the two shops of this name. The other is at 4 Rue du Lavoir. A rare outlet so deep in the southern Ardennes.

NAMUR

NAMUR

TABLE DE WALLONIE

6 Rue de la Halle
Tel: 081 220683
Excellent off-licence, also selling cheeses and other Walloon fare. More expensive than the warehouses but a very good selection of Wallonian ales in 75 cl bottles. Managed by the owners of La Caracole brewery.
Tuesday to Friday 10.00 – 18.30
Saturday 12.00 – 18.30
CLOSED SUNDAY & MONDAY

WEST FLANDERS

BRUGES

HOEFIJZERTJE
12 Walplein
Tel: 050 330604
It is surprising that the town which epitomises Flemish culture for millions of tourists each year should have no beer hypermarket. The nearest thing we have found is this small specialist beer shop attached to a bar of the same name (see Belgian Cafés: West Flanders). Quite expensive. Wide range of glasses.

POPERINGE

BEER STORE
30 Abelestationsplein
Tel: 057 333305
Noel Cuveleir's beer shop is 3 km out of town off the N38 in the direction of Abele. A lonely signpost in a field is the only indication that the distant farmhouse stocks nearly 300 different beers. Pretty convenient for the autoroute from Lille to the French coastal ports, it sits just inside the Belgian border. The opening times we quote come fourth hand.
Daily 09.30 – 18.30
CLOSED MONDAY

ROESELARE

Conveniently for anyone touring West Flanders, Roeselare has three major beer warehouses. **Delicia** (stocking 300 beers) is at 323 Rumbeeksesteenweg, **Reyntjens** (350 beers) is at 96 Populierstraat and **Yves** (600 beers) is at 1 Onze Lieve Vrouwmarkt. You will find one or all of them open between 08.00

and 19.00 from Monday to Saturday and 09.30 to 12.00 on Sunday.

GELDERLAND

ARNHEM

WIJNHANDEL BARRIQUE
9 Pauwstraat
Tel: 085 515167
Fax: 085 435170
Stocks 300 beers.
Thursday 09.30 – 21.00
Saturday 09.00 – 17.00
Other days 09.30 – 18.00
CLOSED SUNDAY

GRONINGEN

GRONINGEN

BIERWINKEL
Oude Kijk in 't Jatstraat
Tel: 050 189706
Small off-licence in the same block as the St. Martinus brewery and a bar called Paard van Troje (see Dutch Cafés: Groningen). Claims to stock nearly 500 beers and must have one of the best selections of Dutch beers in the country, especially from the smaller, more obscure breweries. Its opening hours vary a bit but those listed are the minimum.
Thursday 13.00 – 18.00
Friday 10.00 – 18.00
Saturday 10.00 – 17.00

LIMBURG (DUTCH)

MAASTRICHT

VAN WISSEM
40 Acht Zaligheden
Tel: 043 430290
Stocks up to 600 beers.
Daily 10.00 – 18.00
CLOSED SUNDAY

NORTH BRABANT

EINDHOVEN

BIEREN EN PINTELIEREN
2 Pasqualinastraat
Tel: 040 435422
Stocks up to 500 beers. Specialises in beers from all over the world.
Friday 10.00 – 20.00
Other days 10.00 – 18.00
CLOSED SUNDAY & MONDAY

NORTH HOLLAND

AMSTERDAM

BIER EN CO
23 Piet Heinkade
Tel: 020 626 8025
Strictly speaking, a wholesaler but will sell directly to the public, though only by the case. Stocks 600 beers and definitely worth knowing about if you are living in Amsterdam for any time.
Weekdays 08.00 – 18.00
CLOSED SATURDAY &
SUNDAY

BIER KONING
125 Paleisstraat
Tel: 020 625 6336
Fax: 020 627 0654
An exceptional beer shop in the heart of Amsterdam, just off Dam Square towards Raadhuisstraat. Said to stock 750 different beers, the emphasis is on Belgian with many other imports. It also sells just about every beer book on the market and a selection of glasses.
Monday 13.00 – 18.00
Thursday 11.00 – 21.00
Saturday 11.00 – 17.00
Other days 11.00 – 18.00
CLOSED SUNDAY

BERT'S BIERHUIS
2e/3 Hugo de Grootstraat
Tel: 020 684 3127
Sells 600 beers. No further details.

HAARLEM

DEUX BIERES
83 Gierstraat
Tel: 023 314180
Stocks 300 beers.
Monday 13.00 – 18.00
Tuesday to Friday 10.00 – 18.00
Saturday 10.00 – 17.00
CLOSED SUNDAY

UITGEEST

DRANKENMARKT VREEBURG
7 Lange Buurt
Tel: 02513 12617
Said to stock over 650 beers. Next door to the Café Thijs (see Dutch Cafés: North Holland).
Tuesday to Friday 09.00 – 12.30
Monday to Friday 13.30 – 18.00

Thursday 19.00 – 21.00
Saturday 08.30 – 17.00
CLOSED SUNDAY

ZAANDIJK

KONINCKSPLEIN
13 Lagedijk
Tel: 075 215367
Next door to a café of the same name (see Dutch Cafés: North Holland). Stocks a wide selection of beers, wines and jenevers. Also stocks home-brew kits for making abbey beers, wheat beers and altbier.
Monday 13.30 – 18.00
Tuesday to Friday 09.00 – 18.00
Saturday 09.00 – 17.00
CLOSED SUNDAY

OVERIJSSEL

DEVENTER

TEMPELIER
17 Kleine Overstraat
Tel: 05700 18294
Fax: 05700 41950
Stocks 360 different beers and also home brew items.
Tuesday to Thursday 11.00 – 18.00
Friday 09.00 – 18.00
Saturday 09.00 – 17.00
CLOSED SUNDAY & MONDAY

SOUTH HOLLAND

DELFT

BIERWINKEL
58 Nieuwe Langedijk
Tel: 015 134047
Stocks 400 beers.
Monday 13.00 – 18.00
Tuesday to Friday 10.00 – 18.00
Saturday 10.00 – 17.00
CLOSED SUNDAY

LEIDEN

BIERWINKEL

13 Hartsesteeg
Tel: 071 122813
Brilliantly well-stocked off-licence with over 400 varieties of beer. In a small alley off the square in which St Pancras' church squats. Strong on Belgian beers. Closed for

improvements at the time of going to press.
Tuesday 13.00 – 18.00
Wednesday to Friday 11.00 – 18.00
Friday & Saturday 10.00 – 17.00
CLOSED SUNDAY & MONDAY

MAASSLUIS

OPORTO
7 Noorddijk
Tel: 01899 20247
In the basement of a beer bar of the same name (see Dutch Cafés: South Holland). Note the limited opening hours. Conveniently situated for the Hook of Holland ferry. Stocks over 200 beers.
Friday 10.00 – 21.00
Saturday 10.00 – 17.00
CLOSED SUNDAY TO THURSDAY

ROTTERDAM

DISCOUNT DRANKEN VAN SCHAAGEN
95 Nieuwe Binnenweg
Tel: 010 436 2676
One km from the city centre. Stocks 350 beers. Further out of town along the same road at no. 425 is **Radder Horecare**, another store stocking 300 beers, which has the advantage of being open on Saturday (09.00 to 17.00).
Weekdays 09.00 – 18.00
CLOSED SATURDAY & SUNDAY

UTRECHT

UTRECHT

BERT'S BIERHUIS
83 Voorstraat
Tel: 030 341339
Stocks 700 beers. Lots of presentation packs and ideas for gifts.
Monday 13.00 – 18.00
Thursday 10.00 – 21.00
Saturday 10.00 – 17.00
Other days 10.00 – 18.00
CLOSED SUNDAY

Consumer Organisations

WITH THE EMERGENCE of a single European market in beer, it is inevitable that brewery companies have started to operate on a Europe-wide basis. In response, beer consumer organisations have also started to operate on a European level.

EBCU, the European Beer Consumers' Union, was founded in 1990 and is made up of national consumer groups from Britain, Belgium, the Netherlands, Sweden and Finland. There are hopes that organisations from France and Czechoslovakia may also join soon.

The German brewing industry has not yet been demolished to a sufficient extent to make the emergence of a national consumer group likely, though the first beer guides to that country are now being published, among them The Good Beer Guide to Bavaria (CAMRA Books: ISBN 1 85249 114 0) by Graham Lees, a founder member of the Campaign for Real Ale, who worked for many years in Munich.

CAMRA BRUSSELS

The Campaign for Real Ale (CAMRA) was founded in 1971. Its first group in Europe was formed in 1990 by three CAMRA members who had moved to work in Brussels. They are an industrious but sociable crew. As well as making major contributions to this Guide, they produce a local café guide (see above), run regular trips to breweries and outings to towns and sites of interest to beer lovers. They always welcome contact from other interested groups.

CAMRA Brussels holds regular meetings advertised through the CAMRA newspaper, What's Brewing. There is no membership fee and members are not even required to join CAMRA (UK). More details and copies of the Brussels guide can be obtained from:

CAMRA Brussels
Boite no 5
Rue des Atrèbates 67
1040 Bruxelles
Belgium

OBJECTIEVE BIERPROEVERS (OBP)

The Belgian equivalent of CAMRA is OBP, the "objective beer tasters", formed by the confederation of a number of local groups in 1984.

There have been organisations of beer lovers in various provinces of Belgium for many years but it has only been recently that these have come together as an effective consumer force under a single umbrella.

The concentration of interest has traditionally been in East Flanders, Antwerp and Limburg but the eventual aim is to piece together a fully national organisation. They seem to be achieving this by a steady build-up of issues which clearly affect all Belgian beer drinkers.

Some of the main campaigns at present are:

● Promoting the success of regional artisan breweries

● Monitoring the advance of Interbrew, Alken-Maes (BSN), Riva and other expansionist companies

● Combatting the closure of small artisanal breweries

● Promoting traditional beer styles such as lambic and gueuze

● Limiting the spread of "etiket" beers, the relabelled versions of existing products

Where OBP varies from CAMRA is that its roots lie in discovering and enjoying all beers, rather than promoting a particular style. Where the two organisations are remarkably similar is in the breadth of beer-related activities which are offered to members.

OBP runs or promotes beer festivals, brewery tours and beer tasting evenings on a regular basis. They produce an informative monthly magazine, De Bierproever, published only in Flemish. English-speaking beer drinkers are always made welcome at their events and foreign membership is slowly growing.

Overseas membership of OBP costs BFr 600 for 1994. It includes four editions of their magazine, De Bierproever. Enquiries and Eurocheques should be addressed to:
Objectieve Bierproevers
Postbus 32
2600 Berchem 5
Belgium

PROMOTIE INFORMATIE TRADITIONEEL BIER
(PINT)

The Dutch beer consumers' organisation, PINT, pronounces its name like "sprint". The initials derive from "Promotion INformation (about) Traditional beer". It was founded in 1980 and has been a national movement right from the start.

The Dutch beer scene owes a lot to imported beers and PINT has always differed from CAMRA and OBP in having a European and international outlook on the world of beer, rather than fully devoted to its own country's beers. Nonetheless it tries hard to promote the interests of Dutch breweries, especially in the production of ales and bokbiers.

PINT sponsors, or helps to promote, a number of beer festivals every year, including the national bokbier festival held in Amsterdam in October or November. It also publishes a bi-monthly national magazine, PINT Nieuws.

Overseas annual membership, which includes four editions of PINT Nieuws, cost Nfl 35 for 1994. Further details can be obtained from:
PINT
Postbus 3757
1001 AN Amsterdam
Netherlands

READING LIST

IF THIS GUIDE has whetted your appetite for Belgian beers and you want to know more, we suggest the following:

Bierjaarboek [6th edition]
Peter Crombecq
(Kosmos: ISBN 90 215 1909 7, BFr 595)
The Belgian beer drinker's bible. Peter Crombecq was the founding father of OBP and is a highly respected figure in the European beer consumers' movement. Although his book is only available in Flemish, it describes every Belgian and Dutch beer on the market in the past five years and is essential

reading for any beer lover domiciled in either country.

Bier in Belgie
Geert van Lierde
(Lannoo: ISBN 90-209-1960-1, BFr 495.)
Geert van Lerde is a journalist on the Gazet van Antwerpen. In 1992 he produced this guide in Flemish to the breweries and beer culture of his home country. The only disadvantage apart from the

language is that the layout is town by town, rather than section by section.

The Great Beers of Belgium
Michael Jackson
(MMC: ISBN 90 5373 003 6,
£ 14.95)
Michael Jackson is probably the best known beer writer in the world. This hardback, an introduction to some of Belgium's finest beers and their brewing, is worth buying for the photographs alone. Not a rival but a complementary tome. Copies can be bought from CAMRA Ltd, 34 Alma Road, St Albans AL1 3BW.

Het Nederlands Bierboek
Dave Vlam
(Elmar: ISBN 90 6120 588 4)
This hardback, full colour, illustrated guide to all the beers and breweries functioning in the Netherlands in 1991 is out of print now but is still sometimes found in bookshops. Dave Vlam is a freelance journalist, public relations consultant and beer revolutionaries' handyman. His book gives a clear classification of all the brews and a potted history of every brewery.

Het Mysterie van Gueuze
Jos Cels
(Roularta: BFr 1,295)
A lavishly illustrated book about lambic brewing, gueuze and the brewers of Pajottenland. Underwritten by Alken-Maes it contains little negative comment but is nonetheless a work of great devotion.

Gueuze, Faro et Kriek
Raymond Buren
(Editions Glénat: BFr 295)
An altogether more lightweight tome but humorous and informative nonetheless.

Trappistes et Bières d'Abbayes
Raymond Buren
(Editions Glénat: BFr 295)
Aims to be an accurate and comprehensive guide to the monastic beers of Belgium, the Netherlands and Germany.
A Selective Guide to Brussels Bars
Stephen D'Arcy
(CAMRA Brussels: BFr 100)
The frequently up-dated, 30-page broadsheet of CAMRA's Brussels-based beer enthusiasts. Includes all the latest news about what is new and what has closed down, as well as advice on how to get there and what to avoid.

Of the travel guides, the ones which correspondents and Guide inspectors have found most useful are the books in the Baedeker's series:

Baedeker's Belgium
(AA Books: ISBN 0 7495 0674 1.
£11.99)
An attractive, well-presented, easy-to-follow guidebook with reasonable judgement and reliable facts. Ignore the article on beers unless you want to see the effects of partial understanding!

Baedeker's Netherlands
(AA Books: ISBN 0 7495 0405 6.
£11.99)
The same for the Netherlands.

The Provinces of
Belgium &
The Netherlands

To Hull

NORTH
SEA

To Felixstowe

To Harwich

To Ramsgate

To
Dover

Calais

Dunkirk

Ostend

Zeebrugge

Bruges

WEST
FLANDERS

EAST
FLANDERS

Ghent

Mons

HAINAUT

Charleroi

B E L

G

BRABANT

Brussels

NAMUR

Namur

Arlon

LUXEMBOURG

GD. DUCHY
LUXEMBOURG

Bastogne

LUXEMBOURG

Antwerp

ANTWERP

BELGIAN
LIMBURG

Liege

LIEGE

Maastricht

DUTCH
LIMBURG

Eindhoven

NORTH
BRABANT

Breda

ZEELAND

Rotterdam Europoort

Rotterdam

SOUTH
HOLLAND

Hoek Van Holland

Den
Haag

Amsterdam

NORTH
HOLLAND

Utrecht

UTRECHT

HOLLAND

Arnhem

GELDERLAND

Nijmegen

Apeldoorn

Enschede

OVERIJSSEL

FLEVOLAND

Leeuwarden

FRIESLAND

DRENTE

GRONINGEN

Groningen

NETHERLAND

GERMANY

FRANCE

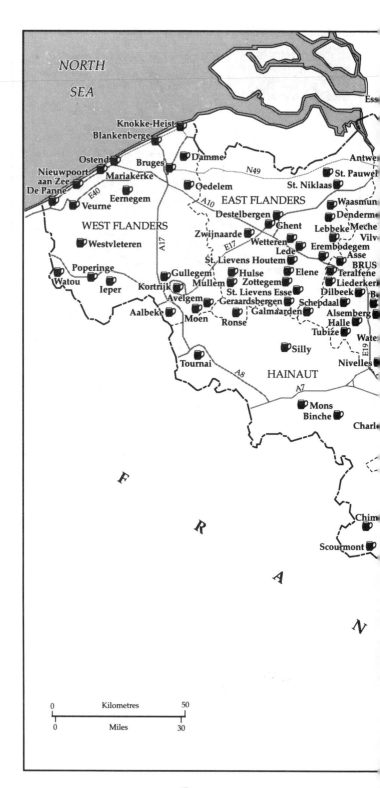

NORTH SEA

Ess

Knokke-Heist
Blankenberge

Ostend
Bruges
Damme

N49
Antwe

St. Pauwel

Nieuwpoort
aan Zee
Mariakerke
Oedelem
St. Niklaas

De Panne
Eernegem
Veurne
A10
EAST FLANDERS
Waasmun

E40
Destelbergen
Denderm
Meche

WEST FLANDERS
Zwijnaarde
Ghent
Lebbeke
Vilv

A17
Wetteren
Erembodegem
Asse

Westvleteren
Lede
St. Lievens Houtem
BRUS

E17
Teralfene

Poperinge
Gullegem
Hulse
Elene
Liederker

Watou
Mullem
Zottegem
Dilbeek
B

Ieper
Kortrijk
St. Lievens Esse
Schepdaal

Avelgem
Geraardsbergen
Alsemberg

Aalbeke
Moen
Galmaarden
Halle

Ronse
Tubize
Wate

Silly
E19
Nivelles

Tournai
A8
HAINAUT

F
A7
Mons
Binche
Charl

R

Chim

Scourmont

A

N

| 0 | Kilometres | 50 |
| 0 | Miles | 30 |

Belgium

NETHERLANDS

GERMANY

Baarle-Hertog

vmoer
stmalle
A21
Turnhout
em
Zoersel
Poederlee
ersel
NTWERP
Itegem
Tessenderlo
BELGIAN
LIMBURG
Paal
A2
Rillaar
Diest
uken
Hasselt
euven
Linden
A13
Maastricht
St Truiden
Zepperen
Landen
Tongeren
BRABANT
ain-la-Neuve
A3
A3
Avennes
Eupen
Liège
E42
Verviers
Seraing
LIEGE
E42
Huy
Xhoffraix
E42
Spa
Namur
A4
Floreffe
Vyle-et-Tharoul
Malmèdy
E25
Lustin
Stavelot
hée-Denée
Durbuy
NAMUR
Dinant
Hastière-Lavaux
La Roche-en-Ardenne
Rochefort
Han-sur-Lesse
Achouffe
St Hubert
A4
Bastogne
LUXEMBOURG
Bouillon
N40
GD. DUCHY
OF
LUXEMBOURG
Florenville
Arlon

E

Netherlands

TERSCHELLIN

VLIELAND

W A D

TEXEL

Den Burg

Den Helder

NORTH
SEA

NORTH
HOLLAND

Hoo

Alkmaar

A9   A7

Uitgeest

Zaandijk

Haarlem   AMSTER

Zandvoort

Amstelveen

A4   A9   Naard

Sassenheim

A44   A4   Leiden   A2

UTREC

Den Haag   SOUTH   Utrecht
A12
A12

Delft   HOLLAND

Maassluis

Schiedam   Rotterdam   Heukelun

Brielle   Gorinchem

Spijkenisse   A16   Dordrecht

A27

ZEELAND   Oosterhout   NORTI

A17   A58   Breda   A58   Oisterwi

Middelburg   Goes   Tilbur

Vlissingen

Terneuzen

B   E   L   G   I   U   M

Beers index

Listed here are key words in alphabetical order. The aim is to make it easier to find a beer in the brewery sections. We have excluded words which are common to many beer names. Where the beer is a label brew believed to be based on an existing beer, we have indicated the beer name in brackets after the name of the brewery.

A completely accurate listing would never be possible. The quarterly magazine of OBP, Den Bierproever, lists around 50 new products in each issue and makes it a policy not to list those which have been discontinued.

Label beers are generally commissioned by a wholesaler or retailer. Often the contract lasts only for one brew and if a new order is placed the beer may be brewed to a different recipe or even by another brewery. Therefore all statements made about the brew on which a label beer is based, while made in good faith, should not be taken as necessarily accurate.

If a beer name cannot be located here it may be that it is (1) neither Belgian nor Dutch, (2) a label beer found only in a small part of the country, (3) new since October 1993, (4) old stock, (5) not known to our researchers or (6) mislabelled.

Join CAMRA!

Help the fight for good beer and pubs. CAMRA has 38,000 members organised countrywide, lobbying brewers and government.

Members get What's Brewing, CAMRA's national newspaper, free every month.
Big discounts on the annual Good Beer Guide and other CAMRA titles.

Free entry to CAMRA beer festivals.

Annual membership: £12/$20. Cheques to "CAMRA Ltd".

I wish to join CAMRA and agree to abide by the Memorandum and Articles of Association. I enclosed a cheque for £12/$20.

Name...

Address ....

....

.... Post or Zip Code ....

Send to CAMRA,
34 Alma Road, St Albans, Herts AL1 3BW, Great Britain
